T0126682

Analecta Gregoriana
Cura Pontificiae Universitatis Gregorianae edita

VOL. LXIV
SERIES FACULTATIS THEOLOGICAE
Sectio A (n. 10)

Cardinal Robert Pullen

An English Theologian of the Twelfth Century

by

F. Courtney, S. J.

ROMAE
APUD AEDES UNIVERSITATIS GREGORIANAE
1954

IMPRIMI POTEST

Romae, die 4 Sept. 1954.

P. PETRUS M. ABELLÁN, S. I.
Rector Universitatis

IMPRIMATUR

Romae, die 10 Novembris 1954.

† ALOYSIUS TRAGLIA
Archiep. Caesarien., Vicesgerens

ROMAE - TYPIS PONTIFICIAE UNIVERSITATIS GREGORIANAE

ACKNOWLEDGEMENTS

I desire to express my sincere thanks to all who have in various ways helped me to complete this study. Among my colleagues on the staff of Heythrop College I must mention especially Fr. William Dempsey S. J., Fr. Maurice Bévenot S. J. and Fr. Edmund Sutcliffe, S. J. I am especialy grateful to Fr. F. Pelster S. J. of the Gregorian University, Rome, for his kindness in reading my manuscript and making a number of helpful suggestions. Among those who have kindly provided me with bibliographical information are Fr. Z. Alszeghy, S. J. of the Gregorian University, Fr. A. Gwynn S. J., Professor of Medieval History in University College, Dublin, Fr. Daniel Callus, O. P. of Blackfriars, Oxford, Dom. J. Leclercq O. S. B. of Clervaux Abbey, Luxembourg, Dr. R. W. Hunt, Keeper of the Western Manuscripts in the Bodleian Library, Oxford, Mr Neil Ker, Lecturer in Paleography in the University of Oxford, Dr Beryl Smalley of St Hilda's College, Oxford, Mlle. M.-T. d'Alverny of the Bibliothèque Nationale, Paris, Mlle. Le Breton of the Institut de Recherche et d'Histoire des Textes, Paris. To all of these I am most grateful, and apologize to any others whose names may have been inadvertently omitted. I should like also to record my appreciation of the courtesy and efficiency of the numerous librarians who have placed their collections and their knowledge at my service.

For permission to quote from my edition of Pullen's *Sermo de omnibus humanae uite necessariis* I am indebted to the Editor of *Gregorianum;* for some quotations from his article ' Some Unknown Writings of the Early Scholastic Period, ' to his Excellency Bishop Artur M. Landgraf, Auxiliary Bishop of Bamberg; for an extract from a MS of Robert Courçon printed in his book *La théologie du sacrement de pénitence au XIIe siècle* I am obliged to the Reverend P. Anciaux of the Grand Séminaire, Malines; for three extracts from his edition of the *Sententie Atrebatenses,* published in the *Recherches de théologie ancienne et médiévale,* to the editor Dom. Odon Lottin, as well as for authorization to cite from texts published in the same periodical by the late F. Bliemetzrieder. By courtesy of the publishers, Verlag Aschendorff, Münster, Westfalen, Germany,

of the *Beiträge zur Geschichte der Philosophie und Theologie des Mittelalters,* I have been able to quote from Band XVIII, Heft 2-3, F. Bliemetzrieder, Anselms von Laon systematische Sentenzen. 1919, and from Band VII, Heft 2-3, B. Geyer, Die Sententiae Divinitatis, ein Sentenzenbuch der Gilbertschen Schule. 1909. Also with permission of Verlag Aschendorff I have quoted a passage from the series *Opuscula et textus historiam ecclesiae eiusque vitam atque doctrinam illustrantia,* Fasc. VII, Tractatus de sex principiis Gilbertano Porretano adscriptus, ad fidem manuscriptorum edidit Albanus Heysse, O. F. M., 1929, recognovit Damianus van den Eynde, O. F. M., 1953. I acknowledge with thanks permission from Messrs Routledge and Kegan Paul, London, to quote from *Plato's Cosmology, The Timaeus of Plato,* translated by Francis Macdonald Cornford, London, 1937.

For his assistance in the preparation of my manuscript for the press I am greatly obliged to Fr. Hugh Thwaites S. J.

Heythrop College, Chipping Norton, Oxon.

F. COURTNEY, S. J.

CONTENTS

INTRODUCTION

It has often been remarked that the twelfth century was an age of intellectual ferment. The observation is certainly true of the study of theology which, under the impulse of teachers such as Anselm of Canterbury, Anselm of Laon, Peter Abelard, Hugh of St. Victor, Gilbert Porreta, Peter Lombard and many others, made greater progress in fifty years than it had in the whole period since the death of St. Augustine. Among the early scholastic theologians the first English name of note is that of Robert Pullen, who taught at Oxford and Paris and was the first Englishman to become a Cardinal [1]. In his day he was renowned as a teacher, and certain of his opinions were fruitful in later theological speculation. He was the author of a number of theological works, including one of the earliest and most elaborate of the twelfth-century books of *Sentences*. This is the earliest comprehensive theological work to be produced by an English writer.

Nevertheless, as Dr. Landgraf has observed, « his importance has till now been far too little appreciated even by scholars » [2]. This neglect has been due to various causes. Pullen's unsystematic arrangement of the material in his *Sentences* must be reckoned among them. Another one was certainly the dominating influence of the *Sentences* of Peter Lombard, which were completed in 1152, probably about ten years later than those of Pullen. The enormous success which the Lombard's work enjoyed in the schools up to the sixteenth century made for the neglect of his immediate predecessors to whom he owed so much. Modern students of medieval theology have, however, uncovered many of the Lombard's sources. Among these we must include the *Sentences* of Pullen, though not to the extent claimed by Mathoud, Pullen's seventeenth-century editor. Mathoud's edition of the *Sentences*

---

1 There is no evidence to support the statement of A. Ciaconius (Vitae Pontif. Roman. et S. R. E. Cardinal. ed. A. Oldini, Rome, 1677) that Cardinal Ulricus, papal legate in England in 1109 was an Englishman.

2 See, 'Some Unknown Writings of the Early Scholastic Period', *The New Scholasticism,* IV, 1930, 11-14.

was excellent for its time, but it is now unsatisfactory and needs replacement. Since its appearance in 1655 it has provoked biographical and theological notices of Pullen in works of reference, but up to the present there is no complete and trustworthy account of his life and work available. In the present study I have tried to make good this deficiency, in so far as the surviving material has permitted. For the details of Pullen's life the material is very scanty. Of his writings we posses the *Sentences,* a number of manuscript sermons and a minor spiritual treatise. In them there is discernible an individuality of thought and style which, it is hoped, will justify an attempt to rescue their author from the neglect which he has endured. In order that this personal quality of his writing might be more clearly appreciated I have quoted freely from it, and, wherever it seemed desirable, followed his arguments in some detail. By this method I have tried also to convey something of the characteristic style of early scholasticism, and to indicate its considerable differences from the fully-developed scholastic theology of the following century.

Scholastic theology was not entirely a growth of the twelfth century. Already in the ninth century the idea of utilising dialectic in theological discussion was familiar, and a distinction was already drawn between simple and liberal, or strictly scholastic, disputation. The latter presupposed a training in the liberal arts [3]. But it was with the opening of the twelfth century and the renewed interest in dialectic which culminated in the development of the theological *quaestio* that scholasticism came into its own, and the 'modern' masters began to acquire an 'authority' of their own, alongside that of the Fathers of the Church, though of course, on a lower level. Some of the 'moderns' acquired their influence by their skill in the selection and arrangement of theological material rather than by the originality of their thought. To this group belong Anselm of Laon and Peter Lombard. Others became recognised as leaders of schools of thought more by the originality and daring of their solutions of theological problems. In the following pages, Pullen's thought will, where possible, be placed in its setting of contemporary schools of thought. Only thus can his own contribution be rightly evaluated. One must not expect too much of the early scholastics. What were exciting discoveries in their day have since become part of the common stock of ideas.

---

[3] See A. Landgraf, *Einführung in die Geschichte der theologischen Literatur der Frühscholastik*, Regensburg, 1948, 11-12; Zum Begriff der Scholastik, *Coll. Franc.* XI (1941) 487 ff.

They did not possess the knowledge of Aristotle available to their thirteenth-century successors. As a result they were incapable of establishing great theological syntheses based on all-embracing metaphysical principles. Their originality is seen chiefly in the ingenuity with which they solved a succession of individual problems which arose in their commentaries on the Bible. Yet their work was an indispensable preparation for the thirteenth century. The materials on which they worked were inadequate, their criticism of sources almost non-existent, but this was offset by their enthusiasm, and by their skill in the use they made of the tools at their disposal.

In the following account of Pullen's theology I have made use chiefly of his most important theological work, the *Libri Sententiarum VIII,* but have also, where it appeared relevant, appealed to the unpublished sermons, and to my edition of his *De Contemptu Mundi*[4]. In studying the *Sentences* I have used the 1655 edition of Mathoud and the two surviving MSS, but have given all references to Migne's edition, which is more likely to be generally accessible[5].

---

[4] Gregorianum XXXI (1950) 192-223.

[5] The references are given to the column, the volume number (186) being omitted.

ABBREVIATIONS

A. H. D.	Archives d'histoire doctrinale et littéraire du Moyen Age, Paris.
Beiträge	Beiträge zur Geschichte der Philosophie und Theologie des Mittelalters, Münster i. W.
C. J. C. Frdbg.	Corpus Juris Canonici, editio Lipsiensis, A. Friedberg, Leipzig, 1879-1881.
Coll. Fran.	Collectanea Franciscana, Assisi.
C. S. E. L.	Corpus Scriptorum Ecclesiasticorum Latinorum.
Denz	Enchiridion Symbolorum Definitionum et Declarationum de Rebus Fidei et Morum, ed. H. Denzinger etc. ed. 24, 1946.
D. T. C.	Dictionnaire de théologie catholique, Paris.
Div. Th. Fr.	Divus Thomas, Freiburg.
E. H. R.	English Historical Review, London.
G. C. S.	Die griechischen christlichen Schriftsteller.
Greg.	Gregorianum, Rome.
M. G. H.	Monumenta Germaniae Historica.
N. R. T.	Nouvelle Revue Théologique, Tournai.
P. G.	J. P. Migne, Patrologia Latina.
R. bibl.	Revue biblique, Paris.
R. H. E.	Revue d'histoire ecclésiastique, Louvain.
R. S. R.	Recherches de science religieuse, Paris.
R. T. A. M.	Recherches de théologie ancienne et médiévale, Louvain.
R. S.	Rolls Series, London.
Schol.	Scholastik, Eupen, Freiburg i. Breisgau.
Z. K. G.	Zeitschrift für Kirchengeschichte, Stuttgart.
Z. k. Th.	Zeitschrift für katholische Theologie, Innsbruck.

SOURCES

1. *Manuscripts*. See Chapter II.

2. *Ancient and medieval printed texts.*

Adso, Liber de Anti-Christo, P. L. 40 & P. L. 101.

Alan of Lille, Liber Paenitentialis, P. L. 210.

Albert the Great, Liber de Sex Principiis, Opera I, Paris, 1890.

Alcuin, De Fide Sanctae et Individuae Trinitatis, P. L. 107.

Annales Monasterii de Oseneia, ed. H. E. Luard, Rolls Series, London, 1869.

Anselm of Canterbury, Monologium, P. L. 158, Liber de Fide Trinitatis et de Incarnatione Verbi, ibid.

Anselm of Laon, Enarrationes in Matthaeum, P. L. 162, Epistola ad Heribrandum Abbatem S. Laurentii Leodiensis, ibid.
Sententiae. Anselms von Laon systematische Sentenzen, ed. F. Bliemezrieder, Beiträge, xviii 2-3 Münster, 1919, 3-46, Sententie divine pagine; 47-153, Sententie Anselmi [1].
Trente-trois pièces inédites de l'oeuvre théologique d'Anselme de Laon, ed. F. Bliemetzrieder, Rech. Théol. anc. méd. ii (1930).

Aristotle, Categoriae, ed. Imm. Bekker, Berlin, 1831.

Athanasius, Contra Gentes, P. G. 25. English translation cited from Nicene and Post-Nicene Fathers of the Christian Church. Second Series. Vol. iv, ed. H. Wace and P. Schaff, Oxford, 1892.

Athenagoras, Legatio pro Christianis, P. G. 6.

Augustine, Contra Adversarium Legis et Prophetarum, P. L. 42.
Contra Faustum Manichaeum, P. L. 42, C. S. E. L. 25.
Contra Julianum, P. L. 44.
De Agone Christiano, P. L. 40. C. S. E. L. 41.
De Baptismo contra Donatistas, C. S. E. L. 51.
De Bono Conjugali, C. S. E. L. 41.

---

[1] The Sententie Anselmi are no longer regarded as the work of Anselm himself, though deriving from his school. H. Weisweiller holds that the same is true of the Sententie Divine Pagine. See H. Weisweiller, Das Schrifttum der Schule Anselms von Laon und Wilhelms von Champeaux in deutschen Bibliotheken, *Beiträge*, XXXIII, 1-2 (1936), 253.

De Civitate Dei, C. S. E. L. 40.
De Correptione et Gratia, P. L. 44.
De Diversis Quaestionibus ad Simplicianum, P. L. 40.
De Diversis Quaestionibus LXXXIII, P. L. 40.
De Doctrina Christiana, P. L. 34.
De Genesi ad Litteram, C. S. E. L. 28.
De Libero Arbitrio, P. L. 32.
De Natura Boni, P. L. 42, C. S. E. L. 25.
De Nuptiis et Concupiscentia, C. S. E. L. 25.
De Trinitate, P. L. 42.
De Symbolo ad Catechumenos, P. L. 40.
De Vera Religione, P. L. 34.
Enarrationes in Psalmos, P. L. 36.
Enchiridion, P. L. 40.
De Peccatorum Meritis et Remissione, P. L. 44.
Epistolae, C. S. E. L. 33, 34.
In Epistolam Joannis Tractatus P. L. 35.
In Epistolam Joannis Tractatus P. L. 35.
Sermones, P. L. 37-39.

Bede, Hexameron, P. L. 91.

Bernard of Clairvaux, Epistolae, P. L. 182.
Epistola de Erroribus Abelardi, ibid.

Boethius, In Categorias Aristotelis, P. L. 64.
In Isagogen Porphyrii Commenta, Editio Secunda, Lib. III, P. L. 64, C. S. E. L. 48.
De Interpretatione, P. L. 64.

Cassian, Conlationes C. S. E. L. XIII, II, P. L. 49.

Cassiodorus, In Psalterium Expositio, P. L. 70.

Clarembald of Arras, Der Kommentar des Clarembald von Arras zu Boethius de Trinitate, ed. W. Janssen, Breslau, 1926.

Cyprian, Quod Idola Dii non Sint, P. L. 4. C. S. E. L. 3.

Disputatio (Catholicorum Patrum) Adversus Dogmata Petri Abaelardi, P. L. 182.

Duns Scotus, Ordinatio, I Vatican City, 1950.

Eadmer, Historiae Novorum ed. M. Rule, Rolls Series, London, 1886.

Florence of Worcester, Chronicon ex Chronicis, ed. B. Thorpe, London, 1849.

Fulgentius, De Trinitate, P. L. 66.

Gandulphus of Bologna, Sententiarum libri IV. ed. J. de Walter, Vienna, 1924.

Geoffrey of Auxerre, Libellus contra Capitula Gilberti.
Pictaviensis Episcopi, P. L. 185.
Vita (Prima) Sancti Bernardi, Lib. III, ibid.

Gilbert Porreta, Commentaria in Librum Boethii de Trinitate, P. L. 64.
Commentaria in Librum Boethii de Duabus Naturis et Una Persona Christi, ibid.
Commentaria in Librum (Boethii) de Praedicatione Trium Personarum, ibid.
Liber sex principiorum, ed A. Heysse, Münster, 1929.

Glossa Ordinaria, P. L. 113.

Gratian, Decretum, C. I. C. Frdbg.

Gregory the Great, Homilia XXXIV in Evang. P. L. 76.
Moralia, P. L. 75.

Hermannus Monachus, De Miraculis S. Mariae Laudunensis, P. L. 156.

Hildebert of Mans, Carmina Miscellanea, P. L. 171.
Epistola 18, ibid.

Honorius of Autun, Elucidarium, P. L. 172.

Hugh of St. Victor, Commentaria in Hierarchiam Coelestem Dionysii Areopagitae, P. L. 175.
Eruditio Didascalica, P. L. 176.
De Sacramentis Christianae Fidei, ibid.
Libellus de Potentia et Voluntate Dei, ibid.

Isidore of Seville, Sententiae, P. L. 83.
Synonyma, P. L. 83.

Ivo of Chartres, Decretum, P. L. 161.

Jerome, Epistola xxii ad Eustochium, C. S. E. L. 54.
Commentaria in Isaiam, P. L. 24.
Liber de Nominibus Hebraicis, P. L. 23.

John Chrysostom, Hom, in Matt. P. G. 51.

John of Hexham, Continuation of Symeon of Durham, vol. ii, ed. T. Arnold, Rolls Series, London, 1885.

John of Salisbury, Epistolae, P. L. 199.
Historia Pontificalis M. G. H. SS. XX. ed. W. Arndt, Hanover, 1868.
Metalogicon, ed C. C. J. Webb, Oxford, 1929.
Policraticus, ed. C. C. J. Webb, Oxford, 1909.

Lactantius, Divinae Institutiones, P. L. 6, C. S. E. L. 19.

Leo the Great, Ep. 16 (ad Rusticum) P. L. 54.

Liber de Vera et Falsa Paenitentia, P. L. 40.

Metamorphosis Goliae Episcopi in 'Latin Poems attributed to Walter Mapes', ed. T. Wright, London, 1841.

Minucius Felix, Octavius, P. L. 3. C. S. E. L. 2.

Otto of Freising, De Gestis Fredericis Imperatoris, M. G. H. XX SS., ed. R. Wilmans, Hanover, 1868.

Origen, Homilia IX in Genesin, G. C. S. 29.

Peter Abelard, Apologia seu Fidei Confessio, P. L. 178
Dialectica, ed. V. Cousin, Ouvrages inédits d'Abélard, Paris, 1836.
Expositio in Epistolam ad Romanos, ibid.
Expositio in Hexaemeron, ibid.
Historia Calamitatum, ibid.
Theologia Scholarium ibid.
Sic et Non, ibid.
Theologia Christiana, ibid.
H. Ostlender, Peter Abelard's Theologia « Summi Boni » Beiträge zur Geschichte der Philosophie und Theologie des Mittelalters, Bd. 35, Heft. 2-3, Münster i. W. 1939.

Peter Damian, De Divina Omnipotentia, P. L. 145.
Sermon 69, P. L. 144.

Peter Lombard, Libri IV Sententiarum, ad Claras Aquas (Quaracchi), 1916.

Peter of Poitiers, Sententiae, ed P. S. Moore and M. Dulong, Notre Dame, Indiana, 1943.

Plato's Cosmology, The Timaeus of Plato, Translated by Francis Macdonald Cornford, London, 1937.

Priscian, Institutiones Grammaticae, Ed. A. Krehl, Leipzig, 1819-20.

Registrum Roffense, ed. J. Thorpe, London, 1769.

Robert of Melun, Oeuvres de Robert de Melun, ed. R. M.
Martin, Tome 1, Questiones de Divina Pagina (Spicilegium Sacrum Lovaniense 13), Louvain, 1932; Tome 2. Questiones (Theologice) de Epistolis Pauli (Spicilegium Sacrum Lovaniense 18), Louvain, 1938.

Robert Pullen, Sententiarum Libri VIII, ed. H. Mathoud, Paris 1655 (reprinted in P. L. 186).
Sermo de Omnibus Humanae Uite Necessariis or De Contemptu Mundi, ed. F. Courtney, Gregorianum, XXXI (1950).

Roger of Hoveden, (Howden) annalium, pars prior, Frankfort, 1601.

Roland Bandinelli (Pope Alexander III), Sententiae, ed. A. M. Gietl, Die Sentenzen Rolands, Freiburg im Bresgau, 1891.

Rupert of Deutz, De Voluntate Dei, P. L. 170.
De Omnipotentia Dei, ibid.
In Regulam Sancti Benedicti, ibid.

Sarum Charters and Documents, selected by W. R. Jones, ed. W. Dunn, Rolls Series, London, 1891.

Sententie Abtrebatenses, ed. D. O. Lottin, Rech. Théol. anc. méd. X (1938).

Sententie Berolinenses, ed. F. Stegmüller, Rech. Théol. anc. méd. XI (1939).

Sententiae Divinitatis, ed. B. Geyer, Die Sententiae Divinitatis, ein Sentenzenbuch der Gilbertischen Schule, Beiträge, VII, 2-3, Münster, 1909.

Sententiae Florianenses, ed. H. Ostlender, Florilegium Patristicum, 19, Bonn, 1929.

Sententiae Hermanii i. e. Epitome Theologiae Christianae, P. L. 178 (where it is attributed to Abelard).

Sententiae Parisienses, ed. A. Landgraf, Ecrits théologiques de l'école d'Abélard (Spicilegium Sacrum Lovaniense 14), Louvain, 1934, 1-60.

Thomas Aquinas, Summa Theologiae; In Quattuor Libros Sententiarum Commentum; Summa Contra Gentiles.

Thomas Malden, Doctrinale Fidei, Venice, 1757.

Summa Sententiarum, P. L. 176.

Walter of Mortagne, Liber de Trinitate, ed. B. Pez. Thesauri Anecdotorum II, 2, Augustae Vindelicorum (Augsburg), 1721.
Epistola ad Abaelardum ed. L. d'Achéry, Spicilegium, tom. II, ed. III, p. 524, Paris, 1723.

William of Champeaux Sententiae Excerptae, ed. G. Lefèvre, Les Variations de Guillaume de Champeaux et la question des Universaux (Travaux et Mémoires, n. 20), Lille, 1898.

William of Conches, De Philosophia Mundi, P. L. 172 (where it is attributed to Honorius of Autun).

William of St. Theodoric, Disputatio adversus Petrum Abaelardum, P. L. 180.
Expositio in Epistolam ad Romanos, ibid.

Ysagoge in Theologiam, ed. A. Landgraf (see under Sententie Parisienses, l. c., 61-285).

3. *Studies and works of reference*

Only works cited in the text are mentioned in this list.

Anciaux, P., La théologie du sacrement de pénitence au XIIe siècle, Louvain, 1949.

Bale,J., Index Brittaniae Scriptorum, ed. R. L. Poole and M. Bateson, Oxford, 1902.

Bardy, G., La Littérature patristique des *Questiones et Responsiones* sur l'Ecriture sainte, R. bibl. XLI 1932 - XLII (1933).

Bateson, M., Catalogue of the Library of Syon Monastery, Isleworth, Cambridge, 1898.

Baumgartner, M., Die Philosophie des Alanus de Insulis, Beiträge, II, IV (1898).

Beumer, J., Ekklesiologische Probleme der Frühscholastik, Schol. XXVIII (1952).

Bliemetzrieder, F., Autour de l'œuvre théologique d'Anselme de Laon, R. T. A. M. i (1929).
vii (1935).
Robert von Melun und die Schule Anselms von Laon, Z. K. G. xxxiii 1934).
Isaac de Stella. Sa Spéculation théologique, ibid, iv (1932)).
L'œuvre d'Anselme de Laon et la littérature contemporaine, ibid.,

Chossat M., La Somme des Sentences, oeuvre de Hugues de Mortagne vers 1155. (Spicilegium Sacrum Lovaniense, 5), Louvain, 1923.
Dieu: sa nature selon les scolastiques, D. T. C. IV, 1152-1243, Paris 1911.

Chenu, M. D., Grammaire et théologie aux XIIe et XIIIe siècles. A. H. D. x (1935-6).

Ciaconius (Chacon) A., Vitae Pontificum Romanorum et S. R. E. Cardinalium, ed. A. Oldoini, Rome, 1677.

Corblet, J., Histoire du sacrement de l'Eucharistie, Paris, 1855.

Cottiaux, J., La conception de la théologie chez Abélard, R. H. E. xxviii (1932).

Denzinger, H., Bannwart C., Umberg, J. B., Enchiridion Symbolorum Definitionum et Declarationum de Rebus Fidei et Morum edn. 24 Barcelona, 1946.

Deutsch. S. M., Peter Abaelard, ein kritischer Theologe des zwölften Jahrhunderts, Leipzig, 1883.

Dickinson, J. C., The Origins of the Austin Canons and their Introduction into England, London, 1950.

Ducange, C. D., Glossarium Mediae et Infimae Latinitatis, ed. G. A. L. Henschel, Paris, 1842.

Dugdale, W., Monasticon Anglicanum, augmented edition, London, 1817-30.

Feret, P., La faculté de théologie de Paris et ses docteurs les plus illustres, Paris, 1894.

Fourier-Bonnard., Histoire de l'abbaye royale et de l'Ordre des chanoines réguliers de Saint-Victor de Paris, Paris, 1904.

Ghellinck,, J. de., Le mouvement théologique du XIIe siècle, éd. 1, Paris, 1914.

Gilson, J. P., The Library of Sir Henry Savile of Banks, in Transactions of the Bibliographical Society, ix, London, 1908.

Grabmann, M., Die Geschichte der katholische Theologie, Freiburg im Breisgau, 1933.
Die Geschichte der scholastischen Methode, ibid. 1911.

Hauréau, B., De la philosophie scolastique, Paris, 1850. Histoire de la philosophie scolastique, Paris, 1872.
Articles on MS. Paris B. N. 2945 in Notices et Extraits XXXIII, Paris, 1903.

Holtzmann, W., Papsturkunden in England, Bd. 3, Göttingen, 1952.

Jaffé P., Regesta Pontificum Romanorum, ed 2, Leipzig, 1885.

James, M. R., A Catalogue of the Manuscripts in Jesus College, Cambridge, Cambridge, 1895.

Joyce, G. H., Christian Marriage, ed. 2, London, 1948.

Knowles, D. and Hadcock R. N., Medieval Religious Houses - England and Wales, London, 1953.

Landgraf, A., Einführung in die Geschichte der theologischen Literatur der Frühscholastik, Regensburg, 1948.
Dogmengeschichte der Frühscholastik, I-II, i, Regensburg, 1952-3.
Literarhistorische Bemerkungen zu den Sentenzen des Robertus Pullus, Traditio 1 (1943).
Die Abhängigkeit der Sünde von Gott nach der Lehre der Frühscholastik, Scholastik, X (1935).
Some Unknown Writings of the Early Scholastic Period, The New Scholasticism IV (1930).
Zum Begriff der Scholastik, Coll. Fran. XI (1941).
Zur Technik und Überlieferung der Disputation, Coll. Fran. XX (1950).
Untersuchungen zu den Eigenlehren Gilberts de la Porrée, Z. k. Th. LIV (1930).
Die Linderung der Höllenstrafen nach der Lehre der Frühscholastik, Z. k. Th. LX (1936).
Die Vererbung der Sünden der Eltern auf die Kinder nach der Lehre des 12. Jahrhunderts, Greg. XXI (1940).
Die Einführung des Begriffspaares opus operans und opus operatum in die Theologie, Div. Th. Fr. XXIX (1951).
Die Gnadensökonomie des Alten Bundes nach der Lehre der Frühscholastik, Z. k. Th. LVII (1933).
Das Axiom « Verbum assumpsit carnem mediante anima » in der Frühscholastik, Acta Pont. Academiae Romanae S. Thomae et Religionis Catholicae, IX, Rome, 1944).
Die Sterblichkeit Christi nach der Lehre der Frühscholastik, Z. k. Th. LXXIII (1951).
Die Unsündbarkeit Christi in den Frühesten Schulen der Scholastik, Scholastik, XIII (1938).
Die Erkenntnis der heiligmachenden Gnade in der Frühscholastik, Scholastik, III (1928).
Glaube und Werk in der Frühscolastik, Greg. XVII (1936).
Die Lehre der Frühscholastik von der knechtischen Furcht, Div. Th, Fr. XV (1937).

Familienbildung bei Paulinenkommentaren des 12 Jahrhunderts, Biblica, XIII (1932).
Die Erkenntnis der helfenden Gnade in der Frühscholastik, Z. k. Th. LV (1931).
Die Bestimmung des Verdienstgrades in der Frühscholastik, Scholastik, VIII 1933).
Der Frühscholastische Streit um die Potestas quam Christus potuit dare servis et non dedit, Greg. XV (1934).
Beiträge der Frühscholastik zur Terminologie der allgemeinen Sakramentenlehre, Div. Th. Fr. (1951).
Zur Frage von der Wiederholbarkeit der Sakramente, Div. Th. Fr. XXIX (1951).
Die Frühscholastiche Definition der Taufe, Greg. XXVII (1946).
Kindertaufe und Glaube in der Frühscholastik, Greg. IX (1928).
Grundlagen für ein Verständnis der Buszlehre der Scholastik, Z. k. Th. LI (1927).
Sünde und Trennung von der Kirche in der Frühscholastik, Scholastik, V (1930).
Die frühscholastische Streitfrage vom Wiederaufleben der Sünden, Z. k. Th. LXI (1931).
Zur Lehre der Konsekrationsgewalt des von der Kirche getrennten Priesters im 12. Jahrhundert, Scholastik, XV (1940).
Zwei Probleme der frühscholastischen Sakramentenlehre, Z. k. Th. LXVI (1942).

Lecler J., L'Argument des deux glaives, R. S. R. XXI (1931).

Leclercq, J., Recherches sur d'anciens sermons monastiques, Revue Mabillon, XXXVI (1946).

Lefèvre, G., De Anselmo Laudunensi Scholastico (1050-1117), Evreux, 1895.

Liebeschütz, H., Medieval Humanism in the Life and Writings of John of Salisbury, Studies of the Warburg Institute, vol. 17, London, 1950.

Lottin, O., Les théories du péché originel au XIIe siècle, R. T. A. M. XI 1939); XII (1940).
Psychologie et morale au XIIe siècle, I-III, Louvain, 1942-49.

Mansi J. D., Sacrorum Conciliorum Nova et Amplissima Collectio, XXi, Paris, 1903.

Martène-Durand, Thesaurus Novus Anecdotorum, Paris, 1717.

Mignon, A., Les origines de la scolastique et Hugues de Saint-Victor, Paris, 1895.

Noyon, A., Inventaire des écrits théologiques du XIIe siècle, Rev. des bibliothèques, 1912-13.

Maldonatus, J., Commentaria in Quattuor Evangelia ed. J. M. Raich, Moguntiae (Mainz), 1874.

Ott, L., Untersuchungen zur theologischen Briefliteratur der Frühscholastik. Beiträge, xxxiv, (1937).

Oudinus, C., Commentarius de Scriptoribus Ecclesiae Antiquis, Leipzig, 1722.

Paré G., Brunet A., Tremblay P., La renaissance du XIIe siècle: les écoles et l'enseignement, Paris and Ottawa, 1933.

Pelster, F., Leben und Schriften des Robertus Pullus, Scholastik, xii (1937).

Petavius (Pétau), D., De Theologicis Dogmatibus, ed. C. Passaglia, and C. Schraeder, Rome, 1857.

Pflugk-Hartung, J. v., Acta Pontificum Inedita III, Urkunden der Päpste, 590 (c) - 1197, Stuttgart, 1886.

Poole, R. L., Illustrations of the History of Medieval Thought and Learning, London, 1920.
John of Salisbury at the Papal Court, English Historical Review, xxxviii (1923).
Lectures on the History of the Papal Chancery, Cambridge, 1915.
Masters of the Schools at Paris and Chartres in John of Salisbury's Time, E. H. R. xxv (1920).
The Early Lives of Robert Pullen and Nicholas Breakspear in Essays in Medieval History presented to Thomas Frederick Tout, ed. A. G. Little and F. M. Powicke, Manchester, 1925.

Rashdall, H., The Universities of Europe in the Middle Ages. New edn. of F. M. Powicke and A. B. Emden, Oxford, 1936.

art. Robert Pullen, in the Dictionary of National Biography, vol. XLVII.

Robert, G., Les écoles et l'enseignement de la théologie pendant la première moitié du XIIe siècle, Paris, 1909.

Salter, H. E., The Medieval University of Oxford, History, N. S. XIV. 53 (1929).

Smalley, B., The Study of the Bible in the Middle Ages, ed. 1. Oxford, 1941.
La Glossa Ordinaria, R. T. A. M. ix (1937).

Silva-Tarouca, C., Fontes Historiae Ecclesiasticae Medii Aevi, Rome, 1930.

Stegmüller, F., Sententiae Berolinenses, R. T. A. M. xi (1939).

Sylvester, W., The Communions with Three Blades of Grass of the Knights-Errant, Dublin Review, CXXI (1897).

Tanner, T., Bibliotheca Brittanico-Hibernica, London, 1748.

Vercellone, G., Variae Lectiones Vulgatae Latinae Bibliorum, Rome, 1860.

Vregille, B de., L'attente des Saints d'après Saint Bernard N. R. T. LXX (1948).

Weisweiller, H., Das Schriften der Schule Anselms von Laon und Wilhelm von Champeaux in deutschen Bibliotheken, Beiträge, XXXIII, 1-2 (1936).

La Summa Sententiarum source de Pierre Lombard, R. T. A. M. vi (1934).

L'école d'Anselme de Laon et de Guillaume de Champeaux. Nouveaux documents, ibid., iv. (1932).

Wilkins, D., Concilia Magnae Britanniae, London, 1737.

Williams, M. E., The Teaching of Gilbert Porreta on the Trinity, Rome, 1951.

CHAPTER I.

THE LIFE OF CARDINAL ROBERT PULLEN

THE NAME PULLEN.

The name Pullen appears under a number of different forms, Latin and English. St. Bernard, who was well acquainted with the Cardinal, refers to him as Pullus [1]. This has become the usual Latin form of his name and is the one employed in the manuscript used by Pullen's editor Mathoud for the 1655 edition of the *Sentences*. In Mathoud's opinion this manuscript dated from Pullen's own day [2]. Geoffrey of Auxerre, St. Bernard's secretary, used the form Pullanus [3], as also does John of Hexham, who wrote about ten years after Pullen's death [4]. This form is clearly but a Latin equivalent for Pulein which occurs in the Annals of Oseney Abbey [5]. A manuscript dating from about the middle of the twelfth century which is cited by Dr. A. Landgraf, refers to Master Robert as R(obertus) Pollet and R(oberti) Poldi [6]. Another manuscript, also mentioned by Dr. Landgraf, uses the form R(obertus) Polanus [7]. The collection of his sermons in MS. Paris, B.N. 2945 contains the form Pulo Further variants of the name which occur in sixteenth and seventeenth-century historians are recorded by Mathoud [8].

---

[1] *Ep.* 205, *P.L.*, 182, 372. John of Salisbury, Pullen's pupil, speaks of his master as Rodbertus Pullus, *Metalogicon*, I, 5; II, 10.

[2] See *P.L.*, 186, 633.

[3] *Libellus contra Capitula Gilberti Pictaviensis Episcopi, P.L.*, 185, 616. It is also used in the MSS of Pullen's sermons.

[4] *Continuation of Symeon of Durham*, II, 319, R. S., London, 1885.

[5] *Annales Monastici*, IV, 19, R. S., (London, 1869).

[6] 'Some Unknown Writings of the Early Scholastic Period', in *The New Scholasticism* IV (1930) 11-4.

[7] *Ibid.* This form also appears in the Treatise of Pullen De Omnibus Humane Uite Necessariis (De Contemptu Mundi) my edition in *Gregorianum* xxxi (1950) 192-223.

[8] *P. L.*, 186, 634-9.

The meaning of the surname Pullus is uncertain. Dr. R. L. Poole wrote that the name « may indeed be the adjective ' brown '; but almost certainly it is the substantive meaning the young of any animal, as a colt or a cockerel, because very early the surname appears as Pullanus, the French *poulain* » [9]. The same scholar went on to suggest that Pullanus « had a depreciative implication, and was used to mean a poor sort of person ». Poole found this interpretation of the name confirmed by what he considered to be an allusion to Robert Pullen by the anonymous author of a twelfth-century poem entitled *Metamorphosis Goliae Episcopi* [10]. In this poem there are references, more or less veiled, to some of the leading Parisian masters of the fourth and fifth decades of the twelfth century, including two of the name of Robert who are thus described:

« Robertus theologus corde vivens mundo
adest ...
et Robertus Amiclas simile secutus ».

Dr. Poole identified Robert the theologian whose purity of life is here signalised, with Robert of Melun who, in 1163, became Bishop of Hereford, and the other Robert to whom the surname Amiclas is given, with Robert Pullen.

The name Amiclas, says Poole, had come to acquire the depreciative sense which may have been implied by Pullus; it was in connotation the opposite to Croesus, so that the term *pauper Amiclas* had become a synonym for a poor man. The fact that, according to John of Hexham [11], Robert Pullen had refused a bishopric offered him by Henry I, being content to lead the life of a poor teacher, is to Dr. Poole further evidence in favour of this identification. The arguments in favour of seeing an allusion to Pullen in ' Robertus Amiclas ' and to Robert of Melun in ' Robertus Theologus ' did not appeal to F. Bliemetzrieder who proposed that these identifications should be reversed [12].

The term ' theologian ' says Bliemetzrieder, is more appropriately applied to Robert Pullen than to Robert of Melun. The

---

9 ' Masters of the Schools at Paris and Chartres in John of Salisbury 's Time ' in *E.H.R.* XXXV (1920), 339 ff.

10 In Latin Poems attributed to Walter Mapes, Ed. T. Wright, (London, 1841).

11 *Loc. cit.*

12 Robert von Melun und die Schule Anselms von Laon', *Z.K.G.* LIII (1934), 116.

words of John of Salisbury[13], who tells us that he listened to Pullen's lectures, but only in theology, suggest that Pullen was known only as a theologian; the references to his teaching at Oxford only make mention of his activity in the promotion of biblical studies. On the other hand, continues Bliemetzrieder, the identification of 'Robertus Amiclas simile secutus' with Robert of Melun, though not certain, is better warranted than with Robert Pullen. Among other possible meanings the name 'Amiclas' might signify either a person of Spartan habits or one devoted to dialectic. No certain identification can be founded on these various meanings. More light, however, is thrown on the problem by the phrase 'simile secutus', which, he contends, is a veiled allusion indicating an adherent of the school of Abelard. The use of similes for the illustration of theological argument was characteristic of that school, as is evident both from Abelard's own work and from that of his pupils, Masters Roland Bandinelli and Odo of Soissons. It is natural to think, therefore, of an allusion to Robert of Melun in the passage in question, since there is no doubt that he owed much to the writings of Abelard[14]. The term *Amiclas* would also be not inappropriate as applied to him, since, according to John of Salisbury[15], when he was a master in the schools he had a reputation for despising money which was only equalled by his love of honour and applause. On the other hand, Bliemetzrieder admits that, in the fragments so far published from the *Sentences* of Robert of Melun, there is no trace of the use of the illustrative simile. Since Bliemetzrieder wrote, however, Père R. M. Martin, O. P. has published the *Questiones de Epistolis Pauli* of Robert of Melun, in which there is ample use of the Abelardian similes[16]. Père Martin notes that they are also to be found in the *Sentences*, the relevant parts of which he published in 1933[17]. The title of *theologus* would not be entirely inappropriate to designate Robert of Melun, Bliemetzrieder acknowledges, since after a short period of teaching dialectic at Mont Ste.-Geneviève, he devoted himself exclusively to theology at Melun.

On the whole, I think the balance of probability is in favour of identifying 'Robertus Theologus' with Pullen and 'Robertus Amiclas' with Robert of Melun. That Pullen was entirely detached

---

13 *Metalogicon*, II, 10.

14 See R. M. Martin, *Oeuvres de Robert de Melun*, II, xxxvii-xxxviii (Louvain, 1938). *Questiones* (Theologice) *de Epistolis Pauli*.

15 *Ep. 183* (*Ad Thomam Archiep. Cantuar.*), P. L., 199, 186A.

16 *Op. cit.*, 26-7.

17 Ibid., note.

from concern with money matters is not borne out by the history of his controversy with Ascelin, Bishop of Rochester. The description 'corde vivens mundo', which is attached to Robert the Theologian, might well apply to Pullen, for St. Bernard says that after his departure for Rome his memory was held in benediction in Paris [18], and John of Salisbury does not confine himself to praising his learning, but also eulogises his character: 'quem vita pariter et scientia commendabant' [19].

Pullen's origin and education.

Pullen was born in Britain, as we learn on the authority of John of Hexham, writing of the year 1146. He says that Pullen refused the offer of a bishopric by Henry I [20]. Whether he was of Anglo-Saxon or Anglo-Norman stock is uncertain, as also is the part of England from which he hailed. Most probably he belonged to the South-West of England, as we find him writing in 1145, when he had become cardinal and papal chancellor, that Prior Joseph of the Benedictine monastery of Sherborne is his first cousin, 'filius anunculi nostri', and that a number of his near relations belong to the same monastery, 'et plures in eodem monasterio uicina nobis propinquitate iunguntur' [21]. This suggests that the family of Robert Pullen was established somewhere in the neighbourhood of Sherborne.

In the twelfth [22] and thirteenth [23] centuries the name Pulayn and its equivalent Puleyn is found in documents associated with the South-West of England.

---

18 *Ep. 352 (Ad Robertum Pullum) P. L.*, 182, 563.

19 *Metalogicon*, II, 10.

20 'Praeminuit his diebus in clero Romano Rodbertus Pullanus, cancellarius apostolicae sedis, in omni sapientia et doctrina experientissimus, Brittania oriundus, ab ineunte aetate philosophiae deditus, ejusque obtentu episcopalem honorem ab Henrico rege oblatum respuens, victum habens his contentus fuit. *loc. cit.*

21 Cartulary of Sherborne, s. xii, Brit. Mus. Add. 46481, fol. 33 v. ed. W. Holtzmann, *Papsturkunden in England*, Bd. 3, 173 (Göttingen 1952).

22 About the year 1200 a certain Reginald Pulayn is mentioned as a witness to an agreement betwween John de Cnoll and the Abbot of St. Augustine's, Bristol, concerning the Church of Wapley, *Sarum Charters ad Documents*, 58-9, R. S., (London, 1891).

23 On Oct. 16th, 1243, one of the witnesses to a document on the fealty due to the Church of Bedminster from the hospital of St. John, Bristol, bears the name Robert Pule(y)n. *Ibid.*, 286-8.

As to the social status of Pullen evidence is likewise wanting. No value can be attached to the speculations of seventeenth-century writers, who, building on the simple statement in the Oseney Annals that he restored the study of Scripture at Oxford, make him out to have been a wealthy benefactor, who out of his own resources supported a number of professors and students from various parts of England. Pullen's own extant writings contain no information on this point. Dr. R. L. Poole was of the opinion that Robert did not spring from an influential family. His conviction rested, apparently, on John of Hexham's testimony to the poverty which marked his life, and on the more questionable identification of Pullen with 'Robertus Amiclas' [24].

The date of Robert's birth is not known. Poole argues that the offer of a bishopric would not have been made by Henry I while Pullen was yet at an early age, since he had no powerful family connections. He assigns his birth to some time in the last quarter of the eleventh century [25]. As he died in 1146 after having been Cardinal for about two years, and apparently after a long career as a teacher [26], and as he had a nephew who by 1145 was already ordained deacon and who was old enough to administer his property in Rochester, the year 1080 would probably not be far out as the date of his birth.

According to traditions recorded by sixteenth and seventeenth-century writers, Pullen received his early education in England and then proceeded to Paris to complete his studies [27]. Both of these statements are likely enough, since at the beginning of the twelfth century England had in comparison few facilities for higher studies. Nevertheless, the assertion that it was under Stephen that Pullen left England to continue his studies abroad, which Pits [28] says he learns on the authority of the fifteenth-century bibliophile, John Boston of Bury, is manifestly erroneous, since Pullen had already begun to teach at Oxford under Henry I. The close acquaintance which Pullen manifests in his *Sentences* with the questions which were most keenly debated in the French schools during the first four decades of the twelfth century, together with his appointment to teach theology in the Cathedral school at Paris make it almost

---

24 'The Early Lives of Robert Pullen and Nicholas Breakspear', in *Essays Presented to T. F. Tout* (Manchester, 1925), 61.

25 The Early Lives, etc., 61.

26 This is suggested by a passage in St. Bernard's letter to Pullen, *infra*, 18.

27 See Mathoud, *P. L.* 186, 634; 639.

28 *Relatio Historica de Rebus Anglicis* (Paris, 1619), 210.

certain that it was in France that he received his theological formation. If the older historians were right in making Paris the centre of Robert's studies, it is probable that he came under the influence of William of Champeaux who was head of the Cathedral school at Paris from 1103 until his entry into the Abbey of St. Victor in 1108, where after a time he resumed his teaching. William was the pupil and in most questions the faithful echo of Anselm of Laon, the most famous teacher of theology between the years 1090 and 1115.

His lectures at Oxford.

The earliest facts in Robert's life of which we have certain knowledge, are those related in the Annals of Oseney Abbey under the year 1133. Mention is there made of his lecturing on the bible at Oxford, of the services which he rendered by his learning to the English and French church, and of his promotion to the cardinalate and chancellorship of the Roman Church [29]. Dr. R. L. Poole, who transcribed the passage from the surviving manuscript, makes it clear that the abbreviated form Oxon is the one used by the copyist. Another source, the *Continuatio Bedae,* gives an expanded sion [30]. The value of this document, if realiable, lies in its association of Robert Pullen with Exeter and in the dating of his teaching at Oxford. It was written for Robert Wyvil, bishop of Salisbury, 1330-75. For the details which it supplies concerning Oxford and Oseney it is based on the Annals of Oseney [31]. Dr. Poole pointed out that for the notice concerning Robert Pullen the compiler was using two sources; one of them, he held, gave the information that Master Robert taught at Exeter, the other, at Oxford. The compiler, in Poole's opinion, endeavoured to reconcile

---

29 'Magister Robertus Pulein scripturas divinas, quae in Anglia obsoluerant apud Oxoniam legere coepit. Qui postea, cum ex doctrina ejus ecclesia tam Anglicana quam Gallicana plurimum profecisset, a Papa Lucio secundo vocatus et in cancellarium Sanctae Romanae ecclesiae promotus est'. *Annales Monastici,* IV R. S. (London, 1869), 19 f.

30 « Eodem anno (1133) venit magister Robertus cognomento pullus de civitate Exonia Oxenfordiam ibique scripturas divinas, que per idem tempus in Anglia (MS. Angliam) absolute erant et scolasticis quippe neglecte fuerant, per quinquennium legit. Omnique die dominico verbum Dei populo predicavit; ex cujus doctrina plurimum profecerunt. Qui postea ob eximiam doctrinam et religiosam famam a papa Lucio vocatus et in cancellarium Romane ecclesie promotus est ». Cited by R. L. Poole, *The Early Lives,* etc. 62.

31 *Ibid.*

his sources by making Robert come from Exeter to Oxford [32]. On the whole, Poole considered it more likely that Master Robert taught at Exeter than at Oxford. He argues that in the Oseney Annals the words *oxon* and *exon* are written very much alike; that cases are known in which they contain *oxon* where the reading should undoubtedly be *exon;* that the existing manuscript from which Luard's edition is printed, where we have the reading *oxon,* is itself but a fourteenth-century transcript of an older book, Vitellius E. 15, which was damaged by a fire in the Cottonian library at Ashburnham House in 1731. Only the first two letters of the word in dispute remain in the fragments of the book which survived the fire. From these Dr. Poole says that it is certain that Robert's teaching was described as ' ap. ox. ', but suggests that this is an error for ' ap. ex(on) '.

In reply to Dr. Poole, Dr. H. E. Salter remarks that ' the original edition of the Annals of Oseney — written about 1196 — did not use Oxonia, a word which had not been invented at that time, but Oxeneford ', and that ' Brian Twyne, who saw the manuscript before it was burnt, gives the word in full ' [33].

A further reason advanced by Poole in support of his opinion that Exeter rather than Oxford was the scene of Robert's teaching, is that ' there is no well-attested instance of any literary activity at Oxford between the isolated appearance of Theobald of Etampes, probably in the first decade of the twelfth century, and some time after 1167 ' [34]. Dr. Salter was able to point to sufficient evidence to invalidate this reason [35].

We may, therefore, take it as well established that Pullen taught at Oxford. The author of the *Continuatio Bedae* must have been drawing on some source other than the Oseney Annals for his information about the length of Pullen's stay in Oxford and for the detail that he came thither from Exeter. Before leaving this point, it is worthy of note that the mention in the Oseney Annals of Pullen's having been called to Rome, and made Chancellor of the Church by Pope Lucius II, has also been called in question by certain historians, but that the accuracy of the Annals has been vindicated here also.

Around the simple mention of Master Robert's activity as teacher of Scripture at Oxford a legend arose which credited him

---

32 *Ibid.*

33 ' The Medieval University of Oxford ' in *History,* N. N., XLV, 53 (1929) 57.

34 *The Early Lives,* etc., 62.

35 *Art. cit.*

with the restoration of learning in the University [36]. As the University of Oxford was not as yet in existence, it is probable that he taught in some school attached to one of the Oxford Churches, perhaps St. George-in-the-Castle [37]. This conjecture is confirmed by the existence of a papal grant in favour of this church issued during Pullen's tenure of the office of Chancellor of the Roman Church [38].

Association with Exeter.

It is possible that before coming to Oxford Master Robert had already acquired a reputation as a teacher at Exeter. Dr. R. L. Poole argued that about the beginning of the fourth decade of the twelfth century Exeter must have been a centre of learning. He relied partly on traces of literary activity, dating from the twelfth century, which had its origin there, partly on the fact that the master and clerks who were there around the year 1160 would have been pupils about 1133 [39]. This argument gains in probability from the fact that in the year 1113 there was an archdeacon at Exeter, a certain Master Robert, who had spent a long time at Laon listening to the lectures of the famous Master Anselm of Laon. When in that year a deputation of canons of Laon passed over to England to solicit alms for the rebuilding of the church of Our Lady of Laon, they spent ten days at Exeter where they were most hospitably received by Master Robert and the citizens [40].

It has been suggested that this Master Robert is none other than Robert Pullen [41]. There can be no certainty about the identification, but it is at least possible. If, as seems likely, Pullen was born about the year 1080, he might well have been archdeacon of Exeter by 1113. Much of Pullen's theology is in harmony with the ideas of Anselm of Laon, as will be indicated in the succeeding

---

[36] See Mathoud, *P. L.*, 633-40.

[37] See Rashdall's *Medieval Universities*, ed. F. M. Powicke and A. B. Emden, III, 9, n. 3; Knowles and Hadcock, *Medieval Religious Houses*, 338.

[38] See W. Holtzmann, *op. cit.*, 182.

[39] *The Early Lives*, etc., 63.

[40] 'Inde venimus ad urbem quae dicitur Essecestra, ubi erat Robertus archidiaconus, qui diu manserat Lauduni pro audienda lectione magistri Anselmi. A quo gratantissime suscepti mansimus ibi per decem dies'. Hermanni Monachi, *De miraculis S. Mariae Laudunensis*, II, 13, *P. L.*, 156, 982 A.

[41] By F. Bliemetzrieder, in *Z. K. G.* 53 (1934) 116, 'Robert von Melun und die Schule Anselms von Laon'.

chapters of this study; Pullen is clearly associated with the more famous theologians of the school of Anselm of Laon and William of Champeaux by Geoffrey of Auxerre [42]; the relations of Pullen with St. Bernard strengthen the case for this association. These indications, taken together with the statement of the *Continuatio Bedae* that Master Robert Pullen came to Oxford from Exeter, all tend to support the conjecture that it was he who was archdeacon of Exeter in 1113.

Lecturer in Paris.

According to the *Continuatio Bedae* Robert taught for five years at Oxford. This brings us to the year 1138. When we next hear of him he is engaged in teaching theology at Paris. The source of our information here is John of Salisbury, who, while giving an account of his own studies, says that Robert became his master in theology in succession to Gilbert Porreta. The year was 1142, when Gilbert was elected Bishop of Poitiers [43]. The school in which Pullen lectured would be that attached to the Cathedral [44].

Archdeacon of Rochester.

In addition to his position as a teacher Pullen held at this time the office of archdeacon of Rochester. For some time between the years 1137 and 1142 the see of Rochester was vacant. For part of this period it was administered by John, bishop of Séez in Normandy. According to the monastic chronicler whose work is incorporated in the *Registrum Roffense,* John of Séez had come to England with Stephen on the latter's succession to Henry I in 1135 [45]. Bishop John of Séez ceased to be administrator on the election of Ascelin, formerly prior of Dover, to the see of Rochester in 1142 [46]. Bishop John of Séez had had charge of the see for

---

[42] *Libell. Contr. Capit. Gilbert. Pictav. Episc., P. L.* 185, 616 C.

[43] *Metalogicon,* II, 10.

[44] P. Feret, *La Faculté de théologie de Paris et ses docteurs les plus illustres,* I (Paris, 1894). 40.

[45] *Registrum Roffense,* ed. J. Thorpe, London, 1769.

[46] A. Saltman defends the opinion that there was a diocesan bishop (John II) of Rochester between 1137 (when John I died) and 1142 (when Ascelin was consecrated), and that this John II was not Bishop John of Séez as adminis-

three years, 1139-42. During that period, adds the chronicler, he appointed Master Robert Pullus as archdeacon. It looks, therefore, as if Master Robert, after spending about five years at Oxford, 1133-8, had been summoned thence to Rochester by Bishop John almost as soon as the latter took over the administration of the see [47]. Both Bishop John and his brother Arnulphus, archdeacon of Séez and later bishop of Lisieux, were intimately associated with the Victorines of Paris. It was John of Séez who established the Victorine canons in his own cathedral at Séez [48]. Arnulphus is remembered as the source from whom Walter of Mortagne obtained the information that Hugh of St. Victor held what Walter considered erroneous views on the human knowledge of Christ. In a letter written about 1133-5 Walter, still perhaps engaged in teaching at Laon, wrote to Hugh of St. Victor attempting to refute his opinion on the point in question [49]. In answer to this letter Hught wrote his treatise *De Sapientia Animae Christi* [50]. It is likely enough that John of Séez and Robert Pullen had been acquainted with each other by contact in academic circles in Paris or Laon long before Master Robert was appointed to the archdeaconry of Rochester. It would appear that it was by permission of Bishop John that Master Robert was lecturing in Paris in 1142, while still retaining his office of archdeacon. Had the permission been granted by the new bishop of Rochester, Ascelin, it is not likely that he would have demanded Pullen's return from Paris so soon as he did.

---

trator. It seems most likely that John II was bishop from 1137-1139, and that Bishop John of Séez was administrator from 1139-1142. For Saltman's view see *Engl. Hist. Rev.* (1951) 71-75.

[47] In 1139. Le Neve, *Fasti Ecclesiae Anglicanae,* contin. T. Duffus Hardy, 2, (Oxford 1854) 579, records Pullen as already archdeacon of Rochester in 1134. This date seems impossible, (i) in view of the information given in the *Registrum Roffense,* (ii) because at that time Pullen was teaching at Oxford. As F. Pelster observes, 'Leben und Schriften des Robertus Pullus', in *Scholastik* XII (1937) 241, an absence prolonged over several years at Oxford could hardly have been compatible with the discharge of the duties of an archdeacon of Rochester. Hence Pelster made the tentative suggestion that Richard Tillesley, on whose testimony the date 1134 is based, (according to Cave, *Historia Litteraria,* 2, Oxford, 1743, 222 f.) misread the last figure of the date in question, taking a IX for a IV. This hypothesis seems to be confirmed by the evidence of the *Registrum Roffense* concerning Pullen's appointment to the archdeaconry.

[48] Fournier-Bonnard, *Histoire de l'abbaye royale de Saint-Victor de Paris,* I, 143 ff.

[49] The letter was published by Mathoud in the notes to his edition of Pullen's *Sentences, P.L.,* 186, 1052-4.

[50] *P.L.* 176, 845.

PULLEN'S DISPUTE WITH ASCELIN.

Robert's non-residence was but one of the reasons which led to his dispute with Ascelin. The history of the affair is contained in several documents printed in the *Registrum Roffense,* and there is an allusion to it in a letter of St. Bernard to Ascelin, in which he asks the bishop to reconsider his decision to recall Master Robert from Paris [51].

During the time of Bishop John I of Rochester, before the vacancy of the see, there had been celebrations in Rochester to celebrate the consecration of the Cathedral [52]. In the course of the festivities a fire broke out in the city, and both the new cathedral church of St. Andrew, and the monastery which was attached to it, received much damage. Shortly afterwards, in June 1137, occurred the death of Bishop John I. As a result of the damage done to their monastery, the monks were compelled to seek refuge in neighbouring monasteries; some of them, we are told, returned home. Presumably it is meant that they returned to their mother-house. After the departure of the monks Bishop John of Séez bestowed several churches of which they had formerly held the revenues on his new archdeacon, Master Robert Pullen. The monastic chronicler, who is clearly biased against the administrator and his archdeacon, describes the bishop as 'more like a plunderer than a pastor of another's flock'. On his election to the see of Rochester, Ascelin supported the monks in their demand for the restoration of their churches. Ascelin also had personal grievances against Master Robert. In a letter written to Pope Eugenius III, shortly after Pullen's death, he accused the Archdeacon of usurping episcopal rights in certain matters: 'quaedam sibi ad episcopale jus spectantia usurparet' [53], and also of being wanting in proper submission to his bishop: 'Nullaque michi, ut proprio episcopo, subderetur obedientia, nullo deferret obsequio' [54]. Robert's attitude, he maintained, was dictated by consciousness of his great learning: 'multe literarum scientie confisus'. Reading between the lines, one gathers that the Archdeacon had made out a strong case in canon law for the legitimacy of the position he had taken up. The rights

---

[51] *Ep.* 205, *P. L.,* 182, 372.

[52] This detail is supplied by Dugdale, *Monasticon Anglicanum,* Augmented Edn. I (London, 1817) 155.

[53] *Registrum Roffense,* 39.

[54] *Ibid.* Ascelin's claim on Pullen's obedience does not preclude the possibility that the latter was a regular canon. See *infra* 37 f.

of the Bishop, which Robert is said to have usurped, evidently refer to certain revenues which the Bishop claimed for himself, and which apparently the archdeacon had received from John of Séez. In the letter to Pope Eugenius they are referred to as 'duos denarios — episcopalis specialiter justitiae'; in the Bull of Celestine II, which promulgated the first settlement of the dispute, they are called 'duos nummos de justitia episcopi' [55]. The charge of insubordination evidently refers to Robert's unwillingness to give up his teaching in Paris and return to Rochester. St. Bernard's letter, written about the end of 1142 or the beginning of 1143, makes it evident that he was responsible for Pullen's prolonged absence in Paris [56].

Allusions in the letter make it certain that Bernard had already sought permission of Ascelin for Master Robert to remain in Paris, but without success. After denying that he had counselled the archdeacon in any way to oppose the will of his Bishop, he renews his request that Pullen be granted leave of absence in order to lecture in Paris. He renews his warning to Ascelin that Master Robert has powerful friends in the Roman curia, and expresses his regret that already, while the appeal to Rome has not as yet come up for hearing, the Bishop should have confiscated the property of the Archdeacon [57]. The property in dispute between the bishop and the archdeacon included the Church of Boxley, the Church of St. Margaret, and the parochial altar of St. Nicholas in the cathedral church of St. Andrew, of all of which the monks had formerly had direct control, together with the Church of Aylesford which had been held of the monks by a chaplain named Jordan, and the church of Southfleet held of them by a certain priest called John. In addition there were the revenues claimed of Robert by the bishop as belonging to himself [58].

The dispute was referred to Rome while as yet Innocent II was pope. Before the case came up for hearing Innocent died, and was succeeded by Celestine II, who had been reputed to favour

---

[55] *Registrum Roffense,* 40.

[56] 'Dure scribitis non merenti. Quid peccavi? Si monui magistrum Robertum Pullum aliquantum tempus facere Parisiis, ob sanam doctrinam quae apud illum esse dignoscitur; id putavi necessarium, et adhuc puto'. *Ep.* 205, *P. L.,* 182, 372A.

[57] 'Si dixi hominem fultum gratia amicorum, quorum in curia non minima est; id dixi, quod vobis formidavi, et adhuc formido. Nam quod post appellationem factam extendistis manum (ut accepimus) ad res appellantis, nec laudavi nec laudo'. *Ibid.*

[58] *Registrum Roffense,* 40.

Abelard, and with whom, therefore, one of St. Bernard's circle, such as Pullen, was not likely to find favour. The Bull which Celestine issued in settlement of the question confirms the impression given by St. Bernard's letter to Ascelin that it was Pullen who had been the first to appeal to Rome. Ascelin, we learn, had been summoned to Rome by Pope Innocent II to answer a complaint which had been made against him [59]. His action in confiscating the property of his archdeacon before the appeal had been heard, was, as St. Bernard implied, quite unjustifiable. Ascelin presented himself in Rome by the appointed day, the octave of St. Martin, November 18th, 1143. In his letter to Pope Eugenius III, written about three years later, Ascelin makes it appear that his journey to Rome had been made spontaneously in order to obtain redress for his grievances, and that he himself had appealed to the Holy See as well as the archdeacon [60]. When the day of hearing arrived Master Robert did not appear, nor did he send a proctor to negotiate on his behalf.

The reason for this non-attendance would appear to have been Robert's conviction that he was unlikely to gain a favourable decision from the pro-Abelardian Pope Celestine, though Ascelin in his letter to Eugenius III attributed Robert's absence to fear arising out of consciousness of guilt [61].

The Bull which contains Celestine's decision is dated November 28th, 1143. From it we learn that, besides Ascelin, certain monks and other persons from Rochester had appeared at Rome for the suit, and that Ascelin had been able to clear himself of the charges brought against him. It enjoined that the churches in dispute should be restored to their former possessors, and that Robert should be summoned to Rochester by the following Pentecost. Bishop Ascelin was left free either to retain him in his office of archdeacon or to select another [62]. Ascelin's letter to the parties concerned in which, on his return to England, he announced the result of his journey to Rome, bears an unmistakable note of triumph [63].

---

59 'super his quae adversus eum dicta fuerant, se in nostra praesentia excusavit'. *Ibid.*

60 'tanta permotus injuria Romanam sedem expetii, sperans illum eo venturum, praefixoque termino communem appellationem executurum'. *Registrum Roffense,* 39.

61 'Se (sed?) me praesente venire nollet, vel potius conscientia accusante, formidaret'. *Ibid.*

62 *Registrum Roffense,* 40.

63 'Notum sit omnibus vobis quod in plena curia Romana, praesente Papa Celestino, ostenderim justam esse querelam monachorum ecclesie nostre'. *Ibid.*

His success was, however, but shortlived. Pope Celestine II died a few months later. His successor, Lucius II, was elected in March 1144, some two months before Master Robert was due to return to England. Probably Robert never again set foot in England, for he was summoned to Rome by the new Pope, and created Cardinal the same year. One of the first results of his appointment was the reversal of the verdict given against him by the previous Pope. The first official document which the new Cardinal is known to have signed is a papal Bull dated the 4th of January 1145. This documents bears the signature of Robert as Cardinal priest of St. Martin's[64]. By the 31st of the same month Robert had become papal Chancellor. Thus, as Dr. Poole observed, the accuracy of the Oseney chronicler who distinguished carefully between these two appointments is vindicated[65]. The letter of Ascelin to the successor of Lucius, Eugenius III, makes the same clear distinction[66]. Hoping that Eugenius would undo the settlement made by Lucius and re-affirm that of Celestine, Ascelin mentions the summons of Master Robert to Rome by Lucius and the reversal of the decision of Pope Celestine; the news that Pullen had been appointed Chancellor, he adds, came shortly afterwards. From this letter it is evident that Robert was already active in Rome by November 18th, 1144, since that was the last date allowed Ascelin for making restitution to Robert of his property. The writer continued that it was only fear of Robert's influence, and reverence for the Roman curia, in which after the Pope himself the Chancellor was the most important personage, that induced him to comply with the settlement ordered by Lucius. He adds that he handed over the property, as well as the archdeaconry, to a nephew of Cardinal Robert, by name Parisius, whom, he says, Eugenius might know. This reference to Parisius is also included by the monastic chronicler of the dispute, who adds the detail that Parisius had been ordained deacon at Rome.

The freedom with which Ascelin speaks of the Cardinal Chancellor, his former archdeacon, in the letter to Eugenius makes it impossible to hold that it was written in Pullen's lifetime. Probably it was composed immediately after news of Pullen's death had reached Rochester[67]. The monastic chronicler, who

---

[64] *Kehr, Papsturkunden in Parma und Piacenza*; (Göttingen 1900) 40.

[65] *Art. cit.*

[66] *Registrum Roffense*, 39.

[67] Pullen died, almost certainly, between September and December 1146, Ascelin in January 1147 or 1148.

evidently had access to a copy of this letter, says that it was taken to Rome by certain monks of Rochester and other interested claimants, but that the mission was a failure. Eugenius III refused to alter the decision of his predecessor Lucius. The ill-success of the mission is attributed by the chronicler to the opposition of Cardinal Robert, but this accusation is without foundation, and made by a writer who wrote many years after the events he was chronicling, and who failed to understand the significance of the documents he was using. Still writing from the standpoint of the monks, the chronicler tells how the unhappy business was finally settled. Parisius, we are told, realising the injustice that had been done to the monks, presented himself at their chapter, and an agreement was reached by which he was to retain the disputed property for his lifetime, after which it was to revert to the monks. Parisius lived for many years after this agreement, says the chronicler, 'right down to the time of Bishop Gilbert' (1185-1214) 'and for several years after'[68].

Papal Chancellor.

As papal Chancellor Cardinal Robert dated papal documents from January 1145 until September 1146; he served both under Pope Lucius II and his successor, Eugenius III, who became Pope in February 1145. Some of these documents deal with English affairs. Of special interest are those from Viterbo, 8th June, 1145, and 4th and 5th February 1146, which concern the Benedictine Abbey of Sherborne in which were a number of Pullen's kinsmen, among them his first cousin Joseph, Prior of the monastery. The monks of Sherborne had become involved in a dispute with Jocelin, Bishop of Salisbury, who had prevented them from holding a free election of a new abbot in succession to their deceased abbot, Robert, and had imposed on them as their abbot, John, Prior of Farleigh. The dispute had been aggravated by Bishop Jocelin's seizure of the property of the monastery. The monks sought redress by sending Prior Joseph to Rome to lay their case before Pope Eugenius III. Eugenius took up the cause of the monks with promptitude. He entrusted Theobald, Archbishop of Canterbury and Robert, Bishop of Hereford with the settlement of the dispute,

---

68 '... et supervixit usque ad tempora domini Gilberti episcopi, et post plures annos', *Registrum Roffense,* 10.

and ordered Bishop Jocelin to grant the monks complete freedom in the election of an abbot, and to restore the confiscated monastic property. He also issued a document placing the abbey under the protection of the Holy See and confirming its rights and possessions. With the official document entrusting the hearing of the dispute to the Primate and the Bishop of Hereford a private letter to the same prelates was enclosed by Cardinal Pullen. In this he recommends the just complaint of the monks to their diligent attention, indicating his personal interest in the case, and expressing the hope that his intervention will be seen to have been of service to the monks, adding that he will thus be in a position to express his personal gratitude for their services [69].

Among other papal documents signed by Cardinal Robert during his tenure of the office of Papal Chancellor are grants in favour of St. Peter's, Dorchester, Oxon, St. Mary's, Thame and St. George's, Oxford [70]. As has already been noted, it may have been at the school attached to St. George's that Pullen lectured during his period of teaching at Oxford.

It has been asserted that the last date on which his name appears in the records is September 2nd, 1146 [71]. It is true that Jaffé notes no subscription by Cardinal Robert later than that date, even though he has used among the sources of his lists the *Acta Pontificum Romanorum Inedita* of Pflugk-Hartung. In the third volume of Pflugk-Hartung's collection [72] the text is given of a Bull in which Eugenius III grants a favour to the monastery of Staffarda in the diocese of Turin. The date of this document is September 22nd, 1146, and it is signed by Cardinal Robert. In the same collection there is a Bull with the same date of September 22nd, which is dated not by the Cardinal but by a sub-deacon acting as a substitute [73]. It was customary at this period for a sub-deacon or other official to act for the Chancellor when the latter was absent through illness or for reasons of other business, if the absence

---

69 W. Holzmann, *Papsturkunden in England,* III, 1952, 171-175.

70 *Ibid,* 176-182.

71 By R. L. Poole in *The Early Lives,* etc. 64, relying on Jaffé's *Regesta Pontificum Romanorum,* ed. 2, Leipzig 1885. According to this work the Bulls issued under Eugenius III are given 'per manus Roberti S. R. E. presb. cardinal. et cancellarii' from March 1145 until the 2nd September 1146. Then from the 18th September until the 17th November 1146, they are issued 'per manus Baronis, subdiaconi'. The new Chancellor, the Cardinal Deacon Guido, appears on the 17th of December 1146.

72 J. v. *Pflugk-Hartung, Acta Pontificum Inedita* III. *Urkunden der Päpste* 590 (c)-1197, Dritter Band Stuttgart, 1886, 79.

73 *Ibid.,* 80.

were but for a brief period[74]. The explanation of Robert's signing one document on September 22nd and the sub-deacon the other on the same day is uncertain. It is probable, however, that his health had broken down about the beginning of that month and that he could no longer perform the duties of his office. His death must have taken place some time between September 22nd and December 17th 1146, when the new Chancellor was already at work, since it was usual for the Chancellor to hold his office until death, or, as happened in several cases, until his elevation to the Papacy.

The appointment of Robert Pullen to the papal chancellorship is proof of his ability as an administrator as well as a thinker. The Chancellor had a very responsible position, for it was his business to supervise the vast amount of secretarial work which was involved in the management of the Roman court[75].

Apart from the numerous official documents which bear his signature little is known of Cardinal Robert during this period. It has been suggested by R. L. Poole, with high probability, that it was he who introduced John of Salisbury to the papal court in the year 1146. Another interesting suggestion was made by the same scholar, that it was Cardinal Robert who, at the instance of Bishop John of Séez, was responsible for the advancement of Nicholas Breakspear to the cardinal-bishopric of Albano[76]. Later Breakspear became Pope under the title of Adrian IV, and is the only Englishman to have held that dignity.

Relations with St. Bernard.

A letter written by St. Bernard to Cardinal Pullen shortly after the election of Bernard's former monk to the papacy as Eugenius III is of interest because of the evidence it affords of the cordiality that existed between them[77]. The Abbot of Clairvaux informs the Cardinal that he has received certain writings 'scripta', (letters or possibly some treatise composed by Pullen) from him and remarks that his memory is always held in benediction in his circle ('apud nos'). The Spirit of Truth, he continues, gives testimony to their mutual affection. The summons of Pullen from Paris to Rome had at first caused him pain, he says,

74 R. L. Poole, *Lectures on the Papal Chancery*, 139.
75 R. L. Poole, *The Papal Chancery*, 139.
76 R. L. Poole, *The Early Lives*, etc. 68.
77 *Ep. 352, P. L.*, 182, 563.

but now he understands that it was part of God's plan for the welfare of the Church.

He begs his friend to be solicitous on behalf of Eugenius, the new Pope. To him, he adds, the Chancellor has been given as a consoler and counsellor. The wisdom that God has given him the Cardinal must make use of to prevent the Pope from being so overwhelmed by the cares of his office as to lose sight of his own spiritual welfare. The Cardinal is also admonished to make use of his high dignity to advance the divine glory, his own salvation and the good of the Church. Up to the present, continues the Saint, the Cardinal had laboured faithfully and successfully in his work of education; now it was his task to strive on behalf of God Himself, lest His law be rendered void by His enemies. Adressing him with affection and respect as 'Father most beloved and greatly missed' — 'dilectissime et desideratissime Pater' — he begs the Cardinal to show himself in his new vocation a faithful and prudent servant of the Lord. He will require, he continues, the simplicity of the dove in the conduct of his own affairs, but on behalf of the Church, which in a special way is confided to his charge, he will need the prudence of the serpent in the struggle against the wiles of the devil. Although he has much to say, he concludes, he will not prolong the letter, since both he and his correspondent are busy men. The bearers of the letter will also bring with them oral messages, and he urges the Cardinal to heed what they have to say as he would Bernard himself.

At the side of this implicit tribute to Pullen's character we may place the witness of John of Salisbury who on each of the two occasions on which he mentions the name of his old master makes particular mention of his goodness [78].

To Pullen's theology St. Bernard had applied the epithet 'sane' [79]. It has been pointed out that Bernard applies the same adjective to describe the theology of William of Champeaux [80], and it has been argued that in his use of the term the Saint meant a theology based on the methods and tradition of Anselm of Laon, the master of William of Champeaux. Such a theology was taught in the Abbey of St. Victor, where the first theological lessons had been given by William of Champeaux. When Bishop Otho of Lucca recommended his protegé Peter Lombard to St. Bernard, it was to the Abbey of St. Victor that the Saint directed him. It was,

78 *Metalogicon,* I, 5; II, 10.
79 *Ep. 205, P.L.,* 182, 372.
80 By F. Bliemetzrieder, *Z.K.G.* 53, (1934) 16.

Bliemetzrieder maintains, because of its connection with the Laon tradition that Pullen's theology was acceptable to the Abbot of Clairvaux. He attributes it to the influence of St. Bernard that for a number of years from 1140 onwards the occupants of the chair of theology in the Cathedral School at Paris were also associated either directly or indirectly with the Laon school. Among these teachers of theology were Gilbert Porreta who had heard Anselm of Laon himself, Robert Pullen, who may have been one of Anselm's pupils, and Peter Lombard, who, though not a pupil of Anselm, had profited by his work. The contention of Bliemetzrieder is borne out by Bernard's letter to Ascelin, which proves how solicitously he watched over the theological teaching in Paris. That letter, which must have been written about the end of 1142 or the beginning of 1143, is marked by great urgency. Bernard must have felt that a teacher of Pullen's ability could render more valuable service to the Church by remaining in Paris than by returning to Rochester. Bernard's *bête noire,* Abelard, had been condemned at Sens in 1140, but his influence was still strong even after his death on April 22nd, 1142. Hugh of St. Victor had died in 1141, and with his death the orthodox theologians had lost their greatest representative. It is likely that it was to fill the gap in their ranks caused by the death of Hugh of St. Victor that Pullen left Rochester for Paris; and it seems probable that he went there at the instance of St. Bernard.

CHAPTER II.

PULLEN'S THEOLOGICAL WORKS

THE SENTENCES.

Among the writings attributed to Pullen by the older bibliographers [1] is the imposing work known as *Sententiarum Libri VIII*. This work was edited from a manuscript formerly belonging to the Benedictine monastery of St. Remigius at Rheims, and published in 1655 by the Maurist, Dom Hugo Mathoud, O. S. B. Mathoud's edition is reproduced in Migne, *Patrologia Latina*, vol. 186. Existing manuscripts of this work are:

(i) London, British Museum, Royal 10 B. V. ff 173, 2 col. late 12th c.; ff. 1^v-3^v Prologus and Capitula: incipit prologus capitulorum sententiarum magistri Roberti Pulli: *Ut in hoc volumine lectori facile quod quesierit occurrat;* f. 4: incipiunt sententie magistri Roberti Pulli sancte Romane ecclesie presbiteri cardinalis et cancellarii. Primo Deum esse demonstrat: *Irrationabilium rationabilis progressus.*

(ii) Troyes, Bibliothèque de la Ville, Cod. 459 (12th-13th c. ff. 1 + 142, 2 col). This MS was at one time in the library of the abbey of Clairvaux. Unlike the London B. M. MS, of which the last few lines are illegible, it preserves the complete text with *explicit,* ' ubi tormentorum mutabilis miseria perseverabit. Sententie magistri Roberti Pulli '. The incipits of the prologue and of the text are the same in both MSS. The Sentences are Pullen's most important surviving work. They are a comprehensive synthesis of early scholastic theology. The treatment is dogmatic, but there are certain passages which could be described as moral or pastoral theology. As yet, however, apart from the earlier penitentials, there was no clear-cut distinction between books covering these different branches of theological science. In addition,

---

[1] See John Bale, *Index Brittaniae Scriptorum*, ed. R. L. Poole and M. Bateson (Oxford, 1902) 385 f.; H. Mathoud, *P. L.*, 186, 635 ff.

there are some chapters which deal with philosophical rather than theological questions. The broad plan of the work is drawn on the following lines:

Book I: God's existence and attributes, the Trinity.
Book II: The work of creation, the nature of man and of the angels, the fall of man and the origin of evil; the nature and mode of transmission of original sin.
Book III: The restoration of man in Christ, grace and the Law; the incarnation and life of Christ.
Book IV: The life of Christ continued, His passion and death; the virtues of faith, hope and charity; Christ's descent into hell; the nature of hell and purgatory.
Book V: The Resurrection of Christ; the Ascension and sending of the Holy Ghost; the preaching of Christianity to Jew and Gentile; faith and justification; baptism and the forgiveness of sins, confirmation; the sacrament of penance; concupiscence and the nature of sin; meritorious works; the inamissibility of charity; mortal sin.
Book VI: Ignorance and imputability of sin; the problem of evil and suffering; the operations of angels and demons; the relation of the human will to good and evil; the relation of the human will to divine grace; loss and recovery of grace; confession and excommunication; priest and penitent; judges and offenders; theories on the sacrament of penance.
Book VII: The sacrament of penance continued; prayer and works of satisfaction; almsgiving and tithes; the relation of Church and State; the duties and rights of soldiers and servants; entry into the clerical state; obligations of clerics, the sacrament of Holy Order; the states of prelacy, virginity and marriage; the contemplative and the active life; the sacrament of marriage.
Book VIII: The Holy Eucharist as sacrifice and sacrament; Antichrist and the second coming of Christ; the end of the world and the resurrection of the body; the last judgment; the final state of the elect and the lost.

As the outline indicates, the plan of the work is not perfect; there is a certain amount of overlapping and repetition, and the arrangement of individual chapters appears at times haphazard. The number of questions treated is very large, so large that Grabmann was of opinion that the reader loses the thread of Pullen's thought. For this reason, he said, it was hardly possible to give an idea of the arrangement of the work [2]. Nevertheless, taken

[2] *Geschichte der katholischen Theologie*, (Freiburg im Breisgau, 1933), 40.

as a whole, the work is an impressive achievement. It is more extensive and comprehensive than any theological work composed by Abelard. For comprehensiveness, depth of thought and doctrinal reliability its only superior among collections of *Sentences* composed before those of Peter Lombard is the *De Sacramentis* of Hugh of St. Victor. There is a general similarity between the arrangement of the material in the *Sentences* of the Victorine and in those of Master Robert, in spite of divergences in the placing of certain questions. No doubt both authors owed something to their predecessors in the arrangement of their work, notably to Isidore of Seville who, apparently, was the first to group extracts from patristic sources under doctrinal headings. The arrangement of the material in the first book of the *Sentences* of Isidore corresponds roughly to the order of the articles in the Apostles' Creed. It will be seen that this is approximately the ground-plan on which Pullen's *Sentences* are built. Pullen's *Sentences* are slightly less extensive than the *De Sacramentis;* they take up 370 columns of Migne, as against 445. The *Sentences* of the Lombard printed in the same collection, though in a slightly smaller type, run to 440 columns.

Pullen's *Sentences* cannot be dated with complete certainty. They have been attributed to the period between the appearance of the *De Sacramentis* (1140) of Hugh of St. Victor and the *Sentences* of the Lombard (1150-2) [3]. Pullen succeeded Gilbert Porreta as a lecturer in theology at the Cathedral School in Paris in 1142; by the end of the year 1144 he had given up teaching for the duties of papal Chancellor. The years 1142 to 1144 are most likely to have seen the final elaboration of his *Sentences*.

The term *Sentences* is an equivocal one. It covers a variety of theological literature ranging from haphazard extracts devoid of any doctrinal or chronological relationship to the masterly works of Hugh of St. Victor, Robert Pullen and, most famous of all, Peter the Lombard. The one purpose common to all the collections was to furnish assistance in understanding the content of revelation, especially as contained in Scripture.

---

[3] M. Grabmann, *op. cit.* 40. F. Pelster is inclined to fix the date before 1142 and is in favour of their having been composed in England art. cit. 245 (*supra* 10, n. 47). A. Landgraf, 'Literarhistorische Bemerkungen zu den Sentenzen des Robertus Pullus', *Traditio,* I (1943) 210-22 argues that the earliest date for Pullen's work is after the appearance of the second redaction of Abelard's *Theologia Scholarium* (the so-called *Introductio ad Theologiam*). This work was known by 1138 and seems to date from 1136-38.

The earliest examples of *Sentences* consist of compilations of texts from patristic writings. There is no unity about these collections; they are mere excerpts from successive pages of the originals. A typical example is the *Liber Sententiarum ex Operibus S. Augustini Delibatarum* [4]. Gradually such extracts were grouped according to subject-matter, or according to the order of the books of the Bible. With the *Sententiarum Libri Tres* of St. Isidore of Seville, in which the dogmatic extracts are separated from those concerned with moral theology, and the former arranged according to a rational plan, we see the main outlines of the fully developed *Sentence* books already taking shape. The next step was the inclusion of the comments of accredited teachers (*magistri moderni*) at the side of the extracts from the patristic writings. These comments were of various kinds: mere lists of contents, exegetical explanations, attempts at harmonising conflicting passages in patristic works, or independent judgments. Gradually, the contribution of the 'modern' master becomes more important. His expositions take the form of *theses,* and the extracts from the Fathers are used as proofs for his teaching. This stage had been reached by the beginning of the twelfth century with the work of Anselm of Laon and his pupil William of Champeaux. The emphasis in this school was still on 'authority'. Although the revived interest in dialectic manifests itself in the clear theological concepts and systematic arrangement of material which mark the productions of Anselm and his pupils, the school as a whole avoided speculation. Nevertheless, Anselm was more than a compiler. There is a real individuality about the productions of the Anselmian school. They are brief, systematic, more or less complete expositions of Christian doctrine which on disputed questions generally offer solutions deriving from Anselm himself. The individuality of the *Sentence* books associated with the name of Anselm is, however, that of a school rather than that of original thinkers. They suggest text-books drawn up on a certain pattern offering the same opinions and very often the same words. This is what distinguishes them from the theological works of Abelard, Hugh of St. Victor and Robert Pullen, quite apart from any question of length. They are the first syntheses on which these later writers worked. The *Summa Sententiarum,* of which the most likely au-

---

[4] For the historical development of the Sentence - book literature see G. Paré, A. Brunet, P. Tremblay, *Le Renaissance du XIIe Siècle,* Paris & Ottawa, 1933, 242 ff., 67 ff. F. Stegmüller, 'Sententie Berolinenses' *R. T. A. M.* xi (1939) 33 ff.

thor seems to be Otho of Lucca [5], is a more impersonal work than the syntheses of the three writers mentioned. It resembles more closely the works directly associated with the school of Laon, and it is evident that it owes much to that school [6].

An important and difficult question is the relation of the twelfth-century *Sentence* books to the teaching in the schools. There is no doubt that up to the twelfth century theological instruction consisted almost entirely in glossing the various books of the Bible; in addition there was a certain amount of glossing of patristic texts and of the Athanasian creed [7]. The stress was on positive rather than on systematic speculative theology. The treatises of St. Anselm of Canterbury are an exception by virtue of their insistence on the place of reason as distinct from authority; but it is uncertain to what extent they represented the actual pedagogical method of Anselm. In any case they found no immediate imitators, and they are individual masterpieces rather than elements in a complete theological synthesis. In the explanation of the sacred text teachers generally distinguished three senses: the literal or historical sense, the allegorical or doctrinal sense, and the tropological or moral sense [8]. The third of these senses tended to be expounded in the pulpit rather than in the classroom. The literal or primary meaning was sometimes known as the *sensus;* the deeper doctrinal meaning which was obtained by an allegorical interpretation of the text (*littera*) was spoken of as the *sententia.* The liberal arts of the *trivium* and the *quadrivium* were expected to aid the student in understanding the various senses. As the studies of the *trivium* dealt with words and their arrangement, they were considered as of special value for the understanding of the literal sense; those of the *quadrivium,* which had for their object number, measure, and material objects and the symbolism which these objects were supposed to contain, were regarded as a valuable preparation for the allegorical sense. The allegorical interpretations were not left entirely to the arbitrary choice of individual masters. They were to be made in conformity with ecclesiastical traditions; hence much use was made of glosses and

---

5 See H. Weisweiller, 'La *Summa Sententiarum,* source de Pierre Lombard', *R.T.A.M.* vi (1934) 181.

6 See H. Weisweiller, 'L'école d'Anselme de Laon et de Guillaume de Champeaux. Nouveaux documents', *ibid,* iv (1932) 383.

7 B. Smalley, *The Study of the Bible in the Middle Ages,* ed. 1 (Oxford, 1941) 53.

8 E. g. Hugh of St. Victor, *Eruditio Didascalica,* V. 2; VI, 2-5; *P.L.,* 176, 789 ff; 799 ff.

commentaries based on the works of the Fathers and early ecclesiastical authorities. The disadvantages of this method were that the student was often overwhelmed with a mass of 'authoritative' interpretations which burdened the memory without always satisfying the intellect; there was no synthesis of doctrinal knowledge, no ground-plan on which the allegorical explanation would be safely erected; and there were inevitable gaps in the theological equipment of the student, since a number of points of doctrine would almost certainly not find treatment in the Bible glossing. Hugh of St. Victor proposed a remedy for this weakness in the system. This was to interpose a course of systematic doctrinal instruction between the literal and allegorical reading of the sacred text. The remedy proposed in the *Didascalicon* was carried into effect in his *Sentence* book, the *De Sacramentis,* parts of which had been given at St. Victor in a course of lectures [9].

Hugh was not the first to lecture on a text-book other than the Bible. One of the charges made against Abelard at his first condemnation at Soissons was of having lectured on a book unauthorised by the Roman Pontiff or by the Church [10]. This book, which was consigned to the flames, is generally taken to be the *Theologia Summi Boni* [11]. Abelard's motive, so he tells us, was to explain the fundamental articles of the faith in the light of illustrations furnished by human reason, and so satisfy the petitions of his pupils, who said that to utter words which the mind did not understand was vain; that nothing could be believed unless it was first understood; and that it was ridiculous to preach to others what neither the preacher nor his audience could understand [12]. Out of this equivocal beginning arose first the *Theologia Summi Boni,* then the *Theologia Christiana* and its later recension the *Theologia Scholarium,* the so-called *Introductio ad Theologiam.* The range of subjects handled in these treatises — they can hardly be called *Summas* — is much narrower than in the *De Sacramentis* of Hugh of St. Victor or the *Sentences* of Pullen; indeed they are confined almost entirely to discussion of God's existence and attributes and of the Trinity of Persons. On the strength of Abelard's priority in time, however, and in virtue of the principles expounded in the *Sic et Non,* he has been hailed by many as the most influen-

---

9 See his *De Sacramentis,* Praefatiuncula, P. L., 176, 173.

10 Abelard, *Historia Calamitatum, P. L.,* 178, 149.

11 Ed. H. Ostlender, Münster i. w. 1939.

12 *Hist. Cal.,* 141-2.

tial figure in the development of the scholastic method [13]. One well-known modern scholar, the late F. Bliemetzrieder, has attempted to dethrone Abelard from his eminent position, and challenged his claim to priority in the composition of a manual or text-book of theological instruction. Having devoted himself to the study and editing of theological texts deriving from the school of Laon, Bliemetzrieder came to the conclusion that Anselm of Laon must be regarded more than any other single master as the founder of the scholastic method. There is no doubt possible of Anselm's importance for the systematic arrangement of theological questions and the collection of patristic texts, but it was Abelard's original genius which was more than any other responsible for putting the questions, and developing the dialectical method for their solution. Abelard's attitude to Anselm may in part explain Bliemetzrieder's verdict that it is a grave error to regard ' cette petite révolution pédagogique d'Abélard ' as originating out of the vacuity of the teaching of Anselm of Laon [14]. The same scholar held that in Anselm's time a distinction had already been made between Bible studies (divina pagina), doctrine (fides catholica) and canon law (lex ecclesiastica) [15]. He was inclined to see in the *Sentence* book which he edited under the name of *Sententiae Divinae Paginae* and regarded as the work of Anselm himself, a manual of doctrinal instruction designed for the young clerics of the diocese of Laon [16].

In spite of what we know of the practice of Hugh of St. Victor and Abelard, both of whom were contemporaries of Pullen, and of the work of Anselm of Laon, it would be rash to assume that Pullen's *Sentences* were delivered to a class just as they stand. Parts of them may have been, and it is possible that John of Salisbury, when he wrote that he had heard Pullen ' in theologicis ' [17], meant instruction in doctrine, and not lectures on the Bible. For the latter he would have used, perhaps, some such expression as ' in sacra pagina '. The theological method of Pullen's *Sentences* inclines one to the belief that part of the work was delivered in its present form as oral instruction in Christian doctrine, while the remainder may, perhaps, represent the *questiones* which he had

---

13 See G. Robert, *Les écoles et l'enseignement de la théologie pendant la première moitié du XIIe siècle*; and G. Paré, A. Brunet, P. Tremblay, *La Renaissance du XIIe siècle.*

14 'L'œuvre d'Anselme de Laon et la littérature contemporaine', II, *R. T. A. M.* vii (1935) 28-51.

15 ' Autour de l'oeuvre théologique d'Anselme de Laon ', *ibid.*, i (1929) 480.

16 *Op. cit.*, see note 14.

17 Metalogicon, II, 10. See *infra* 262, n. 23.

treated in the course of his lectures on the text of the Bible, and finally arranged in a body of doctrine [18].

The *questio* was a dialectical discussion of a problem which had arisen out of the explanation of the sacred text in the course of the *lectio* [19]. With continual glossing of the text problems of readings, of interpretation of or harmonising conflicting 'authorities' inevitably arose. Here we have the elements of the technical *questio.* Precedent for the application of philosophy to biblical problems can be found already in patristic literature and the practice seems to have survived intermittently before it was revived in a more technical form in the twelfth century [20]. Abelard was not, as has been thought, the person responsible for the revival, though he seems to have contributed most to its dialectical development. The lost commentary of Anselm of Laon on St. Paul apparently contained *questiones;* and Gilbert the Universal uses the form in his gloss on the Psalter. During the second quarter of the century with the increasing interest in dialectic the number and length of theological *questiones* show considerable development. The theological expositions composed at this period consist both of explanations of the text and of theological questions [21].

Abelard expresses clearly his idea of the questio [22], as also does Gilbert Porreta [23]. In its simplest form the technique consists merely of question — 'queritur', and solution — 'solutio'. In the twelfth century the simple form is developed considerably; arguments from authority as well as from reason are employed on both sides of the question. Gilbert Porreta notes that not every contradiction is a question. For a true question there must be arguments

---

18 Cf. *Sent.* 792C: 'Audisti; quid iterum vis audire?'

19 On the origin of the *questio* see R. M. Martin, *Oeuvres de Robert de Melun, I. Questiones de Divina Pagina,* XXXIV ff.; G. Paré, A. Brunet, P. Tremblay, *op. cit.,* 109-33; B. Smalley, *op. cit.,* 45-57.

20 See G. Bardy, 'La littérature patristique des questiones et responsiones sur l'Ecriture sainte', *R. bibl.,* XLI (1932) 210-36; A. Landgraf, Zur Technik und Überlieferung der Disputation ,*Coll. Fran.* XX (1950) 173-188.

21 B. Smalley, *op. cit.,* 50-1.

22 *Sic et Non,* Prologus, *P. L.,* 178, 1349, A-B, — 'placet, ut instituimus, diversa sanctorum Patrum dicta colligere ... aliqua ex dissonantia, quam habere videntur, questionem contrahentia, quae teneros lectores ad maximum inquirendae veritatis exercitium provocent et acutiores ex inquisitione reddant ... Dubitando enim ad inquisitionem venimus; inquirendo veritatem percipimus'.

23 'commemorandum est, quod ex affirmatione et ejus contradictoria negatione questio constat'. *Commentaria in Librum Boethii de Trinitate, P. L.* 64, 1253A.

in favour of and against each of the contradictory propositions [24].

It is evident from the discussions of the *questio* furnished by Gilbert Porreta, John of Salisbury [25] and Clarembald of Arras [26] that the *Topics* and *Sophistical Elenchi* of Aristotle which were entering into circulation in the schools about the middle of the century, exercised a decisive influence in the technical development of the *questio* .The arguments on both sides in these discussions are drawn up in syllogistic form; the solution involves not merely the simple interpretation of an author's meaning, but also a scientific refutation of the rejected opinion. 'Authority' is retained as a proof in various degrees by the authors, but is taken up into dialectical structure of the argument, sometimes as a premise in a syllogism [27].

Clarembald justifies the extension of the method of the *questio* to every proposition ,even the most unchallengeable. As a result, what had once been a real problem becomes a technical method of examining unversally admitted truths. Not all the lecturers on the Bible between the years 1130 and 1140 approved of the introduction of the *questio* in the *lectio*. William of St. Theodoric expressly excluded them from his *Exposition of St. Pauls's Epistle to the Romans* [28]. The dialectical *questio* was not favoured in the Abbey of St. Victor, nor is the dialectical development much in evidence in the *Questiones* which the Lombard included in his *Commentary on St. Paul.* His method was less dialectical than positive; when he engaged in dialectic it was because he was constrained against his choice to meet his adversaries on their own ground [29]. Nevertheless, the new technique had come to stay. In the work of Robert of Melun, who disliked the habit of glossing, the *questio* became more important than the exposition of the biblical text. The *Questiones de Epistolis Pauli* of Robert of Melun were issued with the biblical text but without the usual explanatory comment [30]; his

---

24 'non omnis contradictio quaestio est. Cum enim altera contradictionis pars esse vera; altera vero nulla prorsus habere argumenta veritatis videtur, ut « omnis homo est corporeus, non omnis homo est corporeus » ... aut cum neutra pars veritatis et falsitatis argumenta potest habere, ut « astra paria sunt, astra paria non sunt » tunc contradictio non est questio; cujus vero utraque pars argumenta veritatis habere videtur, questio est », *ibid.*

25 *Metalogicon,* II, 15.

26 See his Commentary on Boethius' *De Trinitate, Der Kommentar des Clarenbaldus von Arras zu Boethius de Trinitate,* ed. W. Jansen (Breslau, 1926) 34.

27 R. M. Martin, *op. cit.* I, XXXIX.

28 *Expositio in Ep. ad Rom. Praefatio, P. L.* 180, 547.

29 R. M. Martin, *op. cit.* I, XXXVIII.

30 R. M. Martin, Louvain, 1932.

Questiones de Divina Pagina[31], which apparently derive from a commentary of his on St. Matthew, appeared even without the biblical text on which the questions were based. His editor, R. M. Martin, is convinced that the greatest theological *Summa* of Robert of Melun, his *Sententiae,* consists largely of developments of the questions which appear in the two collections of *questiones.* Père Martin concludes, « Peut-être sommes-nous ainsi dans la vrai voie pour établir la genèse des grandes Sommes théologiques du moyen âge. Si on parvenait à prouver le fait, à tout le moins pour la majorité des cas, l'importance du rôle de la *questio* en théologie serait bien placé en belle lumière »[32].

Before one could affirm with complete confidence that Pullen's method of explaining the Bible determined the structure and method of his *Sentences,* it would be necessary to examine his missing commentaries on the Psalter and the Apocalypse. In default of these works one can only examine the structure, subject-matter and method of the *Sentences*, and compare the results with what is known of the theological *questio* in the works of other writers.

The structure of the *Sentences* suggests that much, if not all, of the work consists of questions or developments of questions which had arisen in the course of lectures on the Bible. Each of the eight books is divided into a number of chapters. Some of the successive chapters are closely linked by a chain of continuous thought; others are more or less independent of what precedes or follows. Within each chapter a number of questions, which generally arise out of each other, are raised and answered. The subject matter of many of them is based on some text of Scripture. Sometimes the text provides the proof of some doctrinal point; at others it is a question of reconciling apparently conflicting texts. The *Praenotationes* which are prefixed to the text of the *Sentences* indicate the principal questions considered in the various chapters, and give an idea of the structure of the whole. A typical example of these *Praenotationes* is the following summary which describes the contents of Book I, Chapter XI: 'Supradictis adjicitur quod Deus nihil eorum odit quae fecit, et qualiter omnes diligat; et quod ejus dilectio non variatur, et quod supradicta exposita non obviant huic *Odisti omnes qui operantur iniquitatem;* et Deum malos, et ipsos eum odio habere. Et qualiter malos, bonos futuros diligit; et unde sit quod quosdam a malitia eripit, quosdam non. Et quid fieret de malo quem diligit, si malus moreretur; et utrum

---

31 R. M. Martin, Louvain, 1938.

32 *Op. cit.* I: *Quaestiones de Divina Pagina,* XLVI.

bonum futurum malum odio habeat. Et quod damnandum etiam antequam esset oderit; et quod praescit praevult, et perdendum dum bonus est amat; non, e contra, iniquum semper odit '[33].

Sometimes it is a text of the Athanasian Creed which appears to have given rise to the question[34].

The method of treating the questions which we observe in the *Sentences* is marked by the technique of the *questio* as described above, and as it appears in the *questiones* of Robert of Melun. The influence of dialectic is everywhere apparent. Arguments in favour of both sides of the question are given. Sometimes the opposite position to that of the author is introduced by the words ' Dices ' or ' Respondes '.

Both problem and objection are at times formulated in strict syllogistic form[35]. Various forms of the syllogism are employed: simple, composite, hypothetical, disjunctive[36]. The reasoning is acute and precise. In certain chapters argument and counter-argument are so managed as to produce something resembling a complete disputation[37]. In his replies Robert Pullen generally refutes the erroneous opinion by a careful exposition of the true position, making precise distinctions of ambiguous or alternative sense of texts and phrases[38]. At times he indicates the logical flaw in the argument he is attacking; occasionally he dismisses a piece of reasoning as mere sophistry; sometimes, when the opposite view is manifestly absurd, he employs the method of *reductio ad absurdum* or indulges in elaborate irony[39].

At times a reference is made to the *Gloss* in order to establish the sense of a text; most frequently the text is left to speak for itself.

The explicit references in Pullen's *Sentences* to Fathers of the Church are by comparison with contemporary writers surprisingly rare. Even Abelard in his theological treatises makes many more appeals to authority than does Pullen. The Athanasian Creed is cited from time to time, and on philosophical questions there

---

33 641D-642A.

34 e. g. 734B, 785C, 808C.

35 e. g. I, 10 in the discussion of the mode of the soul's presence in the body; *ibid.* 15, on the question of the divine omnipotence, 690A ff; 709 ff.

36 e. g. 712C. 709C. 690A-B, 693B.

37 e. g. I, 10, 15.

38 ' Sed aliud est proprie uti dictionibus, aliud improprie, nusquam reprehensa auctoritate ', 679C; ' Scio tamen figuras et dictiones alias et alias habere interpretationes ', 779B.

39 680C, 712B, 691C-D, 715A.

are one or two references to Plato and Aristotle and Boethius. It is not that Pullen despised authority. For him the authority of the Catholic Church was final. The following passage is characteristic of his attitude: 'Rationi ergo et auctoritati assentientes, imo Catholicae fidei qua Catholici sumus obviare timentes, fatemur ac certissime asserimus'[40]. He delights in bold speculation, but recognizes that the solution of certain problems lies in submission to the voice of authority rather than in the conclusions of reason[41]. The teaching of faith on divine things, he insists, is certain; human reason can assert only what is probable: 'Dei tamen de potentia timide disputandum puto, nec quod ipse valeat penes se, verum quid de eo senserimus asserendum. Nam cujusmodi sit apud se propter (praeter?) quod fide capitur, quasi in caligine opinamur'[42]. The same warning is sounded elsewhere[43]. When he refers to St. Augustine or other accredited authorities it is always with respect, but he avoids the tedious habit of making a chain of 'authorities'; rather his method is so to absorb the teaching of authority that he can express it again in his own language.

There are, therefore, indications that much of the material in the *Sentences* is a reproduction or development of *questiones* treated by Pullen in his lectures on the Bible. Some of it seems to be the result of glossing rather than of questioning; but even here, to judge by the expository method used in the *Sentences*, Pullen was not one of those glossators like Anselm of Laon and William of St. Theodoric whose method was to reproduce *in extenso* or in summary the comments of the Fathers and other ecclesiastical writers, but an original thinker who set down also his own reflections.

Sermons.

Nineteen sermons attributed to Robert Pullen, '*Sermones doctoris Roberti pullani*' are preserved in a late 12th-century MS, no. 458, in the library of Lambeth Palace, London. The same collection is to be found under his name in a 13th-century MS, O. 2. viii, belonging to Hereford Cathedral Library. These sermons are certainly authentic, as the contemporary attribution in the MSS

---

40 801B. *Cf.* also 964C.

41 See 676B-C, 694A-B.

42 717A.

43 *E. g.* 694A.

to Pullen is supported by internal evidence, at least in a number of cases. I have found no other complete collection of these sermons but have been able to identify a number of them in various miscellanies. Eton College MS 38 attributes the eight which it contains to Pullen; the remainder are anonymous, with the exception of no. 14, which in Florence, Biblioteca Laurenziana, MS Strozzi 28 is included in a collection of sermons attributed to St. Bernard [44]. The following list shews that the manuscripts of these sermons of Pullen are not numerous. A number of them belonged to Cistercian libraries and they often occur in proximity to sermons of St. Bernard or of his secretaries, a detail which confirms the evidence of St. Bernard's letters for the close association of these two contemporaries. The sermons are here listed according to the order which they have in the Lambeth and Hereford MSS.

1. *inc. Magnum quidem et difficile est nostrum propositum, sed utile attendentibus et salubre ...*
   exp. Nec minus lectulus qui inter manus domini est domum subuerteret diaboli. MSS Lambeth 458, Hereford Cath. 0. 2. viii, Paris B. N. Lat. 12413. 12414, 18096, 13572. 3730.
2. *inc. Heri, fratres karissimi, de bono conscientiae uobiscum sermonem habuimus ...*
   exp. ... Reuertere, ergo, reuertere ad cor, cognosce te. Quid facis in mundo, qui maior es mundo? MSS Lambeth 458, Hereford 0. 2. viii, Eton College 38, Paris B. N. Lat. 12413, 12414, 18096, 13572, 3730.
3. *inc. Discipuli cum domino appropinquantes ierusalem uenerunt Betsage ad montem Oliueti ... Pax illa quam ierusalem, que uisio pacis interpretatur, significat, non est hic ...*
   exp. ... docens nos, ut non nostram, sed dei in omnibus gloriam queramus. Ipse ergo benedictus qui uenit in nomine domini. MSS Lambeth 458, Hereford 0, 2. viii, Paris, B. N. Lat. 12413, 12414, 18096, 3730.
4. *inc. Dicit dominus Ecce ego demetam posteriora baasa ... Non mirum si iniqui iniquitatem dominus puniuit ...*
   exp. ... et nos ipse resuscitare dignetur qui uiuit et regnat per infinita secula, amen. MSS Lambeth 458, Hereford, 0. 2. viii, Eton College 38. Paris B. N. Lat. 12413, 12414, 18096, 13572.
5. *inc.* Quattuor reges aduersus quinque insurrexerunt ... Huius prophetie misterium expondituri altius ordiendum censuimus ...
   exp. ... quia si quid perfectum in nobis est, non a nobis, sed a deo illud esse sciamus. MSS Lambeth 458, Hereford 0. 2. viii, Eton College 38, Paris B. N. Lat. 12413, 18096, 13572.

---

[44] See Bandini, *Catalogus*, Florence, 1792, t. II p. 325.

6. *inc.* Sacerdotes nescientes dominum, neque officium *suum ad populum, abstrahebant populum a sacrificio dei...*
exp. ...*Duplicatus est quinarius, quia ad seruiendum deo uterque sexus est inuitatus.* MSS Lambeth 458, Hereford 0. 2. viii, Lincoln Cathedral 201, Troyes, Bib. de la Ville 1562, Paris B. N. Lat. 12414, 18096.

7. *inc. Dominus eduxit filios israel... Res hic gesta fratres karissimi, magnum nostri profectus insinuat sacramentum...*
exp. ...*ut sint nobis quasi exemplaria credendi et bene operandi, unde dictum est, in medio animalium cognosceris.* MSS Lambeth 458, Hereford 0. 2. viii, Paris B. N. Lat. 12414, 18096, 13572.

8. *inc. Ait Samuel, congregate uniuersum israel in Masphat... Samuel bonos significat prelatos...*
exp. ...*Tu quoque fac simile, si in aliquo bono noueris te profecisse.* MSS Lambeth 458, Hereford 0. 2. vii, Paris B. N. Lat. 12414, 18096.

9. *inc. Intrauit iesus in quoddam castellum... Mundus, fratres karissimi, leges sibi a deo positas custodit...*
exp. ...*Quos ipse pro mortuis nostris exaudire dignetur, qui uiuit et regnat per infinita secula seculorum, amen.* MSS Lambeth, 458, Hereford 0. 2. viii, Troyes Bib. de la Ville 1562, Paris B. N. Lat. 12414, 18096, 13572.

10. *inc. Aiel de Bethel edificauit Iericho et in primogenito suo fundauit eam. Aiel bonos figurat in hac uita deo seruientes...*
exp. ...*finem uero pessimum euitemus, adiuuante eo qui uiuit et regnat per secula, amen.* MSS Lambeth 458, Hereford 0. 2. viii, Paris B. N. Lat. 12413, 12414, 18096, 13572.

11. *inc. Egredimini, filie ierusalem... adhuc infirmis et delicatis ista exhortatio proponitur...*
exp. ...*quatenus peruenire mereamini ad plenariam cognitionem tanti in diademate patris.* MSS Lambeth 458, Hereford 0. 2. viii, Eton College 38, Douai 371, Lincoln Cath. 201, Paris B. N. Lat. 13586, 12413, 12414, 18096, 2531A, 3730, 2945.

12. *inc. Cantate domino canticum nouum, quia mirabilia fecit... Uestrum est nouum cantare canticum et non uetus...*
exp. tunc digne nouum istud canticum cantare poterimus. MSS Lambeth 458, Hereford 0. 2.viii, Paris B. N. Lat. 12413, 12414, 18096, 3730.

13. *inc. Arbor si ceciderit ad aquilonem uel ad austrum ibi erit... Graue dictum, uera tamen et immutabilis sentencia...*
exp. ...*et sic introducet nos rex in cellam uinariam, et arbor nostra cadet ad austrum.* MSS Lambeth 458, Hereford 0. 2. viii, Paris B. N. Lat. 12413, 124-4, 18096, 3730.

14. *inc. En lectulum salamonis ambiunt ex fortissimis israel... Salamon, qui pacificus interpretatur, Christus est...*
exp. ...*Unde si dictum est multe filie congregauerunt diuitias, sed tu supergressa es uniuersas.* MSS Lambeth 458, Hereford

O. 2. viii, Alençon 149, Florence Bib. Laurenziana, Strozzi 28, Paris B. N. Lat. 12414, 18096, 13572.

15. *inc.* *Que est ista que ascendit per desertum sicut uirgula fumi ... Admiratur de ascensu ecclesie que in fragili corpore ...*
exp. *... tanquam sapiens medicus conficit, quod nobis concedat iesus christus, qui cum patre et spiritu sancto uiuit et regnat per omnia secula seculorum, amen.* MSS Lambeth 458, Hereford 4. 2. viii.

16. *inc.* *Legimus in libro regum quod rex sirie cum exercitu suo obsedit ciuitatem samarie ... Sicut sacra scriptura nobis loquitur siria elatio interpretatur ...*
exp. *... sed nichili pendentes tanquam uilissima sub pedibus conterunt.* MSS Lambeth 458, Hereford O. 2. viii, Eton College 38.

17. *inc.* *Apud ueteres in libro numeri quando amoreorum populus ab israelitis percussus est ...*
exp. *... uidelicet usque ad illam natiuitatem qua renascuntur cum deo et agno in uitam eternam, amen.* MSS Lambeth 458, Hereford O. 2. viii, Eton College 38.

18. *inc.* *Postquam israel de terra egypti est egressus ...*
exp. *... propter hoc uestram dulcedinem admonet nostra dilectio non ut subuertatur, sed ut a nobis terra predicta possideatur, quod nobis concedat domnus noster iesus christus qui cum patre et spiritu sancto uiuit et regnat per omnia secula seculorum, amen.* MSS Lambeth 458, Hereford O. 2. viii, Eton College 38.

19. *inc.* *In exodo. Uenit autem amelech et pugnabat contra israel in raphadim ... Amelech pugnabat contra israel in raphadim. Rex iste paganus qui pugnabat contra israel diabolum significat ...*
exp. *... Tunc autem os habere dicitur cum oratio funditur et uerbum dei audientibus exponitur.* MSS Lambeth 458, Hereford O. 2. viii, Eton College 38.

A completely different set of sermons, with one exception which is the same as no. 11 in the list already given, is attributed to ' Magister Robertus Pulo ' in Paris, B. N. Lat. 2945, fol. 46v-95v: The MS dates from the late 12th, or early 13th century, as does also the hand which attributes the sermons to Magister Robertus Pulo. Are these sermons authentic? In favour of Pullen's authorship there is strong evidence, both external and internal. The name Pulo is sufficiently close to the more usual Pullus, Pullanus or Polanus. The case for authenticity is strengthened by the fact that the same hand correctly assigns f. 1-46v of the same book, *Epistola domni willelmi quondam abbatis S. Theodorici ad fratres de Monte Dei,* to its real author, although elsewhere it is ascribed to St. Bernard. This MS was seen and described by C. Oudin in the seventeenth century. At that time it belonged to the Colbert

Library. Originally it came from the Abbey of Foucarmont. Oudin notes that another copy of the same set of sermons was contained in MS 1434 of the library of Alexander Pétau, but afterwards passed into the possession of Queen Christina of Sweden [45]. Hauréau adds that later they were acquired by the Vatican Library.

Unlike the Lambeth and Hereford collections, these sermons in Paris B. N. 2945 are *sermones de communi sanctorum,* short homilies based on texts of the gospels which were read at the masses of martyrs, confessors and virgins. Internal evidence proves that at least some of them were delivered to monks. The Lambeth and Hereford sermons contain no allusion to the monastic life, and appear to have been preached before an audience of young clerics engaged in study. Nos. 1-26 of the B. N. 2945 sermons are all based on a New Testament text; no. 27 is the same sermon as no. 11 in the Lambeth and Hereford collections.

B. Hauréau decided against Pullen's authorship of the B. N. 2945 sermons, on the grounds that the preacher was himself a monk, whereas there is no proof that Robert Pullen was ever a member of a monastic order [46]. The assertion that the author of the sermons was a monk is chiefly based on a couple of phrases in the sermons: 'Quando huc intrauimus mundum in maligno positum exuimus' (fol. 48) and 'sed quia monachis monachi loquimur, de mercibus monastice uite conuenientibus dicemus' (fol. 80v).

Both of these passages are strong evidence in favour of the opinion that the preacher was a monk, though not necessarily belonging to the same monastery as his congregation, since there is also a suggestion in his expression 'claustris uestris', that he was a visiting preacher: 'Itaque, fratres, licet uos hortentur ut in claustris uestris quieti sedeatis, ego tamen moneo ut negotiatores ad nundinas eatis' (fol. 80v). Elsewhere he warns his hearers against accepting ecclesiastical office with its attendant cares: 'quia re uera spiritualis anima plurimum sue deuotionis et reuelationis periculum incurrit cum a paradiso claustri propter prelationem exiens in turbinem et procellas populares se mitti permittit' (fol. 50v-51). Hauréau saw here an additional reason against Pullen's authorship of the sermons, since one who became Cardinal

---

[45] Casimiri Oudini, *Commentarius de Scriptoribus Ecclesiae Antiquis* II, 1120, (Leipzig, 1722). On MS Paris. B. N. Lat. 2945 see also B. Hauréau, *Notices et extraits,* XXXIII (Paris, 1903) 406-410, A. Noyon, *Revue des bibliothèques,* XXI (1913), 309-312, *Catalogue Général des Manuscrits Latins,* (Paris, Bibliothèque Nationale, 1952, III, 318), J. Leclercq, Recherches sur d'anciens sermons monastiques, *Revue Mabillon* XXXVI (1946) 11.

[46] Notices et extraits, *l. c.*

and Chancellor of the Church would thereby have proved himself unfaithful to the counsels which he had given others. This reason is unconvincing, as there may have been urgent reasons relieving the preacher of the necessity of adhering to his own counsels. In any case preachers do not always practise what they recommend to others.

The difficulty may be met by assuming that Pullen, though not a Benedictine or Cistercian monk, was a regular Augustinian canon. There is no direct proof of this, but there are, as I shall show, indications in his career and writings that make it probable. Theoretically, regular canons were not monks, but the two types of religious had much in common. The former were sometimes called monks, and their convents were sometimes referred to as monasteries [47]. These resemblances would be sufficient to justify Pullen's use in a sermon of the phrase 'monachi monachis loquimur' if he, as a regular canon were preaching either to monks or to his own brethren.

Indications that Pullen was a regular canon may be thus summarised:

1. In his discussion of religious life in his *Sentences* he speaks of religious superiors as 'praepositi' [48]. Now 'praepositus' was the term employed by the regular canons to designate the superiors of their communities during their earliest period [49].

2. During Pullen's five years of lecturing at Oxford, 1133-38, the Augustinian canons were already established there in the two priories of St. Frideswide's and Oseney. No other religious had as yet any Oxford foundations. There were still surviving at St. George's -in-the-Castle some secular canons, but these clergy were generally married [50]. As a vigorous opponent of married priests Pullen is not likely to have been of their number [51].

3. Pullen's patron, Bishop John of Séez, who had appointed him archdeacon of Rochester, was an intimate associate of the

---

[47] Iohannes de Columpna Mari Lib. VII cap. 92 (MS Paris B. N. Lat. 4915 f. 370 cd) writes: 'Preterea circa idem tempus claruit magister Ricardus de Sancto Victore parisiensis canonicus regularis ... Scripsit idem monachus Ricardus de contemplatione, de patriarchis, de mystico sompnio nabugodonosor ...' See also Ducange-Henschel, *Glossarium Med. et Inf. Latinitatis,* art. 'canonicus'; J. C. Dickinson, *The Origins of the Austin Canons and their Introduction into England* (London, 1950) 192-223; Powicke-Emden, *Rashdall's Medieval Universities* III, 17f. n. 2.

[48] 941B: « Sunt aliqui praepositis suis inobedientes ».

[49] Dickinson, *op. cit.* 80, 201.

[50] Powicke-Emden *loc. cit.*

[51] See *infra* 248.

Victorine canons of Paris, and had installed them in his own cathedral [52]. At the instance of the same Bishop, Pullen appears to have become himself the patron of the English Augustinian canon, Nicholas Brakespear, when the latter appeared at Rome during Pullen's tenure of the papal chancellorship [53].

4. The fact that Bishop Ascelin of Rochester claimed to be Pullen's diocesan does not invalidate this hypothesis, since it was recognised that the regular canons were subject to the local bishop [54]. Nor was the status of a regular canon incompatible with Pullen's activity as a teacher and administrator.

5. The audience to which the sermons were addressed included religious who would have the duty of preaching to the people [55]. This suggests that they were canons rather than monks, as being more likely to have a cure of souls. If this were so, the sentence, 'Quando huc intrauimus mundum in maligno positum exuimus, et exiuimus in quemdam paradisum, ut dicit S. Augustinus', (fol. 48), would come naturally from a preacher of the Augustinian order.

6. The fact that the ultimate primary source for Pullen's activity in Oxford is the Annals of the Augustinian Abbey of Oseney may be explicable as a manifestation of a legitimate *esprit de corps*.

Internal evidence of thought and style favours the MS attribution of the sermons to Robert Pullen. We may compare certain passages from these sermons with others taken from undoubted writings of Pullen.

(1) On purity of intention, fol. 79: 'Solet in scripturis lucerne nomine mentis intentio designari. Quod aperte docet cum subdit, « si oculus tuus fuerit simplex totum corpus lucidum erit, si nequam, et tenebrosum », quia scilicet qualis intentio talis iudicatur et actio. Unde et Sanctus Gregorius dicit quod intentio ponit nomen operi'.

On the same subject *Sententiae,* 5, 35, (P. L. 186, 857 B): 'affectus enim tuus operi tuo nomen imponit. Unde Dominus: « si oculus tuus fuerit simplex, totum corpus tuum lucidum erit, si autem nequam fuerit etiam corpus tuum tenebrosum erit »'.

Similarly, De Contemptu Mundi, (D. C. M.) my edition, *Gregorianum,* XXXI (1950) 218: 'Audi Dominum: lucerna corporis tui est oculus tuus. Oculus est intentio, sine qua quecunque fiunt

---

[52] *supra* 10.

[53] *supra* 17.

[54] Dickinson, *op. cit.* 162, 200.

[55] 'Si docens Ecclesiam dei increpes tantummodo, et arguas et castiges, et exprobes peccata populi ...' (fol. 75v).

erronea sunt ... Arbor enim mala fructus malos facit. Arbor intentio; fructus, operatio. Secundum arboris naturam fructus contrahit proprietatem. Sic affectus intentionis operi nomen imponit, uel uitii, uel uirtutis '.

(2) Similar resemblances of thought and phraseology are to be seen in his favourite topic of the contrast between prosperity and adversity.

Fol. 68: 'A dextris et sinistris hostes sentimus. A dextris dum prosperis extollimur; a sinistris dum aduersis deicimur'.

In the D. C. M. we read (ed. cit. 209): 'Pertinent igitur prospera dum alleuantur deitiendum; aduersa dum deitiuntur alleuandum'.

In sermon 11: 'Prima (uisio Christi) spem generat ne deiciamur in aduersis; secunda timorem parit ne erigamur in prosperis'.

(3) Fol. 83 on detachment from this world: 'dum suspirantes ad patriam omnia transitoria desiderio amoris transuolamus'. On the same topic D. C. M. ed. cit. 200: 'Tandem ergo tedeat nos uite nostre supernam spirantes patriam ... ut deliciis non hereamus solo, puncti uero sepius auolemus polo'.

(4) Fol. 67v contains a warning against the love of riches: 'quia, si amas, times habere carere, et si non amas non times, quia sine dolore amittitur quod sine amore possidebatur'.

Compare D. C. M. (ed. cit. 210): 'Quocirca cum amiseris doliturus, tum habes diligis insanus que nec tecum permanere queant'.

(5) Fol. 90v contains a warning to monks to refrain from 'muliercularum conspectibus', 'muliercularum obtutibus'. Several times Pullen returns to this theme in his other works: Sermon 6 'Alii (clerici) muliercula amplexantur'; Sermon 7: 'Visu enim mulierum ... etsi ab his contineant, solent moueri sancti donec proficiant'; Sermon 15: 'si, instigante spiritu fornicationis, mulierem ad concupiscendum quandoque uiderit'; D. C. M.: (ed. cit. 202) 'Quem uero mulierem seu pecuniam contemplari delectat ... quasi catenam nectat'.

(6) Temptations of the five senses, allegorically the five kings of Genesis, XIV, 1 ff., are thus described on fol. à8v: 'Uisus enim cuiusque de regibus istis intendit concupiscentie, auditus fabulis, gustus edului, odoratus nidoribus, tactus spurcitie'.

The same allegory, with some verbal resemblance, occurs in sermon 5: 'Contingit autem uisum per exteriora uagari et false speciei illecebris detineri ... auditus similiter nugis canoris sepissime irretitur, odoratus, nidorem culine aut aliorum odoramentorum dulcedinem comprehendens, eum sequitur. Gustus autem, nonne in saporibus nimis delectatur? Sed tactu in duobus peccamus ...

Sic isti quinque reges in conflictu quattuor regum succumbunt'. Cf. D. C. M. ed. cit. 202.

(7) Certain of Pullen's favourite, and in some cases rare, words appear in this M. S:

a) *debriari*: fol. 49^{v}, 50: 'anima diuino spiritu debriata', Cf. sermon 6: 'nisi debriatus ante mortem surrexerit'; sermon 17: 'uitiorum amaritudine debriantur';

b) *exorbitare*: fol. 58: 'qui de religionum puritate exorbitans'; Cf. sermon 18: 'multi quidem in hoc seculo rectitudinis orbitam tenere uidentur, qui uelud distorti exorbitant'. This word was probably due to the influence of St. Augustine, though it also occurs in Tertullian.

c) *agonista*: fol. 60; 'Tu, strenuus (sic) agonista, abnega et hanc et ceteras passiones': Cf. D. C. M. (ed. cit. 203): 'Agonista obnitens uiriliter age'. Sententiae II, 31: P. L. 186, 763: 'Agonistas ergo aut decoros efficit aut inglorios'.

d) *fastus*: fol. 68: 'Si quis superbo fastu elatus'; Cf. sermon 18: 'si quandoque accidat ut in pompa et fastu regio ingredi templum Dei dignemini'; D. C. M. (ed. cit. 206): 'Arguente eum (David) propheta Nathan, non regio fastu indignatus intumuit'.

e) *qua fronte*: fol. 66; 'Nam si equus procul odoratur bellum, eques qua fronte pertimescit?' Cf. D. C. M. (ed. cit. 207): 'nisi militie ducem nostrum stipemus, domi regnantem qua fronte uidebimus?'.

(8) Pullen's prose is marked by its rhetorical balance, antithesis, and play on words. These characteristics appear also in MS 2945, e. g. fol. 54^{v}-55: 'maior non inter homines, sed inter humiles, maior non honore sed onere, maior non potentia sed patientia'. Another rhetorical device found in this MS and in other works of Pullen is that of sentence elaboration by means of the repetition in the past participle of a verb already used in some other form,, e. g. fol. 84: 'He uoluptates quasi Syrenes undique ante nos saltant, ut incaute aspicientes, immo cecos sopiant, sopitos decipiant, deceptos dilanient'; cf. sermon 19: 'Quo uiso, Seon ad alia certaminis temtamenta se preparans, statim ad arma ministros conuocat, conuocatos ordinat, excitat ordinatos, excitatos inire bellum imperat'; similarly D. C. M. (ed. cit. 222): 'Credenda fides erudit; erudita spes petit; petita caritas acquirit'.

(9) More general features of style common to this MS and Pullen's undisputed works are the methodological opposition of texts of scripture with the intention of stimulating attention and focussing a problem, and the introduction of direct speech in the narrative part of the sermons.

(10) The thought and general atmosphere of the sermons suggest those of Pullen. The preacher is well acquainted with the works of St. Augustine. His teaching on grace is that of a trained theologian, and the points stressed are precisely those emphasised by Pullen in his Sentences.

Summing up the evidence in favour of Pullen's authorship of these sermons we have:

1) The explicit attribution of the MS. The form 'Pulo' employed here in place of the more usual 'Pullus', 'Pullanus' and 'Polanus' creates no real difficulty. Still more divergent forms than 'Pulo' are found, which, nevertheless, certainly refer to Robert Pullen [56].

2) The occurrence in B. N. 2945 of a sermon which is also found in the other collections of Pullen's sermons, viz. No. 11 in the list already given (= no. 27 in B. N. 2945).

3) Notable resemblances of thought and style between B. N. 2945 and the undisputed writings of Pullen. It would appear therefore, that B. N. 2945 contains 27 genuine sermons of Pullen.

The following list contains the list of *incipits* and *explicits* of the 27 sermons, arranged in the order of their occurrence in MS. 2945. For convenience they are numbered in sequence to those already given above.

20	*inc.*	*fol.*	46v	*Hoc est preceptum meum ut diligatis inuicem sicut dilexi uos ... Tria sunt diligenda: Deus proximus et nos ipsi ...*
	exp.	»	47v	*... et glorificauerunt Patrem, qui in celis est benedictus in secula seculorum, amen.*
21	*inc.*	»	48	*Hec mando uobis ut diligatis inuicem ... Uerba sunt, in quibus admonet hec duo ut alterutrum amenus ...*
	exp.	»	49v	*... potestatem nostram, qui est benedictus in secula seculorum, amen.*
22	*inc.*	»	49v	*Ego sum uitis uera ... In scriptura sacra per pitem aliquando significatur Christus, aliquando anima a Deo degenerans ...*
	exp.	»	52	*... manserit uite que est Christus Iesus benedictus in secula seculorum, amen.*
23	*inc.*	»	52	*Ego sum uitis uera ... Abominatur deus omnes qui confidunt in uirtute sua. Unde et hoc loco sancti euangelii uocat se uitem ...*

[56] e. g. Pollet, Poldi, cf. *supra* p. 1.

	exp.	»	53v	*... ut fructum afferamus et totum ad eum referamus cui est et potestas in secula seculorum, amen.*
24	*inc.*	»	53v	*Facta est contentio inter discipulos ... Quia propter nos haec scripta sunt uideamus ...*
	exp.	»	56	*... et dedit nobis uictoriam per Dominum nostrum Iesum Christum. Qui uiuit.*
25	*inc.*	»	56	*Misit Dominus Iesus duodecim apostolos ... Quomodo hic prohibet Dominus ne discipuli in uiam gentium abeant ...*
	exp.	»	58v	*... precibus peruenire adiuuet ipso prestante qui uiuit et regnat in secula seculorum, amen.*
26	*inc.*	»	58v	*Si quis uult post me uenire ... Sequentium Dominum due michi species esse uidentur ...*
	exp.	»	61	*... ad terram sortis sanctorum ipso prestante qui uiuit et regnat in secula seculorum, amen.*
27	*inc.*	»	61	*Nichil opertum est quod non reuelabitur ... Legimus quod Raab meretrix abscondit exploratores Iericho in solario ...*
	exp.	»	62v	*... laus erit unicuique a Deo et honor cui est imperium in secula seculorum, amen.*
28	*inc.*	»	63	*Nolite arbitrari quod uenerim pacem mittere ... Ex apostolica doctrina habemus ...*
	exp.	»	63v	*... dedit uictoriam per Dominum nostrum Iesum Christum cui est honor et gloria in secula, amen.*
29	*inc.*	»	63v	*Si quis uult post me uenire ... Tria proposuit ualde necessaria in quibus totius securitatis et perfectionis summa consistit ...*
	exp.	»		*... Quod a nobis auertat ipse qui uiuit et regnat per omnia secula.*
30	*inc.*	»	66	*Cum audieritis prelia et seditiones ... Cum, ut perhibet scriptura, militia sit uita hominis super terram ...*
	exp.	»	68	*... in quo uincemus et nos. Ipsi honor et imperium.*
31	*inc.*	»	68	*Ponite in cordibus uestris non premeditari ... Huius sententie sic moderanda est intelligentia ...*
	exp.	»	70	*... Ergo operaris gratia Dei non uiribus tuis. Ipsi gloria et imperium in secula seculorum, amen.*
32	*inc.*	»	70	*Ue uobis qui edificatis monumenta prophetarum ... Infructuosa est sine ueritate species sanctitatis ...*

	exp.	»	72v	*... qui nos perducet ad eorum consortium in secula seculorum.*
33	*inc.*	»	72v	*Cum persequentur uos in ciuitate ista fugite in aliam ... Quid est, fratres, quod Dominus hic fugere moneat ...*
	exp.	»	74r	*... id est peccatum, et accedit ad Deum. Ipsi honor et imperium per omnia secula seculorum.*
34	*inc.*	»	74	*Attendite a fermento phariseorum ... Fermentum, ut ait apostolus, etiam modicum, totam massam corrumpit ...*
	exp.	»	75r	*Felicem quietem concedat nobis Dominus Iesus Christus qui uiuit et regnat per omnia secula seculorum.*
35	*inc.*	»	75	*Sint lumbi uestri precincti ... Lumbos ut ait beatus Gregorius, precingimus ...*
	exp.	»	76r	*... ad salutem nobis adimplere concedat Iesus Christus, qui uiuit et regnat per omnia secula seculorum.*
36	*inc.*	»	76	*Uigilate quia nescitis quā hora Dominus uester uenturus sit ... Si bonum est uigilare in hoc seculo ...*
	exp.	»	77v	*... Nescitis quando Dominus uester uenturus sit. Ipsi honor et gloria in secula seculorum.*
37	*inc.*	»	77v	*Estote parati, quia qua hora non putatis ... Solent celebres et sublime potentie uiri ...*
	exp.	»	79r	*... quod auertat ipse filius hominis, qui uiuit et regnat per omnia secula seculorum.*
38	*inc.*	»	79	*Nemo lucernam accendit et in abscondito ponit ... Solet in scripturis lucerne nomine mentis intentio designari ...*
	exp.	»	80v	*... non sibi uiuat sed ei pro quo Christus mortuus est. Ipsi honor et gloria in secula seculorum.*
39	*inc.*	»	80	*Negotiamini dum uenio ... Rerum celorum, fratres mei, quantum in diuina pagina legimus ...*
	exp.	»	82r	*... et reddam tibi centuplum in presenti, uitam eternam in futuro seculo, amen.*
40	*inc.*	»	82	*Homo quidam peregre proficiscens ... Omnes peregre profecti sumus ...*
	exp.	»	83r	*... eodem tramite perducat Iesus Christus, qui uiuit et regnat per omnia secula seculorum.*
41	*inc.*	»	83	*Uidete, uigilate et orate ... hec tria omni homini ad salutem necessaria sunt ...*

	exp.	»	85	*... Sanctus iste sic uidit, sic uigilauit, sic orauit, prestante Domino nostro Iesus Christo, qui uiuit et regnat per omnia secula seculorum.*
42	*inc.*	»	85	*Uos estis sal terre ... Experto didicimus sal condimentum esse ciborum ...*
	exp.	»	86v	*... et bene utatur malis. Ipsi honor et imperium per omnia secula seculorum.*
43	*inc.*	»	86v	*Simile est regnum celorum decem uirginibus ... Certum est in diuina pagina aliquantulum eruditis ...*
	exp.	»	88	*... Quarum periculo nos eximat Iesus Christus, qui uiuit et regnat per omnia secula.*
44	*inc.*	»	88	*Prudentes uirgines aptate lampades uestras ... Omnes anime que suo creatori in mentis puritate ...*
	exp.	»	89v	*... sed etiam coram hominibus, ipso prestante qui uiuit et regnat per omnia secula seculorum.*
45	*inc.*	»	89v	*Simile est regnum celorum homini negotiatori ... Omnes debemus esse dei negotiatores ...*
	exp.	»	90v	*... prudenter facere nos doceat Iesus Christus Dominus noster qui uiuit et regnat per omnia secula seculorum, amen.*
46	*inc.*	»	90v	*Egredimini, fili Ierusalem, et uidete regem Salamones ... Adhuc infirmis et delicatis ista salutaris exhortacio proponitur ...*
	exp.	»	93v	*... quatinus peruenire mereamini ad plenariam cognitionem tanti diadematis, amen.*

Sermons 1 and 2 were preached on successive days, and it seems probable that they and the remainder of the Lambeth-Hereford collection were addressed to the same congregation. This appears to have consisted of clerics engaged in the study of philosophy and the liberal art [57].

Fifteen of the sermons are inspired by events of the Old Testament, the remaining four have texts of the New Testament as their starting point [58].

---

[57] ... nostre professionis reducamus ad memoriam quod clerici sumus: serm. 12. Rami siquidem uestri studia uestra sunt: scilicet studia philosophorum, studia artium liberalium, dialectice, grammatice etc., quibus intenditis, et in quibus totum tempus et studium uestrum consumitis: *ibid.*

[58] The O. T. texts are 3 Kings (Vg.), XVI, 3, serm. 4: Gen. XIV, ff. serm. 5: 1 Kings (Vg.) II-VI, serm. 6: Jos., V, 2 ff., serm. 7; 1 Kings (Vg.) VII, 5 f. serm. 8; 3 Kings (Vg.), XVI, 34, serm. 10; Cant. III, 11, serm. 11; Isai.

However, given the allegorical method of scriptural interpretation, which in the twelfth century reached its fullest development, it did not much matter which texts furnished the starting point of the sermon. The chief aim of the preacher was moral instruction suited to the needs of his congregation. By means of *testimonia,* or confirmatory passages of scripture, he soon passed from his initial text to others suited to his purpose, subjecting each in turn to allegorical interpretation. Where other preachers clearly distinguished three or four distinct senses, Pullen was usually content with two, the literal and the spiritual senses. The former he refers to as *historia* or *littera.* It may or may not be concerned with morality. If it is an historical event it is treated summarily at the beginning of the sermon. The main body of the discourse is devoted to the elucidation of the spiritual meaning, whether it be doctrinal or moral. Pullen is chiefly interested in the moral application. This spiritual sense he calls the mystical meaning, *sensus mysticus,* or the deeper meaning, *sensus altior,* the mystery, *mysterium,* or the sentence, *sententia.* He compares the elucidation of this meaning to the crunching of a hard bone to get at the marrow. (Serm. 17. His allegorical interpretations are extremely ingenious. Most of them appear to be traditional, but he allows himself to coin a few new allegories, which he introduces by some such phrase as 'non incongrue dicitur', 'competenter dicitur'. St. Gregory the Great appears to have influenced him most in his construction of sermons. Occasionally other patristic sources are mentioned such as St. Augustine, Origen, and the Clementine Recognitions. The allegory of Hebrew names shows the influence of St. Jerome's *Liber de Nominibus Hebraicis,* and in one or two passages Latin poetry is quoted.

By making use of the allegorical technique Pullen ranges over all the traditional themes of ascetical theology with great earnestness and his usual vigour and outspokenness, laying special stress on the obligations of priests and prelates. Bishops are the guardians of the Church. They must be well versed in the knowledge both of the Old and the New Testament, resplendent in good works, and able to defend the faith against opponents. (Serm. 14). They must appoint suitable archdeacons as their coadjutors, and take

---

XLII, 10, serm. 12; Eccle. XI, 3, serm. 13; Cant. III, 7, serm. 14; Cant. III, 6, ff. serm. 15; 4 Kings (Vg.) serm. 16; Num. XXI, 26 ff., serm. 17; Num. XXI, 22 ff. serm. 18; Exod. XVII, 8-13, serm. 19.

The N. T. texts are Apoc. II, 17, serm. 1; II Cor. I, 12, serm. 2; Mt. XXI, 1, serm. 3; Lc. X, 38, serm. 9.

care that parishes and monasteries have good parish priests and abbots. (Serm. 8, 9). Prelacy should not be the object of ambition, but should be accepted only with reluctance, with the intention of promoting the honour of God and the salvation of men. At times a prelate should withdraw from external occupations to enter into himself and meditate on divine truths, that thus spiritually refreshed he might be the better able to nourish others. (Serm. 9). Like a shepherd's dogs they must watch over the flock of Christ; as the sheepdogs bark and snap at straying sheep, so prelates must rebuke and punish their subjects, proceeding even to excommunication, nor must they be too easy in loosing what they have bound. (Serm. 4, 6, 19).

Priests should study the scriptures, from which the truths of faith can be drawn by much toil and care, as a fish is taken from the water. (Serm.6). For scripture is a well of divine truth, from which a just man can gain power to defend the poor and give counsel to the desolate. (Serm. 19). It may also be likened to a tree from which choice fruit may be picked, far superior to the bitter acorns, the food of swine, which fall from the oaks of Basan, which typify the writings of the pagan philosophers and other gentile writers. But care must be taken when expounding scripture not to obscure its teaching by excessive flights of fancy, or to waste time by commenting on unprofitable or thorny passages. (Serm. 3). For the purpose of scripture is to procure moral improvement by its threats of punishment and promises of rewards. It is regrettable that some find the plain style of scripture distasteful, and lacking in Ciceronian elegance. These are tempted to return to the Egyptian fleshpots of secular literature. (Serm. 7).

Of those who study scripture the vast majority are led by unworthy motives. With some it is a vain desire to appear learned that is the attraction; with others mere curiosity and an appetite for knowledge; with others a simoniacal desire to employ their knowledge in securing some worldly emolument. (Serm. 13). Among the comparatively few sincere students of scripture Pullen distinguishes those who have been instructed by the great doctors, presumably the commentaries of the Fathers of the Church, and others who have studied under ordinary teachers. The former attain to so profound an understanding of scripture that when they consult the sacred page they seem to hold converse with God Himself. Others less well instructed should beware of aspiring to equality with these adepts. (Serm. 9).

Various warnings are given to clerical students. They must pay no heed to those who would deter them from hearing sermons

or studying scripture, or discourage them from putting into practice what they have learned. (Serm. 16). Dialectic and the liberal arts are to be studied, but care must be taken not to be seduced by them. They are but interim studies, which in time must be forsaken for the study of the scriptures which point the way to the knowledge of God [59]. Dialecticians are notorious for irreligion and captiousness [60].

Hunting, hawking, chess playing are pursuits unbecoming in clerics, and should be avoided. (Serm. 6). The clerical obligation of preserving chastity is several times insisted on (Serm. 6, 7, 15, 17). A tranquil conscience should be developed by the use of the sacrament of penance; (Serm. 2, 3), and the three theological virtues of faith, hope and charity, together with the four moral virtues of prudence, justice, fortitude and temperance should be assiduously cultivated (Serm. 4, 5, 9). Those who have the care of souls will be held responsible by God for the proper instruction of their flocks (Serm. 6). Both the active and the contemplative life have their place in the Church, but the latter is to be preferred. (Serm. 10). Joy, love, justice and holy fear are praised as the four characteristic marks of the Christian spirit (Serm. 11), and simplicity in dress together with modesty in behaviour are recommended to those who have embraced the clerical state. (Serm. 12). Priests and prelates who live unworthy lives aggravate their sin by persisting in their ministry, and their prayers are profitless for others (Serm. 15); whereas holy teachers truly have God dwelling in them as He is in heaven. (Serm. 16). Care must be taken that good works are performed for the love of God, and not for a purely mercenary desire of a heavenly reward. (Serm. 19).

---

59 'Si inuenerit te studium assiduitatis impendentem in grammatica uel dialectica, dicet uobis, *non noui uos*. Scola enim Christi non suscipit dialecticum uel oratorem neque philosophum, neque in regno Dei legetur dialectica'. Serm. 13 ...

60 'Hii autem sunt grammatici et dialectici siue philosophi, qui studium assiduitatis artibus et philosophicis rationibus impendunt, eisque innituntur, et in eis confidunt, refragantes et resistentes eternis bonis. Philosophica namque ratio contraria est eternis bonis, et solum naturam sequitur, id est cursum nature, dum non patitur uirginem esse post partum, idem corpus in diuersis locis'... ibid. 'Noctes namque diebus laborando continuant, dum isti de dialectica disputant, illi uero de arte sophistica litigant. Nec desunt qui Platonem ceterosque philosophos sompniant. Student sophismatibus implicare socios, nec uolunt a nodis peccatorum abstrahere se miseros'... Serm. 19.

'Est quoque indigna uiris et stulta scientia. Hac inflati potentes ac diuites consuetudinum nouitates ad devorandos pauperes constituunt. Hac gloriantur peruertere uerum pro falso falsum pro uero fallacibus argumentis comprobare ... pro tali scientia horrendos cruciatus sine fine patientur ' Serm. 18.

The same earnest moral tone pervades the sermons in Paris B. N. MS 2945. Similar lessons are drawn from scripture, but at times direct application of the texts is made to the monastic life. Idleness, gluttony, unchastity and hypocrisy are the vices which the preacher singles out for special denunciation [61]. He urges those who have the duty of preaching to hold a balance between instruction and reproof in their sermons [62].

As in the *Sentences* so in these sermons Pullen affirms that it is the soul which constitutes a man [63].

His teaching on grace in these sermons is also in keeping with the doctrine in his *Sentences*. In both he shows a close knowledge of St. Augustine [64].

---

61 'Hostes uestri occia sunt. Hostem hunc captiuum tenes cum timore humano uel iudiciali horrore opera eius non imples. Sed adhuc spirat si in te titillatio eius locum habet. Ipse motus, quamuis debilis et torpens intus langueat indecens est ei qui sub Iesu duce militat ... (Serm. 24).

...'scire oportet esse monachos phariseos qui ornant sepulchra et quorum uita et studium totum est sepulchra dealbare et reedificare Ierico non reueriti ... (Serm. 32).

62 'Si docens Ecclesiam dei increpes tantummodo et arguas et castiges et exprobes peccata populi, nichil autem consolationis proferas de scripturis diuinis, obscurum nichil explanes, nichil scientiae profundioris attingas, nec aliquid intelligentiae secretioris apprehendas, obtulisti quidem coccum, sed non duplicatum; tenuisti in manibus lingue lucernas, sed non ardentes. Ignis enim tuus incendit tantummodo, non illuminat. Et rursus si docens mysteria legis aperias, discutias archana secretorum, seueritate uero disciplinae non teneas, obtulisti quidem coccum, sed non duplicatum. Tenuisti lucernam, sed non ardentem. Ignis enim tuus tantum illuminat, non accendit. Qui ergo recte offert et recte diuidit coccum offert duplicatum, ut sic lucernas doctrine per exemplum uite ardentes teneat, quatenus cum scientie lumine igniculum seueritatis admisceat ...' (Serm. 35).

63 'Unde quidam philosophus dicit animus cuiusque is est quisque, non forma illa que digito demonstrari potest. (Serm. 26. cf. *infra* Ch. IX).

64 ...'Omne enim bonum ad gratiam dei est referendum. Et notandum quod non ait, ut plenius et perfectius credatis in eum, nec se misericordiam consecutum dixit ut fidelior, sed ut fidelis esset, quia sciebat non se initium fidei sue priorem dedisse deo, et retributum sibi ab illo eius augmentum, sed ab illo se factum fidelem a quo et apostolum. Ipsius itaque est dare os et sapientiam, quia ut recte loqui aut operari uelimus, operatur incipiens, qui uolentibus cooperatur perficiens. Propter quod ait apostolus: *Certus sum quoniam qui cepit in uobis opus bonum perficiet.* Ut ergo uelimus sine nobis operatur. Cum autem uolumus, et sic uolumus ut faciamus, nobiscum cooperatur. Tamen sine illo uel operante ut uelimus, uel cooperante cum uolumus, bona pietatis opera nichil ualemus. Proprium quippe arbitrium nisi dei gratia iuuetur nec ipsa bona uoluntas in homine esse potest. Ipsa operatur et uelle et perficere non tantummodo scientiam reuelando ut nouerimus quid agere debeamus, sed etiam inspirando caritatem ut ea que discendo nouimus etiam diligendo faciamus. Alioquin iners est bona nostra uoluntas, quam ex nature creatione prima adhuc retine-

The learned character of these sermons, Paris B. N. 2945, appears also in the references to the Septuagint[65], and to Latin classical poets (fol. 46, 48, 80). Similar classical allusions appear in sermons 17 and 19. In classical literature he finds models for his spirited descriptions of the spiritual combat[66].

---

mus. Nam, ut perhibet Augustinus in ultimo libro de ciuitate dei, post peccatum primi parentis nec felicitatem nec potestatem felicitatis tenuimus, nec tamen amissa felicitate voluntatem felicitatis amisimus. Sed, ut dixi, hec uoluntas est prorsus inefficax sine gratie efficacia. Quid igitur agit liberum arbitrium? Ut gratiam cooperantem sequamur, ne in uacuum accipiatur. Alioquin non diceret apostolatus: *hortamur uos ne in uacuum gratiam dei accipiatis.* Ut quid enim eos moneret quod in eorum potestate non esset? Audiens in prima radice malignos suggestores incidisti in latrones, qui, plagis penalium corruptionum impositis, abierunt, te semiuiuo relicto. Quasi enim totus uiuus eras quando posse mori et posse non mori habebas, sed dum meliori parte uite que est posse non mori priuatus es, quasi semiuiuus relictus es. Immo reputandus es fere exanimis, cui est inflicta necessitas mortis. Sic te intueor letalium uulnerum dolore prostratum, ut surgere nec uales ipse, nec uelis. Uiribus enim premortuis mauis in ceno uolutari quam in surgendo fatigari. Nichil cogitare aut affectare permittit anxietas nisi ut in ipso luto quiescas. Reformidas medicum accedentem, et repellis. Execraris enim ferrum uitale tanquam letale. Itaque surgere nec uis nec potes, nec si surrexeris erectus subsistere necdum incedere potes. Quare necessaria est gratia samaritani, qui custodit isrel, ad hec singula scilicet inspirans ut uelis, efficiens ut uolens possis, protegens euntem, perducens peruenientem. Tamen auxiliarem manum ductricis gratiae si uolueris sponte recidere nec omnino annui aut coherere, in uacuum recepisti. Et in hac cohesione liberum consideramus arbitrium. Unde dicit apostolus: *Coadiutores dei sumus, et gratia eius in me uacua non fuit* Utrumque et liberum arbitrium et gratiam complexus apostolus ait philippensibus: *Cum metu et tremore uestram salutem operamini, deus est enim qui operatur in uobis.* Quando iubet ut operentur, liberum eorum conuenitur arbitrium. Sed ideo cum tremore et timore, ne extollaris de bonis tanquam de tuis. Si gaudes, et time, ne forte quod datum est humili auferatur superbo. *Deus enim operatur.* Ecce gratia. Ergo operaris gratia Dei, non uiribus tuis. Ipsi gloria et imperium in saecula saeculorum'. (Serm. 31, Cf. *infra* Ch. XI).

65 'Unde et Jesus ille; moysi successor, in figura ueri Jesu uestri precepit omni populo unanimiter uociferari, uel iuxta septuaginta interpretes iubilare' (Jos. VI, 16) fol. 54. Cf. 60v.

66 In hoc exercitu superbi et immundi, fornicatores et adulteri in prima fronte regis signa preferunt. Subsequuntur auari et cupidi, et ceteri prout principis calliditas disposuit. Alii ira precipites aperte seuiunt, et cominus in gladio malignitates totis uiribus feriunt. Alii simulatores et callidi ex insidiis tela toxicata iaculantur eminus. Nec desunt tibicines, qui per classica lituorum musice dulcedinis audacibus augent et pauidis dant animos. In hoc bello uibrat tela suggestio, consensus uoluntatis sauciat, occidit post consensum operis perpetracio. Israel autem prius per speculatores prudentie apparatum et aduentum amoreorum edoctus, in iasa montem propinquum et excelsum ad terrorem inimicorum et munimen suorum ordinata acie conscenderat, unde tucius et leuius inimicorum impetum sustinebat, et fortius illorum agmina dirumpens passim cateruatimque sternebat. (Serm. 18).

THE DE CONTEMPTU MUNDI.

Of this work, which is attributed to Pullen by the older bibliographers, there did not appear to be any surviving manuscript. However in T. K. Abbott's catalogue of the Manuscripts in Trinity College, Dublin, I found mention of a work by Pullen, bound up with several others in MS. C. 4. 21 (Abbott n. 330) which on examination proved to have the title *Sermo elegantissimus magistri Rodberti polani de omnibus humane uite necessariis.* This title does not appear in the traditional lists of Pullen's writings, nor is the work included in the collections of his sermons preserved in manuscript in various English libraries. Its omission from these collections is not surprising, since it is not a sermon in the strict sense of the word, but rather an ascetical treatise, apparently addressed to a single person. It is about twice the length of the average sermon of Pullen. The *incipit,* « Care frater considera » is identical with that assigned to the *De Contemptu Mundi* of the same author. It is reasonable, therefore, to suppose that the *Sermo* and the *De Contemptu Mundi* are but different titles for the same work.

The Dublin manuscript, C. 4. 21., forms part of a miscellany made up of two distinct sections, which were only bound together in the seventeenth century. The first of these, a small vellum MS of 19 ff, is written in a late fourteenth-century hand, and is an apocalyptic tract dating from the early years of the Great Schism. The second consists of 128 ff (vellum quarto) and contains MSS of the letters of Hidelbert of Mans (ff. 19-54), the Dialogues of St. Gregory (ff. 54-136), the Pullen text (ff. 136^{v}-143), the Rule of St. Augustine (143^{v}-146). The whole of this section was compiled as a single volume, as is proved by its title: 'Incipiunt epistule Hildeberti cenomanensis episcopi, cum dialogo gregorii, et quodam sermone magistri Roberti pulani'. There are, however, two distinct hands discernible, both belonging to the early thirteenth century. The Pullen text is written in a rather narrow English hand.

Both sections of the Dublin miscellany belonged at one time to Henry Savile of Banke (d. 1617) [67]. Savile's collection came largely from the Yorkshire monasteries of Rievaulx, Byland, Fountains, Mount Grace, etc. It is, therefore, of interest to find that the only other reference, as far as can be ascertained, to the *Sermo*

[67] Cf. Gilson in *Transactions of the Bibliographical Society,* IX, (1908) 139-210, nos. 119, 170.

de omnibus humane uite necessariis occurs in the thirteenth-century catalogue of the library of Rievaulx, which was printed by M. R. James [68]. There the title of Pullen's work is given as *Sermo magistri Roberti pullani de omnibus Christiane uite necessariis.* Unfortunately, only the title of the Rievaulx copy survives, all trace having been lost of the text. It seems probable, however, that the Dublin copy was related to it, and that it came from one of the monasteries in the neighbourhood of Rievaulx. The alternative title, *De Contemptu Mundi,* appears in the early sixteenth-century catalogue of the library of Syon monastery, Isleworth, near London [69]. This copy has also vanished. It would appear, therefore, that the Dublin manuscript is the only one surviving of this work of Cardinal Pullen [70].

Although a variety of topics are treated, the text may be described in general as a treatise on conversion and amendment or life. For convenience of reference I have divided the text into thirteen sections according to the principal subjects discussed. The development of the thought in the various sections may be outlined as follows:

(I) The trials of this life must be endured with patience, in order to make satisfaction for sin, and obtain detachment from the world.

(II) Good works are necessary, as well as immunity from sin. Complete sinlessness is impossible amid the temptations of this life. Nevertheless, there are varying degrees of guilt. Temptations arise either from within or from the devil.

(III) Contrition must be sincere and universal. Perfect contrition suffices to obtain forgiveness without confession and satisfaction, if these are morally impossible. In such a case confession must be made later. When it is possible, confession must not be omitted. It should be humble, sincere, and accompanied by trust in God.

(IV) Confidence in God must be joined with distrust of self.

(V) Gratitude to God is a motive for submission to the trials of this life.

---

68 Catalogue of The Manuscripts in Jesus College, Cambridge, Cambridge, 1895.

69 Ed. M. Bateson, Cambridge, 1898.

70 For valuable information regarding the Dublin MS. I am indebted to Father Aubrey Gwynn, Professor of Medieval History in University College Dublin, and to Mr. Neil Ker, Lecturer on Paleography in the University of Oxford. I desire also to express my thanks for much help received from Father Maurice Bévenot, Professor of Theology at Heythrop College.

(VI) The thought of death should withdraw men from worldliness and self-indulgence.

(VII) Love of God and of one's neighbour are essential for salvation. Fraternal charity must be universal, but admits of different degrees of intensity. Riches are to be used as a trust from God.

(VIII) Evangelical poverty is commended, and restitution of ill-gotten goods is enjoined.

(IX) Voluntary mortification is held to be more meritorious than sacramental satisfaction, but prudence is recommended in its practice.

(X) Purity of intention is required, as sinful motives completely corrupt good works and merit hell. Mixed motives render good works profitless, but after repentance the merit inherent in such works can revive.

(XI) Until it is perfected by charity, fear of God is servile,, and avails only to exclude the outward execution of sin. Fear and self-interest are useful, but not the highest motives.

(XII) Holy Viaticum should be received before death. Care must be taken to avoid a sacrilegious communion by true repentance and satisfaction.

(XIII) The essence of the Christian religion lies in the practice of the theological virtues of faith, hope and charity.

There can be no doubt that the text is an authentic work of Cardinal Pullen. I have given in the notes to my edition references to, and citations from, the *Sentences* and the unpublished sermons which reveal not only similarities of thought, but also of verbal expression, and which establish this conclusion. The same result is obtained if the style of composition is considered. As in the other writings, we find here a gift of forceful and terse expression, and a fondness for balanced and antithetical phraseology, which reveal clearly the rhetorical education of the author. It was, no doubt, these literary devices which induced whoever was responsible for the title to describe the treatise as a ' sermo elegantissimus '.

Writings no longer extant.

Among the recorded works of Pullen of which no manuscripts appear to have survived are:

i. Super Doctorum Dictis ... incip. *' Hostis humani generis undique '.*
ii. Praelectionum suarum liber 1.

iii. In Apocalypsin Joannis liber 1 ... incip. '*Sopitam plerumque concupiscent*'.

iv. Super aliquot psalmos liber. 1. London Brit. Mus. Royal MS 3. C. V. which is attributed in a 16th century hand to 'Pullus', and contains a commentary on Pss. 1-50 has been shewn to be the work of Ivo of Chartres [71].

v. *Exortacio Roberti Pulli de carne et spiritu.* This work is listed in the medieval catalogue of the library of St. Augustine's, Canterbury (ed. M. R. James, no. 468), as part of a volume which is in Oxford, Bodleian, Laud. misc. 385. Unfortunately the *Exortacio* no longer forms part of the volume.

iv. *Exortacio ad penitentiam M. R. Pulli.* This work is also mentioned in the catalogue of St. Augustine's. (ed. cit. no. 824).

---

71 See B. Smalley, La Glossa Ordinaria, *R.T.A.M.* ix (1937) 374 n .29.

CHAPTER III.

GOD'S EXISTENCE AND ESSENCE. ATTRIBUTES RELATING TO THE DIVINE NATURE

Proof of God's existence.

For his demonstration of the existence of God, Pullen appeals to the evidence of design in the material universe [1]. He does not develop or illustrate his argument. He is content to indicate its fundamentals: the harmonious co-ordination of a multitude of irrational creatures, and the ceaseless recurrence of similar phenomena. The argument is meant to imply that the universe had a beginning. He then goes on to enquire whether the Author of the ordered universe Himself had a beginning [2]. He replies that if God also had a beginning He would be dependent on a being superior and prior to Himself, 'aut excellentius se et antiquius habebit' [3]. He concludes that God exists and is without beginning: 'Constat itaque Deum esse et initium subsistendi non habere' [4].

The argument from design was, and is the common property of theistic philosophers; but the conciseness and pithiness with which Pullen formulates it are characteristically his. It was, along with the argument from efficient causality, far more popular with twelfth-century writers than the ontological argument of St. Anselm [5].

Among Pullen's contemporaries Abelard made effective use of the argument from design [6]. If, however, we are to assign any particular source for our author's reasoning the most likely would

---

1 'Irrationabilium rationabilis progressus, et indefessus in se recursus, dispositorem suae praesidere machinae indubitanter evincit'. 673D.

2 674D.

3 675A.

4 Ibid.

5 M. Baumgartner, 'Die Philosophie des Alanus de Insulis', *Beiträge*, II, iv. (1898), 107.

6 *Expos. in Ep. ad Rom.*, *P. L.* 178, 804A *Theologia Schol. III. P. L. 1085-1088.*

appear to be the *De Sacramentis* of Hugh of St. Victor. In the ninth chapter of the first book the Victorine proves the eternal existence of God in a manner which closely resembles that employed by Master Robert [7]. Whatever the relationship between Abelard, Hugh and Robert Pullen, all three show an advance in theological method on the work associated with the earlier school of Laon [8]. All three, unlike the writers of the earlier school, preface their discussion of the divine attributes and the Trinity with a philosophical proof of God's existence and unicity.

The divine essence.

For the early scholastics the question which perfection is to be regarded as the metaphysical essence of God did not exist in the form in which it was discussed by later writers. The early twelfth-century scholastics approached the question from a logical and grammatical rather than from a metaphysical point of view. For them the question was, in what sense, if any, can God be called a substance. By their speculations on this question they prepared the way for the development of the doctrine of analogy and its application to the problems of the divine essence and attributes.

Pullen approaches the question of the essence of God by the assertion that, if we are to follow Aristotle, we must admit that all forms of being are comprised in the categories of substance or accident [9]. If we assign accidental being to God we make the source of all being dependent on another [10]. If God is a substance He cannot be immutable, for a substance is by definition the substratum of accidents and susceptible of contrary modifications. Pullen then asks whether God, even though He has no accidents, should not be put in the category of substance on the ground that He exists in His own right [11].

It is probable that the meaning of the clause, 'quia per se et non per aliud existat', is, that God may be called a substance because He is uncaused being, and not merely because He exists

---

[7] *P. L.* 176, 219C-D.

[8] For a list of printed texts of this school see F. Stegmüller, *art. cit.*, *R.T.A.M.* xi, (1939) 33 ff.

[9] 675A.

[10] 'per aliud est, qui ceteris esse confert'. *Ibid.*

[11] 'An dicemus substantiam, non quia alii se subjiciat, sed quia per se et non per aliud existat?', 675A.

in His own right without inhering in another. If this interpretation be correct, Pullen's idea of the metaphysical essence or ' definition ' of God is substantially the same as that put forward by the majority of later scholastics, and his phrase, ' ens per se et non per aliud ', is equivalent to their ' ens a se et non ab alio '. There is some support for this interpretation if we compare Pullen's words with the treatment of the same question to be found in the *Monologium* of his predecessor, St. Anselm of Canterbury [12]. In the twenty-sixth chapter of that treatise St. Anselm employs indifferently the phrases *a se* and *per se* in reference to the uncaused existence of God in the course of an argument very similar in development to that of Pullen [13].

The logical and grammatical point of view is evident in the concluding sentences of Pullen's first chapter. If, he continues, God is to be regarded as a substance in this second way, He is unique, since all the substances of our experience are the *substrata* of accidents. Consequently, He cannot be designated by a name, for all names signify a substance with a quality. It follows that the dissyllable ' Deus ', God, is not a part of speech, since He is not that which a noun seems most properly to express: ' quia de quo magis videtur nomen non est '. A noun should express a substance with a quality. If this dissyllable is a part of speech, he continues, and consequently a noun, we must enquire what is its substance that is the subject of quality; for a name, as Aristotle remarks, determines the quality with reference to substance [14].

The thought behind this dialectical quibbling is clear: names cannot be predicated univocally of God and creatures. As yet, however, the Scholastics, not excepting Abelard, the ablest logician of the first half of the twelfth century, had very rudimentary ideas on the nature of analogy, and were unable to formulate a completely satisfactory answer to the difficulties they felt in predicating the same terms of God and creatures. Often they were content to echo those passages of the Fathers which stressed the ineffability of the nature of God [15]. In discussing the substantiality

---

[12] XXVI-VII, *P. L.*, 158, 179.

[13] That Pullen was aware of the concept of God as self-subsistent being is evident from his proof of the unity of God.

[14] 675A-B.

[15] ' Possunt et alia generis ejusdem innumera proferri loca veterum patrum, quae divinam essentiam nulla prorsus Φάσει vel καταφάσει, hoc est affirmatione, declarari posse persuadent, adeoque nec ipsum esse aut οὐσίαν de illa praedicari ', Petavius, *De Theologicis Dogmatibus*, Vol. I, cap. vi; see

of God they did no more than transcribe or paraphrase the relevant patristic texts which were in circulation [16]. As a result of the encyclopaedic activity of the compilers of *Florilegia* and collections of canons between the ninth and the twelfth century, these texts were very numerous [17]. A notable exception to the general unanimity of early twelfth-century Scholastics on the divine substance was Gilbert Porreta.

In addition to the works of the Latin Fathers and translations of certain parts of the works of some of the Greeks, the early Scholastics had access to the first part of the *Organon* in the translations and commentaries of Boethius. The Latin grammarians, particularly Priscian, were also much studied. By making use of Boethius and Priscian they were able to eke out the resources of the patristic texts and develop a rudimentary theory of the names of God. The danger was, and not all escaped it, of an illegitimate transition from the purely conceptual or grammatical sphere to the ontological order, or at least of some confusion between the two. In Pullen's discussion of the definition of the divine essence we can see the influence of Boethius and the grammarians at work, and note the tendency to confuse the sphere of the grammarian with that of the metaphysician. In his translation of and commentary on the *Categories* of Aristotle Boethius observes:

---

also Vol. VIII, cc. vi-viii. For Augustine see *De Doctrina Christiana,* 1, vi, 6, *P. L.,* 34, 21; *De Genesi ad Litteram* V, xvi, *P. L.,* 34, 333; *De Diversis Quaestionibus ad Simplicianum,* II, 2, P. L. 40, 138; *Contra Adversarium Legis et Prophetarum,* I xx, 40, P. L. 42, 627.

For the scholastics of the first half of the twelfth century, see P. Lombard, *Sent.* I. D. viii.

16 'Ut autem de essentia Latini Patres nec minus Graeci de οὐσῖα ad Deum accommodanda varie locuti sunt ob eas quas dixi causas, sic in substantia Latini duntaxat eandem loquendi varietatem usurparunt. Nam ambobus istis nominibus eadem in graeco sermone vox respondet οὐσίας. Itaque substantiam nonnulli Deo tribuunt, alii abjudicant. Hujus autem denegandae (causa) ... peculiaris in hoc cernitur, quod οὐσία, cujusmodi a philosophis et principe illorum Aristotele describitur, subjecta sit accidentibus, unde et substantia dicitur. Ita Marius Victorinus ... Idem et Boethius asserit ... Cum igitur in Deo nullum sit accidens, ideo substantiam proprie illi non tribui docuit Augustinus (Lib. VII *De Trinitate,* cap. v. *P. L.* 42, 942) et post eum Anselmus et alii' Petavius, *op. cit.* Lib. I, cap. vi.

17 'Ces restrictions faites, il n'en est pas moins vrai que les essais de systématisation théologique que nous présente le XIIIe siècle, sont allés prendre les *auctoritates* qu'ils utilisent dans l'arsenal offert par les collections canoniques. Les ressources de documentation présentées par ces recueils étaient beaucoup trop abondantes pour ne pas exercer une réelle fascination sur les théologiens', J. de Ghellinck, *Le mouvement théologique du XIIe siècle,* ed. 1 (Paris 1914), 312-3.

'Hic Aristoteles sermonum omnium multitudinem in parvissimam colligit divisionem ... omnis enim res aut substantia est aut accidens'[18]. Pullen echoes this with his 'quidquid autem est, vel substantia, si Aristotelem sequimur, vel accidens est'[19]. Translating Aristotle, Boethius writes: 'Maxime vero substantiae proprium esse videtur cum unum et idem numero sit, contrariorum susceptibilem esse'[20]. Pullen argues that God 'si substantia est, susceptibilis contrariorum est'[21]. The conclusion that the term *God* is not part of speech which Pullen deduces from the Aristotelian *Categories*[22], depends on Boethius' translation: 'genus autem et species circa substantiam qualitatem determinant, qualem enim quamdam substantiam determinant'[23]. More immediately Pullen's expression, 'Nomen ... circa substantiam qualitatem determinat', seems to derive from a definition which the medieval grammarians found in Priscian: 'Nominis est proprium significare substantiam cum qualitate'[24]. To the grammarians this meant that all nouns were conceived as denoting things with forms or qualities. The meaning was to be derived from a combination of the formal and substantial elements. The theory held good even of abstract nouns, e. g. of the noun *albedo,* and did not imply that the noun always represented a substance really existing. Hence, where the logicians spoke of *suppositum* and *significatum,* the grammarians preferred the terms *substantia* and *qualitas.*

The application of this grammatical theory to the names of God ultimately led to the elaboration of the doctrine of analogy. To the grammarian a name which loses its *qualitas* or formal element ceases to be a name; it becomes, as it were, a reality without a form. Now it was evident that in God there could be no composition of substance and quality; *id quod* and *id quo* were identical. As Père Chenu remarks, the grammarians were at one with the Areopagite in his mystic negations[25]. It was reserved to St. Thomas to find a metaphysical solution for the agnosticism of the grammarians. Pending that solution the mental confusion evident in the process of thought which from the onto-

---

18 In *Categorias Aristotelis,* Lib. I, *P. L.,* 64, 169C.

19 675A.

20 *Ibid.,* 198B.

21 675A.

22 *Categoriae,* 3b, 20.

23 *Op. cit.,* 1, *P. L.* 64, 194C.

24 *Grammatica,* II, v.

25 M. D. Chenu, Grammaire et théologie aux XIIe et XIIIe siècles, *A. H. D.,* 1936.

logical simplicity of God deduces the grammatical non-existence of the dissyllable *Deus* is excusable. It is possible that Pullen in asserting that 'the dissyllable *Deus* is not a part of speech', aimed at cutting away the ground from the grammarians and dialecticians who raised difficulties against the doctrine of the Trinity, basing their objections on a rigid interpretation of the Aristotelian categories. To meet their objections it was necessary to show that God was not subject to the rules of dialectic which were founded on these categories. For this reason Pullen showed that God was not a substance nor an accident in the accepted sense of these terms. When he went further and said that the word God was not a part of speech, he may have had in mind the formal propositions in which these pseudo-dialecticians set forth their conclusions.

This interpretation seems to be confirmed by a comparison of Pullen's treatment of this topic with that of Abelard. The latter in three successive works [26] inveighed against Roscelin and his supporters who had attacked the orthodox statement of the mystery of the Trinity [27]. Before answering their objections in detail, Abelard proved that all sound authorities on dialectic admitted that God could not be included in the Aristotelian categories. He stressed also that terms and rules of speech could not be used of God in the same way as of creatures [28].

The unity of God.

The second chapter of the *Sentences* is devoted to proving that there is but one God. If there were more Gods than one, argues Master Robert, they would be equal in perfection, since God cannot be inferior to any other being. Since God is without beginning, He is without limit. Whatever has a limit or end has had a beginning. It is possible that a being may come into existence and exist without end, but this would be due to the good pleasure of its creator. Every being which is intrinsically limited — 'quae ab esse ad non esse nativo properat defectu' — owes its existence to another. If it had existed from all eternity it would be essentially

---

[26] *Tractatus Summi Boni; Theologia Christiana; Theologia Scholarium.*

[27] 'Quorum tanta est arrogantia, ut nihil esse opinentur, quod eorum ratiunculis comprehendi aut edisseri nequeat, contemptisque universis auctoritatibus, solis sibi credere gloriantur'. *Theol. Chr. P. L.*, 178, 1218C.

[28] *Ibid.*, 1241B.

incapable of ceasing to exist. Now God exists from all eternity; consequently there is not any limit to His goodness, knowledge, immensity and power: 'nihil aliud decet, nisi ut intransgressibili, imo, inaccessibili decoretur bonitate, scientia, immensitate, potentia'. Consequently, if there were more Gods than one, they could not differ in age and power as the idolators foolishly assert [29].

Curiously enough, Pullen does not seem to perceive that he has proved enough for his purpose: that the concept of more than one infinite being involves a contradiction in terms. Other contemporary writers did not fail to draw this conclusion [30].

In order to dispose of the difficulty arising from the hypothesis of more Gods than one all equal in power, Pullen introduces quite a new line of argument. The created universe, he proceeds, can have but one author. Now if there is but one creator, it follows that there can be but one God. That there is but one creator is evident from the existence of but one universe. The creation of the universe had its cause in the intrinsic goodness of God; its completion was the work of His infinite perfection. On the hypothesis of more Gods than one of equal goodness and power, there would have been created more worlds than one [31].

It cannot be objected, he continues, that more than one God co-operated in the creation of the single world of which we have knowledge. A self-sufficient and self-subsistent being does not require any such co-operation. Co-operation, he admits, is intelligible where there is identity of nature, as between the Persons of the Trinity, for with them there is perfect unity of will, operation, knowledge and power. It is also intelligible when conferred as a grace on man: — 'aut beneficii est, ut cum sancto sanctus est Dominus'. Between two distinct divine natures, he implies, co-operation is unintelligible. Not even the bond of charity could make such co-operation conceivable. He concludes that, as Father, Son and Holy Ghost, being one God, effect one and the same work of creation, so, if there were more than one God, a number of distinct works of creation would be in existence. Since it is beyond the power of our minds to establish the existence of any such other works of creation, faith, based on authority, comes to the assistance of reason, affirming that there is but one God [32].

---

29 675B-C.

30 E. g., the author of the *Summa Sententiarum*, P. L., 186, 47C; P. Lombard, *Sent.* I D. iii, cap. 3; Roland Bandinelli, *Sent.*, ed. Gietl., p. 16; Hugh of St. Victor, *De Sacr.*, Lib. I, P. iii, c. 12, *P. L.* 176, 220 B.

31 676A.

32 676B-C.

There is nothing, as far as I know, quite like this argument in the works of the early Scholastics. The nearest approximation to it, perhaps, is Abelard's reasoning in the *Theologia Scholarium* [33] where we have an argument from the harmony of the world-order to the unity of its Creator and Author. But Abelard has nothing corresponding to Pullen's speculations on the existence of more than one universe. He is content to argue that God is the Supreme Good; that the Supreme Good avoids the superfluous, and that, if more than one supremely perfect being were the author of the universe, we would be face to face with such superfluity.

Underlying the argument of Master Robert there are two suppositions: that the created world is a manifestation of the goodness of the Creator; and that no other universe exists beyond the visible universe which, he has already indicated [34], is clearly one harmoniously-regulated system. Both of these presuppositions are of Platonic ancestry. To the early twelfth-century Scholastics, who possessed a fragmentary version of the *Timaeus* in the translation of Chalcidius, they were familiar ideas. The study of St. Augustine would also familiarise them with some of the leading ideas of Plato and the Neo-Platonists. In translation and commentary the thought of the Greek philosopher was at times distorted, and the medieval philosophers and theologians often interpreted him in the light of the Christian revelation.

In the *Timaeus* Plato explains the purpose of the demiurge in making the world:

> Tim. 'Let us, then, state for what reason becoming and this universe were framed by him who framed them. He was good; and in the good no jealousy in any matter can ever arise. So, being without jealousy, he desired that all things should come as near as possible to being like himself' [35].

When St. Augustine argues that it is fitting that God should have made the world, he is thinking in terms of the philosophy of Plato: 'Sed bona facere, si non posset, nulla esset potentia; si autem posset, nec faceret, magna esset invidentia' [36]. It is to be noted that neither to St. Augustine nor to his medieval disciples did the idea of the communication of the divine goodness through

---

[33] Lib. III, cap. ii, *P. L.*, 178, 1088 ff.

[34] 673D.

[35] *Plato's Cosmology - The Timaeus of Plato,* translated by Francis MacDonald, Cornford (London, 1937) 37.

[36] *De Gen. ad Litt.*, IV, xvi, 27, *P. L.*, 34, 307A.

creation imply any moral or physical necessity in the creative act. Typical of the conservative interpreters of Augustine is the following extract from the *Sententiae Divinae Paginae* of the school of Laon:

> 'Cum divina essentia sit summe bona et ab ea, teste Augustino, etiam omnis invidia relegata esset, essetque in ea plenitudo caritatis, necessitas erat non exigens, sed decens, ut quod caritatis erat, exequeretur. Sed quia caritas non vult sola esse, nec sola frui suis rebus, ideo decuit, eum velle aliquos fieri participes sue glorie '[37].

It is certain that Pullen did not regard the creative activity of God as in any way compulsory. He could write in his treatise on the work of creation: 'God made the world when it was His good pleasure. It lay in his power first to make this world and then to add as many others to it as can be conceived. Whence could compulsion be brought to bear on a Maker of infinite power, that He should begin his work sooner? How could He be prevented from making many worlds, after creating one from nothing? God had no need of the world; before it existed He was infinitely blessed. Evidently, God made the world, not for his own advantage, but that others might share in his goodness[38]. What is essential to Pullen's argument for the existence of one God is that the free creative impulse, which is the cause of the existence of the world of our experience, would also be present in any other god.

On the existence of a single universe Plato had written in the *Timaeus*: 'For the god, wishing to make this world most nearly like that intelligible thing which is best and in every way complete, fashioned it as a single, visible, living creature, containing within itself all living things whose nature is of the same order '[39]. Another passage contains the same thought: 'Have we, then, been right to call it one Heaven, or would it have been true rather to speak of many and indeed of an indefinite number? One we must call it, if we are to hold that it was made according to its pattern '[40].

Starting from this assumption that the world was one, early Christian apologists in the East and the West argued against the pagan philosophers that there could be but one God. Their reasoning followed two main lines; to postulate more than one author of

37 ed. F. Bliemetzrieder. *Beiträge* XVIII (1919) 10. Similar ideas are expressed by William of Conches in the *De Philosophia Mundi, P. L.*, 172, 51B (where the work is attributed to Honorius of Autun).

38 *Sent.*, II, i, 717C.

39 Trans. F. M. Cornford, *op. cit.*, 40.

40 *Ibid.*, 41.

a single world is derogatory to the infinite perfection of the divine nature; and the harmony which is maintained among the conflicting and irrational elements that go to make up this universe points to the superintendence of the whole by one supreme intellect and will [41].

The early Scholastics were acquainted with these arguments of the Fathers either at first hand or through the medium of the numerous *florilegia*. Clearly Abelard and his school owe the substance of their proofs of the unity of God to patristic sources. It is not possible to say with certainty whence Pullen derived his argument. He was not a mere compiler laboriously transcribing the *Sententiae* of the traditional authorities with a *verbatim* fidelity. He was a thinker who repaid his sources by an intelligent and original treatment of the material with which they furnished him. He may have found the starting point for the second stage of his argument in certain words of Augustine [42]. A much closer parallel to his argument is to be found in the *Contra Gentes* of St. Athanasius. There can be, of course, no question of Pullen having had first-hand acquaintance with this work, but it is possible that his reasoning is dependent on that of Athanasius through the medium of some Latin work [43].

Having argued for the unity of God, the cause of the harmony of creation, Athanasius continues:

> ' For the fact that there is one universe only and not more is a conclusive proof thas its Maker is one. For if there were a plurality of Gods, there would necessarily be also more universes than one. For neither were it reasonable for more than one God to make a single universe, nor for the one universe to be made by more than one, because of the absurdities which would result from this. Firstly, if the one universe were made by a plurality of gods, that would mean weakness on the part of those who made it, because many contributed to a single result; which would be a strong proof of the imperfect creative skill of each. For if one were sufficient, the many would not supplement each other's deficiency. But to say that there is any deficiency in God is not only impious,

---

[41] E. g. Lactantius, *Instit.* I, iii, *P. L.*, 6, 122-27; Minucius Felix, *Octav.*, *P. L.*, 3, 287-92; Ps. Cypr., *De Idolorum Vanitate*, VIII, *P. L.*, 4, 576A; Athenagoras, *Legat. Pro Christ.*, VIII, *P. G.*, 6, 906C.

[42] ' Unum dominum communis natura testatur, quia unus est mundus '. *Serm. de Sanct. Innocent.*, *P. L.*, 39, 2151. (The authenticity of this work is doubtful).

[43] According to Alcuin (Versus de Sanctis Eboracensis Ecclesiae, M. G. H. Poet. 1, vv. 1535 sqq., cited in Silva Tarouca, *Fontes Hist. Eccles.* 1. 329) Athanasius was represented in York Library.

> but even beyond all sacrilege. ... Again, if each one were sufficient for the creation of the whole, what need of more than one, one being self-sufficient for the universe. Moreover it would be evidently impious and grotesque, to make the thing created one, while the creators were many and different, it being a maxim of science that what is one and complete is higher than things that are diverse. ... Creation, then, being one, and the universe one, and its order one, we must perceive that its King and Artificer also is one ... Nor does it follow from the unity of the Maker that the universe must be one, for God might have made others as well. But because the universe that has been made is one, it is necessary to believe that its Maker also is one '[44].

The argument is interesting, but evidently of limited value. St. Athanasius takes it for granted that there is but one universe, and Pullen admits candidly that this assumption cannot be verified. Faith has to support reason at this point.

THE SIMPLICITY AND IMMUTABILITY OF GOD.

Pullen's treatment of his subject makes it desirable to follow him in taking these two attributes together[45]. Judged by the standards of a more fully developed Scholasticism his method of discussion is faulty and his range limited. He does not separate with sufficient precision problems affecting God considered as a unity from those relating to the Trinity. He is inclined to devote a disproportionately large amount of attention to discussing composition of substance and accident in reference to the simplicity of God and to neglect other forms of composition. Both of these faults he shares with other writers of his age.

He begins by insisting that the attributes of God are not accidental modifications but identical with the divine essence. With St. Augustine, whose words he incorporates into his text, he asserts that God is great without being subject to quantity, beautiful without addition of form[46].

Thus God differs from creatures, whose perfection implies the advent of formal causes and the operation of a superior efficient

---

[44] *Contra Gentes,* II, 39, *P. G.,* 25, 77, 79. The translation is taken from *Nicene and Post-Nicene Fathers of the Christian Church,* Second Series, Vol. IV, ed. H. Wace, D. D. and P. Schaff, D. D., LL. D. (Oxford, 1892) 25-6.

[45] 680-83.

[46] 'Sed magnum dicimus et pulchrum sine ratione, si potest intelligi, et quantitate'. 680C. See St. Augustine, *De Trinitate,* V, i, *P. L.* 42, 912.

cause. God, the Supreme Good, can have none other than Himself as the source of His infinite perfection.

The contrast of human and divine perfection suggests a difficulty. If human perfections are not forms inhering in the human substance, in other words, if in the dispute over universals the anti-realists are right, it would appear that creatures share the divine prerogative of essential simplicity. The rest of the fourth chapter is taken up with the solution of this problem.

First he states the position of the anti-realists. Can we say, he begins, that creatures are simple and formless in essence like God, and that what we take to be accidents are but mental concepts devoid of objective reality? [47] In favour of this view he argues that the mind has the power of conceiving an object in various ways, even though different objective forms do not correspond to each different mode of the object as conceived. A remarkable example of this power had been given by Abelard in his attempt to defend against the dialecticians the co-existence of three Persons in one divine essence [48]. Pullen admits that this theory which denies the objective existence of accidents is difficult to understand and more difficult to explain. On the other hand, attempts to explain qualities in terms of a realist philosophy break down for various reasons [49]. For the sake of argument he adopts the hypothesis

---

47 'An sicut Deum, sine quantitate magnum, sine qualitate, bonum; ita hominem omnemque rem vere informem discretione cogitatuum, non varietate formarum, distinguimus?: 680D. It seems better to use the term anti-realists rather than nominalists or conceptualists. The objection formulated by Pullen can be maintained on both the nominalist and conceptualist philosophy. John of Salisbury, *Met.* II, ch. XVII, ed C. C. J. Webb, 92, describes an anti-realist view similar to the one Pullen formulates: 'Alius versatur in intellectibus, et eos dumtaxat genera dicit esse et species'.

48 *Theol. Chr.*, III, *P. L.*, 178, 1257D-58B.

49 'Haec enim est vis mentis, ut concipiat diversis modis rem, licet formis non diversam. Quod dico, difficile est videre, difficilius explanare. Nam concolores per quid inter se conveniunt, per quid a discoloribus differunt, si accidentia non sunt? An, ut quidam aiunt, conveniunt et differunt, sed in nullo, ut albi similantur sibi, sed in quo? An in participata specie? (The realist view.) Sed ratio evincet universalia non esse. An in dividua albedine? Sed singuli cernuntur suam, non alterius habere. Verumtamen sibi similes esse liquet quia licet diversas, habent tamen albedines. Sed si formas tollimus, unde similes? Sic dico, in consuetudine loquor, auctores tam divinos quam mundanos videor habere adversos' (680D-681A).

It seems certain from this passage that Pullen rejected exaggerated realism, without, however, deciding in favour of any other theory. He suggests that the anti-realist view is fashionable, and makes use of it to bring up an objection to his doctrine of the divine simplicity, but his attitude to this merely philosophical dispute is agnostic. Some light is thrown on the phrase, *indivi-*

that the anti-realist view is true, while admitting that, although it is fashionable, it has against it the authority of Scripture and of profane authors [50].

On the anti-realist hypothesis, he urges, it would seem that creatures not only participate in the divine simplicity but also in the divine immutability, since they would not be subject to accidental forms [51]. He replies that it is a fact that creatures are subject to all the variations of growth and decay, emotion and other physical changes; that whatever permanence is found in them is the free gift of the Creator. This dependence is sufficient to differentiate creature and Creator [52].

Having established the mutability and contingency of creatures he proceeds to urge certain traditional objections against the divine immutability. How can God remain unchanged after the work of creation, or after the bestowal and withdrawal of His grace from the Jews? How could the eternal Son of God become incarnate in time without the reception of some accidental form [53]. A solution is suggested, only to be rejected as unsatisfactory. According to this solution, God, like His creation, is the subject of actions, but these actions remain external to His essence which remains unaltered [54].

Against this solution he argues, that if the divine essence is distinguished from its actions, it is made subject to accidents. It thus becomes no less mutable than creatures. Consequently, before God could have approved the work of creation, He would have had to love justice, hate the contrary, and be disposed in various other ways. Thus the Creator would not have preceded the creation in solitary state, but accompanied by a family of acts [55]. Moreover, on this view it would be necessary to admit that the divine attributes of goodness, beauty, immensity are identical with the di-

---

dua albedine by the following passage which occurs in Gilbert Porreta's commentary *In Librum de Duabus Naturis et Una Persona Christi*, P. L. 64, 1372B: ‘ Homo et sol a grammaticis appellativa nomina, a dialecticis vero dividua vocantur. Plato vero et ejus singularis albedo, ab ejusdem (iisdem?) grammaticis propria, a dialecticis vero individua ». *Dividua albedo,* therefore, means the universal form of whiteness; *individua albedo* signifies the form of whiteness inhering in a particular substance.

50 681A.

51 *Ibid.*

52 *Ibid.*, B.

53 681B.

54 *Ibid.*, C.

55 *Ibid.*, D. ‘Constat quia non solus, imo actuum familia stipatus, Creator creaturam antecessit ’.

vinity, for this is the teaching of authority; whereas the divine actions are distinct. To say, however, that the act of being wise, for example, is distinct from the divine essence, while the divine wisdom is identical with it, is unreasonable [56]. Without attempting a solution of the objections he has raised against the divine immutability he terminates the discussion abruptly by asserting that the divine substance has nothing distinct from itself, nothing which in the slightest degree could make it the subject of mutability. Creatures, however, are so constituted as to be liable to change, whether they are formless, which seems less likely, or whether they are subject to forms, which seems more likely [57].

In chapter five the topic of the divine simplicity is resumed [58]. What we regard as forms, he begins, are for all sane persons nothing else but God Himself. When we speak of God as omnipotent, just or wise, we are designating solely the divine essence, upon the various aspects of which we meditate in various ways. The results of this kind of meditation are expressed in various verbal expressions. Such expressions have for their object not only those truths which we understand concerning the unity of God's being, but also those concerning the Blessed Trinity. Although these truths are manifold, and become known to human minds in divers ways, nevertheless all the divine attributes, though apparently inhering in the divine essence after the manner of forms, cannot be other than God Himself, who though resplendent by many various titles, is none the less simple and one [59].

All this insistence on the divine simplicity suggests that Pullen has some definite adversaries in view. It is known that there were heterodox views prevalent among certain Masters in the early twelfth century. In the *Theologia Christiana* and later in the *Theologia Scholarium* Abelard refers to the error of Ulger, who taught at Angers that the divine attributes are realities distinct from the divine essence[60]. Against this error Walter of Mortagne also inveighed, though without reference to individual opponents [61]. Now there seems to be a certain resemblance in a few sections of the first book of the *Sentences* of Pullen to parts of the *De Trinitate* of Walter of

---

56 681D.

57 ‘ Creatura autem, sive informis sit, quod minus, sive formata, quod videtur amplius, eo modo se habet, vel habere valet ut mutetur ». 682A.

58 *Ibid.*

59 682A-B.

60 *P. L.*, 178, 1285B. See G. Robert, *Les Ecoles*, etc. 198-203.

61 *Liber de Trinitate*, ed. B. Pez, in *Thesaurus Anecdotorum*, (Augusburg, 1721) II, ii, cc. 8 & 11.

Mortagne. The resemblance between the two works is close where the authors are engaged in refuting certain erroneous doctrines on the divine relations and the simplicity of the divine essence. Thanks to hints given by Abelard ,it is known that Walter of Mortagne had definite adversaries in view, among them Master Ulger. It is reasonable to suppose that Pullen had the same opponents in mind.

Walter of Mortagne followed the Laon tradition. Though not a pupil of Master Anselm he was one of his successors who directed the school at Laon; later he became bishop of the diocese of Laon. In his refutation of Ulger, Walter made use of the principle, stressed in the school of Laon, that the divine attributes are distinguished in virtue of the diverse effects produced by God: « ex diversitate effectuum » [62]. Here, too, Pullen is at one with him, as he explains the names of God on the same principle: « juxta suos se habendi modos » [63]

Another principle constantly emphasized by the Laon school was « Quidquid est in Deo Deus est ». Though he does not use the exact words, Pullen holds fast to the principle they contain, when advancing as his decisive argument against all composition in God that composition would involve polytheism [64].

The omnipresence of God

The treatment of this attribute is very concise [65]. Master Robert begins with a question: Is God's abode in heaven, according to the letter of the text, '*The Lord's throne is in heaven*' (Ps. x. 5)? Or are we to look for the deeper sense of these words, evident in such texts as '*The Spirit of the Lord hath filled the whole world*' (Wisd. i. 7) and '*The whole earth shall be filled with His majesty*' (Ps. lxxi. 19) and '*If I ascend into heaven, Thou art there; if I descend into hell, Thou art present*' (Ps. cxxxviii. 8)? The distinction between the literal meaning — 'an secundum litteram' — and the deeper sense — 'an secundum sententiam' — was natural to a teacher of the Middle Ages. In Pullen's day texts, sacred and profane, received a threefold explanation when read in the schools.

---

62 *Op. cit.*, cap. vii.

63 682A-B.

64 'Quas formas, ut supra dictum est, ideo idem aut cum unitate divinitatis, aut cum qualibet personarum dicimus, ne si nostro more, singulae aliud sint ab eo in quo sunt, plurima sit copia rerum veneranda'. 682C.

65 689C-90A.

The grammatical construction was the explanation 'secundum litteram'; the 'sensus' was the *prima-facie* meaning of the 'littera'; the 'sententia' implied the profounder understanding of the thought of an author, or the perception of the doctrinal content of a text [66]. Interpreting these texts in accordance with their deeper meaning Pullen maintains that there is no place where God is not present, not only by His power — 'potentialiter' — but also by His essence — 'essentialiter'. He is not divided by parts, but wholly in every place, not gaining in purity from what is pure, nor suffering defilement from what is unclean [67].

In keeping with his usual method Pullen now suggests an objection. According to Scripture, '*The Holy Spirit of Discipline will flee from the deceitful*' (Wisd. i. 5). God is in the sinner by His substantial presence, he answers, but not dwelling in him by grace. God cannot be in one place and not in another, he continues, otherwise He would be limited and circumscribed by place; whereas Scripture testifies that '*of his greatness there is no end*' (Ps. cxliv. 3). He quotes with approval Isidore of Seville's description of the divine onnipresence: 'In mundo est, sed non inclusus, extra mundum, sed non exclusus' [68]. The simplicity of the divine essence, he explains, excludes from God all notion of spatial extension. He concludes that God has no more need of place now that it exists than He had before it was made.

In all this there is nothing that is not orthodox and traditional. As for so much of his theology, St. Augustine is the ultimate source here of the principal points raised.

Pullen's teaching that God is essentially present in every place has its foundation in the oft-repeated assertion of St Augustine that God is wholly present everywhere. In particular is the

---

[66] See Hugh of St. Victor, *Erudit. Didascal.* VI, *P.L.*, 176, 807-809.

[67] 689D. Pullen here supplies for a deficiency in his treatment of the divine simplicity.

[68] *Sent.*, I, ii, *P.L.*, 83, 541. The passage was part of a compilation made by Isidore from earlier writers.

Hildebert of Mans († c. 1134), a famous writer of verses on theological subjects, incorporates and develops the words of Isidore in one of his poems addressed to the Trinity:

'Extra cuncta, intra cuncta,
Intra cuncta, nec inclusus,
Extra cuncta, nec exclusus ...
Extra totus, complectendo;
Intra totus es, implendo'.

P.L., 171, 1411.

Augustinian doctrine clearly developed in the *Epistola ad Dardanum de Praesentia Dei*[69], a text much used by the early Scholastics[70]. In the same work Augustine also provides material on which the Scholastics drew for their discussions of the indwelling of God in the soul by grace. A further point treated by them — the impossibility of the divinity being defiled by contact with what is sordid or unclean — goes back to Augustine's controversies with the Manichees in the *De Agone Christiano* and the *De Natura Boni*[71].

The ideas of St. Augustine were transmitted through Alcuin[72] and especially through the work of St. Anselm of Canterbury[73]. In the writings which derive from the school of Laon[74], these ideas are clearly stated and maintained, as also in the later and more elaborate syntheses of Otho of Lucca[75], and Hugh of St. Victor[76], writers who had affiliations with that school.

By the middle of the third decade of the twelfth century, the question of the omnipresence of God had become a matter of controversy. In his *Theologia Scholarium* Abelard appeared to defend a merely potential presence of God in the universe[77]. It has been argued that the difference between his position and that of the more conservative theologians was almost entirely a matter of terminology, and that his opponents failed to understand his thought[78]. However that may be, his expressions were such as to justify the alarm and the polemic of the conservatives. Even if it be admitted that Abelard's own views were fundamentally

---

69 *P. L.*, 33, 837.

70 See *Summa Sent.*, *P.L.*, 176, 49A; P. Lombard, *Sent.*, I, xxxvii, i and iii.

71 *De Agon. Chr.*, XVIII, *P. L.*, 40, 300; *De Nat. Bon.*, XXIX, *P. L.*, 42,560.

72 *De Fid. S. et Indiv. Trin.*, *P. L.*, 101, 27.

73 *Monolog.*, XX-XXIII, *P. L.*, 158, 169 sqq.; *Ep. de Incarn. Verbi*, *P. L.*, 158, 273.

74 E. G. *Sent. Anselmi*, ed. F. Bliemetzrieder, *Beiträge* (1919), XVIII, 2-3.

75 *Summa Sent.*, *loc. cit.*, 48.

76 *De Sacr.*, *loc. cit.*, 223.

77 'Quod tamen ubique esse per substantiam dicitur, juxta ejus potentiam vel operationem dici arbitror, ac si videlicet diceretur ita ei cuncta loca esse praesentia, ut in eis aliquid operari nunquam cesset, nec ejus potentia sit alicubi otiosa. Nam et ipsa loca, et quidquid est in eis, nisi per ipsum conserventur, manere non possunt, et per substantiam in eis esse dicitur, ubi per propriam virtutem substantiae aliquid nunquam operari cesset, vel ea ipsa, ut dictum est, servando, vel aliquid in eis per se ipsum ministrando', *Theol. Schol.*, III, 6, *P. L.*, 178, 1106A.

78 By Dr. L. Ott in 'Untersuchungen zur Theologischen Briefliteratur der Frühscholastik', *Beiträge*, XXXIV (1937) 199.

orthodox on this point, it is certain that they gave rise to error among his immediate disciples [79].

Among the leaders of the opposition to the views of the Abelardians was Walter of Mortagne. Writing in 1136 or 1137 to Abelard himself, Walter asks if he still maintains the opinion which he expressed to him in a recent conversation that God was not everywhere essentially present [80].

In a letter addressed to Theodoric of Chartres, dating probably from about the same period, Walter informs him that it is reported that he is accustomed to deny the essential omnipresense of God [81]. Although, he continues, he does not believe these reports, he has decided to formulate the arguments for the traditional doctrine. Dr. Ott maintains that, even if this letter was written to Theodoric, which is doubtful, there can be no doubt that on the divine omnipresence the ideas of Theodoric were entirely orthodox, and that the Abelardians are the object of Walter's polemic in this epistle [82].

Before the publication of the third book of the *Theologia Scholarium* [83] there may have been some uncertainty about Abelard's own position; but there could no longer be any doubt in the minds of the conservatives once that work had become generally accessible. By 1138 Abelard's third book was in the hands of his opponents [84].

By about the end of the fourth decade of the century the question of the divine omnipresence was warmly debated in the schools. This is evident from the amount of attention it receives in the works of the Masters who were engaged in teaching theo-

---

79 See *Sententiae Florianenses,* ed. H. Ostlender (Bonn, 1929) 9 sqq., n. 22; *Epitome Theol. Christianae,* the work of Abelard's disciple Hermann, *P. L.,* 178, 1723, 1738 and edit. of Rheinwald *Sent. Hermanni,* cc. 19 & 27, pp. 50 sq. 76 sq.; *Sententiae Parisienses* ed. A. Landgraf in *Ecrits théologiques de l'école d'Abélard* (Louvain, 1934) 15. In this work, the most extreme of the writings of the Abelardian school on this point, there is a return to the old difficulty raised by the Manichees of a defilement of the divine essence through contact with the unclean. Dr. Landgraf dates the work 1139-41, at which period Hugh of St. Victor and most probably Pullen were teaching in Paris.

80 See L. d'Achéry, *Spicilegium,* tom. III, ed. 3 (Paris, 1723) 524.

81 *Ibid.* 522.

82 *Ibid.* 522.

83 1136-8. See J. Cottiaux, 'La conception de la théologie chez Abélard', *R.H.E.* xxviii (1932) 254 ff.

84 See William of St. Theodoric's *Disputatio adversus Petrum Abelardum, P.L.,* 170, 249 sqq. This work dates from the end of the year 1138. See G. Robert, *Les écoles,* etc., 206.

logy at that time [85]. Among those works the most important is the *De Sacramentis* of Hugh of St. Victor. There can be no doubt that the chapters which treat of God's presence in the universe and with the allied question of the soul's presence in the body are intended to be an answer to the equivocal assertions of the Abelardians [86]. In close dependence on and agreement with the work of Hugh is the *Summa Sententiarum,* which adds, however, to the arguments of the Victorine some additional material from patristis sources [87]. The most complete treatment of the question is to be found in the *Sentences* of the Lombard. While dependent on the school of St. Victor for part of his exposition, the Lombard shows a juster appreciation of the actual teaching of Abelard and his disciples [88]. Although his treatment of the divine omnipresence is less copious than that of the Lombard,, Robert Pullen shows more originality. He is in substantial agreement with Hugh of St. Victor, without, however, manifesting any verbal dependence. Following on his exposition of the omnipresence of God, Robert devotes a long chapter to a discussion of the manner of the presence of the soul in the body [89]. The ostensible purpose of this discussion is to provide an illustration of the divine omnipresence in the universe. There can, however, be no doubt that the chapter had a polemical bearing in addition to its function as an illustration. Nor can there be any doubt that it is Abelard whom Pullen is attacking. In his *Dialectica,* Abelard had denied the Augustinian explanation of the soul's presence in the body [90]. He refused to admit that the soul was either *localis* or *in loco.* It was this heterodoxy on the part of Abelard and his followers which was the principal motive for the inclusion of a chapter on the soul in the theological works of the conservatives. Pullen's chapter on the subject is very original and in places enlivened by humour and

---

85 e. g. Hugh of St. Victor († 1141), P. Lombard, who, although a teacher of theology in the Cathedral school at Paris in 1140, did not complete his *Sentences* until 1150 or 1152.

86 *De Sacr.,* I, iii, *P. L.,* 176, 223 f.

87 *P. L.,* 176, 48 sq.

88 *Sent.* I. D. XXXVII.

89 690-603.

90 'At vero, mihi non aliter videtur posse dici in singulis partibus existere, nisi secundum vim et potestatem ipsius quae quidem, dum in una tantum parte corporis essentialiter manet, vires suas per omnia membra diffundit, unoque et eodem loco consistens omnia simul membra *regit* atque vivificat ...', *Dialectica,* Pars. I, Lib. II, ed. V. Cousin, *Ouvrages inédits d'Abélard* (Paris, 1836) 193.

keen irony. There is good evidence in it that he was acquainted with the *Dialectica* of his opponent [91].

Although Pullen and the other teachers associated with Hugh of St. Victor had the views of the Abelardians in mind, at least for the greater part, in their polemical handling of the question of the divine omnipresence, it is certain that the novelties which they were attacking did not originate in the school f Abelard. Some years before that school came into existence, St. Anselm had attributed to Roscelin of Compiègne the error which was now fastened on Abelard [92]. Honorius of Autun, who in other respects has much in common with the conservative school of Laon, taught that God was substantially present only in the 'intellectual heaven', i. e. the third heaven in which the Trinity is beheld face to face [93]. However, to set the fires of controversy burning fiercely the provocative genius of Abelard was needed.

---

[91] Pullen retorts: 'Si autem anima humanae machinae *regina regiae excellentiae* decreta subditis mandatura, suae non immemor simplicitatis simplex sibi solium elegit; quomodo, si ipsa non est in reliquis *regni* partibus, quae fiunt sentire potest?' 691A.

[92] *Ep. de Incarn. Verbi*, VII, *P. L.*, 158, 273 f.

[93] *Elucidarium*, III, *P. L.*, 172, 4. Honorius died about 1130. On his relationship to the school of Laon see Bliemetzrieder, 'L'Oeuvre d'Anselme de Laon et la littérature contemporaine' in *R. T. A. M.* (1933) 275 ff.

CHAPTER IV

THE DIVINE WILL AND THE PROBLEM OF PREDESTINATION

THE IMMUTABILITY OF THE DIVINE WILL.

True to the principle of the school of Laon, ' Quidquid est in Deo Deus est ', Robert Pullen maintains that the divine will is identical with the divine essence [1]. In its dealings with creatures this divine will manifests approval and disapproval. For this reason Scripture speaks of God's love, and of His hatred, anger and fury [2]. These terms, however, do not mean that God is subject to passion, for passion implies mutability. The divine anger or mercy is eternal in its volition, though temporal in its effect [3]. Making use of this principle Pullen disposes without difficulty of the objection that God has willed in the past many things which He wills no longer, such as the passion of Christ [4].

A problem requiring solution is, how to conciliate two apparently conflicting texts of Scripture. In the book of Wisdom we read, '*For thou lovest all things that are, and hatest none of the things which thou hast made*' (xi. 25); in the Psalms, on the other hand, '*Thou hatest all the workers of iniquity*' (Ps. v. 7).

Considering the first of these two texts, he observes that the mere fact that creatures continue to exist is an argument in support of its truth. Were anything the obiect of the divine hatred, it would surely be annihilated. Hence, so far from hating any

---

1 714B.

2 697A-B. The chapter (XII) beginning at this point is entitled *De ira furore Dei et voluntate.* The opening words of Pss. vi and xxxvii in the Vulgate ' Domine ne in furore tuo arguas me, neque in ira tua corripias me ' may have suggested the title. Cf. also Ps. ii. 5, ' Tunc loquetur ad eos in ira sua et in furore suo conturbabit eos '. The chapter is a good example of how systematic theology arose out of commentary on the Bible made with material taken from the Fathers. Here Pullen appears to be indebted to St. Augustine, especially to *Enarrat. in Ps. v*, *Enchirid.*, and *Contr. Adver. Legis.*

3 *Ibid.*, B-C.

4 *Ibid.*

of His creatures, it appears that God loves them all, since He preserves them all in being [5].

This conclusion, he proceeds, involves grave difficulties. The lost, both angels and men, still retain existence. Are they loved by God? Moreover, God's love for creation will either be of an equal degree of intensity towards individuals or of varying degrees. If of varying degrees, He will love what is good more intensely than what is evil. But more and less, equality and inequality, cannot be predicated of God. It follows that God cannot love creatures with varying degrees of love. Hence God must love all in the same degree, Judas as much as Peter, Satan as much as Michael the archangel of the only-begotten Son [6].

This conclusion is clearly unacceptable. Either the love of God is free or it is necessitated. If free, the above conclusion would make it imprudent and unworthy of God; if necessitated, God ceases to be divine [7].

The first of these dilemmas must be solved. The method of solution is found in the use of the argument *a pari* or *a simili*. This type of argument was a favourite with Abelard, who, however, did not see in it much more than a way of scoring debating points against other dialecticians who raised objections against the Faith. He did not claim by the aid of dialectic the power of plucking the heart out of the mystery of the Faith [8].

You admit, begins Master Robert, that the divine knowledge is more extensive than the revelation given to men. This does not entail accidental modification in varying degree in God. The two states — more extensive knowledge and less extensive revelation — can be eo-existent without detriment to the divine simplicity. So, too, God can simultaneously be giving more to men and owing them less than He gives. Consequently, He can, *a pari*, be simultaneously loving one man more than another without being inconsistent or liable to change. The passage in question, is a typical example of Pullen's dialectical method [9]. The very fact

---

5 693A-B.

6 693C.

7 *Ibid.*

8 i. e. in his later works. See J. Cottiaux, 'La conception de la théologie chez Abelard', in *Rev. d'Hist. ecclés.*, XXVIII (1932), 533 ff.

9 'Nonne sciens plus, suos docet minus? An, ne plus minusve sit penes eum, mentiemur non plus scire quam docere? An, ut plus sciat quam doceat, mentiemur per plus et minus inaequalem sibi et a se diversum esse? Fatebimur ergo plus scire, cum suos minus doceat hunc diligere, cum illum minus diligat. Nec quia hic plus minusve agit, major minorve erit, non ob hoc mutatus, sed potius justus'. 693D.

that God's goodness transcends that of men requires that He love one man more than another, since, Pullen implies, even men love the greater good more than the less.

Evidently, Pullen feels that his solution is not entirely adequate. Nevertheless, he continues, if we are unable to find a complete solution for our difficulties, we are not thereby justified in propounding absurd theories that are no part of our Faith. Better, he asserts, to remain in pious ignorance than indulge in stupid speculation. He has recourse to a text of Gregory the Great which was the constant refuge of theologians when faced with an insoluble problem: 'That faith is without merit which (only) accepts what reason can prove'[10]. Quoting the Epistle to the Hebrews, he reminds his readers, or audience, that evident truths and propositions of the Faith are different matters: '*Now faith is the substance of things to be hoped for, the evidence of things that appear not*'[11]. He admits candidly that our knowledge of heavenly truths is limited in this life. Can there not be in God secrets too profound for our minds to penetrate, he asks. Shall men, who are still ignorant of earthly things, presume to comprehend those of heaven? Shall a mind which as yet does not know itself, claim to be familiar with Him in whose image it was created? Coming from one who was far from decrying the power of the human intellect or forbidding its legitimate exercise, this outburst is remarkable. It seems likely that some definite opponents are envisaged. Who these are it is not possible to say with certainty. Most probably they were to be found among those addicted to an excessive use of dialectic. Even Abelard felt obliged to rebuke such spirits. Possibly the followers of Abelard, if not Abelard himself, are the object of Pullen's polemic. Even where Abelard himself kept within the bounds of orthodoxy, his disciples, misunderstanding and over-simplifying his thought, tended to overstep them.

After this attack on the innovators, Master Robert again addresses himself to the problem, using the same method of argument *a pari*. If a man loves one person more than another, he begins, this does not mean that there is mutability in his will, provided he has always maintained this difference in the degrees of his love. The same holds good of God. Mutability is in evidence, he admits, if there is development in one man's love for another. However, this proviso does not apply to God. What appears to be mutability when God loves a person with greater love than

---

[10] 694A. St. Gregory, *Hom. xxvi in Evang., P. L.*, 76, 1197C.
[11] Hebr. ii. 1.

before is not so in fact. It is the person beloved who is subject to change, inasmuch as he has become better disposed to receive of God's unchanging love. He attempts to make the point clear by a comparison. Just as men of strong eyesight gaze at the sun with pleasure and those of weak sight at the same unchanging source of light and heat with distress, so it is with those who receive of the one unchanging love of God. Those who are at various times better disposed, receive more of the light and heat that is the love of God. So God, he concludes, whose essence remains simple and immutable, accommodates Himself to the varying merits of men. So God can love the just in varying degree and hate the wicked; but, whereas the source of His hatred is man's guilt, that of his love is his own goodness. Consequently, although Scripture asserts that God does not hate anything which He has made, it also declares, and with greater frequency, that He hates all the workers of iniquity (Ps. v. 7) [12].

Pullen now states that it is necessary to harmonise these two texts. Clearly, he says, that text which is of frequent occurrence, and of which the meaning shines forth without ambiguity, namely, that God hates all the workers of iniquity, needs no modification. Consequently, the other text, which teaches apparently that God hates nothing which He has made, is the one requiring interpretation. God, he argues, hates the injustice performed by man or angel; but injustice is something negative: 'injustitia est nihil'. Consequently, he who becomes involved in injustice himself becomes nothing, as authority declares. Now Scripture teaches that God is not the author of evil: '*sine ipso factum est nihil*' [13]. Two interpretations are therefore possible of the text, '*and* (*Thou*) *hatest none of the things which thou hast made*'. The first is to understand these words as applying to creatures only while they remain obedient to the divine ordinances: 'perstantium in ordine assignatio'. The second is as follows: God hates nothing, i. e.

---

[12] 694C.

[13] John i. 3. Pullen, in common with his contemporaries, places a stop after *nihil*, making it the end of vs. 3. The arrangement of John i. 3-4 has always been matter of dispute. In the West the division of the verses followed by Pullen remained in general favour up to the end of the sixteenth century. Of it Maldonatus wrote: 'Prima est quam quotidiano sequimur usu, ut post illud *nihil* sententia puncto claudatur', *Commentarium in Quattuor Evangelistas*, II, ed. J. M. Raich (Moguntiae (Mainz) 1874), 393. The great authority of Augustine, and in particular the definition of evil which he transmited to the Scholastics: 'Quid est autem aliud, quod malum dicitur, nisi privatio boni' (*Enchirid.*, II, 10, *P. L.* 40, 236) tended to perpetuate this arrangement.

the presence of evil, among the things which He created. This hatred may last only for time, if God deign to recall to existence a soul which, as it were, has by sin become non-existent. But he who has irrevocably turned away from God becomes the object of God's eternal hatred and punishment. In Hell there is no hope of amendment for such a soul: perpetually it cleaves to evil with all its will, hating the Author of its pain. In this life, on the other hand, sinners may still be said in a certain sense to love God, that is, while they retain hope of pardon and conversion. It is true, as Scripture testifies, that even in this life there are some men who are filled with hatred of God: '*The pride of them that hate thee ascendeth continually*' (Ps. lxxiii. 3). How much more so in hell; for if he that is lesser in the kingdom of God is greater than John the Baptist (cf. Lk. vii. 28), in like manner those in hell of least malice are, it would seem, more wicked than the most depraved among the living [14].

The harmony which Master Robert has established between the two classes of texts is a good example of what has been called the *Sic et Non* method of treatment [15]. It is a favourite method of Master Robert for the elucidation of theological problems [16].

The question of reconciling God's love of men in varying degree with the divine simplicity and immutability had been treated by St. Augustine in the *De Trinitate,* but not at any length [17]. Pullen has taken the leading ideas of Augustine, developed them, and thrown them into the form of a closely-reasoned dialectical discussion. Even St. Augustine's illustration has been taken over — that of human beings of varying powers of eyesight gazing at

---

14 695A-B.

15 So called after the *Sic et Non* of Abelard, in the prologue of which rules are given for harmonising apparently conflicting texts of Scripture and the Fathers, *P. L.,* 178, 1339-49. The principles there laid down have been given an exaggerated importance in the development of the Scholastic method of exposition: statement of problem, arguments for the opposite view, counter arguments, solution, criticism of the arguments for the opposite view. Grabmann has shown that the method of Scholastic exposition, as perfected in the thirteenth century, owes more to Aristotle than to Abelard; that Abelard's method in the *Sic et Non* is borrowed from the canonists; that the introduction of the Scholastic method of exposition was only indirectly influenced by Abelard's *Sic et Non.* See his *Geschichte der scholastischen Methode,* II, 199-221.

16 See above, pp. 30 ff. The features of the *Sic et Non* method evident in this chapter are the use of dialectic and the distinction between the various senses of one and the same term.

17 V. xvi, *P. L.,* 42, 924.

the sun. The question must have been a popular one in the schools round about the middle of the twelfth century, since it is discussed by the author of the *Summa Sententiarum* [18], by Peter Lombard in his *Sentences* [19] and by Hermann, who is generally taken to be the author of the *Epitome Theologiae Christianae,* a work formerly ascribed to Abelard [20]. The first two of these writers are in substantial agreement with Pullen in their conclusions, but the discussions do not approach his in liveliness or subtlety. The treatment of the question by Hermann has hardly anything in common with that of Master Robert. All three differ from him in placing the question in connection with their treatment of the virtue of charity, instead of in the treatise on God. The Lombard shows an advance on the others by the employment of a more precise and scientific terminology which later became the type for the school.

The question of reconciling the texts of Scripture which speak of God's hate and of His universal love is not treated expressly by any of the other three writers, though the Lombard refers to a text of Augustine in which it is briefly discussed [21]. It is possible, but by no means certain, that Robert Pullen used this tract of Augustine. There we find the distinction between the sin of man which God hates, and the goodness in his nature which is the work of God, as well as the two texts from the Psalms and the Book of Wisdom used by Pullen, but that is all. There is no trace of verbal transcription.

The problem of predestination

The author of the *Summa Sententiarum* remarks that the love of God for man is also called election, i. e. predestination to glory, and that God's hatred is the same thing as the reprobation of the sinner [22]. It is, therefore, intelligible that Pullen should include in the same chapter as the foregoing discussion some considerations on the problem of predestination [23].

We shall be disappointed if we look for a systematic exposition of the whole question, even in the brief form in which we

18 *P. L.*, 176, 126.
19 *Sent.*, III. D. xxxii.
20 *P. L.*, 178, 1748.
21 *Tr. cx in Joh., P. L.* 35, 1923.
22 *Loc. cit.*
23 XII, 697-700.

find it in the *Sentences* of the school of Laon and in those of William of Champeaux who was closely connected with that school [24]. Still less must we hope for the careful definitions and distinctions which mark the more developed theology of the next century. What we find in Pullen is a discussion of a number of problems arising out of the Augustinian theory of predestination which was taught in the schools of his day.

First he enquires how can God justify a sinner if he is not the object of His love; and how can God love one who, as he has already shown, is worthy of hate? Yet it is clear, he continues, that the sinner must be the object of God's love; otherwise God would never convert him, nor would the words of Scripture be true that God '*hath first loved us*' (1 John iv. 10). He replies that God loves the sinner not because of the sinner's wickedness, but because He Himself is good. The sinner is loved that he may be made good, and the love with which God loves him is not merely a present love, but one which reaches from eternity. So it would seem, he concludes, that the sinner who is destined to be converted and saved is the object of the same eternal love as the faithful friend of God. God is not subject to change, he implies, when He converts a sinner [25].

Next he considers very briefly the most difficult problem arising out of this subject: if none are saved except those elected by God, why is it that some are left to perish, others saved? On this point he is in agreement with his contemporaries deriving from the school of Laon and the Augustinian tradition. All men, he says, being defiled by original sin, are liable to perdition; but, whereas the divine mercy remits the debt to one man, the divine justice hands over another to reprobation [26].

---

[24] For the texts of the school of Laon see F. Stegmüller, *art. cit. supra*, p. 24 n. 4; for William of Champeaux see G. Lefèvre, Les Variations de Guillaume de Champeaux: *Sententiae vel Quaestiones*, 28 ff.

[25] 695B-C.

[26] 695C. This conclusion Pullen derives from Rom. ix. 13: 'As it is written: Jacob I have loved, but Esau I have hated'. The *Sententiae Anselmi* (which though deriving from the school of Laon are no longer regarded as the work of Anselm himself) observe on the same text: 'Quaeritur ergo, quare istum reprobaverit, illumque elegerit, cum ex eisdem patribus et eodem concubitu nati sint, et neuter eorum adhuc in propria persona aliquid boni sive mali egerit. Credendum est ergo quod hunc sola gratia elegerit, quod est predestinare, illum autem reprobaverit juste, id est, non elegerit. Nam si hunc propter futura opera remunerasset, videretur insipientia; si propter preterita, iam utique injustitia esset, cum aeque ambo nichil meruissent. *Hunc ergo per gratiam elegit, illum per justitiam non elegit.* Quaeritur autem,

The next question to be raised concerns the fate of a sinner whom God loves with a view to his salvation, but who dies before being converted. He admits that this fantastic hypothesis will never be verified. Nevertheless, he considers it possible, and gravely decides that the man would be lost, since God's love will not go so far as to induce Him to admit the wicked into heaven. The divine love only makes the sinner worthy of Heaven after his conversion, not while he is still in his sin. The loss such a sinner would therefore have to be attributed to an eternal decree of reprobation. This is all the more evident, he adds, seeing that the divine will and the divine foresight are never frustrated [27].

A new question is now taken up. Since, he begins, the final conversion and salvation of a sinner are to be attributed to the eternal love of God, and since this involves the consequence that such a sinner is always in a certain sense the object of God's love, are we to say that the converse holds good? Is the just man who is foreseen by God as falling into sin, and ultimately losing his soul, the object of God's hatred while yet he is in a state of justice? He proposes a tentative solution, only to reject it after examination. According to this solution such a man was never really just. In its favour might be adduced, he suggests, the text of *John*: '*They went out from us, but they were not of us*' (1 John ii. 19). This text might suggest the possibility of a merely specious justice in those ultimately destined for reprobation. Possibly Pullen is referring to an opinion which was attributed to Gilbert Porreta at the Council of Rheims (A. D. 1148) according to which baptism is inefficacious in the case of those destined for reprobation. On that occasion Gilbert vehemently denied ever having taught such a blasphemous doctrine, and the charge was dropped by order of Pope Eugenius III. However, the doctrine was current among some of his disciples [28]. Pullen argues against the theory of a merely specious justification that baptism was efficacious to cleanse Christians from the stain of original sin, as circumcision cleansed Jews like Esau; and while they were yet infants no other sin could defile them. Consequently, if they were cleansed, they were not wicked; if not wicked, they could not be objects of hate to a just judge.

---

quare non magis hunc quam illum elegerit. Penes ipsum est; nobis autem sufficit dicere cum apostolo: *Quam investigabiles viae ejus*', *Sent. Anselmi*, ed. F. Bliemetzrieder in *Beiträge*, XVIII (1919) 89-90. P. Lombard teaches the same doctrine in *Sent.* I. D. XLI.

27 695D.

28 See John of Salisbury, *Hist. Pontif.* 10, *Mon. Germ. Hist.*, *Script.* XX, 524, A. Landgraf, *Z. k. Th.* LIV (1930) 192, 202 ff.

Still the question is not yet settled. God, he objects evidently has the intention of condemning those destined to reprobation, not merely while they are in the innocence of infancy, but even before they are born; consequently He must hate the reprobate even while they are in a state of innocence. He condemns them because even while they are yet unborn He foresees their guilt [29], not because of any arbitrary choice of souls for salvation or reprobation. 'Non enim personam accipit, sed merita praescit, et secundum ea damnare disponit'. This is why God felt hatred for Esau, a hatred evinced by the punishment decreed for him. This punishment, and that of all the lost, is vouched for by Scripture and foreseen by God, and that which God foresees He will do, He has willed to do. Moreover, he continues, if it be maintained that God, Who from all eternity has decreed the reprobation of the sinner, does not decide that condemnation (and so loves the sinner) while he is yet innocent, it would appear that God, provoked by subsequent sins, begins to will the condemnation which ultimately He carries into effect. This consequence is clearly incompatible with the immutability of God.

On the other hand, to admit that God hates the reprobate while they are still persevering in goodness appears to contradict Scripture, according to which God neither punishes a person before he is guilty nor rewards him before he has merited his crown. Should we say, therefore, he continues, that God neither hates nor loves a person before he has merited one or the other, i. e. while he is yet unborn. Against such a simple solution the words of our Lord to the just on the Day of Judgement are decisive: *'Come, ye blessed of my Father, possess you the kingdom prepared for you from the foundation of the world.'* The preparation of an eternal crown in heaven bespeaks an eternal love, he says, prior to actual personal merits; so too the preparation of eternal fire for the devil and his angels betokens an eternal hatred. For the good, God has prepared heaven; for the wicked, hell: but His actual choice of those who by His grace are to be saved and of those

---

[29] 696B. This was the orthodox view, see William of Champeaux, *Sententiae,* ed. G. Lefèvre in *Les Variations,* etc.; so too Anselm of Laon: 'Ergo quos vult salvat, non tamen sine eorum voluntate libera, quia ipse non vult, nisi ipsi velint. Malos vult perire, non tamen sine eorum voluntate, quia aliter injuste; itaque Deus praevidit de hominibus futura, licet sint necessaria, non tamen implentur, nisi facientium voluntate libera', cited by F. Bliemetzrieder in 'Trente-trois pièces inédites de l'oeuvre théologique d'Anselme de Laon', in *R. T. A. M.* II, (1930) 61, n. 20. Similarly, P. Lombard, *Sent.,* I. D. XLI.

who (through their guilt) are to be lost He could have reversed, since '*He hath mercy on whom He will: and whom He will, He hardeneth*' (Rom. ix. 18). Nevertheless, the Scriptural teaching that God neither punishes nor rewards anyone before personal sin or merit troubles him. If reprobation and election are eternal, with God's justice in evidence in the former and His mercy in the latter state, and if they are equivalently punishment and reward, we seem to be at an impasse. He solves the dilemma very ingeniously, by suggesting that texts of Scripture which speak of God as rewarding or punishing only after personal merit or demerit are to be understood of the final state of the elect or the reprobate; that it is inexact to use the terms punishment and crown of the divine reprobation or election until it is consummated [30].

It might appear that he has decided that God has no love for the reprobate even while as yet innocent, given the principle of predestination antecedent to actual personal merit which he has just enuntiated. Still, he maintains that God may be said to love such a soul and that in no absurd sense. The reason is that God must love a person of holy life. God loves what is good in the man who is to be lost, just as He detests what is evil in the one who is to be saved. To the difficulty how God can simultaneously love sin, he answers that as long as the soul is still innocent God acts towards it as is fitting towards a good man, but that this loving treatment ceases on the development of personal malice. It is worth remembering that, earlier in the discussion, Pullen has forestalled an objection to the effect that this solution is inconsistent with the divine immutability. He concludes this chapter with the remark that though in this way God loves the reprobate while innocent, He does not feel complacency in the elect soul while it is still in a state of sin. [31].

The whole chapter is very characteristic of its author with his taste for speculation and use of dialectic for the statement and resolution of objections.

THE CONCILIATION OF MERCY AND JUSTICE.

Master Robert opens the discussion of this problem by reaffirming his conviction that souls destined to perdition are ne-

---

30 'An praetextatae satis faciemus quaestioni, poenam coronamque asserentes tantummodo existentis esse et permanentis, et vel de dolore gementis, vel de gaudio jucundantis?' 696D.

31 697A.

vertheless justified by the sacrament of baptism and worthy of heaven while they persevere in goodness. He establishes this conclusion on the authority of the text, '*Rejoice in this that your names are written in heaven*' (Luke x. 20), words which were spoken to some who afterwards fell away. Such souls would have been received into heaven had they died while yet in God's favour, just as the elect would have been condemned to hell if death had overtaken them before their conversion. God judges a man according to the state in which death finds him, notes Pullen, and he adds that a distinction must be drawn between the divine foresight which has in view the final state of all things, and the divine judgment which assesses the present state of men. This distinction permits one to say that God can simultaneously adjudge a soul to hell in virtue of His foresight and to heaven according to His judgment of the present state of the soul [32]. This distinction was also made use of by Anselm of Laon [33].

It would follow, Pullen implies, that God loves the reprobate, while they are as yet innocent. But at once he objects, how can God be said to love a creature whom, instead of allowing to perish, He reserves to be a vessel of His wrath in the place of torment?

He suggests that God's love manifests itself by tempering with mercy the punishment which it imposes out of justice, according to the text '*All the ways of the Lord are mercy and truth*' (Ps. xxiv. 10). Whether he is suggesting an intermittent mitigation of the pains of the damned or stating a general principle governing the divine punishments is not clear. Relying on the autho-

---

[32] 700C.

[33] See 'Trente-trois pièces inédites de l'oeuvre théologique d'Anselme de Laon', no. 18, ed. F. Bliemetzrieder, in *R. T. A. M.* II (1930) 58-9: 'Unde Ambrosius de prescientia Pharaonem damnandum censuit, sciens eum se non correcturum. Apostolum vero Paulum elegit, presciens utique quod futurus esset fidelis. Quibusdam autem gratia data est in usum, ut Sauli ... Jude, illis quibus dixit: esse nomina vestra scripta sunt in celo, et post abierunt retro. De quibus Ambrosius: sed hoc propter justitiam, quia hoc est justum, ut unicuique pro merito respondeat, quia erant boni, et nomina eorum erant scripta in celo propter justitiam, cui deserviebant, propter prescientiam vero in numero erant malorum. De justitia enim judicat Deus, non de prescientia tia. Unde et Moysi dicitur. Si quis peccaverit ante me, delebo eum de libro vitae, ut secundum justiciam judicis tunc videatur deleri cum peccat, juxta prescientiam vero nunquam in libro vite fuerat. E contra tunc aliquis videtur ascribi, cum malus esse desinit, qui secundum prescientiam nunquam defuit'. Here we have undoubtedly the starting-point for Pullen's speculations on the present question. Though not decisive by itself it helps to strengthen the view associating Pullen with the school of Anselm of Laon.

rity of Cassiodorus [34] and an opinion which St. Augustine regards as tolerable [35], Peter Lombard favours the view which attributes to the divine mercy an intermittent relaxation of the pains of the lost [36]. Pullen, however, objects that, if mitigation is evidence of divine love, the eternal duration of hell is even more striking testimony of His hatred. In support of his objection he quotes the text, '*Judgment without mercy to him that hath not done mercy*' (James ii. 13). In accordance with his usual method he now proceeds to try to conciliate this text with that from the Psalms '*All the ways of the Lord are mercy and truth*'.

Considering the latter text, he observes that *truth* means the judgment of divine justice, and in the punishment of the wicked this punishment is so much in evidence as to overshadow the mercy of God [37]. In this sense God's judgments may be said to be without mercy [38].

A second explanation of this text he gives as follows. There is no work of God which does not proceed either from his mercy or his justice. In this life His mercy is visible in His endurance of the wicked, and conversion of penitents; in the next life His justice is in evidence in the equitable distribution to all of rewards and punishments according to their works [39]. Even in the recompense of the elect, he adds, God's justice is tempered by His mercy, since human merits are temporal and exiguous when compared with eternal life.

This consideration leads him to enquire whether, conversely, there is any proportion between eternal punishment and temporal guilt. If, he argues, it be maintained that the rigour of divine justice supplies what is wanting to human guilt, this would be to make of divine justice mere tyranny and oppression. He solves the difficulty by an appeal to the mysterious and inscrutable element in the divine operations. Justice, he says, is operative in the reward of the elect, even though its working transcends our understanding. The same holds good of the eternal punishment

---

[34] Cassiodorus, *Super Ps. L.* 15, P. L., 70, 368 and *Expos. in Ps. C.* 1, *P. L.*, 40, 289.

[35] *Enchir.* CXXII, *P. L.*, 40, 289.

[36] *Sent.* IV, D. XLVI.

[37] 'Dicamusne adesse misericordiam, sed quasi sopitam, quasi tepidam?' 701A.

[38] 'ac per hoc judicium sine misericordia, quia adeo est modica, ut sit quasi nulla ». *Ibid.*

[39] 701B.

of the wicked [40]. We have a clue to the understanding of the mystery, Pullen now suggests, in the words of Our Lord that the lesser in the kingdom of heaven is greater than John the Baptist (Matt. ii. 2); for these words appear to suggest that after this life, charity and sanctity are perfected, so that they become commensurate with beatitude of eternal duration.

It might be argued, he continues, in parallel fashion that the malice of the wicked continues to increase after death; the difference between the blessed and the damned being that the growth in charity of the former is the gift of the divine goodness; whereas the hardening of the latter in evil comes from themselves. The increasing malice would justify an eternal punishment.

Criticising this reasoning, he remarks that if it were sound it would mean that the saved and the lost are repaid, not merely for their deeds done in this life, but also for what they do in the next. Not unexpectedly he rejects this conclusion as contrary to St. Paul's declaration that only deeds done in this life are the object of the divine judgment, '*For we must all be manifested before the judgment seat of Christ, that every one may receive the proper things of the body, according as he hath done, whether it be good or evil*'. (2 Cor. v. 10).

Before abandoning the attempt to solve the problem along these lines he considers one more argument. The dispositions of the will are the most important element affecting our sentence at God's hands. Now surely it is strange, he urges, if the will as it was in this life should be taken into account, and not as it will be in the next; for then it will be more deeply rooted in good or evil. Moreover, we would then see a certain parallelism between the wills of men and of angels; the latter immune from death and with wills inflexibly set in good or evil, were recompensed with heaven or hell. Why should not the wills of human beings after death be taken into account?

Very briefly he dismisses this piece of sophistry with the remark made in his characteristic tentative manner. 'An potius temporalis aeternae voluntas vindicabit voluntati recompensationem?' — the will as it was in time merits the reward of the will in eternity. He ends with the emphatic conclusion: 'Transiens namque manentis causa est voluntas voluntatis' — 'the will that passes is the explanation of the will that abides for ever' [41].

---

40 'At sicut praesens bonum acquirit futurum, Deo miserante et justo, licet latenter, Judice; ita scelus mundi finiendum infinita sibi vindicat cruciamenta justissimo judicante, sed justitiam nobis celante'. 701D.

41 702C.

In the following chapter Pullen resumes the subject and offers his solution of the problem of conciliating God's mercy with His Justice [42]. He observes that if we are saved it is by the mercy of God; if lost, it is through our own fault. Though we cease not after death to be entitled to reward or punishment, the term *merit* is more properly used of our actions here below. Our activity in the next life is rather to be called the reward of merit. In this life we perform meritorious actions, but not heareafter, though we enjoy in the next life activity of mind and will [43].

Since in the next life the will remains eternally fixed in good or evil, eternal punishment for adults, he urges, is intelligible. The lot of infants, not purified from the stain of original sin, is harder to understand. Nevertheless, in keeping with the Augustinian teaching, he maintains that such souls are with justice consigned to the region of the lost; the eternity of their suffering implies the eternal existence of their guilt [44]. Once the soul of the infant has quitted the prisn of the body it will have the use of reason. If regenerated by baptism, its soul, being adorned with charity will be worthy of heaven; if it has not charity, it is justly deprived of that bliss [45].

From this it follows, he continues, that the justice of God which assigns heaven to the saints is blended with mercy; whereas the justice which condemns the reprobate is unmixed with clemency. But if his mercy is never found without justice, how comes it that his justice can be found without mercy? [46].

To the solution of this difficulty he now addresses himself. He premises that in the conversion of the wicked which is effected without regard to personal merits, and in the salvation of infants by baptism, God's tender mercy is in evidence rather than the strictness of his justice [47]. On other occasions it is justice that turns the scale to the exclusion of mercy [48]. On yet other occasions both mercy and justice are manifested simultaneously as when what is wanting to a man's merits is supplied by the grace of God [49].

In reply to a possible objection to the effect that it is presumptuous to attribute to God any work which is not a work of justice or

[42] Ch. 14, entitled 'Quod hic meremur in futuro recipiemus' (701-708).

[43] 'Huic vitae actionem, alteri do voluntatem. Nam defunctis operum cessante opera, sola cogitatio erit reliqua'. 703A.

[44] *Ibid.*, B.

[45] *Ibid.*, C.

[46] 703C.

[47] *Ibid.*, C-D.

[48] 704A.

[49] *Ibid.*

a work of mercy, he answers that God always possesses the one and the other, although certain operations proceed from the one attribute, certain others from the second and yet others from both [50].

This statement represents his considered view; and it was evidently known as his teaching among his contemporaries [51]. Already in substance it had been taught by William of Champeaux, who almost without exception took his opinions from his master, Anselm of Laon [52].

Although he has made his own position clear, Master Robert is still willing to see what can be said for the other opinion, namely, that in all God's dealings both mercy and justice are operative. He is willing to concede for the sake of argument that God treats the damned with greater mildness than their wickedness merits [53]. Nevertheless, he refuses to admit that such souls are the object of God's love, or that such indulgence is to be called mercy in any real

---

50 'Habet enim semper utramque, verum generanda quaedam producit ab una, quaedam ab altera; alia, autem, ut dictum est, ab utraque'. 704B.

51 The Lombard discusses the question of the justice and mercy of God in the fourth book of his *Sentences,* Dist. XLVI sqq. In the fifth chapter of this distinction he enquires, 'Quomodo universae viae Domini dicuntur misericordia et veritas'. He distinguishes two schools of thought: 'Quibusdam placuit, non in omni opere Domini haec duo concurrere, secundum effectum dico; nam secundum essentiam non dividitur misericordia a justitia, sed unum est; verum secundum effectum non in omni opere dicunt esse misericordiam et justitiam, sed in quibusdam tantum misericordiam, in aliis justitiam, atque in aliis misericordiam et justitiam'. With this opinion he identifies himself since he continues: '*Fatemur* tamen, Deum omnia quae facit, misericorditer agere et juste, referentes rationem dicti ad Dei voluntatem, quae justitia est et misericordia, non ad effectus misericordiae et justitiae qui sunt in rebus ». That this opinion was recognised as the teaching of Pullen is proved by a gloss on the text of this chapter of the Lombard which is found in a manuscript (Cod. Patr. 128) of the Bamberg Government Library. The gloss appears after the statement of the opinion, and is as follows: *Post hec* etc. 'Quibusdam placuit', scilicet m(agistro) Roberto Pol(lacuna) m(agistro) Mauritio ... This interesting extract was published by Dr. A. Landgraf in his article, 'Some Unknown writings of the Early Scholastic Period' in *The New Scholasticism,* IV (1930).

The second school of thought is described by the Lombard without comment. 'Aliis autem videtur quod sicut dicitur Deus omnia opera sua facere juste et misericorditer, ita concedendum sit in omni opere Domini justitiam esse et misericordiam id est clementiam, secundum effectum vel signum, quia nullum opus Dei est, in quo non sit effectus vel signum aequitatis et clementiae, sive occulte, sive aperte: aliquando enim manifesta est clementia sive benignitas, et occulta aequitas, aliquando e converso.

52 ...'Omnibus etiam divina gratia suam aequaliter opem offerebat, ut quicumque ea uti vellet, misericors in eo et justitia Dei in eo inveniretur'. See *Sententiae vel Quaestiones* in *Les Variations* etc. ed. G. Lefèvre.

53 704C.

sense. The same holds good of the reprobate once they are hardened in sin in this life. It seems, he says, that just as the elect are chastised by God for their correction, but without hatred on His part, so the reprobate are indulged, not out of love, but rather like a sick patient, hope of whose cure has been abandoned. If God loved such hardened sinners, he insists, He would wish them well; if this wish were in any way real it would lead to their conversion, since God is omnipotent [54].

As for those already in hell, it may be admitted, he continues, that if God mitigates their pain, it is a sign that He wishes well to them to a certain extent. Compared with the fact of eternal loss, any such mitigation must, however, be regarded as negligible. The suggestion that God could be well-disposed towards such souls without their feeling any effects of such a love, must be rejected as senseless. Were God well-disposed to the lost they should be able to rejoice in hell; but Scripture testifies that in hell there is no joy: '*There shall be weeping and gnashing of teeth*' (Matt. viii. 12) [55]. He concludes that God is not well-disposed to the lost, but hostile to them, especially to the worst among them. Whether, however, He is less ill-disposed to them than their deserts merit he will neither obstinately deny nor hastily affirm [56]. Even if they are punished less severely than they deserve, it remains certain that they are not the objects of God's love.

Neither in the *Summa Sententiarum* nor in the *De Sacramentis* is there to be found anything similar in method or completeness to Pullen's discussion of the relation between the divine justice and mercy. In the former work all we are given is the brief statement that these attributes are distinguiished in virtue of their different effects, but that each is one with the divine essence [57]. In the *De Sacramentis* Hugh of St. Victor is content to remark that the will of God is just because He is the first cause and wholly self-sufficient [58]. To this he adds, in his treatment of the problems of eschatology, a brief demonstration of the justice of eternal punishment, relying for his principal argument on Gregory the Great [59]. The closest resemblance to Pullen's work is to be found in the *Sentences* of the Lombard [60]. Here the question is treated in a more positive and less spe-

---

54 704C-705B.
55 705C.
56 *Ibid.*
57 *P. L.*, 176, 65A.
58 *P. L.*, 176, 235A.
59 *Ibid.*, 610D-611D.
60 *Loc. cit.*

culative style. The various questions which Pullen raises are divided into different chapters. There is a gain here in pedagogical method, but the Lombard does not approach Pullen in vividness of presentation or in literary excellence.

God's salvific will and the attitude of the living to the reprobate

The former of these questions is not considered for its own sake but in relation to the latter. Having established that God does not love the reprobate, Master Robert enquires whether a Christian should love them. Clearly, he begins, men may not love the Devil. No love that we could feel for him would avail him anything. To hope for his conversion would be to go against the divine will; to pray for his forgiveness would be wicked, since he is impenitent. He considers that what he said of the attitude of Christians to the devil should also apply to human beings who are among the reprobate, provided we are certain that they are suffering their deserts in hell[61].

As for those now in hell whose lives on earth were not without some merit, he considers that they may be afforded some relief from their pains through the merits of those still living. This, he says, is conjectured by certain authors[62].

---

[61] 706C.

[62] 706C. This opinion, which Pullen proposes not without hesitation, found some favour before the time of St. Thomas, because it seemed to be tolerated by St. Augustine. In the *Enchiridion*, CIX, *P. L.* 40, 283, Augustine points out that the dead are aided by the suffrages of the living, if they stand in need of them, provided that their lives on earth were not so evil as to deprive them of the power of profiting by them. St. Thomas is clearly right when he points out that the mitigation of which St. Augustine speaks in the *Enchiridion* refers to the pains of purgatory (*Suppl.* Q. 71, art. 5). This interpretation is confirmed by Augustine's sermon no. 172 (alias 32), *P. L.* 38, 936, *De Verbis Apostoli.* Here Augustine makes it quite clear that those who depart this life without charity are excluded from the benefits of the suffrages of the living.

In the *Enchiridion*, CXXII, St. Augustine, replying to those who maintained that the eternity of Hell is incompatible with the divine mercy, rejects their principal assertion, but tolerates, without himself accepting, their opinion that the mercy of God brings at certain times some mitigation of the pains of the damned: 'Sed poenas damnatorum certis temporibus aestiment, si eis hoc placet, aliquatenus mitigari'. After citing this passage the Lombard remarks: 'Unde non incongrue dici potest, Deum, etsi juste id possit

As for the reprobate who are still living, we must remember that their ultimate fate is at present hidden from us. Even though they are the objects of the divine hatred, we must not prejudge them, nor exclude them from the common observances of charity. If we act in this way we shall not be setting our wills in opposition to the Divine will which is to cast them off as reprobate, since God wills us to desire their salvation. This is evident from the text, '*Who will have all men to be saved and to come to the knowledge of the truth*' (1 Tim. ii. 4). This text, he continues, applies not to the Will of God in itself, which effects all that it desires, but rather to God's Will that all men should pray for the conversion of sinners [63]. This

---

non omnino tantum punire malos in futuro quantum meruerunt, sed aliquid eis, quantumcumque mali sint, de poena relaxare', *Sent.* IV. D. xlvi.

In addition to these texts of St. Augustine there were others which induced medieval writers to speculate about diminutions in the pains of the lost. St. Thomas (*Suppl.* l. c.) mentions a legend associated with St. Macarius, a sermon attributed to St. John Damascene, which is probably spurious, and a passage from the Περὶ ἀρχῶν of Origen.

In his life of St. Gregory the Great (lib. II, c. iv, *P.L.* 75, 105) John the Deacon relates that the Emperor Trajan was released from hell through the tears of the saint. It was probably this story which induced Pullen to believe that in certain exceptional cases souls have been delivered from hell by the mercy of God, and, having been restored to this life, have in the end gained salvation. (See *Sent.* lib. VII, c. xxvii, *P.L.* 186, 944f.). On the whole question of early-scholastic ideas on the mitigation of the pains of hell see A. Landgraf, Die Linderung der Höllenstrafen nach der Lehre der Frühscholastik, *Z.k.Th.* LX (1936) 299-370.

[63] 'non in se, quia quaecunque voluit fecit, sed in cunctis, quos ita facit velle, ut pius effectus pium moveat judicem, impium expiare'. 707B. Pullen's interpretation is based on St. Augustine. Altogether the Saint proposed four different, but related, interpretations of the text. A literal interpretation according to which the text is to be understood of all men, is to be found in the *De Spiritu et Littera,* XXXIII, *P.L.* 44, 238. Thus interpreted, the text has reference to the Will of God considered as antecedent to God's prevision of final impenitence on the part of men. Theologians of Pullen's day do not seem to have been familiar with this text of Augustine. In the controversy with the Pelagians, who appealed to this text in support of their teaching that free will universally given to men can attain salvation unassisted by supernatural grace, Augustine proposed somewhat different interpretations of the text, 1 Tim. ii. 4. He ceased to interpret it of the Will of God considered as antecedent to, and conditioned by, the prevision of the use made by men of free will assisted by grace; instead, he applied it to the Will of God considered as consequent on the prevision of the final state of men in this life. Regarded in this way, it is evident that the salvific Will of God is not universal in scope; it applies to the elect only. Only by accommodation can the text, if applied to the 'consequent' Will of God be said to have reference to all men. In various works Augustine proposes three such accommodations.

interpretation he justifies from the fact that the Divine Will has from all eternity intended the intercession of the saints to be the proximate cause of the conversion of sinners.

In heaven the wills of the saints will be entirely at one with the divine Will, since all ignorance will there be dispelled[64]. The spectacle of the lost will not distress them, for they will appreciate the justice of God's judgments on the wicked[65].

The question is now raised as to the legitimacy of hating those who have not the Faith, both Jews and Gentiles, since it is certain,

---

(1) God may be said to desire the salvation of all men in the sense that He inspires the faithful to desire and pray for the salvation of all men. This interpretation of which Pullen avails himself occurs in the *De Correptione et Gratia*, XV, *P. L.* 44, 945.

(2) All who are saved owe their salvation to the Will of God. This interpretation is suggested in *Epis.* CCXVII, *P. L.*, 33, 985; *Contra Julianum, Lib. IV*, cap. viii. *P. L.*, 44, 760; *Enchiridion*, CIII, *P. L.*, 40, 280; *De Praedestinatione Sanctorum*, VIII, *P. L.*, 44, 971.

(3) God may be said to desire the salvation of all men since those who attain salvation belong to all classes and conditions of men. Thus in the *Enchiridion*, CIII, *P. L.*, 40, 280; *De Correptione et Gratia*, XIV, *P. L.*, 44, 943.

All three accommodated interpretations were used in the School of Laon. See the *Sententiae Anselmi*, ed. F. Bliemetzrieder, *op. cit.* (*supra*, 81 n. 28) 63-4, and the *Sententiae Berolinenses*, ed. Stegmuller, *art. cit.* (*supra*, 24, n. 4). Of special interest is an extract published by Bliemetzrieder in 'Trente-trois pièces inédites de l'oeuvre théologique d'Anselme de Laon', *loc. cit.* (*supra*, 85). 'Anselmus de voluntate Dei ... Voluntas autem Dei tribus modis accipitur. Dicitur enim voluntas essentiae, que est in ipso deo, scilicet dispositio vel ordinatio secundum quam disponit omnia vel bona vel mala, de qua dicitur: *omnia quaecumque voluit fecit*, et: *voluntati ejus quis resistet?* Dicitur enim voluntas dei bona, qua operatur in sanctis, quia videlicet fecit sanctos benevolos erga deum et proximum, secundum quod dicitur: *vult deus omnes salvos* fieri, id est facit sanctos suos velle. Si enim *sancti diligunt* proximos sicut seipsos, volunt itaque illos salvos fieri, et hec habent a domino. In qua voluntate, *illud mirum est, quod sancti discordant partim a voluntate dei: deus enim non vult, id est, non disponit omnes salvare, quos sancti tamen volunt fieri salvos. Circa igitur malos proximos cum illa dei voluntate conveniunt, quia deo resistere nolunt, et ex affectu caritatis disconveniunt ...*

Here we have not merely the interpretation of Augustine used by Pullen, but also the very problem discussed by him: how to reconcile our duty of charity towards all with our obligation of seeking in all things conformity to the Will of God. So he writes: 'Monet Apostolus in omnibus probare quae sit voluntas Dei (Rom. XII. 2), hoc enim solum inter omnia debet servo placere, quod probaverit Dominum suum velle. Dominus autem vult malos male perdere (Matt. xxi. 41); nonne igitur placebit servo malorum perditio? Quomodo autem fratres diligit si eos damnari volet? Aut si id fratribus nolit, nonne Dominum contemnit cujus voluntati contradicit?' (706D-707A).

64 707B.

65 707C. This idea probably derives from Gregory the Great's *Homil. XL. in Evang.*, *P. L.*, 76, 1309A-B.

argues Pullen, that those who die without faith are destined to Hell; this on the authority of the text, '*He that doth not believe is already judged*' (John iii. 18). In virtue of the interpretation of 1 Tim. iv. 4 that he has adopted, he forbids such hatred.

As for the reprobate in general who belong to the Church, he suggests two more reasons for not excluding them from our charity. Granted that '*many are called, but few are chosen*', he justifies a universal charity for the reason that in any given age of the Church all the members may be destined for salvation and consequently beloved of God. If this reason appears unacceptable, he continues, to one who holds that the reprobate are to be found in all ages, we must continue to pray for the salvation of all, in accordance with the interpretation of the Pauline text. At the same time, it is possible to say that our wills are all the time in conformity with the divine Will; because we can hate the multitude of the reprobate in general, while remaining in ignorance of the individuals comprising it, and, consequently, continuing to love all our contemporaries [66]. At times it has happened that holy men have received a revelation of the future perdition of certain reprobate souls. In such cases the just could not help desiring what they knew to be the divine will in regard to those souls. The general rule is, however, that we must love all men until it is certain that they are numbered among the reprobate [67].

Finally he examines the possibility of loving and hating the reprobate simultaneously. The concept is a difficult one, he says [68]. Although unaware of their identity, one would conform one's will with the divine will and desire their perdition, at the same time endeavouring by the merit of one's own charity to secure some mitigation of their pains [69]. He admits that this would be a very distant kind of love (perexilis amor), not love in the true sense of the word, but only sympathy.

Among the theologians contemporary with Pullen who adopted the same interpretation of 1 Tim. ii. 4. was the author of the *Summa Sententiarum* [70]. The Lombard preferred the third explanation [71]. Hugh of St. Victor does not discuss the point in the *De Sacramentis.*

---

66 708A.

67 'nisi si cui quempiam ad populum sinistre innotuit pertinere'. *Ibid.*, C.

68 708C.

69 *Ibid.*, He means a milder sentence than their deserts warrant.

70 *P. L.*, 176, 65C.

71 *Sent.*, I. D. XLVI, cap. 2.

CHAPTER V.

OMNIPOTENCE AND PROVIDENCE

GOD'S OMNIPOTENCE: DISPUTE WITH THE ABELARDIANS

God's omnipotence is clearly affirmed [1]. Nevertheless, adds Pullen, God cannot perform any action which is irrational or evil: for this very reason is He called omnipotent, since the capacity for evil implies limitation. Consequently, however great a creature may be, its power is negligible in comparison with that of the Creator [2].

This doctrine of the essential incompatibility of omnipotence and the capacity for evil was derived by the scholastics from St. Augustine [3]. It was known and expounded in the School of Laon [4], whence it passed into the *Summa Sententiarum* [5] and the *Sentences* of the Lombard [6].

A necessary concomitant of omnipotence, continues Pullen, is foreknowledge; thus is the divine omnipotence preserved from all approach to evil. This foreknowledge has been in God from all eternity, since God cannot grow in perfection. Whatever comes into existence has had an eternal pre-existence in the mind of God, according to the text, '*Quod factum est in ipso vita erat*' [7]. Whatever, therefore, God foresees from all eternity He will in due time bring to

---

1 708D.

2 709A.

3 See *De Trin.*, lib. XV, cap. xv, *P. L.*, 42, 1077; *Enchiridion*, cap. XCVI, *P. L.*, 40, 276; *De Symbolo ad Catech.*, cap. 1, *P. L.*, 40, 627 (this work is of doubtful authenticity).

4 See e. g. *Sententiae Berolinenses*, ed. Stegmüller, *loc. cit.* (*supra*, p. 24 n. 4).

5 *P. L.*, 176, 68.

6 *Sent.*, I. D. XLII, cap. II.

7 This arrangement and interpretation of the text of John was customary in Pullen's day. It was accepted on the authority of St. Augustine. See, e. g. *De Gen. ad Litt.*, Lib. V, cap. XVIII, n. 36, *P. L.*, 34, 333. On this point the Lombard writes: (*Sent.*, I. D. XXXV, cap. 9). 'Ex hoc igitur sensu omnia dicuntur in Deo et omne quod factum est dicitur esse vita in ipso; non ideo quod creatura sit Creator, vel quod ista temporalia essentialiter sint in Deo, sed quia in ejus scientia semper sunt, quae vita est'.

pass. Any precipitate alteration of the course of providence would be evil and irrational, and, consequently, not possible to God [8]. The importance of this conclusion lies in the fact that it effectually removes from the sphere of the divine operations any effect in time which has not been foreseen and willed by God from all eternity. A like conclusion had been drawn, as was to be expected, by Abelard, who, however, went further and maintained that the present order of providence is the only one possible, and, since it derives from the mind of an infinitely perfect being, the best one possible. Pullen was evidently well acquainted with the work of Abelard, and it is to the refutation of his opinions on the divine omnipotence and providence that he devotes the remainder of this chapter [9].

He begins by formulating an objection against the orthodox position which contains the essence of the Abelardian theory. If anything which occurs apart from what God has ordained is irrational, it is evident that God can do nothing which lies outside the order of His providence; but His providence only has in view that which actually occurs: consequently he can only do that which He actually does do. The divine providence, action, power and will are necessarily linked and proportioned one to another [10]. This objection does not appear to be a quotation from any particular work belonging to the school of Abelard but a forceful statement of one of the arguments in favour of the Abelardian position. That position was defended by arguments drawn from 'authority', or what its defenders took to be the meaning of their authorities, and also by philosophical reasons [11].

---

[8] 709B-C. 'Quocirca quidquid divinae providentiae sinceritatem praecipitanter actum evacuaret, illud malum et irrationabile videretur; quidquid autem irrationabiliter fieret, illud Deum non posse supra dicebatur'.

[9] Cap. XV, 708-714.

[10] 'Si ergo quidquid aliter se haberet, quam Deus ordinavit, irrationabile esset, nullum autem irrationabile potest, liquet ipsum nihil posse nisi quod veritas habet providentiae; sed nihil providit nisi quod contingit: nihil igitur potest nisi quod fit. Imo nihil potest, nisi quod vult et facit. Id enim solum facere disposuit, quod per voluntatem effectum reddit. Haec ergo quattuor tali sibi vinculo connectantur, ut nec se deserant, nec excedant, quippe et providentiae divine actus aequalis est potestas, et potestati adaequatur cum actione voluntas, unde aiunt (sc. the Abelardians) voluntate Dei potestatem non esse majorem'. 709C.

[11] Master Roland Bandinelli, afterwards Pope Alexander III, who had been a pupil of Abelard's and whose *Sentences* (ed. Gietl, *op. cit.*) show the influence of the ideas of his master, did not follow Abelard on this point. After stating a number of arguments of the Abelardians, he gives his *determination* in favour of the orthodox teaching (pp. 56-58). Among the arguments for the opposite opinion which he adduces is one based on the equivalence of the di-

In reply to his statement of the Abelardian objection Pullen admits that for any event to take place which God has not foreseen and pre-ordained from all eternity would be irrational and wrong in the present order of Providence. Nevertheless, he asserts, God could have planned another and different order in which effects other than those of the present order would be good and reasonable [12].

Abelard had not failed to see that his argument might be thus answered [13]. It is of interest to compare Abelard's statement with the actual words used by Pullen [14].

Besides the general similarity of the thought there is a certain

---

vine will, power, and operation which resembles the objection proposed by Pullen. '*Augustinus*: non enim dicitur Deus omnipotens, eo quod omnia possit, sed quia quidquid vult potest, scilicet quicquic vult operatur' (p. 50) (these words are apparently not in Augustine, but are an enlargement and misinterpretation of passages in the *De Civ. Dei*, lib. XXI, cap. vii, *P. L.*, 41, 719, and *Serm. I ad Catech.*, *ibid.* o0, 627. — 'Si quicquic potest operatur: ergo non potest plura facere quam faciat' (*ibid.*). '*Augustinus super 'Quicumque vult'*: idem est Deo velle et posse: ergo quicquic vult potest et quicquid potest vult. Quicquic autem vult operatur: ergo quicquic potest operatur. Si quicquid potest operatur: ergo non potest plura facere quam faciat. (*ibid.*). Cf. also *Summa Sententiarum*, Tract. I, cap. xiv, *P. L.*, 176, 68-69; *Ysagoge in Theologiam*, ed. A. Landgraf in *Ecrits théologiques de l'école d'Abélard*, pp. 265-268. P. Lombard, *Sentences*, I. D. XLIII.

Abelard himself, who maintained his unorthodox ideas on this question in the *Theologia Christiana* Lib. V (*P. L.*, 178, 1324 ff.) as well as in the later *Theologia Scholarium*, Lib. III (*P. L.*, 178, 1098), argued from Plato's *Timaeus*: 'Si enim ponamus ut plura vel pauciora facere possit, vel ab his quae ponit cessare, profecto multum summae ejus bonitati derogabimus. Constat quippe eam non nisi bona facere posse; si autem bona, cum possit, non faciat, et ab aliquibus quae facienda essent se retrahat, quis eum tanquam aemulum vel iniquum non arguat... Hinc est illa Platonis verissima ratio, qua scilicet probat Deum nullatenus mundum meliorem potuisse facere quam fecerit; sic quippe in *Timaeo* suo ait: 'Dicendum', inquit, 'cur conditor, fabricatorque geniturae omne hoc instituendum putaverit. Optimus erat. Ab optimo porro invidia longe relegata est, itaque consequenter sui similia cuncta, prout cuiusque natura capax beatitudinis esse potuerit». *l. c.* 1094A. This reasoning he supports with arguments from other 'authorities' and from reason. Later he retracted his opinions on this question in his *Fideĭ Confessio* (*P. L.*, 178, 107).

12 709D.

13 'Sed fortassis inquies quod sicut justum est aut bonum seu rationabile id quod modo facit, ita bonum esset atque aeque bonum si illud faceret et hoc dimitteret'. *Theol. Chr.* 1324B. The same passage occurs in the *Theologia Scholarium*, *l. c.*, 1095D, but as printed in Migne it is hopelessly corrupt.

14 'Quod si dixerim quae Deus, ut modo sunt, providet, aliter providere potuit, ut juxta illam providentiam aliud quam nunc velit et agat, libere potuerit; quod quidem secundum id quod tunc providentia sic haberet, bonum et rationabile esset; verum secundum id quod nunc est, malum et irrationabile est'. 709D.

verbal resemblance between the two passages. The phrase 'bonum et rationabile' in Pullen's passage has for its counterpart the 'bonum seu rationabile' of that of Abelard. This is but one of several indications in this chapter that Pullen was acquainted with the actual writings of Abelard.

Against his first reply to the objections of the Abelardians, Pullen raises a new difficulty. He urges that it is impossible to think of another possible order of providence in the divine mind. The reason is that the actual order has been present to the mind of God from all eternity, and it is impossible to think of another and contradictory order being simultaneously present [15].

This statement is not to be found in so many words in the writings of Abelard, but it is implicit in his theory. Master Roland Bandinelli states an argument of the Abelardians which closely resembles that formulated by Pullen [16].

To the objection he has raised Pullen replies that it is destructive of the very idea of divine justice and mercy, and that it inevitably leads to the conclusion that the will of God is not free [17]. This logically leads to the denial of the divine omnipotence, pursues Pullen, and removes from us all ground for gratitude to God who cannot act otherwise than He in fact does [18].

This type of objection had not escaped Abelard [19], and he had countered it in advance [20]. In particular, to the objection that

---

[15] 709D-710A.

[16] *Sententia,* ed. Gietl, p. 52.

[17] 'Si ergo dispositio Dei res aliter ac fiunt, nec prius ordinare, nec post ordinatas immutare valet, quomodo Sanctorum studium, et pro studio salus, impiorum perversitas et pro ea infernus rite deputatur, inde gratiae, hinc, divinae justitiae?... Nunquid aliud videam nisi necessitatis violentiam, cum nec unquam Petro negare, nec Judae conferre potuerit perseverantem gratiam?' 710A.

[18] 710B. *Theologia Scholarium.*

[19] In the *Theologia Scholarium,* lib. III, cap. v (*P. L.,* 178, 1096D) he formulates it as follows: 'Si enim hic damnandus omnino salvari non posset, nec ea facere per quae a Deo salvaretur; utique arguendus non esset, nec reus constituendus, quod ea non faceret quae facere non posset. Sed nec ea bene illi praeciperentur a Deo, per quae salvaretur, cum nullatenus facere posset'. Further on he writes: 'Hoc quippe, inquiunt, aestimare, multum derogat divinae excellentiae, ut videlicet id solummodo facere possit quod quandoque facit, et id solum dimittere quod dimittit'. *ibid.,* 1098. He also anticipates the objection that we owe no gratitude to God on his theory of providence: 'Alioquin nequaquam de eis quae facit grates ei referendae essent, cum ea quae dimittere non potest, necessitate magis quadam propriae naturae compulsus quam gratuita voluntate ad haec facienda inductus agat', *ibid.,* 1097B. Cf. also *Theol. Chr.,* lib. V, *P. L.,* 178, 1328-1329.

[20] Cols. 1099 ff.

gratitude is not due to a God whose power is restricted to that which He actually effects, he replies that the statement is frivolous. The beneficient activity of God, he maintains, though necessarily expressing itself in an unalterable order of providence, is not an activity which imposes itself on God against His will, but the spontaneous and willed outflowing of His goodness. Cnsequently, gratitude is due to Him no less than it would be to one who succoured us, moved by an irresistible instinct of kindness [21].

This reply was not unknown to Pullen, for he formulates the next objection against his own position in this sense. Gratitude is due to God, since, although He could not act otherwise, what He does, He does willingly [22]. This is, evidently, a concise summary of Abelard's reply. In answer to this assertion of Abelard's Pullen retorts that we cannot be grateful for what God effects, since this is inevitable; nor can the godness of the divine will be matter for special thankfulness, since that too cannot be otherwise. Gratitude is the due of him who, while conferring a benefit, retains the power of witholding it [23].

Pullen next proposes by way of objection that God, if He wished, could act otherwise than in fact He does; but that He could not allow such a will to have effect, since, if He did allow it, His providence in regard to a soul destined for perdition might become mutable, and, being convicted of error, God would cease to be God [24].

An argument similar to this is adduced by the author of the

---

21 'Quod autem novissime opponebatur, nullas scilicet grates Deo referendas esse pro eis quae facit, cum ea nequaquam dimittere possit, et quadam necessitate id potius agat quam voluntate omnino frivolum est ... Si autem ita aliquid necessario ageret, ut vellet nollet, id facere cogeretur, tunc ei profecto nullae hinc gratiae deberentur. Cum vero ejus tanta sit bonitas atque optima voluntas, ut ad id faciendum *non invitum eum*, sed spontaneum inclinent, tanto amplius ex propria natura diligendus est, atque hinc glorificandus, quanto haec bonitas ejus non per accidens, sed substantialiter inest. Tanto quippe hinc melior existit, quanto in ea firmius persistit. Nunquid enim alicui subvenienti nobis grates non haberemus, si tantae is pietatis esset, ut cum nos affligi violenter videret, a subveniendo abstinere non posset, ipsa eum scilicet pietate ad hoc compellente?', *l. c.*, 1101B-D.

22 710B.

23 710B-C.

24 'Dices forsan: Et Deus, si velit, aliter agat ac facit; sed, etiamsi velit, voluntati effectum habere non licuerit, alioquin ratio providentiae in anima ruitura vacillet, et Deus nota falsitatis turpatus, non amplius queat esse Deus'. 710C.

Sententie Parisienses [25] who was a defender of the Abelardian doctrine.

Pullen replies that the power of willing another order of providence does not mean that God will use that power. Only that which is to have actuality is willed by God. He then attacks the position of the Abelardians with vigour, maintaining that it leads either to a denial of original sin or to the imputation of responsibility for it to God [26]. Unaided human nature, he continues, can neither avoid sin nor practise virtue without the help of God. Now Adam sinned, and, according to the Abelardians, God could not have preserved him from sin, since in their opinion the divine power is limited to effecting actual reality [27].

This argument had also been foreseen, or at least answered, by Abelard [28]. The answer he suggested was quite unsatisfactory, and was founded on a sophistical distinction between the phrases ' Deum posse salvare ' and ' posse salvari a Deo '. The latter possibility expresses a mere passive potentiality of human nature which Abelard is willing to allow to every human being. The former, he held, only applies to the elect, since he interprets it as meaning that it is not repugnant that God should save a person [29]. He affects to see something monstrous in God being able to save the unworthy. His argument runs as follows [30]: every man can be saved, because grace can be given to all; but God cannot save all, because not all make a worthy use of grace. Later theologians, with their distinctions of the antecedent and consequent aspects of the divine will, and of sufficient and efficacious grace would have made short work of this typical piece of early twelfth-century dialectic. Pullen meets the Abelardians with their own favourite weapons of irony, simile, and the use of the 'reductio ab absurdum '. He summarises their answer as follows. While admitting that it is beyond the divine power to prevent the sinner from falling into sin, they say that God has bestowed grace which, if the sinner had used it, would have preserved him unscathed [31]. The words are not Abelard's but they represent accurately enough his thought as expounded in the *Theologia Scholarium* [32].

---

[25] ed. A. Landgraf, *op. cit.*, (*supra* 97, n. 11) 20.

[26] 711A-B.

[27] *Ibid.*, A.

[28] *Theol. Schol. l. c.*, 1096-1097.

[29] *Theol. Schol.* 1099D-1100A.

[30] This is a summary of his thought as expressed in 1099D-1109B.

[31] 'Sed fortasse dices: licet divinae non fuerit facultatis peccantem ne peccaret praemunire, attamen gratiam contulit qua usus persistere quiret illaesus '. 711B.

[32] *Loc. cit.* 1096D-1097B.

What a marvel, retorts Pullen ironically. So God is capable of beginning, but not of completing the work of salvation. We have here an infant, he continues, who, after being regenerated by baptism, will in adult years fall into sin and be lost, but who, nevertheless, having received grace, retains the power of living holily and, consequently, of reigning with God. Now here is the marvel: on their theory God is neither willing nor able to preserve this soul in innocence, lest his foreknowledge be proved false; at the same time the child retains the power of preserving its innocence and of attaining eternal life, whether God likes it or not: 'velit nolit Deus'[33].

Moreover, it follows from their premises that the redemption of the human race could not have been accomplished except by the Incarnation, and that God was unable to protect the Saviour from the fury of His assailants in the Passion, though Christ as man retained the power of escaping from it. Consequently, God could not have refused us our salvation, though Christ in His human nature retained the power of refusal. To the servant, then, not to the Lord, gratitude is due[34]. The redemption of the world was no more a free act of God in the Abelardian system than its creation[35].

Authority, adds Master Robert, refutes these absurd consequences; it testifies that God could have employed some other means of redemption than the shame of the Passion, even though no other way would have been so well suited to the frailty of human nature[36]. God could have freed captive mankind from the servitude of the devil by His word of command alone. He preferred to show an example of humility to those who glory in power, and manifest His love for those who would serve Him, and being made man to be a leader to His followers in the way, heartening them by precept and example. Though God preferred this way He had others at His disposal. The needed not the Apostles to protect Him against the fury of the Jews. God the Father could have provided Him,

---

33 711B-C.

34 When presented with a text from Scripture which attributed alternative possibilities of action to God a favourite trick of the Abelardians was to distinguish, where possible, between the human and the divine will in Christ. Cf. Master Roland, *Sent.*, *ed. cit.* p. 54: 'Sed auctoritatem istam sic interpretantur secundum quod homo, locutum fuisse, dicentes: et plura potuit facere, secundum quod homo, quam fecerit'. Pullen is here showing the weakness of this argument.

35 711D.

36 Cf. St. Augustine, *De Trin.*, Lib. XIII, cap. x, n. 13, *P.L.*, 42, 1024.

if He had asked for them, with twelve legions of angels. If God could have done this, once again it is evident that He is able to do that which in actual fact He never wills or effects [37].

Pullen admits that in this life it is difficult or even impossible to explain adequately *how* God can do an infinite number of things which in effect He does not do. Nevertheless, Scripture testifies to this power of God, he continues, and he cites St. Augustine, referring to him rather vaguely as ' magnus aliquis ', to the effect that in the next life we shall see how many things God can do which He does not will [38].

God, he adds, can only be deceived if His actions are other than those ordained by the order of His providence. He is not deceived if that different course of action has been prepared according to a different order of providence, an order which would have existed from all eternity. Granted the existence of the present order, God cannot act contrary to it, leaving it incomplete and unfulfilled, but He remains free to have chosen another order [39]. Many possibilities are open to God which, though good in theselves, He cannot morally effect now, because by an eternal and unalterable decree He has resolved that they shall not be given actuality [40].

He concludes with what he recognises to be two bold speculations. God, could, in virtue of His absolute power, give the grace of repentance even now to the devil, and bring him to salvation; in the one person of Christ the divinity could withdraw itself from the humanity, leaving the man Christ to fall into sin and be lost. This fantastic hypothesis he admits will never be verified, because the grace of the hypostatic union precludes all thought of sin in Christ. Nevertheless, he insists, this grace has not limited God's

---

[37] 712A-B. The objection urged by Pullen that God could have procured the redemption of the human race in some way different from the historical one is raised against himself by Abelard in the *Theologia Christiana* (*P. L.*, 178, 1527): ' Scriptum quoque est quod potuerit Deus alio modo quam fecerit humanum genus redimere '. He does not answer the difficulty nor does he raise the question in the later *Theologia Scholarium*.

The objection that the Father could have sent twelve legions of angels to Our Lord's aid is proposed by Abelard in the *Theol. Chr.*, *l. c.*, and again in the *Theol. Schol.* lib. III, 1097-98. His answer, which he gives in the latter work, is very artificial: ' ... non quod videlicet rogare poterat vel impetrare, sed quod impetraret, si rogaret ... Non itaque ex hoc Dominico dicto cogi possumus eum aliquid posse facere quod nunquam faciat '.

[38] 712B.

[39] 712C-713A.

[40] 713A-B.

power in regard to what is intrinsically possible [41]. The glory of the Son of Man is a gratuitous grace conferred by the Son of God. If it is a grace, it is possible for it to be withdrawn. The Prophet speaking in the person of the Messias, '*O my God, be not Thou silent to me: lest ... I become like unto them that go down into the pit*' (Ps. xxvii. 1), testifies that the possibility was not unknown to the Saviour, but Christ also knew that He would merit through His obedience that the union with the Godhead would never be severed [42].

The question of the divine omnipotence as it was argued by Pullen against Abelard was one of the most hotly debated of all theological questions in the first half of the twelfth century [43]. It

---

41 'Audacius dixerim et hodie Deum posse diabolo compunctionem infundere, et poenitenti veniam dare, satisfacientique salutem indulgere. Audacissime adjecerim, in una persona quae est Christus divinitatem humanitate posse se disjungere, et disjunctae gratiam suam retrahere, ut jam purus homo sine Deo ruat in vitium, de vitio in infernum, quod ne unquam fiat beneficium quidem contulit, sed beneficio potentiam suam non inclusit' (713CC).

42 'Omnia sciens homo Jesus nequaquam id peteret, si divinitati impossible foret; sed quia fieri potuit, ne fieret obediendo impetravit, nunquam timens lapsum fastigii sui sine dubio praenovit constantiam, quam se promeriturum sanctissimo militiae suae obsequio nullo modo dubitavit' (714A).

43 M. Chossat in the *D. T. C.* art. 'Dieu, — Sa Nature selon les Scholastiques', col. 1163, mentions the following opponents of Abelard on this question: William of Saint-Theodoric, *Disp. adv. Abel.*, *P. L.*, 180, 256 ff. (Actually this work hardly touches on the point in question, and then only indirectly; see col. 270D-271A); Saint Bernard *Ep. CXC*, c. V, sq., *P. L.*, 182, 1062. (There is nothing on Abelard's optimism in these chapters; they are concerned with his errors on the Redemption which are only remotely connected with our present question); the author of the *Disp. Alt. adv. Abael.*, *P. L.*, 180, 318 (who does treat this question); Rob. Pullen (the reference should be to chapter 15 as well as to Ch. 16); Hugh of St. Victor (the reference given to the *Erudit. Didascal.* is an error for the *Libellus de Pot. et Vol. Dei*).

S. M. Deutsch (*Peter Abaelard*, p. 227, n. 3) while admitting that Pullen in the passages examined above was attacking Abelard, maintained that the distinction between the positions of the two opponents was one of words rather than one of fact. In support of this assertion, which, it will be obvious, finds no support in the chapter just considered, he adduces a passage from the fourth book of the *Sentences* (cap. VI, *P. L.* 186, 811) in which Pullen is discussing the human will of Christ in relation to the Passion: 'Nonne enim utraque natura, majjor (i e. the divine nature of Christ ex se, minor (i. e. the human nature) ex majore, quidquid potest novit, non tamen quidquid novit potest? Nimirum novit mala, nec potest mala. Constat item quod quidquid agit, potest, non tamen quidquid potest, facit: nam pleraque in se considerata, bene fieri poterant, verum ad universitatem relata non fieri melius decet, quippe nonnulla quae facta enitescerent, infecta mavult Deus quoniam in ordine rerum aliud sedet: nimirum Deus, qui res ordinasse alias aliter poterat, hunc, qui fit, sua consultus ratione ordinem elegit, in quo sic magna

was not a dispute of mere academic interest, but one affecting a number of other grave questions such as the liberty of the divine will, and all the inter-related problems of the divine foreknowledge, predestination, providence and the existence of evil. As Chossat well remarks, the formula of Abelard was pregnant with possibilities of error [44]; possibilities which were only too fully realised in the teaching of Wiclef, to mention only one among later thinkers who adopted heterodox opinions on the subject of the divine power [45].

A refutation of the Abelardian errors on this question or of some persons holding similar opinions is to be found in the *Sentences* of William of Champeaux, which cannot have been composed later than 1121. As was usual in the polemic of the time, the names of the opponents envisaged are not mentioned [46]. Even

---

parvis, sic mala contemperavit bonis, ut universitas perspecta, undique delectet intuentem, ut in quamlibet modico mutata decoloret speciem'. On this Deutsch remarked: 'so scheint das ganz die Ansicht Abaelards zu sein, und der Unterschied nur darin zu bestehen, dass Robert die abstrakte Möglichkeit, Abaelard die konkrete Unmöglichkeit betont, was ein Unterschied mehr in den Worten als in der Sache ist'.

His position, is, therefore, that Abelard merely denied that in the concrete any other world order than the actual one is possible to God, and that Pullen admitted this, but asserted that God could, in the abstract, have instituted another order. He finds only a verbal difference in these two positions. The preceding discussion will have shown that this reconciliation suggested by Deutsch is untenable. It fails to take account of the distinction between the absolute power of God (*potentia absoluta*) and the power of God as exercised within a certain limited sphere of activity freely chosen by the divine wisdom and therefore unalterable (*potentia ordinata*). What the divine wisdom has freely chosen to have effect within this sphere cannot be otherwise, since God is immutable. In this sense the power of God is limited, i. e. the *potentia ordinata,* but God remains free to have chosen another order. Of this distinction Pullen, it is evident, was well aware. It was the central point in his dispute with the Abelardians, who denied, for the reasons already reviewed, the distinction as applied to the order of divine providence. So far from being a mere dispute about words it had most far-reaching consequences.

44 *Art. cit., l. c.*

45 Thomas of Walden, a contemporary of Wiclef gives the following passage from the *Trialogus* of Wiclef, lib. I, cap. XI: 'Quod omnipotentia Dei et ejus actualis creatio coaequantur; et inde est Deus omnipotens, quia omne possibile producit; quia nolo (inquit) vagari circa intelligibilitatem sive potentiam producendi res, quae non sunt, concedens quod nihil est producibile nisi quod est', Walden *Doctrinale Fidei,* lib. I, art. I, cap. x, (Venice, 1757) 71.

Another quotation from the same work reads: 'Concede quod Deus nihil potest producere, nisi pro mensura aliqua illud producat, quia aliter non solvitur clare ratio Augustini de Dei invidia' (Walden, *op. cit.* 72).

46 'Sic quidam argumentantur. Si providentiam Dei necesse est esse veram, tunc res impossibile est aliter evenire, quia ita omnia fiunt ex neces-

though William and Abelard had come into conflict over the question of universals we cannot be certain that it was Abelard's teaching in particular that was envisaged by William in his *Sentences*. There is no evidence that at the Council of Soissons in 1121 Abelard was accused of teaching that the divine power is limited to the existing order of providence. Both Abelard himself and Otto of Freising only mention the charge of Sabellianism [47], and no official acts of the council have survived to supplement their information. It was at the Council of Sens in 1141 that Abelard's opinions on the subject of the divine providence were condemned [48].

As for Pullen's refutation of the views of Abelard these conclusions seem well founded: it is an original and independent piece of work, and it is based on a first-hand acquaintance with the work of Abelard. Both of these conclusions are apparent after a comparison of Pullen's treatment of the question with the work of Hugh of St. Victor, Otho of Lucca, Master Roland Bandinelli, and the author of the *Ysagoge in Theologiam* [49]. None of these authors mentions the objection that on the Abelardian theory, gratitude is not due to God, nor do they seem to be aware of Abelard's answed. Pullen, as we have seen, knows both [50].

sitate, quia si possible est res aliter evenire, et providentiam Dei possibile est falli. Quod ita probatur: Si possibile est res aliter evenire, tunc potest non esse quod Deus providit. Si autem hoc est, tunc potest evenire contrarium divinae providentiae. Et si hoc est, tunc potest esse falsa divina providentia. Et si potest esse falsa divina providentia, tunc potest esse non vera. Quod si est, tunc non necesse est eam esse veram ... sic determinamus ... Si possibile est res aliter evenire, tunc potest non esse quod Deus providit — bene sequitur. Iterum si potest non esse quod Deus providit, tum potest evenire contrarium divinae providentiae — bene sequitur. Sed si potest evenire contrarium divinae providentiae, tum providentia Dei potest esse falsa — non sequitur, quia verum est antecedens, et falsum consequens', *Les Variations,* etc., ed. G. Lefèvre, p. 45. The error which William attacks was older than Abelard, though in his hands, as was to be expected, it gained a new lease of life. Already about the middle of the eleventh century, St. Peter Damian had maintained the possibility of alternative providences against the dialecticians; cf. *De Divina Omnipotentia, P. L.*, 145, 595 ff.

47 Abelard, *Hist. Calamitatum, P. L.*, 178, 140-150. Otto of Freising, *De Gestis Frederici Imp.*, Lib. I, cap. 47, *Mon. Germ. Hist.*, XX. Script. 377, ed. R. Wilmans.

48 Mansi, *Coll. Max. Conc.* Tom. XXI, 568; *Denz.*, 374: 'Quod ea solummodo possit Deus facere vel dimittere vel eo modo tantum vel eo tempore, quo facit et non alio'.

49 Hugh, *De Sacr., P. L.*, 176, 214-216; *Lib. de Pot. et Vol. Dei, ibid.*, 839-842. Otho, *Summa Sententiarum, ibid.*, 68-70; Roland, *Sent.*, ed. Gitl, pp. 49-50; *Ysagoge,* ed. Landgraf, *op. cit.*, (*supra*, p. 97 n. 11) 265-268.

50 It is one thing to use another writer's text to combat his views, and quite another to appropriate his work without acknowledgement and publish

If, as seems probable, the *Sentences* of Pullen represent the substance of his theological teaching at Paris, it would appear that his attack on the Abelardian theories dates from some time shortly after Abelard's death in the spring of 1142. It was some time in that year that, as John of Salisbury informs us [51], Robert succeeded Gilbert Porreta as lecturer in theology at Paris. By the beginning of 1145, when he appears as a Cardinal, Robert had ended his teaching activity. Even if his refutation of the heterodox opinions on the divine omnipotence was composed for the first time after Abelard's death, and after the question had been decided authoritatively by the Council of Sens, it was evidently more than a mere scholastic exercice. The controversy seems to have been prolonged between the orthodox theologians and the disciples of Abelard. There is good reason for dating the *Sentences* of Master Roland and the *Ysagoge in Theologiam* later thant the death of Abelard; and both of these works speak of the question as if it were still debated [52]. The same impression is gained from a study of Pullen's work.

God's providence

Pullen's treatment of this subject is closely related to that of the divine omnipotence. From what he has already proved concerning the latter he infers at once that God could have instituted an order of providence different from the existing one [53].

---

it as one's own. The consciences of medieval writers were not very tender in the matter of plagiarism; but it is an unfair charge to bring against Pullen in regard to his use of Abelard's work for the preceding discussion. Throughout, Pullen makes it clear that he is attacking the views of Abelard. He deserves credit for stating them with accuracy. Contemporary readers would be well aware of the object of his polemic even though in keeping with the convention of the time he does not make explicit mention of him. Hauréau's assertion that Pullen plagiarised Abelard, a charge which he grounded on the present chapter, merely proves the superficiality of his own reading of Pullen. See his *De la philosophie scholastique* (Paris, 1850) 329.

51 *Metalogicon*, Lib. II.

52 Roland, *Sent.*, ed. Gietl, p. 54: 'In hoc articulo quidam *a ratione ecclesie dissencientes dicunt*, Deum non posse plura facere quam faciat vel facturus est'. There seems to be an insinuation here that not all the Abelardians have accepted the decision of Sens — 'a ratione ecclesie dissencientes'.

Ysagoge, ed. A. Landgraf, *op. cit.* 265: 'De Potentia Dei. De hac re cum apud omnes constet, de illo, utrum scilicet plura possit Deus quam velit vel faciat, *controversia est*'.

53 714B.

God's providence he defines as the willed arrangement of what He foreknows: 'praenotionis voluntaria dispositio'. This is an advance on the definition in the *Sententiae Divinae Paginae* [54], and is more concise than the definition given by Hugh of St. Victor [55]. God's providence, continues Pullen, is an eternal reality. Even when that which was foreseen and arranged by God has come to pass, His knowledge and will remain unaltered, though they cease to be called foreknowledge and predisposition. All things are present to God, he asserts, not as actually existing, but as clearly known [56]. Things which occur at different times cannot be simultaneous even before God [57].

As Mathoud noticed, this teaching is irreconcilable with what St. Thomas was to teach more than a hundred years later [58]. According to Pullen, God possesses foresight of all events [59]. St Thomas, on the other hand, lays it down that the divine knowledge is not conditioned by time [60]. It is, therefore, inexact to say that God *foresees* events.

The Augustinian view which influenced Pullen is also proposed by Peter the Lombard [61]. It looks as though Pullen were aware of the view afterwards defended by St. Thomas that all events are present to God in their actuality, but failing to understand it, rejected it on the ground that it involved the simultaneous existence of all events in time. You cannot be standing and lying down, awake and asleep, healthy and ailing, alive and dead at the same time, he urges. A man is certain of all this. How then can God be deceived into thinking that all things exist simultaneously? With elaborate irony he breaks into apostrophe: 'And thou, Adam, long since excluded from Paradise and thy body reduced to dust,

---

54 'providentia Dei est praescientia Dei, sive de bono, sive de malo', *ed. cit.* 30.

55 'providentia est cura eorum quae exhibenda sunt subjectis, et quae commissis convenit impertiri' *De Sacr.* l. c. 213 B.

56 'non actu existendi, verum perspicacitate noscendi', 714D.

57 'nam quae diversis temporibus fiunt, simul esse nec apud Deum queunt'. 714D.

58 1022D.

59 'quid est praenotio, quid vero dispositio, nisi *praescientia* futuris suum rebus ordinem oassignans? Praescientia autem omnino est scientia'. 714C.

60 '... ejus cognitio mensuratur aeternitate, sicut etiam suum esse; aeternitas autem tota simul existens ambit totum tempus ... Unde omnia quae sunt in tempore, sunt Deo ab aeterno praesentia, non solum ea ratione qua habet rationes rerum apud se praesentes, ut quidam dicunt, sed quia ejus intuitus fertur ab aeterno supra omnia, prout sunt in sua praesentialitate'. *Summa Theol.*, I, XIV, 13.

61 I. D. XXXVI, cap. ix.

art happy in thy spirit in heaven. How comes it then that in God's sight thou art still mortal, still in Paradise partaking of forbidden fruit? How, I ask, art thou, though unaware of thy plight, even now in hell (i. e. Limbo) without sense of pain, even as aforetime thou wast in heaven and did not feel delight? '[62]. All things, he continues, are present to God, not as having existence but as no more hidden from God than things present: 'non ita ut existant, sed ut non magis quam presentia Deum lateant '[63]. God is said to have made the future, not in the sense that it is an existent reality, but in virtue of this foreknowledge: 'non quidem existente natura, verum praeeunte scientia '[64].

The events of the past and the present did not have actuality because they were the object of the divine knowledge; nor will that knowledge give actuality to events that are still in the future: '(scientia) quae quia existentiae necessitatem non infert praeteritis aut praesentibus, nec est illatura futuris '[65]. Here we see the same confusion as before — the notion that if all things are said to be present in their actuality to God it follows that they must be simultaneous in time.

At the root of Pullen's misconception is a false notion of the mode of the divine knowledge. He thinks of the divine knowledge as if it were a kind of superhuman knowledge, infinitely more perfect than human knowledge inasmuch as its object is every detail of the future as well as of the past and the present, all of which it takes in simultaneously, but resembling the knowledge of created intelligences inasmuch as it is a conceptual knowledge. Quite different is the Thomist teaching on the manner of God's knowledge[66].

Because he conceived the divine knowledge as conceptual after the manner of human knowledge, and was unaware that the medium of the divine knowledge is the divine essence, Pullen could go on to adduce these two analogies in favour of his position. The prophets, he urges, are aware of the future because of a divine revelation, but their knowledge has no effect on actuality: 'num talis notio ad esse cogit? '[67]. We, too, he continues, are acquainted by experience with the changing cycle of the year, are able to

---

[62] 715A.
[63] *Ibid.*
[64] *Ibid.*
[65] 715B.
[66] See *Summa Contra Gentiles* 1. 66.
[67] 715B.

foresee many events for the actual existence of which we are not in the slightest degree responsible [68].

Next he distinguishes a threefold object of the divine providence. Evildoing is foreseen but in no way furthered by God. It is permitted for the sake of the good which God will bring forth from it. Evildoers are made to serve the ends of God's positive providence on behalf of the just [69]. All good works have God for their principal author. Those of nature are entirely from God; those that require the rational activity of creatures are partly from God, partly from the creature responding to the stimulus of grace: ' Futura itaque (quae) Deus ita scit, aut sine eo fiant, qualis est culpa, aut cum eo fiant, qualia sunt rationis consilia, aut per ipsum fiant, qualia sunt naturae opera ' [70].

It is not without significance that the *Sententiae Anselmi* make the same distinctions as Pullen and in a similar context [71].

Now in regard to all its objects, Pullen observes, the divine providence is co-eternal with the divine being. For this reason, he admits that the concept of another possible order of providence is a difficult one, but maintains that it is also a valid one. The reasons that prove that God can do otherwise than in fact He does, prove conclusively, he urges, that there could have been another possible order of providence. To admit that the principle of contradiction has a universal and absolute validity does not in any way derogate from the divine omnipotence. God, he admits, cannot make the present moment or the past different from what it is or was [72]. Before the present has become the past any possible course is open to God to achieve the present. God cannot, he insists, make present that which does not belong to the present [73]. This, he insists, is not to limit the power of God but a proof of the supreme wisdom in His providential dispositions [74]. If con-

---

68 ' Sic et nos, anno jugiter redeunte, rerum innovatione edocti, pleraque praevidemus: praevidentes autem sponte futuris nullam subsistendi causam administramus '. *Ibid.*

69 715B.

70 *Ibid.* C.

71 ' Deus ergo previdit omnia, id est, mala que permissurus tantum fuit, et bona, que facturus fuit, vel per se solum, ut celum et terram, et cetera, vel rationalis creature arbitrario cooperante, ut virtutes '. ed. F. Bliemetzrieder, *op. cit.*, 90.

72 ' Nam quomodo id queat effici, ut idem eodem tempore sit et non sit, utpote me in instante hoc, regem et esse, et non esse '. 716D.

73 ' Deum nego hoc in praesento ad actum perducere, posse quidquam eorum quae ad idem praesens non pertinuerint '. 717A.

74 ' Dum hoc dico divinae potestati non derogo, verum ordinatissimam demonstro '. *Ibid.*

trary states could simultaneously exist, or if that which has happened could cease to have happened then there would be chaos instead of divine order [75].

Here Pullen ranges himself with St. Augustine and St. Jerome. The former had maintained against Faustus that whatever has had reality cannot not have had it. The fact of that reality is a truth which God, the Supreme Truth, cannot but recognise [76]. For the reasons set forth by Augustine Pullen upholds St. Jerome's assertion that, though God can forgive a sinner, He cannot alter the fact that the sinful act has taken place [77].

Against this dictum of St. Jerome, St. Peter Damian had protested in his *De Divina Omnipotentia* [78]. He admitted that the principle of contradiction held good of created natures left to themselves, but maintained that God is not bound by this impossibility. The reason for this assertion is to be found in his metaphysic, which places the ultimate origin of possibility in the divine will, rather than in the divine essence.

Pullen returns at the end to the point where he began. How can the divine will, he enquires, be a cause of what is co-eternal with it, of providence? That it is a cause is implied in the definition he has given [79]. In the same way he replies, as the soul is the cause of life in the body [80].

---

75 'confusioni simile foret quasi chaos rite videretur, si cum ordinatione sua quid esset vel non esset, contrarium statim inducere posset; nec igitur quod fit non fieri possit, nec quod est factum non esse factum'. 714A.

76 *Contra Faustum Manichaeum*, XXV, v. *P. L.* 42, 482.

77 *Ep.* (xxii) *ad Eustochium*, *C. S. E. L.* 54.

78 *P. L.* 145, 596-612.

79 'praenotionis voluntaria dispositio', 714C.

80 'Divinae providentiae divina voluntas quomodo, ut supra assertum est, causa est, si neutram neutra existendo antecedit? Sicut vita in corpore effectus est animae, non praeventus ab efficiente'. 718B.

CHAPTER VI

GOD AND THE PROBLEM OF EVIL

The nature of evil

At the root of Pullen's speculations on this subject are two principles which he, in common with other medieval writers, took over from patristic sources. Of these the first maintained the essentially negative character of evil, particularly of sin or moral evil; the second stressed that all positive reality was essentially good and had its origin in God. The first of these principles was clearly affirmed by St. Augustine [1]. The second principle finds expression in two sentences attributed to Augustine: 'Quidquid est, in quantum est, bonum est' [2] and 'Quidquid est in quantum est, a Deo est ut a summo bono' [3].

In order to obtain an idea of Pullen's thought on this subject it is necessary to go beyond the first book of his *Sentences* and to reduce to some kind of order the various disconnected references which he makes to the existence of physical and moral evil in the later books.

That his ideas on the nature of moral evil followed traditional lines is clear from a passage which we have already examined. In this he declares that injustice is a negation. Consequently, a person who is involved in sin, himself becomes, as it were, a negative entity [4]. He ceases to participate in the goodness that comes from God. At first sight it would seem probable that Pullen held

---

1 'omnia per ipsum facta sunt, et sine ipso factum est nihil ... ... Peccatum quidem non per ipsum factum est ... quia peccatum nihil est, et nihil fiunt homines cum peccant'. Tract. I *in Jo. Ev.* n. 13, *P. L.* 35, 1386. 'Quid est autem aliud, quod malum dicitur, nisi privatio boni, *Enchir.* II, *P. L.* 40, 236.

2 Cf. Aug. *De Div. Quest.* 83, q. 24 (*P. L.*, 40, 17): 'Omne autem quod est, in quantum est, bonum est'.

3 Cf. Aug. *De Div. Quaes.* De vera Religione cap. xviii, n. 35 (*P. L.* 34, 137). See A. Landgraf 'Die Abhängigkeit der Sünde von Gott nach der Lehre der Frühscholastik' *Scholastik,* X, 2-4 (1935), 162; id. *Dogmengeschichte der Frühscholastik* I, ii, 205.

4 '... ergo implicans se injustitiae juxta auctoritatem efficitur et ipse nihil'. 694D.

that the substantial nature of a rational being was corrupted by sin. It is certain that he was aware of the opposite view held by St. Augustine, but he seems to have found it difficult to reconcile that view with certain objections which presented themselves to his mind. In the sixth chapter of the second book he considers the text of St Paul, '*for every creature of God is good*'[5]. With this text he tries to conciliate that from the Psalms, '*The north and the sea thou hast created*'[6]. The difficulty arises from the allegorical interpretation given to the latter text by the Gloss, where we read 'Aquilonem, Diabolus. Mare tu creasti, Saeculum'[7]. He suggest that the devil is good in virtue of his creation, but evil because of his perverse will. However, he finds it difficult to accept that the devil can be really good and at the same time evil. Even if it be replied, he continues, that the substance of the devil remains good and only his will and action are evil, the difficulty remains. For his substance is not distinct from himself[8]. And yet it is absurd to suppose that the devil is wholly good, worthy of the divine love and the veneration of men. Were he good he would not be subject to punishment. To say that it is only what is evil in him that is punished, i. e. his will and action, is equally irrational. Anger is not directed against what is irrational, nor is punishment meted out to what is insensible[9]. It may be answered, he proceeds, that the whole nature is the subject of the divine chastisement, because of the evil elements that have accrued to it[10].

This answer he considers unsatisfying. If the evil elements remain extrinsic to the nature of the devil, they cannot defile it and render it evil in itself. If the devil is evil how can it be maintained that his nature or substance is good?[11]. The devil, he concludes, was originally good; as he now is, neither is his substance good, nor is he a creature of Good. He is his own work, and for this very reason is he the devil[12]. He is well aware that his con-

---

5 1 Tim. iv. 4.

6 Ps. lxxxviii. 13.

7 *P. L.*, 113, 993C.

8 'Illius autem substantia nihil aliud est quam ipse', 725B.

9 725C.

10 *Ibid.*

11 'Utique nunquam recte nocet mali vicinia, nisi cum sui lue inficit vicina. Si ergo diabolum, ut verius est, malum dicis, quomodo substantiam ejus aut naturam bonam asseris?' *Ibid.*

12 'Jam nec substantia ejus bona, nec Dei creatura. Sed proprium opus, ac per hoc diabolus. Quare? qui a Deo optime erat creando formatus, a se pessime est peccando foedatus'.

clusion is not in conformity with the thought of Augustine[13]. So we have, he observes, two contraries simultaneously existing in the same subject on the Augustinian view. He foresees difficulties in interpreting Scripture if the teaching of St. Augustine on this point is followed, but he does not pursue the matter further. 'Let us pass on', he remarks, 'taking this as assured, that if the opinion which this passage of Augustine seems to express must be preferred, then we shall have to distort every statement which is seen to be contrary to it, interpreting these, as it were, by main force'[14].

There was much discussion on the nature of moral evil in Pullen's day. Three theories were current, as the Lombard informs us[15]. Some held that only the internal consent of the will constituted a sin; others that both the act of the will and the external act were sinful; others again that neither the act of the will nor the external act was sinful, since all acts were good and came from God.

The first group referred to by the Lombard is undoubtedly that of Abelard and his followers. The second, includes the Lombard himself, as is evident from the concluding words of the same chapter. To this group Robert Pullen also belongs. The third group includes chiefly the followers of Gilbert Porreta, though the Lombard expresses their position very inadequately. They differed from the second chiefly by insisting that not merely was the faculty, i. e. the will, from God but also the faculty in action that was sinful, though the sinfulness came from man. They tended to speak of sin as a quality or accident. Hence Pullen may be referring to their views when, as already noticed, he cites and rejects the suggestion that the devil is punished in his whole nature because of accidental modifications that have defiled it.

Against Abelard, Pullen defended the opinion that not merely was the internal consent of the will to do evil sinful, but also the

---

[13] 725D.

[14] 726A. A French theologian, De Launoy, consulted by Mathoud on this chapter, wrote an interesting defence of Pullen on the point in question (*P. L.* 186, 1028-9). He pointed out that the opinion that the fall of the angels resulted in an intrisic corruption of their nature was no longer defended in the schools, but that the opposite view was not a matter of faith. He cites William of Auxerre to show that Pullen's view was not without support in the Middle Ages. He shows, too, that the identification of the created substance and its faculties as taught by Scotus Eriugena, and later by the Nominalists, was intimately connected with the opinion favoured by Pullen.

[15] *Sent.* II, D. XXXV, cap. ii. See A. Landgraf, *Dogmengeschichte der Frühscholastik,* I, ii, 240.

external act into which that consent issued [16]. Abelard's ideas on the nature of sin are to be found in his *Ethica* or *Scito Te Ipsum* [17]. It is hardly necessary to prove that Pullen did not consider an external act sinful if the internal act of the will was without blame. His contention was that a guilty will became more guilty if it issued in an unlawful act [18]. The internal sin consists in consent to what is known to be unlawful; culpable ignorance does not excuse a sinner [19]. The rule of morality is to be found in the precepts of God and the dictates of reason [20], and any offence against these norms is of greater or less gravity according to the circumstances [21].

The origin of evil

God cannot have been the cause of the evil in the world, says Pullen, for it is He who is the Author of all that is most desirable for soul and body. God, he says, gave men and angels the power of sinning when He created them with free wills. The power of sinning was but the complement of the power of meriting a reward. God desired that rational creatures should freely serve Him, and, in order to deter them from sin, He kept before them the threat of punishment. Those who are not deterred by the threat of punishment serve as deterrents to others. The power of sinning is a good quality in a rational nature; it is the will to sin that is a defect or vice in nature [22]. Once the will turns to evil the acts which flow from it become evil [23], but God, the Author of the will, has no part in the evil direction that it takes [24].

---

16 '... bina se nobis bona aut mala ingerunt. Prima radicantur in cogitatione, altera ut opera fiant pullulant ex radice. Merito unum et alterum appello, quoniam idem esse non potest, id quod latet in cogitatione, quodque apparet in actione'. 865A.

17 Cf. cap. iii, *P. L.* 178, 645C. See also *Problema Heloissae XXIV, ibid.*, 710D.

18 'Sed utrum culpabilius? Macula utique secunda; quippe cum prima sit plerumque cum altera (i. e. an external sin); nam cum prima (the internal sin) noxia sit ex se, secunda nihil nocet nisi ex altera; operatio enim quae secundo succedit loco, quantumcumque horrenda videatur, sine culpa est, si animus insons est'. 865B.

19 *Ibid.* Cf. 873A, 962B.

20 699B.

21 901D.

22 759D.

23 *Ibid.*

24 760A. Here again there seems to be a reference to the school of Gilbert Porreta.

The first sin of which human nature was guilty was that of our first parents. In Adam all his descendants sinned, because of their solidarity with him. The explanation of this solidarity which Pullen proposes was not one which was to find acceptance among later theologians. It was a too materialistic view, but in extenuation of his opinion it may be pleaded that the transmission of original sin, though accepted by all theologians of his day as a fact, had as yet received no satisfactory theological explanation. Here we are concerned with his opinions on original sin only in so far as they affect the problem of evil in its relation to the providence of God. From this point of view two observations must be made. First, that the sin of our first parents is the ultimate source of all the evil, both physical and moral, in human history. This Pullen teaches explicitly [25]. Secondly, Pullen asserts that, though God foresaw the disobedience of our first parents and the evils that were to come of it, He was entirely justified in imposing on them the duty of obedience [26].

After vindicating the justice of the divine precept given to Adam by a consideration of its intrinsic holiness, Pullen adds a further reason. Out of the suffering and misery that follow in the wake of sin, man learns humility; he realises that to withdraw from God is to tread the way of death; he grows in spiritual wisdom. With the help of divine grace the weakness that is the legacy of original sin becomes a positive advantage [27]. In addition to stimulating to progress in holiness physical evils have a corrective or sometimes a purely penal function. As such they are pleasing to God and permitted by Him for this purpose [28].

THE AGENTS OF THE DIVINE CHASTISEMENT

Whoever is the cause of moral harm to another cannot be regarded as the instrument of God [29]. On the other hand, just as a person is always the instrument of God in rendering assistance to another, in like manner can he be regarded as God's instrument if he is merely the occasion of physical harm [30]. This conclusion follows from Pullen's premises that all good has God for its origin,

25 760A.
26 751C.
27 751D-752A.
28 878B.
29 889D.
30 889D.

and that physical evil has always some good purpose, either penal or corrective, in the divine providence.

Consequently, we must distinguish between an action and the suffering which results from it, if we are to assign to God what is His in any particular case. The mere physical power of inflicting suffering is, as we have already seen, a purely natural power given to all by God [31]. The suffering which results from another's action is from God, in the sense that it is permitted by Him for a Just cause. For this reason the prophet Amos teaches, says Pullen that there is no evil in a city which the Lord hath not done [32]. By which words we are to understand, not sin but physical evil or suffering. Though the suffering be caused by an unjust action it is not in itself morally evil [33]. If the cause of the suffering be just, then God can be regarded as the Author of the cause of the suffering as well as of the suffering itself [34]. By this Pullen means that God approves of the cause as well as of the effect. The union of the human and the divine elements in the infliction of just punishment is comparable to that which is found in the performance of any supernatural good work [35].

The instruments which are used by God for the punishment or for the correction of men include good and evil spirits, other men, and even irrational or inanimate creatures. Both good and wicked instruments subserve the ends of divine justice. The city of Sodom was destroyed by good angels; the first-born of the Egyptians were slain by the wicked spirit known as the Destroyer [36]. It is the wicked spirits that carry the souls of the lost to hell, and the good angels who conduct the just to Paradise. The spirits of evil vex men in various ways: bodily and material harm, famine, plague, and shipwreck are not improbably their work, at any rate in many instances [37]. More especially have the demons liberty to afflict the wiched, save when God intervenes in His inscrutable mercy [38]. Nor are the just immune from their assaults. God permits them to assail men like Job for their trial and per-

---

[31] 759D-760A.

[32] Amos iii. 6, "*Shall there be evil in a city, which the Lord hath not done?*".

[33] 878A.

[34] 878B.

[35] 'Et sicut nunquam es sanctus nisi cum sancto Deo, non enim per te tu ipse benefacis, sed gratia Dei tecum, ut bonum tu edas opus, sed primo Deus: ita tu malum poenale putas inferre, sed infert Deus per te'.

[36] 878D-879A.

[37] 879B, 880B.

[38] 879C.

fection [39]. So we may speak of a mission of the evil spirits, or rather, of a twofold mission. They are sent forth by their leader the devil for the ruin of mankind; they are permitted to exercise their nefarious activity by God, and in this sense are also called His angels [40]. The wicked among men are afflicted by both good and evil spirits, but no case is known, says Pullen, of the good angels afflicting just men, except possibly to stimulate them to further advancement [41].

There is no reason for thinking, adds Pullen prudently, that all the disasters and sufferings that befall men must have angels or men for their authors. Disease and accidents have to be reckoned with, as well as other causes. God does not always require instruments when His purpose is to punish the impenitent, correct the erring or perfect the saints [42]. What is certain, he continues, is that to each human being there is given a guardian angel whose duty it is to protect his charge during life on earth and to help him in practising virtue. The limits to the angelic co-operation are that he must not interfere with the free will of his charge, nor ever forsake the path of righteousness on his behalf [43].

It is also credible, he observes, that various kingdoms have their respective angels. So the archangel Michael once presided over Israel, though now he watches over Christendom [44]. The thought of conflicts between men or states poses a pretty problem for our author. It is wicked, he says, to contend against one whose cause is just. And yet an angel has a duty to his charge. Must he then help him against the angel of the Lord on the opposite side? [45]. He can offer no definitive solution, but suggests than an angel can try to assist his own side or charge, and yet do no harm to the opposite one. It is his duty not to hurt a good man but to help his own protegé in every way that is lawful. Such is the affection of the angels for the souls entrusted to them that we read in the book of Daniel of a holy contention that arose among them, each one striving for his own, while as yet the will of God was unknown [46]. Some writers, he notes, maintain that wicked angels preside over wicked nations, and that they are responsible for wars

[39] 879D.
[40] 880A.
[41] 880D-881A.
[42] 880D-881A.
[43] 881A.
[44] *Ibid.*, C.
[45] *Ibid.*, D.
[46] 881D-882A.

that break out between nations. In favour of this opinion is the speech of the good angel to Daniel, in which he said 'And now I will return to fight against the prince of the Persians'. That the good angels should engage in battle with each other is untenable [47].

War as an aspect of the problem of evil seems to have exercised a special fascination over Master Robert. He gives much more attention to it than to the existence of disease or poverty. The reason for this interest may be that the frequent incidence of feudal warfare in his day brought this problem home to him with particular urgency; possibly too he saw in the vivid contrast between the sordid motives of the human agents and the divine motives which tolerated them, excellent matter for speculation. He held that wars may be waged for just reasons but it is in the problem of unjust wars that he is at the moment interested [48].

Both men and God may be said to be the authors of wars. Men make active preparations for war, but God never permits it to break out except when He wills it for some holy purpose [49]. So, in so far as God is the Author, war is just; in so far as it is the work of men, it is madness. As an example which illustrates his point he cites the destruction of Jerusalem by the Romans. God was pleased that his holy will to punish the Jews for their sins should be carried into effect by means of the wicked will of the Romans. Nevertheless, He in no way approved of the evil motives of the Romans, nor of the wicked methods they employed. It was the good result that was acceptable to Him [50]. When God thus makes use of evil men as his scourges He allows them to enjoy prosperity, and withholds his anger from them; but only for a time, and only in so far as to make them fit instruments of his wrath. When they have fulfilled that function they in their turn are broken and cast aside by God.

God and hereditary suffering

It is a fact of experience, observes Pullen, that both under the Old Law and the New, children have to suffer for the iniquities of their forebears. The spectacle of so much unmerited suf-

---

47 882A; Dan. x. 20.

48 'Scio conflictus certantium nonnunquam juste, sancteque ab hominibus fieri, verum eo mihi modo opus est qui prave subitur'. 876A.

49 876A.

50 877B-D.

fering fills us with distress until we take up the Scriptures and learn that the suffering of children is designed for their own advancement in merit. It is a punishment only for their parents, not for them. With elaborate rhetorical balance and play on words he affirms that it is fitting that criminal fathers should be convicted of sin in this way too, and that saintly children should be afflicted with pain for their advancement in patience [51]. It is commonly held, he continues, that the pains of the lost are aggravated by the spectacle of the suffering of those dear to them, which they are allowed to learn, returning to this world for this purpose [52]. Even if this opinion be groundless and the sufferings of the living are not known to the dead, it is likely that the living have to bear the iniquities of their parents as a warning to others who are still alive. Sometimes the sufferings of the children are intended for the spiritual profit of their parents. Thus it was with those of the children of Job; and those disasters redounded also to the spiritual good of themselves.

But whether good or evil fortune befall the children, it would be unreasonable, he objects, that they should be called to account for another's deserts. Scripture says that '*the soul that sinneth, the same shall die*' [53], and that God will repay each one according to his own merits. To this objection Pullen replies that these texts have reference te the final state of souls after death. If you consider this life, he continues, you will see that the good or evil that is in people affects others in quite different ways [54]. There is no ground for complaint against God on the score of unfair treatment. God is no respecter of persons: He looks to the good of the world as a whole. According as He sees fit, He dispenses either prosperity or adversity. If merely on account of the goodness of their

---

51 'Nam et dignum est *scelestos patres* sic quoque flagitiorum argui; et salubre est, *coelestes filios* in commodum patientiae flagris atteri'. 769B.

52 He introduces this idea in reference to Judas in his *De Contemptu Mundi*, Greg XXXI (1950) 217.

The question of inherited guilt and suffering arose in twelfth-century commentaries on Exod. xx, 5: '*I am the Lord thy God, visiting the iniquity of the Fathers upon the children, unto the third and fourth generation.* Various explanations were current. Pullen rejects any inheritance of the guilt of actual sins, but admits the inheritance of original sin, and of bodily sufferings. See 761f. and A. Landgraf, Die Vererbung der Sünden der Eltern auf die Kinder nach der Lehre des 12. Jahrhunderts, *Greg.* XXI (1940) 203-247.

769C; *De Contemp. Mundi, Greg.* XXXI (1950) 217. In the latter work the idea is applied to Judas.

53 *Ezech* xviii, 4.

54 770B.

parents He showered blessings on some children, and suffering on others, who are the offspring of bad parents, the charge of unfair discrimination might be sustained. As it is, however, the charge is a mere calumny, since in the disposal of His gifts it is not so much the merits of the parents that God has in mind as the profit of those who receive them. Only those who judge by worldly standards, envying the mighty and despising the lowly, could see in the divine distribution of gifts any ground for the charge of injustice [55].

Besides, it is a fact of experience that the moral worth of children does not necessarily correspond to that of their parents. Parents of like excellence have children who differ very considerably from each other; children of equal goodness come from fathers who differed very considerably in character from each other. There is no fixed rule according to which the goodness or happiness of children depends on the character of their parents [56].

Still, he concludes, even though there is no unfair discrimination, it remains true, on the whole, that the children of the good fare happily and those of the wicked have to suffer. God disposes all things in accordance with justice, and his impartiality is seen in this: He never distributes his favours in accordance with the corrupt standards of worldy nobility. This kind of nobility is mere foolishness, inverting right order; it is wont to venerate all things that savour of pride and detest those that are subject to lowliness [57].

The divine omnipotence and the existence of moral evil

In his discussion in the first book of the *Sentences* of questions affecting the divine will Pullen poses the problem of reconciling the existence of moral evil, which is admittedly displeasing to God with the divine omnipotence which, he objects, should be able to avert it. By way of answer, he suggests that we should make a distinction between a positive act of unwillingness, represented by the word 'nolle', and the purely negative state of not willing, signified by the phrase 'non velle'. Clearly, he says, God cannot be said to be positively unwilling that evil should exist in the world, since, if He were, his will would have achieved its object. Should we then be justified in saying that God wills the presence of moral

55 770C.
56 *Ibid.*
57 770D.

evil? [58]. Certain texts of Scripture appear to be in favour of this conclusion. Why do we pray not to be led into temptation if we do not fear that God may so lead us? So, too, the text *'O my God make them like a wheel; and as stubble before the wind'* seems to suggest that God can positively desire the existence of moral evil [59], since it is a prayer that God may harden the heart of the sinner and allow him to be overcome by the tempter. Such a prayer would not be uttered by a soldier of the Lord if he knew it were displeasing to his King [60].

If such interpretations of Scripture are sound, it means that God positively desires evil, and that, consequently, He is pleased by it. Moreover, evil-doers cannot but be pleasing to God, since they are but the instruments of his will. Are we to say that they are God's adversaries because, although fulfilling His will, their actual intention is to please themselves rather than Him? Clearly such self-seeking would be wicked; nevertheless, from what has already been said, it is evident that these evildoers are but the obedient instruments of God who would have them so. How then can God justly punish them? How, on the other hand, can He glorify them for obedience to his will, for in the sight of men they are manifestly scoundrels? [61].

Putting an end to this typical piece of dialectical quibbling, Pullen now offers his definitive solution. Both reason and authority testify to the existence of much evil in the world. This evil cannot possibly be pleasing to God, since in the words of Scripture, *'Thou art not a God that willest iniquity'* (Ps. v. 5), and between God and the sinner, as Holy Writ also testifies, there is no likeness (Ps. xlix. 21). Consequently, whenever we find in the Scriptures passages which seem to derogate from the moral perfection of God, we must interpret them in such a way as does not conflict with

---

58 698A.

59 Ps. lxxxii. 14. The Vulgate reads: 'Deus meus, pone illos ut rotam: et sicut stipulam ante faciem venti'; the Hebrew text means 'make them like the whirling dust; as stubble before the wind (Revised Version, Ps. lxxxiii. 13).

Pullen's interpretation, whether original or borrowed, shows the lengths to which allegorical exegesis was carried. 'Pone illum ut rotam' signifies that the sinner is symbolised by the rim of a wheel. The rise of the rim at the back of the wheel stands for his growth in worldy prosperity, which the just man puts behind him; the fall of the rim in the direction of movement typifies the decline of the sinner in heavenly things, to which the just man presses forward.

60 698B.

61 698C.

any other passage, and in a sense which is entirely worthy of Him [62]. So the text '*Lead us not into temptation*' cannot mean that God helps the sinner to do evil.

Consequently, we may roundly deny that God positively wills our sins, but we may not say that He is absolutely unwilling that we should sin [63]. The Saints, for example, are permitted to fall into sin that they may grow in humility, but God does not desire them to remain in sin. The words 'non nolit' describe this permissive will of God. No one would sin were God altogether unwilling — 'eo nolente'; no one can arise from sin unless He positively so wills — 'eo volente'. The explanation is, as Scripture teaches, that all good comes from God, the supreme Good, whose will is infallibly efficacious. Consequently, if a person falls into sin and is lost it is evident that God did not will him to rise from sin [64]. Can we say, then, he continues, that if God did not positively will the conversion of such a sinner, He was unwilling for him to be converted? Or can we go further and say that God willed positively that He should not be converted? 'Sed si peccatorem nolit converti, velit non converti?' To say either the one or the other would be monstrous, he replies. The responsibility lies with the free will of man who chooses either conversion or obduracy. According to his choice he is justly treated by God.

Since conversion is evidently a desirable thing, and yet all are not converted, it follows that God does not will positively all things to come to pass which are good. What He does will He brings into being, if it is as yet non-existent, or preserves in being if it is already existent. Likewise He is positively unwilling that only thos evils should not be, from which in his providence He would preserve His elect, or, from which in his mercy He would deliver them once they have happened [65].

These principles are now applied by Pullen to a special case, the Passion and Crucifixion of Christ. That the death of Jesus was pleasing to God is apparent, he says, since it was the means of the world's redemption and the way by which the Son manifested His obedience to the will of the Father. Now if the death of the Son was pleasing to the Father He must have willed that

---

[62] 698C-D.

[63] 'Itaque Dominum nostrum scelera nostra velle, omnino, nolle autem, non omnino negabimus'. *Ibid.*

[64] 699A.

[65] 699C; also 811D: 'Quando autem malis inter bona locus non est, ... miseratione provida fieri mala non sinuntur, ne bona propinquitate foeda obfuscentur'.

death to take place only at the hands of the Jews; otherwise that death to take place only at the hands of the Jews; otherwise the divine will was frustrated. It might be objected, he continues, that, although the Father willed the death of the Son, his will was indifferent as to the manner of that death. This objection cannot be maintained, he replies since it argues an improvidence that is out of keeping with the divine will. It remains, therefore, that God willed that his innocent Son should not only die, but that He should be slain, and that at the hands of the Jews. It would seem, therefore, that God must have willed that the Jews should kill Jesus. Unless God had willed it so, the Jews would have been unable to encompass his death. God, therefore, gives to the wicked the power of doing evil, and, unless He willed to give that power it would not be theirs. So, too, Scripture tells us that the Father delivered up the Son; therefore He must have willed Him to be delivered up to sinners.

The solution of this problem lies along the lines already familiar to us. The fact of being slain by persecutors is never sinful replies Master Robert; generally, on the contrary, it is a virtuous and meritorious act. On the other hand, to kill the saints is universally admitted to be gravely sinful. Consequently, though God wills that Christ be slain, He does not will that any person should slay Him [66]. In all that is good the will of God concurs; without the concurrence of that will no good can come. God is willing that man should have the power of doing evil. The possession of this power is not sinful, any more than the capacity for doing good is a virtue. Rather is the capacity for evil an advantage for him who does not avail himself of it. One who refrains from an action because he lacks the power to perform it deserves neither praise nor blame. So in regard to evil, he concludes, only the capacity for action is pleasing to God, for in itself this is good; the evil will and the sinful action displease Him [67].

Peter the Lombard who completed his *Sentences* about five years after Pullen's death discusses the question of God's attitude

---

66 700A. This distinction between the active and passive aspects of one and the same action was soon after Pullen's time formulated as one between the *opus operans* and the *opus operatum*. From the question of Christ's death it was transferred to that of the efficacy of the sacraments. See A. Landgraf, Die Einführung des Begriffspaares opus operans und opus operatum in die Theologie, *Div. Th. Fr.* XXIX (1951) 211-223.

67 700B. 'Sic ergo mali placeat, nempe potentia bona, ut et mali displiceat voluntas et effectus'.

to evil in the world in the forty-sixth distinction of the first book of the *Sentences*. He distinguishes two principal schools of thought [68]. The first school seems to be that of Hugh of St. Victor, The second school was clearly the one to which Pullen belonged, of which perhaps he was the leading thinker.

The difference between the formula used by Pullen and that of the adherents of the Victorine view lies in their different conceptions of the term ' evil '. Pullen tended to reserve the term to the evil in the will and the active execution of that will; the passive reception of that evil was not evil, but generally meritorious. It was only the passive reception of evil that was the object of the divine complacency in his view. Consequently, he could avoid saying that God in any way willed the existence of evil [69]. The first school, represented by Hugh of St. Victor and the author of the *Summa Sententiarum,* did not make the sharp distinction that we find in Pullen between the active and passive elements in one and the same action. These authors tended to regard any individual evil action as a whole, e. g. the Crucifixion, and to say that it was evil, and displeasing to God. Then they attended to the good results which flowed from it, and decided that its existence, though not its essence, was good, because of these results. As God is the author of all good, they concluded that its existence was pleasing to God, not as considered by itself, but in relation to its consequences [70]. Although the Lombard tends to favour the view of Hugh and the author of the *Summa Sententiarum* there is reason for thinking that he is indebted to Pullen in his discussion of the Divine Will and the Crucifixion [71].

It is to be noted that in separating himself from the school of thought which maintained that God approved of the existence of evil because of its good results, Pullen was abandoning the teaching of Anselm of Laon and William of Champeaux, two of the most famous masters of the early twelfth century [72]. It was, no

---

[68] ' Alii enim dicunt, quod Deus vult mala esse vel fieri; non tamen vult mala '. Cap. iii.

[69] Pullen's position is clearly summed up in lib. iv, cap. vi, 811C: ' Homo quia malus, operatur malum. Deus quia bonus, vertit in bonum; *nec curat qui omnipotens est impedire mala, quoniam de malis oriuntur bona. Mala indubitanter a Deo contemnuntur, verum quoniam bona pariunt, merito tolerantur* '.

[70] *l. c.* 66A-C.

[71] *Sent.* I. D. XLVIII, cap. ii.

[72] See G. Lefèvre: *De Anselmo Laudunensi Scholastico, cap. iv*; A. Mignon, *Les Origines de la Scholastique et Hugues de Saint-Victor,* ch. 6; Anselmi Laudunensis, *Enarr. in Matt.* (*P.L.*, 162, 1307B-C); in *Ep. ad Heb.*, *ibid.*, 1587C.

doubt, through the influence of the latter that this teaching had gained currency in the abbey of St. Victor, for it was he who founded there the school of theology. In the lifetime of both Anselm and William their doctrine on this point had been vigorously opposed by the Benedictine, Rupert of Deutz [73]. Rupert rejected as impious a distinction which, he said, he had heard was taught by Anselm and William, namely, that with regard to evil the Will of God could be considered not only permissive, but also approving [74]. So horrified by this report was the Abbot Rupert that he made a journey from Germany to France in order to refute Anselm and William in open debate [75].

Anselm considered the dispute merely one of words [76], and it is possible that to some extent he had been misrepresented. Nevertheless, the assertion that God is willing that evil should exist, taken in any sense which goes beyond mere toleration, was rejected by later theologians. It was the position defended by Rupert of Deutz and Robert Pullen which St. Thomas Aquinas also adopted more than a century later [77].

---

73 See Ruperti Abb. Tuitensis, *De Voluntate Dei* (*P. L.*, 170, 347, sqq.; *De Omnipotentia Dei*, ibid. 437C; *In Reg. St. Bened.*, ibid., 480-483.

74 *De Voluntate Dei*, cap. i, *l. c.*, 937C.

75 *In Reg. S. Bened.*, lib. I, p. 1, *P. L.*, 170, 482C.

76 Cf. Lefèvre, *op. cit.*, *l. c.*; *Anselmi Ep. ad Abb. S. Laurent Leodiensis*, P. L., 162, 1587A.

77 Cf. *Summa Theol.*, Pt. I, Q. 19, art. 9, 'ad primum ergo dicendum quod quidam dixerunt quod, licet Deus non velit mala, vult tamen mala esse vel fieri ... sed hoc non recte dicitur'.

CHAPTER VII

HUMAN REASON AND THE MYSTERY OF THE BLESSED TRINITY

THE EXISTENCE OF THE BLESSED TRINITY

Robert Pullen was more interested in solving theological problems by the aid of dialectic than in straightforward and systematic exposition of dogma. This characteristic is at once apparent in his treatment of the theology of the Blessed Trinity. His second chapter he had devoted to a proof of the unity of God. He had conceded, as we have already noticed, that in the last analysis, the authority of faith supplements the efforts of reason in establishing that there is but one God [1]. In the third chapter he begins by invoking one such 'authority': '*Hear, O Israel, the Lord our God is one Lord*' (Deut. vi. 4). Against this text he sets one which affirms the Trinity of Persons, the Johannine comma, the authenticity of which he takes for granted: '*And there are three who give testimony in heaven, the Father, the Word and the Holy Ghost*' (1 John v. 7).

REJECTION OF RATIONALIST EXPLANATIONS

He infers that the unity that is God is three: 'Ergo unum, id est Deus, est hi tres' [2], that each of the three is God, good and wise [3]. Then he raises the question, why are there not three gods who are good and wise? [4]. The first solution, says Pullen, is that of a dialectician. It is based on the extreme realist answer to the question of universals, according to which species are subsistent realities. In this solution it is affirmed that the species is the entire substance of the individuals that comprise it, and that the species

---

[1] 676C.
[2] 676C.
[3] *Ibid.*
[4] *Ibid.*

is found unchanged and in its entirety in each of these individuals. Consequently, the species is a single substance, and the individuals that comprise it a number of persons, and these many persons are identified with that single substance [5]. Pullen cites this solution only to reject it with scorn. Such an attempt only makes more unintelligible, he says, what is in itself obscure, but which is accepted on the authority of faith [6]. He offers no criticism of the philosophical fallacy underlying this solution, beyond the remark that the Blessed Trinity cannot be conceived as a whole compounded of three integral parts, Father, Son and Holy Ghost, since the divine essence is simple and each of the three Persons is God and equal to the others.

Whether Master Robert had in view any particular dialectician when he formulated this solution is doubtful. It is true that the philosophical presupposition on which it is based, that of exaggerated realism, represents the original doctrine of William of Champeaux; but William had abandoned this position after the damaging attacks made on him by Abelard, and he candidly admitted that he was unable to offer any solution to the problem of reconciling the unity and diversity of the three Persons [7].

It is quite possible that there is no reference to any particular dialectician, and that Pullen is merely elaborating a text of St. Augustine. In the *De Trinitate* Augustine explicity rejects the notion that the relation of the three divine Persons to the divine essence is parallel to that of individual men to the species man [8]. This passage of St. Augustine was known to the theologians contemporary with Robert Pullen: both Abelard [9] and Hugh of St. Victor [10] refer to it.

---

[5] 'Dicet dialecticus: « Species est tota substantia individuorum, totaque species, eademque in singulis reperitur individuis. Itaque species una est substantia; ejus vero individua, multae personae, et hae multae personae sunt illa una substantia » '. 676D-677A.

[6] 677A.

[7] 'Quid ergo vocemus tres illas personas, aut quomodo diversae sint inter se, nondum nobis est manifestum ... Cum autem Deo placuerit, revelabit fidelibus suis, quia haec est vita aeterna '. See Lefèvre, *Les Variations*, etc., p. 28.

[8] 'Si autem species est essentia, sicut species est homo, tres vero illae quas appellamus substantias sive personas, sic eamdem speciem communiter habent, quemadmodum Abraham, Isaac et Jacob speciem quae homo dicitur, communiter habent; non sicut homo subdividitur in Abraham, Isaac et Jacob, ita unus homo et in aliquos singulos homines subdividi potest: omnino enim non potest, quia unus homo jam singulus homo est ... Non itaque secundum genus et species ista dicimus ». Lib. VII, cap. vi. *P. L.*, 42, 944.

[9] *Theologia Scholarium*, II, *P. L.*, 178, 1057D.

[10] *De Sacr.*, *P. L.*, 176, 377D.

Pullen next proceeds to formulate and criticise another attempt at a rationalistic conciliation of the Trinity of Persons and the unity of essence. May it be said, he begins, that just as a genus, which in itself is one, becomes manifold by the assumption of differences, so in the same manner God, who is one substance, becomes several Persons by the assumption of the forms of paternity, filiation and procession from Father and Son? [11]. This explanation is rejected, but not without a careful and philosophical criticism. It is important to realise that it is not the existence of the divine relations that Pullen is rejecting, but the notion that they are forms or properties really distinct from the divine essence. This is evident, both from his own argument and from those of certain of his contemporaries who combated the same error.

The first observation that he has to offer is that if God is three in virtue of these three properties then He will become manifold, nay innumerable, in virtue of all his other attributes [12]. This criticism presupposes that the adversaries whom Pullen has in mind, made, or logically shoud have made, a real distinction between the divine attributes and the divine essence. From such a disposition the consequence drawn by Pullen would follow, since he, in common with all orthodox theologians, held that whatever was in God was God.

In answer to the criticism which he has offered, he proposes two answers, which, he says, the opponents might make. You will reply, he begins, that there are certain forms inhering in *genera* which do not constitute specific differences; so in the same way there are properties (i. e. the attributes, such as immensity, etc.) appertaining to the (divine) substance which do not constitute Persons. Secondly, these attributes of intelligence or immensity are identical with God; consequently, they do not make for diversity of Person. The others, such as paternity, filiation and procession are not identical with God; hence they can constitute Persons [13].

---

[11] 'Utrumne sicut genus, quod in se est unum, assumptis differentiis transit in multa, et est illa, ita Deus, qui est una substantia, paternitate, filiatione, ab utroque processione formatus, est plures, non dii, sed personae; quemadmodum genus est plura, non genera sed species?' 677B.

[12] 'Sed Deus, si ex illis tribus est tres; ex intelligentia immensitate pulchritudine omnipotentia, dulcedine et ceteris fit multo plures, fit, inquam, ex innumerabilibus innumerabiles'. 677B.

[13] 677B. 'Sed dices: Sunt nonnullae formae generum quae ea nequaquam ducunt ad esse specierum. Sunt quoque proprietates pertinentes ad substantiam, sed non efficiunt personam. Aut dices: Hae idem quod Deus sunt, ac

In reply to his opponent's distinction between properties which are not identified with the divine substance and which, consequently, produce multiplicity of Persons, and attributes, which because of their identity with the divine substance do not have this effect, Pullen asks what reason is there for making this distinction. Further, if the substance which is one God, and which, consequently, is itself one, is also three Persons, because these three properties are affixed to it — 'Quia tribus illis afficitur'[14], it would appear that it is the matter of the Persons; and the Persons would appear to be compacted of the divine substance and the properties affixed to it. Consequently, the divine substance would appear the greater, and the Persons less, because the former would be prior and the latter posterior. Hence the Father, who is God, will be less than God who is the matter, and than

---

per hoc diversitatem personae non faciunt; illae idem quod Deus non sunt, ac per hoc id possunt'. Hauréau completely misunderstood the meaning and bearing of this passage. He did not see that it represented an objection proposed against himself by Pullen. Taking it to represent Pullen's own thought, he needlessly altered the punctuation and even the sentence-structure in order to support his assertion that Pullen was a nominalist. Even if this assertion were otherwise well-founded, the present passage lends it no support. Hauréau writes: 'Sur la grave question des universaux Robert Pullus appartient à l'école nominaliste. Il proclame hardiment qu'il n'y a point de substances universelles' (This is true, cf. 677A; but the mere fact that Pullen rejects exaggerated realism does not make him a nominalist. The meaning of this remark of Pullen has been discussed already, see p. 66 n. 49). 'A ses yeux, il est propre à toute substance de faire partie d'une espèce, d'un genre mais on ne doit pas prétendre qu'il existent des espèces, des genres, des substances génériques, spécifiques, à la surface desquelles apparaissent les périssables individus'. In proof of this, Hauréau adduces the passage in question which he re-writes as follows: 'Sunt nonnullae formae generum, quae ea nequaquam ducunt ad esse; specierum sunt quoque proprietates pertinentes ad substantiam, sed non efficiunt personam'. This emendation is completely unwarranted and makes nonsense of this passage. Apart from the fact that it does not in the original represent Pullen's position, if read as Hauréau rewrites it, it has no value as an answer to Pullen's original criticism of the genus-species explanation of the Trinity. The point of Pullen's criticism is that forms in God on this theory multiply Persons; and Persons stand to the genus as distinct species; hence all God's attributes should be productive of Persons and of as many species. The opponent replies that in a genus not all forms, or attributes, are productive of species because they are not specific differences — 'nequaquam ducunt ad esse specierum' — there is nothing to do with the theory of exaggerated realism here. Moreover, the word 'substantia' in the next sentence claerly refers to the divine substance. This sentence is a kind of minor premise following on the general statement made in the preceding one. For Hauréau see his *Histoire de la philosophie scolastique,* 484.

[14] 677C.

paternity which is God too (in virtue of the principle 'Quidquid est in Deo Deus est'). The same would hold good of the Son and of the Holy Ghost. Moreover, if God and a form are conjoined to form a Person, it may be asked, who has conjoined them? Here Master Robert has in mind the axiom, in his day derived from St. Hilary, 'Quidquid autem compositum est, necesse est non fuerit aeternum'[15]. Surely too, he continues, whatever things are conjoined can be separated[16].

Again, he insists, if there are three Persons, and three forms of which they are composed, 'ex quibus conficiantur'[17] — it follows that these three forms are eternally existing, as are the Persons. Moreover, as in the theory in question, these forms are the principles by which the Persons are diversified, they cannot be identified with God, since the Persons themselves are God, and the same reality cannot be both a principle of identity and difference between the same things[18]. The consequence is that on this explanation of the Trinity we have three realities co-eternal with God, viz. the three relations of paternity, filiation and procession, and six coaeval with each other viz. the three Persons and the three realities by which they are constituted[19].

The thoroughness of this refutation and the care with which Pullen states and replies to the answers of the opposite side, make it antecedently probable to anyone familiar with his theological method that he has in view certain definite and contemporary errors. It is true that St. Augustine in that part of the *De Trinitate* with which Pullen seems to have been familiar says that certain persons explain the mystery of the Trinity in terms of the relationship of species to genus[20]. Both Abelard and Hugh of St. Victor, and presumably, therefore, Pullen were familiar with this text of Augustine[21]. Nevertheless, between the refutation which Augustine proposes and that which we find in Pullen there is no resemblance. The whole emphasis in Pullen's treatment of the

---

15 See Abelard, *Theol. Schol. P. L.*, 178, 1058B.

16 See Abelard, *l. c.*, 'Omne, inquit Plato, quod junctum est natura, dissolubile est'.

17 677C.

18 'Nonne cum hae, sicut et personae, aeternae sint, et ut diversae sint personae Deus non sint (idem enim se non posset diversificare, personae autem Deus unus sunt). *Ibid.*, C-D.

19 'nonne, inquam, tres Deo reperiuntur coaeternae, et sex sibi coaevae?' *Ibid.* D.

20 Lib. VII, cap. vi, *P. L.*, 42, 943: 'Nam si genus est essentia, species autem substantia, sive persona, ut nonnulli sentiunt'.

21 Cf. Abelard, *Theol. Schol. l. c.*; Hugh of St. Victor, *De Sacr., l. c.*

question is that the theory of his adversaries leads to a denial of the simplicity of the divine nature. The approach of St. Augustine follows different lines.

There can be little doubt that the teachers whom Pullen is attacking are those referred to by Abelard in the *Theologia Christiana* and the *Theologia Scholarium.* In the former work, which dates from about 1124, Abelard accuses six of his contemporaries of teaching error [22]; in the latter, of which the part in question was completed by 1125, the number is reduced to four [23]. The errors which are laid to the door of a certain Master described as engaged in teaching in Burgundy, include the affirmation that there are three properties in God, in virtue of which the three Persons are distinguished, and which are three essences distinct from the Persons themselves and from the divine nature itself [24]. The master in Burgundy has been identified by G. Robert [25] as Gilbert 'the Universal', a Breton and a famous glossator of the Bible, who in the year 1127 became Bishop of London. All the indications given by Abelard point to the correctness of this identification. Others besides Gilbert are, according to Abelard [26], guilty of these errors. Some of them, including a Master identified by Robert as Ulger or Alger, until 1125 a teacher at Angers, went further than Gilbert, affirming a real distinction between all the divine attributes and the divine essence [27]. With these latter, Pullen is not concerned in the present chapter, thought as we have noticed above, he seems to be refuting them in his sections which deal with the simplicity of the divine essence [28].

Abelard helps to enlighten us on the question why such a respected master as Gilbert taught that the divine relations were realities distinct from the divine essence. As no other evidence seems to be available we have to accept Abelard's assertion that the Master teaching in Burgundy, who is almost certainly Gilbert 'the Universal', really did hold the opinions attributed to him [29].

---

22 *Theol. Chr., P. L.,* 178, 1285-6.

23 *Theol. Schol. l. c.,* 1056-7.

24 *Ibid., l. c.,* 1056D. Cf. also *Theol. Chr. l. c.,* 1254D; 1285B.

25 See *Les écoles,* etc. 198-203.

26 *Theol. Schol.* 1057A-B; *Theol. Chr.,* 1254D; 1285B.

27 *Theol. Schol. l. c.*

28 See above 119f.

29 Robert (*Les écoles,* p. 202) attempts to prove that Gilbert held the opinion attributed to him by Abelard by arguing from a reference made to him during the Council of Rheims just before the hearing of the case against Gilbert Porreta. However, this argument appears indecisive: se J. Cottiaux: 'La conception de la théologie chez Abélard' in *R. H. E.* XXVII (1932), 258, n. 2.

The motive assigned to Gilbert and those who thought as he did, was the conviction that unless the relations or properties, as they were then generally called, were realities distinct from the divine essence, there was no way of distinguishing the three divine Persons [30].

By way of confutation of the errors of Gilbert and the rest, Abelard observes that their theory is useless to attain the purpose intended [31]; that it is contrary to the Augustinian doctrine of the simplicity of the divine essence [32]; that a composite reality is by nature posterior to the elements of which it is compounded, whereas the Trinity cannot be posterior to any other reality; and that whatever is compound in nature can be resolved into its elements [33].

Of these four reasons the last two are also used by Pullen, as we have already noticed. There is, however, no verbal resemblance to suggest that Pullen was dependent on Abelard.

Another writer who attacked the errors attributed by Abelard to the Burgundian Master was Walter of Mortagne. It has been argued that the treatise in which this attack is contained, the *Liber de Trinitate,* was composed about 1125, and that as Walter did not possess at that time Abelard's *Theologia Christiana* or *Theologia Scholarium* their attacks on the same errors are independent of each other [34]. In the eleventh chapter of the *De Trinitate* [35] Walter begins by enquiring whether there are any properties in God which are not identified with God, and maintains that there are no relations which are distinct from the divine essence. He proves his contention first by citing 'authorities' testifying to the simplicity of God, and then by various reasons. Among these reasons he places the incongruity of conceding that, in addition to the three Persons, there are three entities co-eternal with God but not identified with Him [36].

This is much the same kind of argument as that used by Pullen, which we have cited already. It is possible that Pullen used the work of Walter, but there can be no certainty. A notable

---

30 *Theol. Chr., l. c.,* 1254D-1255A.

31 *Ibid.*

32 1255C.

33 *Theol. Schol.* 1058A.

34 See M. Chossat, *La Somme des Sentences,* 86.

35 Ed. B. Pez, *Thesaur, Anecdot.,* Tom. II, p. II, 51-71.

36 *De Trinitate, l. c.,* 68C. 'Item, si tres relationes in Deo sunt, et sunt aliae res quam divina substantia, apparet ab aeterno non fuisse sanctam Trinitatem, quae Deus est, sed cum ea quandam aliam relationum Trinitatem, et ita manifestum est duas esse Trinitates in Deo sibi coaeternas, scilicet unam, quae Deus est, et aliam ab ipso diversam'.

difference between the arguments of the two writers is that Pullen does not make use of the term ' relatio ' but ' forma ' or ' proprietas '. Walter uses ' proprietates », and also ' forma ' in addition to the term ' relatio '. Both of them refer to the relations as ' res '.

Another point of difference between Master Robert and Master Walter of Mortagne is that it is only the former who uses the analogy of genus and species to describe the notion of the Trinity which they are attacking. It should be observed that Pullen does not say that this analogy was used by any of his contemporaries. It seems to be nothing more than a compendious way of expressing what was essential to their systems — a real distinction between the divine essence and the relations constituting the Persons. The same distinction was defended in the trinitarian theology of Gilbert Porreta who in 1148 was summoned before Pope Eugenius III at the Council of Rheims to answer a charge of teaching heresy [37].

Pullen and the Trinitarian Errors of Gilbert Porreta

Was Pullen thinking of the theories of Gilbert Porreta, as well as of those of Gilbert ' the Universal '? It will be worth while to set down reasons which suggest that he had Gilbert Porreta in mind.

(1) The genus-species form into which Pullen throws the theory he is attacking expresses in a summary way the theory of Gilbert Porreta, and indeed is suggested in at least one passage of the latter's works [38].

(2) In reply to his objection that on the theory in question every divine attribute would be productive of a divine Person, Pullen, as we have already seen, suggests that his opponents will distinguish two kinds of ' properties ' in God: personal ' properties ', which are not identified with the divine essence and which are

---

[37] On the Trinitarian teaching of Gilbert Porreta see Michael E. Williams: *The Teaching of Gilbert Porreta on the Trinity*, (Rome, 1951; A. Landgraf, *Untersuchungen zu den Eigenlehren Gilberts de la Porré, Z. k. Th.* LIV (1930).

[38] Discussing how objects may differ in various degrees Gilbert observes: ' Sunt etiam quae conveniunt non dico diversarum numero naturarum suarum imaginaria vel substantiali conformitate, sed unius simplicis atque individuae essentiae singularitate. Differunt autem personalibus proprietatibus, ut Deus Pater, et ejus Filius, et utrorumque Spiritus. Sed, sicut jam diximus, non sunt horum omnium aliqua a se invicem ita diversa, sicut ea quae omni genere totisque personalibus proprietatibus differunt '. Gilbert Porret. *Commentar. in Lib. Boethii de Duabus Naturis et Una Persona Christi, P. L.* 64, 1389B.

capable of leading to distinction of the Persons, and 'properties' appertaining to, or identified with, the divine essence, which do not have that effect. Now this distinction is precisely the distinction made by Gilbert Porreta and his school between the 'proprietates personae et personales' and the 'proprietates personae tantum et non personales'. The former are productive of distinction of persons, but not the latter. The distinction, which is applied both to human and divine persons, is followed both in the *Sententiae Divinitatis,* a work deriving from the school of Gilbert,s and in Gilbert's own writings [39].

---

[39] 'Praeterea sciendum est, quod proprietatum quaedam sunt personae tantum et non personales; quaedam sunt personae et personales. Personae et non personales sicuti humanitas et albedo, quae non faciunt aliquem differentiam a ceteris, quia quicumque est homo albus, humanitate et albedine est homo albus. Personae et personales, sicuti est socratitas vel platonitas, scilicet collectio omnium proprietatum compacta ex omnibus accidentibus partium tam substantialium quam accidentalium, forma videlicet dissimilitudinis, quae facit eum diversum ab omnibus aliis. Nunquam enim talis collectio ita integra et plena in ullo alio reperiri potest. Hoc dicitur persona. Dicitur enim per se sola'.

This distinction is then applied to the divine nature: 'Nunc vero de naturalibus ad theologica transeamus, similiter assignando, quod quaedam proprietas est personae et non personalis et quaedam personae et personalis. Personae et non personalis, sicuti divinitas quae omnium personarum communis est. Sicut enim divinitate Pater est Deus, ita singulae personae. Personalis proprietas est paternitas, filiatio, connexio utriusque. Nam paternitas facit Patrem differre a Filio, et sic de singulis ». *Sententiae Divinitatis,* ed. B. Geyer, Beiträge VII, ii (1909) 162-3.

The same distinction is evident if we take a typical passage from one of Gilbert's own works:

'Quoniam ergo illae proprietates non sunt substantiae (genitive), quod ex eo maxime certum est, quia non singulariter dicuntur de omnibus divisim et collectim suppositis, multo magis non pertinet ad substantiam, id est non est substantialis, Trinitas, videlicet unitates, quibus illae proprietates et illi quorum sunt numerantur, quae nec praedicantur simul omnes nec divisim de singulis. *Ut enim item itemque dicatur, illa est certissima regula qua dicitur, non esse substantiam, quidquid de tribus divisim et simul suppositis non praedicatur.* Quo fit ut neque Pater, neque Filius, neque Spiritus Sanctus, id est quaelibet istarum proprietatum a quibus haec sunt indita nomina, neque Trinitas, qua secundum eas Pater et Filius et Spiritus Sanctus sunt tres, de Deo, scilicet Patre, et Filio, et Spiritu Sancto, substantialiter praedicetur, sed potius (ut supra dictum est) ad aliquid ... *Deus vero, id est divinitas, quae hoc nomine intelligitur, et veritas et justitia et bonitas et omnipotentia et substantia et immutabilitas et virtus et sapientia et quidquid hujusmodi, id est diversum quidem nomine, idem vero re excogitari potest de divinitate, id est, de Patre, et de Filio, et de Spiritu Sancto substantialiter dicuntur*: cum una οὐσία dicuntur, vel divisim, vel simul Deus, verus, justus, bonus, omnipotens, subsistens, immutabilis, fortis, sapiens et hujusmodi aliis ab eadem nominibus

(3) Some of the objections raised against his opponents by Pullen are the same as those raised against Gilbert Porreta in 1148 at the Council of Rheims. Geoffrey of Auxerre, secretary of St. Bernard, states that Gilbert denied that the properties of the Persons (i. e. the relations) were identical with the Persons, and that in his system they were three realities or entities, distinct in number from each other and from the divine substance [40]. The same charge is mentioned by Otto of Freising [41].

(4) There is also a certain amount of external evidence which would seem to make it probable that Robert Pullen was acquainted with the opinions of Gilbert Porreta. Gilbert had composed his principal works on the Trinity by 1141 during the period of his teaching at Chartres, chiefly, it would appear, between 1126 and 1137. From Chartres Gilbert went for one year to Paris to lecture on theology. He was succeeded in the chair of theology by Robert Pullen in 1142. It is most unlikely that Gilbert's peculiar ideas on the divine nature should not have found expression in his teaching or that they could have remained unknown to his immediate successor. The whole character of Pullen's *Sentences* is evidence of his close acquaintance with the theological controversies of the day. If we put the extreme limits of the composition of his *Sentences* as 1138-1146, though 1142-1146 would seem to be a more probable period, we have a time at which opposition to Gilbert might well have begun to show itself, even though matters did not come to a head until 1148. Gilbert's unorthodox ideas were certainly known to Abelard as early as 1140, if we are to accept the authenticity of a remark attributed to him by Geoffrey of Auxerre. During his trial at Sens, Abelard warned Gilbert, who was one of the assessors of the Council, that his own condemnation could not be far distant, using for this purpose a line of Horace. Gilbert, we are told, was struck with fear by Abelard's words [42]. In the same passage

---

esse id quod sunt, praedicantur'. Gilbert Porret., *Commentar. in Librum (Boethii) De Praedicatione Trium Personarum.* P. L., 64, 1310 B-C.

40 '*Capitulum tertium*: quod tres personae tribus unitatibus sunt tria, et distinctae proprietatibus tribus, quae non haec sint, quod ipsae personae, sed sint tria aeterna differentia numero, tam a se invicem, quam a substantia divina' Gaufridus: *Libellus Contra Capitula Gilberti Porretani Pictav. Episcopi, P. L.*, 185,617.

41 'Quod proprietates non sunt ipsae personae' *Gesta Frederici Imp.*, Lib. I, cap. 50, *M. G. H.* SS. XX, p. 379.

42 'Fuit item Gillebertus, quem cognominavere Porretanum. ... Timebat enim quod apud Senonas Petrum ei dixisse ferunt: 'Tunc tua res agitur, paries cum proximus ardet'. Gaufridus, *Vita S. Bernardi, lib. III*, cap. v, *P. L.*, 185. 312 A. Cf. Horace, *Epist.* I, xviii, 84.

we are given to understand that the dissatisfaction with Gilbert's teaching had been developing for some time [43].

Another indication of the widespread currency of the ideas of Gilbert Porreta prior to his examination at Rheims in 1148 comes from the *Sententiae Divinitatis,* a work which, as we have already seen, betrays unmistakeably the influence of his ideas on the Trinity. Dr. B. Geyer has shown cogent reasons for dating this work prior to 1148, but not earlier than 1141 [44]. This work proves not only that Gilbert's ideas were current, but that they had already begun to provoke opposition. Before the work of G. Robert appeared it was accepted that Walter of Mortagne and Abelard were attacking Porretanism. The authority behind this earlier hypothesis was Deutsch [45]. When Robert showed that Gilbert 'the Universal' was almost certainly the Burgundian Master about whom we read in Abelard, Deutsch's opinion was either rejected entirely or modified so as to include both Gilberts. In the modified form it was accepted by M. Chossat [46] and, apparently, by L. Ott [47]. Considerations of time tended rather to favour this modified view. According to John of Salisbury, by the date of the Council of Rheims, 1148, Gilbert had already spent about sixty years in the study of letters [48]. At his death in 1154 he would have been about eighty years of age. Walter of Mortagne must have been a considerably younger man. He did not die until 1174. The exact year of his birth is uncertain, but it was during the last decade of the eleventh century. He began teaching at Laon about the year 1120 [49]. If Chossat is right in attributing the *Liber de Trinitate* of Walter to about the year 1125 — and his argument for this date seems sound enough — it is evident that at that time Gilbert Porreta would have

---

43 'Novissime tamen cum jam fidelium super hoc invalesceret scandalum, cresceret murmur, vocatus ad medium est,' Gaufridus, *op. cit., l. c.*

44 *Sent. Divin., ed. cit.,* 61-2.

45 *Peter Abaelard,* by S. M. Deutsch (Leipzig, 1883), 260-4.

46 *La Somme des Sentences,* pp. 84-6. Chossat was hesitant about including Gilbert Porreta among the adversaries in question, but had no doubt that the author of the *Summa Sententiarum* was aiming at him. It seems certain that the persons attacked in the *Summa Sententiarum* (Tract. I, cap. XI, *P. L.,* 176, 58D-59D) are the same as those against whom Walter of Mortagne wrote (*l. c.*).

47 See 'Untersuchungen zur theologischen Briefliteratur der Frühscholastik' in Beiträge, XXXIV (1937), 318.

48 *Hist. Pontif. ed. cit.,* p. 522, n. 10.

49 For these details of Walter's life I am indebted to L. Ott. 'Untersuchungen zur theologischen Briefliteratur der Frühscholastik' in *Beiträge,* XXXIV (1937), 126 ff.

reached an age at which his theological thought was likely to have attained its full maturity and be known to Walter.

One reason for thinking that the systems of the two Gilberts were not essentially different lies in the motives which impelled them to draw a real distinction between the divine essence and the divine Persons. We have already seen that, according to Abelard, the motive for Gilbert 'The Universal' was the necessity of distinguishing the three Persons from each other [50]. Compare with this statement the Lombard's words in which he is speaking of the School of Gilbert Porreta [51].

Summing up, therefore, it seems certain that on the question of the divine relations Gilbert Porreta and Gilbert 'the Universal' were at one in their principal affirmations, and in the motives which induced them to make those affirmations. External evidence makes it likely that by the time Abelard and Walter of Mortagne engaged in the dispute Gilbert Porreta had elaborated his views; but there is no certain proof that he was included among the false teachers assailed by Walter of Mortagne and Peter Abelard. On the other hand, chronological reasons and circumstances of place make it likely that Robert Pullen had in mind the opinions of Gilbert Porreta [52]. These reasons are considerably strengthened by his apparent acquaintance with one of the fundamental theses of the Porretarists — the distinction between 'proprietates personae et non personales' and 'proprietates personae et personales'.

The Trinity a Mystery

After asserting that the mystery of the Trinity is inexplicable, Pullen lays it down that the reason why we say that there are but three Persons in the Trinity and not more is that we believe this

[50] 'In hanc autem heresim ex hoc maxime sunt inducti quod nisi proprietates istas, per quas scilicet personae differunt diversas res ab ipsa substantia divina ponant, nullo modo assignare valent, in quo sit personarum diversitas, quarum eadem penitus est essentia' *Theol. Chr., l. c.,* 1254D-1255A.

[51] 'Sed iterum addunt: Si proprietates ipsae divinae essentiae sunt, cum essentia non differant tres personae, nec proprietatibus differunt. Quomodo enim differt Pater a Filio, eo quod divina essentia est, cum in essentia unum sint?' *Sent.* I. D. XXXIII, cap. i.

[52] To the reasons given above may be added the fact that Gilbert 'the Universal' died in 1133, whereas Gilbert Porreta was still living ten years later, about which time Pullen's work was completed.

truth on authority [53]. In this life, he asserts, we cannot know God as He is in Himself, but in the next life we shall enjoy an intellectual vision of Him. He explains that the vision of God which is promised to the clean of heart has express reference to the future life and not to the present. In this life God's presence is not manifest even to the heart of man [54].

It is, no doubt, as a result of this conviction that he is utterly silent about the existence of ' necessary reasons ' in virtue of which the human mind could arrive at a knowledge of the Trinity. On this point Hugh of St. Victor's position is heterodox in expression, if not in thought. He spoke of a clear demonstration of the Trinity by reason [55]. In this he was following St. Anselm for whom not merely the existence, but the properties of the Persons are manifested by reason. Such confusion is excusable in the earliest Scholastics. It is, however, remarkable that Pullen's thought should have been so sure as to preserve him following a path which was only abandoned finally in the age of the great masters of the next century. In his *Sentences* there is not even a reference to the analogical illustrations of the mystery of the Trinity which, in their various forms, derive from St. Augustine, and which were in favour among certain early scholastics, such as Walter of Mortagne and the author of the *Summa Sententiarum,* who, however, did not attribute any probative value to them. It is worthy of note that on this question too Robert Pullen abandoned the teaching of Anselm of Laon who in the *Sententiae Divinae Paginae* had declared that a knowledge of the Trinity appeared to be innate in human reason [56].

---

[53] 677D.

[54] 678A.

[55] *De Sacr., P. L.,* 176, 225.

[56] ' Cognitio etiam istius Trinitatis materialiter videtur insita humane rationi '. *Ed. cit.,* 7.

CHAPTER VIII

THE DIVINE PERSONS

The divine processions

The chapter in which Pullen treats of the processions, and especially that section of it which is devoted to the procession of the Holy Ghost, is the most difficult part of his theology of the divine nature. The difficulty arises partly from the undeveloped character of his terminology, partly from occasional obscurities of expression, and partly from an unsystematic arrangement of his material. During the course of his discussion he makes one of two equivocal statements, for example, that the Father and Son are two principles of the Holy Ghost. It will be most convenient, first to expose his ideas without any more comment than is required to elucidate his meaning, and then to consider whether, and to what extent, his statements are at variance with common teaching on this question.

He begins by the affirmation that in the Trinity there are two processions, that of the Son from the Father, and that of the Holy Ghost from Father and Son. The first he proves from Scripture in virtue of the text '*Ego enim a Patre processi*' (John viii. 42); of the procession of the Holy Ghost he gives no formal proof. The distinction between the two processions he finds in the fact that one is a procession from one Person only, the other from two Persons. The procession of the Son is His generation; that of the Holy Ghost, His distinction from the other two Persons. Pullen seems to be ignorant of the term 'spiration'.

Father and Son are both principles in the Trinity: the Son a principle of the Holy Ghost; the Father, of the Son as well as of the Holy Ghost. Substantial, not local, origin indicates dependence on a principle in the Trinity. Hence the Son is a principle from a principle, seeing that He is of the Father.

In the Trinity the three Persons are constituted in different ways. Two of the Persons are processive; two are each a principle; and, in each case, procession and principality arise in dif-

ferent ways. No two of the Persons are simultaneously but one in procession or principality, but two [1]. This is the first of several passages that cause difficulty in the chapter.

The term ‘ principle ’ does not necessarily imply that the principle has a son, but only the existence of one who proceeds from Him. The Father is a principle, but not just because He is God; otherwise the Holy Ghost would be a principle. Hence a Person is a principle in virtue of something that differentiates Him [2]. Pullen next observes that, in order for this differentiation to arise, the Father must be a principle in one way, the Son in another [3]. One difference is that the Father is a principle both of the Son and of the Holy Ghost; the Son, of the Holy Ghost only. Moreover, the Father is a principle of the Son by generation, ‘ ut a se nati ’, but of the Holy Ghost as of one who proceeds from Him, ‘ ut a se procedentis ’ [4].

But, he continues, it would appear that the Father and the Son are both the principle of the Holy Ghost in one and the same way, precisely as the Spirit proceeds equally from both [5]. The question arises, therefore, are the Father and the Son to be considered not as two principles of the Holy Ghost but one, just as they are one in divinity and omnipotence? [6]. Here, it is important to realise, Pullen is stating a difficulty against the conclusion he has already reached. Scripture draws no distinction between the two processions, scil. from the Father and from the Son. How then can it be maintained that the Spirit proceeds in different ways from the Father and the Son, or, conversely, that the Father and Son are two principles of the Holy Ghost? The rest of the chapter is devoted to proving that they are indeed two distinct principles, though Scripture does not say so explicitly.

First he examines what is to be said in favour of the conclusion that they are but one principle. If, he begins, the relation which exists between the Father and the Holy Ghost and that which exists between the Father and Son, taken together, and the Holy Ghost are not merely similar, but one and the same, then it may

---

1 ‘ Duo simul nequaquam sunt unus procedens, principiumve unum, verum duo, et procedentes et principia ’.

2 ‘ Quare quod principium est, ex aliqua distinctione persona est ’. 685A.

3 ‘ ut autem distinctio fiat (siquidem ex ea communio nulla est) aliter Pater aliter Filius principium est ’. 685A.

4 *Ibid.*

5 ‘ Pater autem et Filius uno eodemque modo, uterque Spiritus Sancti principium esse *videtur*, quemadmodum Spiritus ipse indifferenter ab utroque procedere videtur ’. 685A.

6 *Ibid.*, B.

perhaps be said that Father and Son are one principle of the Holy Ghost [7]. Hence, he argues, it could be said that, just as there are certain attributes common to all three Persons (' sicut sunt quaedam communia tribus ') [8] so there are others common to two (' ita quoque alia sunt vere communia duobus ') [9]. Some of these attributes common to two Persons would be in each of them in a different way, as, for example, that of procession in the Son and the Holy Ghost; or that of principle used indeterminately of the Father and the Son. The other attributes common to two Persons would be in each of them in one and the same way, as, for example, that of principle in the Father and the Son with reference to the Holy Ghost. Thus these two Persons would be one principle, just as the three Persons are one in divinity and omnipotence [10]. If this is so, then we should have to say, he adds, that, since procession is an attribute predicated of the Son and the Holy Ghost, they are also one in procession. This he concludes, is inadmissible [11]. He bases his rejection of the conclusion arrived at on the ground that the Persons are one in all that they have in virtue of their common divine nature, but not one in what is theirs as a consequence of their personal distinctions. As we have already seen, his position is that a divine Person is a principle, not in virtue of the divine nature as such, but in consequence of a personal distinction [12].

Another reason for holding that the Father and the Son are two separate principles he finds in the following consideration. Although the triune Godhead possesses many different attributes, yet, since each of these is identified with the divine substance, the Godhead is one nature. Conversely, though it be admitted that two Persons have one and the same personal property, yet, since

---

7 ' Relatio autem, tametsi similis, non una fortasse est ea quae inter Patrem et Spiritum, et illa quae inter Patrem ac Filium, et eundem Spiritum Sanctum; aut si est, non jam fortasse duo, Pater et Filius Spiritus Sancti principia sunt, sed unum '. 685B.

8 685B.

9 *Ibid.*

10 ' ... quorum pars differenter inest, ut processio Filio atque Spiritui Sancto; aut principium quoquo modo habitum, Filio atque Patri. Pars autem (modo tribus communium), uno et indifferenti modo habetur, ut principium in Patre et Filio respectu Spiritus Sancti; atque ideo, sicut tres sunt unus Deus, et unus omnipotens, ita duo sunt unum principium '. *Ibid.*, B-C.

11 ' Et item duo procedens unus est; quod non adeo credibile videtur '. 685B-C.

12 ' Convenit enim ut personae sint unum in omni eo quod ex natura divinitatis suscipiunt, et non sint unum in eo quod ex natura distinctionis assumunt '. 685B-C.

it belongs to them precisely as distinct Persons, in regard of it they are two, not one. The Father and the Son are thus two principles, and the Son and the Holy Ghost two who proceed [13].

Further he continues, if we admit for the sake of argument that the Father and Son are a principle in one way only, and allow that they are different Persons, we may still maintain that they are two principles [14].

If, however, as seems more probable, the Father is a principle in a different way from the Son, there is all the more reason for distinguishing them as two principles [15].

It is not surprising that Pullen's seventeenth-century editor, Dom Hugo Mathoud, O. S. B. felt considerable misgivings over some of the opinions expressed in this chapter. After long hesitating over the interpretation of these statements he consulted a well-known Sorbonne professor of theology, Jacques de Sainte-Beuve [16], whose explanations convinced him of Pullen's orthodoxy.

With regard to the first difficulty, viz. that the Father and the Son are said to be two principles of the Holy Ghost, Sainte-Beuve indicates the ambiguity of the word 'principle'. If the term is used adjectively, he says, there is no more objection to be raised against the phrase 'duo principia' than against 'duo spirantes', which was taken up by the later Scholastics. That Pullen uses the term adjectivally is evident from his assertion that the Father and Son are a principle of the Holy Ghost in one and the same way, and that the Holy Ghost proceeds equally from both of them [17]. From this passage, says St. Beuve, it is clear that Pullen conceived the property of spiration as the same in Father and Son, and that in consequence they produced the Holy Spirit in one and

---

[13] 'quod si sancta Trinitas, tametsi quamplurima suae habeat insignia substantiae, nihilominus tamen in omnibus illis quia una est substantia, una quoque est natura, cur non duae personae, licet illis una concedatur personalis convenire proprietas, attamen quia ad distinctionem pertinet, potius in ea sunt duae quam una, ut Pater et Filius non unum principium sint sed duo, itemque Filius et Spiritus Sanctus procedentes duo sint, non unus?' 685D.

[14] 'Sic quoque Pater atque Filius, si uterque uno solum modo principium esse concedatur, in persona tamen a se differre nullatenus negentur, duoque principia sic quoque esse posse dicantur'. 686C.

[15] 'Sin autem Pater et aliter quam Filius, quod verius putatur, in natura principii se habet, quanto magis aliud hic, aliud ille, si ita est ut videtur, principium esse debet'. *Ibid.*

[16] Born 1613, died 1677. He was the author of treatises on Confirmation and Extreme Unction and was one of the most famous theologians of his day.

[17] 'Pater et Filius uno eodemque modo uterque Spiritus Sancti principium esse videtur, quemadmodum Spiritus ipse indifferenter ab utroque procedere videtur'. 685A.

the same way. Further, Pullen's insistence on two principles is due to his perception that two persons ('duo supposita') are necessarily required for the production of the Holy Ghost who proceeds as love, and as the link of Father and Son 'nexus amborum'). For the same reason later theologians maintained that Father and Son were two Spirators ('duo spiratores'). This was taught by St. Thomas in his *Commentary on the Sentences.* In this view others concurred, such as Gabriel Biel and Ockham, who say that we may speak of one or more principles of the Holy Ghost, though under different respects. So, too, Durandus (in I *Sent.* D. XXIX, Q. 11): 'Si nomen principii accipiatur pro eo quod agit, sic Pater est unum principium; Pater autem et Filius sunt duo principia'[18]. For these reasons, continues Sainte-Beuve, certain theologians, writing after the Councils of Lyons and Florence[19], observe that the Fathers of the Councils did not say that the Holy Ghost proceeds from one principle, but 'as it were' from one principle ('tanquam ab uno'). It is evident, therefore, that the Fathers assembled in these two Councils did not deny that there were two principles, but only that there was a twofold spirative activity[20].

It may be asked, adds Sainte-Beuve, why Pullen alone among theologians of his day defended the existence of two principles. It should be noted, he replies, that he wrote many years before the definitions of Lyons and Florence settled the question. Had he written at a later date there is no doubt that this most loyal of theologians would have submitted to the conciliar decisions with better grace than was manifested by a number of later theologians.

The most interesting explanation which Sainte-Beuve suggests, is that Pullen's anomalous handling of the question is the result of his intention to defend the Latin view of the divine processions

---

18 St. Thomas admitted that one could speak of two 'spirators' in *I Sent.* D. II, q. 1, a. 4. He retracted this statement in the *Summa Theol.,* I, q. 36, a. 4 ad 7, where he maintains that there is but one spirator, although Father and Son are 'duo spirantes'.

19 The second Council of Lyons, 1274, defined that the Holy Ghost proceeds from the Father and the Son 'non tanquam ex duobus principiis, sed tanquam ex uno principio, non duabus spirationibus sed unica spiratione', Denz. 460. The same doctrine was re-affirmed by the Council of Florence (1438-1445); cf. Denz. 691, 704.

20 This interpretation of the word 'tanquam' as used in the definition of the Council of Lyons is of very doubtful validity. J. Slipj points out in his *De Principio Spirationis,* that the Council used this term in the same way as the word 'quasi' (ὡς) is used in the phrase 'quasi unigeniti a Patre' in John i. 14. The argument used here by Sainte-Beuve is precisely that used by Gregory of Rimini (died 1358) to establish his view which, though not heretical, is undoubtedly unsound.

against the Greek schismatics who denied that the Holy Ghost proceeded from the Son as well as from the Father. Pullen, he argues, considered that the procession of the Holy Ghost from the Son could be more effectively defended by attaching the notion of principle, not to the common divine essence, but to the fact of personal distinctions in the Godhead. The fact that the Holy Ghost preceeds as notional love of Father and Son would imply a relationship to the Father and the Son which would demand the activity of both Persons for His production. At the same time, he says, Pullen safeguards the unity of the formal principle of spiration in the manner already indicated.

It may well be that it was zeal for the Latin doctrine that inspired Pullen to show that we can speak of two principles, although he makes no mention of the Greek teaching. But there can be little doubt that Sainte-Beuve's assertion that Pullen in speaking of two principles was using the term in its adjectival sense, as equivalent to 'duo spirantes' will not bear examination. In order to support his contention, Sainte-Beuve relies on Pullen's remark that the Father and the Son are a principle of the Holy Ghost in one and the same way, and the Holy Ghost proceeds equally from both of them [21].

Sainte-Beuve does not seem to realise that here Pullen is not stating his own position, but merely proposing a difficulty to himself. Once this is realised, his elaborate defence of Pullen's argument falls to the ground. The fundamental position of Pullen is to be seen in his assertion that principality arises from, and is differentiated by, personal distinctions in the Godhead [22]. He, therefore, necessarily concuded that the Father and the Son could not be a principle of the Holy Ghost in one and the same way. It is, consequently, impossible to explain his use of the phrase 'duo principia' as if it merely meant 'duo principiantes' or 'duo spirantes'.

A second difficulty mentioned by Mathoud, viz. that the Father and the Son are a principle of the Holy Ghost in virtue of their personal distinction is rightly described by Sainte-Beuve as crucial.

---

[21] 'Pater et Filius uno eodemque modo uterque Spiritus Sancti principium esse videtur, quemadmodum Spiritus ipse indifferenter ab utroque procedere videtur'. 685A.

[22] 'Constat autem quod Patri minime convenit principium, ideo quod Deus est, quia Spiritus Sanctus quoque ipse est Deus, principiumque non est. Quare quod principium est, ex aliqua distinctione persona est; ut autem distinctio fiat (siquidem ex ea communio nulla est) aliter Pater, aliter Filius principium est'. 684D-685A.

To clear the ground for a solution he invokes the principle that ambiguous and obscure passages in an author must be interpreted in the light of other passages on the same subject in which the author's meaning is clear. Now Pullen has plainly stated, he says, that Father and Son produce the Holy Ghost in one and the same way (' uno et indifferenti modo ') [23]. This assumption of Sainte-Beuve cannot be granted, for reasons already stated.

Considering the chapter as a whole, one is impressed by the subtlety of Pullen's speculation, but also at times bewildered by his abrupt transitions. As far as I am aware, no other theologian of repute before the fourteenth century dared to speak of two principles of the Holy Ghost. Pullen's respect for orthodox doctrine was such as to justify Sainte-Beuve's assertion that, had he been writing after the Council of Lyons, Pullen would have abandoned his anomalous position. One must recognise that in Pullen's day theological discussion of the divine processions did not reach a high level.

As there was no authoritative decision before the Council of Lyons condemning the teaching that Father and Son were two principles, Pullen, no doubt, felt free to speculate. There is apparently nothing like his speculation on this question in the fragments that survive of works immediately associated with the School of Laon, nor, as far as I am aware, in any theologian before Peter of Poitiers. This writer, who died about sixty years after Pullen, has a long chapter in his *Sentences* in which he discusses the meaning of the term ' principle ». In the course of the discussion he enquires whether the Father and the Son are to be considered as one Author of the Holy Ghost or as two. He admits that Father and Son may be said to be two authors of the Holy Ghost provided the plurality refers merely to the Persons; but he prefers the expression ' one author ', and expressly refuses to concede that one may speak of two principles as this is contrary to ' authority ' [24].

THE DISTINCTION OF THE PERSONS

The three Persons of the Blessed Trinity are distinguished from each other by their several personal properties. These properties are identified with the Persons they distinguish. Though the Per-

---

23 685A.

24 *Sentences* I, XXX, ed. P. S. Moore and M. Dulong (Notre Dame, Indiana, 1943).

sons are distinct they are in no wise separated from each other [25].

The Son, he continues, describing the circuminsession of the Trinity, is in the Father and the Father in the Son, and the Holy Ghost in both and both in Him. Only three distinguishing properties are to be admitted in the Trinity. Other terms applied to the Persons, and there are a number of them, merely express their personality in an indeterminate manner. Among these general terms he instances the word 'person' itself [26]. The term Father, Son, and Holy Ghost denote their respective properties. These properties which distinguish the Persons, he formulates in the following concrete fashion: The Unbegotten Father begot the Son; the Only-Begotten Son was born of the Father; the Holy Ghost proceeds from both Father and Son. Both here and elsewhere Pullen studiously avoids using the abstract terms paternity, filiation, and procession. It is not that he is ignorant of abstract terminology as applied to the divine Persons, as has been suggested [27]; he has already employed these terms in formulating the heterodox opinion which he criticised in a previous chapter [28]. It is incredible that a famous Parisian Master of the fifth decade of the twelfth century, should have been unaware that abstract terms were in use among others in their description of the divine Persons.

The explanation of his avoidance of the abstract terminology is surely to be found in his feeling that it savoured of Porretanism and tended to suggest that the properties of the Persons were accidental forms. His repugnance was, no doubt, excessive and led him into a certain awkwardness of expression at times, but it is intelligible once we remember the fierce controversies that raged in his day over concrete and abstract terminology as applied to God.

The properties which distinguish the Persons, says Pullen, are not included in the categories of accidental being [29]. In this as-

---

[25] 'Proprietates quoque quibus personarum admiramur distinctionem, quid commode dicemus, nisi personas naturaliter ab invicem distinctas, distinctas utique ut a se alias, non tamen separatas', 682B.

[26] 'Eaedem autem tres (personae), tametsi plurimis distinguantur modis, non tamen amplius quam tres conficiuntur proprietates. Quotquot enim sunt, tres tantum personae distinguere intendunt. Proprietates autem personarum vocabula quaedam designant discrete, alia confuse: Discrete singulas, confuse autem binas vel ternas'. 682D-683A.

[27] 'Einen abstrakten Namen kennt Robertus für die drei Proprietäten nicht', M. Schmaus. 'Der Liber Propugnatorius des Thomas Anglicus. II Teil: Die Trinitarischen Lehrdifferenzen', in *Beiträge,* XXIX, I (1930) 386.

[28] See 677B.

[29] 'Hae sunt proprietates, quas praedicamenta nesciunt'. 697D.

sertion he is in agreement with Master Roland Bandinelli, who thought that the opponents whom he in common with Pullen was attacking, viz. the school of Gilbert Porreta and those who held similar opinions, conceived the properties distinguishing the Persons as accidental modifications of the divine essence [30].

Moreover, continues Pullen, these properties exceed our comprehension [31]. Human generation affords no assistance in understanding the divine and eternal generation of the Son. Human reason cannot comprehend the eternity and equality of Father and Son in one Godhead [32].

This agnosticism in regard to the constitution of the divine persons was typical of theological works deriving from the school of Laon [33].

Our knowledge of Pullen's conception of the properties in virtue of which the three divine Persons are distinguished has been increased by a fragment from an Oxford manuscript published by Dr. A. Landgraf: 'Dicitur autem magister R(obertus) Polanus prohibuisse in cathalogo dici proprietatem factivam personae vel effectivam vel constitutivam; Persona enim eterna, nec facta nec effecta nec constituta' [34].

The expressions which Pullen forbade are to be understood in the sense in which they were used in his day. At that time one who said that the personal properties or relations constituted the Persons was taken to deny the simplicity of God. This is evident from the summary of the questions which Pullen prefixed to his *Sentences*. In the list of questions treated in the third chapter of the first book where, as we have already seen, he is attacking views held among others, by Gilbert Porreta, Pullen writes: 'et *proprietates* pertinere ad substantiam, sed *non efficere personam*' [35].

---

[30] 'Modo queritur de divina essentia, utrum sit susceptibilis aliquarum proprietatum, cum proprietas largo modo accipiatur pro aliquo contento sub aliquo VIII predicamentorum'; '... Si proprietas in Deo est, ergo deitas vel paternitas vel filiatio vel processio'. *Sent.* ed. Gietl, pp. 17-19.

[31] 697D.

[32] 679D-680C.

[33] Cf. F. Bliemetzrieder *R.T.A.M.* IV (1932), p. 158. Cf. also '*Sent. Atrebatenses*', ed. D. O. Lottin, *ibid.*, X (1938) 205 ff. '... filius est genitus; genitura autem ineffabilis; item de Spiritu Sancto tantum dicitur: procedens; que processio ineffabilis est'. William of Champeaux writes: 'Est enim unus Deus et Trinus, unus quidem in substantia, trinus in personis; quod qualiter explicare possim non video, cum in nulla rerum natura simile quid possit inveniri'. See Lefèvre, *Les Variations,* etc. p. 24.

[34] See *art. cit.* in *The New Scholasticism*, IV (1930), 11-14.

[35] 640D.

The whole question of the constitution of the divine Persons was in a very undeveloped state at the time when Pullen wrote. A later writer, Praepositinus, maintained that the personal properties, so far from constituting the three Persons, did not even distinguish them [36]. This opinion, according to which the properties were mere verbal expressions, was at the opposite pole to that assigned to Gilbert Porreta. A conciliation between the two views was attempted by William of Auvergne who taught that the properties of the Persons were neither mere verbal expressions nor external and accidental modifications of the divine Persons [37]. Throughout the thirteenth century the controversy continued, though with the publication of the *Summa Theologiae* of St. Thomas Aquinas, the main positions of Catholic theology on this question were established. The elaboration of the idea of a virtual distinction between the subsistent relations and the divine essence enabled theologians to teach with security what had formerly had an equivocal sense, viz. that the divine Persons were constitued by their personal properties or relations [38].

By that time scholastic theologians were in full possession of the philosophy of Aristotle. In Pullen's day an incomplete Aristotle was eked out with all the resources of medieval grammar and rhetoric. Pullen's power of manipulating words is remarkable. A characteristic example occurs in the eighth chapter of the first book of the *Sentences* which is entitled: 'Alius est Pater quam Filius, non aliud, et similia' [39]. Considering the very rudimentary terminology at his disposal Pullen makes here a very creditable attempt at distinguishing what is common to the three Persons and what is proper to each of them. Commenting on the phrase from the Athanasian Creed, 'Alia est enim persona Patris, alia Filii', he observes that what the Son is, that the Father is: 'Verum id est Pater quod Filius' [40]. The Father is God, omnipotent, wise, good; the Son is all these too: 'omnia eadem est Filius' [41]. Yet the Father is the begetter and unbegotten and a principle that is unoriginated: 'Sed Pater est Genitor; et hoc aliud, Ingenitus; et hoc tertium, Principium sine principio' [42]. The Son is none of these. Hence it appears that the Son is not all that the Father is.

---

36 M. Schmaus, 'Der Liber Propugnatorius des Thomas Anglicus', etc., *Beiträge*, XXXIX, I (1930) 388-99.

37 Schmaus, *ibid.*, p. 391.

38 Cf. *Summa Theol.*, P. I, qu. 40, art. 1 and 2.

39 687C-689C.

40 687C.

41 687D.

42 *Ibid.*

After indicating that Father and Son are one in divinity, but have personal distinctions (' ex divinitate sua quidquid est Pater, est quoque Filius '), Pullen suggests that the dictium ' Quidquid est Pater, est Filius ' requires restriction to the divine essence [43]. Then, characteristically, he offers another solution: the Father is someone who is not the Son — ' aliquis qui non est Filius ' [44] — but not something which the Son is not. The masculine gender, he suggests, insinuates the personal distinction of Father and Son; the neuter, the unity of the divine substance: ' ut masculinum genus insinuet distinctionem Personae, neutrum vero unitatem substantiae '. Even this grammatical solution is not final. The Father is an unoriginated principle: ' Principium sine principio ' [45]. Now the word ' principium ' is of the neuter gender. Hence the foregoing solution would appear to be unsound. It is worth while noting in this passage the ingenuity with which Pullen could continue this grammatical quibbling [46].

The same ingenious quibbling on masculine and neuter pronouns is pursued indefatigably by Pullen; and *alius, aliud,* or *quidam* and *quiddam* are pressed into service to provide a display of verbal fireworks which cannot be adequately represented in English by translation or paraphrase. He concludes by re-affirming his suggestion that the neuter gender signifies the unity of substance of the Persons and the masculine the distinction of Persons, but with a qualification. Whatever is predicated of the Father in the neuter, and not of the Son, is identical with the Father, but it does not imply that the Father is anything (understanding here the divine substance) which the Son is not [47].

---

[43] 688A.

[44] *Ibid.*

[45] 688B.

[46] ' Pater est Principium sine principio, illud non est Filius, sed aliud. Quod? *Principium de Principio*: quid inde consequitur? num quod Pater sit aliud, et aliud Filius? Num quod Pater sit tale quid vel aliquid, aut illud quod non est Filius? Non. Pater enim et Filius sunt unum et idem. Quid ergo? Quid aliud est Pater quam Filius? Quod Pater non est ille qui Filius; quod item Pater est aliquis, aut, si ita dici potest, talis quis qui non est Filius ': 688B.

If this and similar passages were ever delivered in the lecture-room one can imagine the applause with which they would have been received. John of Salisbury insinuates that one of the qualifications essential to a successful lecturer in theology was that he should prove himself a subtle dialectician. He implies that he found Master Robert Pullen satisfactory in this respect. 688B. Cf. John of Salisbury, *Metalogicon,* Lib. II, cap. X.

[47] ' Illud autem aliud quod de Patre enuntiatur, et non de Filio, utique Pater est, et dicitur; Filius vero non est nec dicitur: non tamen ideo aliud est, aut dicitur Pater, quam Filius '. 689A.

In this chapter Pullen had strained the resources of his theological equipment to the utmost. The very brilliance of much that is here, only serves, however, to show the inadequacy of the old logic and the old terminology that were in use in the school of Laon. There was need for development, as Gilbert Porreta had perceived.

Two quotations will show the Laon ancestry of Pullen's chapter on the distinction of the divine persons. The first is from the *Sentences* of William of Champeaux, whose theology is substantially the same as that of Anselm of Laon, whose pupil he had been [48]. Apart from the greater skill and subtlety with which he presents it, Pullen does not add anything essential to this doctrine of William.

The second quotation is taken from the collection of *Sentences* edited by F. Bliemetzrieder, entitled *Sententiae Divinae Paginae* which the editor considered to be the work of Anselm of Laon himself [49].

Here, as elsewhere, Pullen seems to have taken an idea which was familiar in the school of Laon and given it a more elaborate and subtle treatment than we find in the works which have a more immediate relationship to that school.

The chapter closes with the observation that whatever justification there may be for speaking of the three Persons as creating or ruling the universe [50], there is no ground for speaking of three creators or rulers. The reason is that the noun denotes the unity of the divine substance, the plural participle, the plurality of the Persons.

THE EQUALITY OF THE THREE PERSONS

This question occurs as a long digression in the course of Pullen's treatment of the theology of the Incarnate Word. He has concluded in the second chapter of the fourth book of the *Sentences* that the divinity of Christ is superior to the humanity in goodness

[48] 'Dicitur etiam Filius e substantia Patris, non ex persona. Ad quam etiam dicendum distincte, his utimur vocibus alius, aliud, ille, illud: dicimus enim: alius Pater est quam Filius, non aliud, vel illud est Pater quod Filius, non ille, per neutrum quidem substantiam, per masculinum personas significantes'. See Lefèvre, *Les Variations,* etc., 27.

[49] 'Item potest vere dici, pater est alius quam filius, sed non aliud. Item potest dici: pater non est idem cum filio — idem dico masculinum, non neutrum'. *Ed cit.* 10.

[50] 689C. 'Tres regnantes, tres creantes'.

and power. This conclusion gives him the opportunity of formulating an objection. If, he begins, the power of God who assumed a human nature is proved to be different from that of the humanity of Christ because God can do that which the man (Christ) cannot do, it would appear that Father, Son and Holy Ghost cannot have the same power. For that which actually exists must be reckoned possible. Since the Father begets, it is evident that he has the power of begetting; similarly, the Son has the power of being begotten and the Holy Ghost of proceeding from both. Now each of the three Persons has, therefore, His own particular power, but not that which belongs to another. How can it be said, then, that the three Persons have one and the same power? [51]

Omitting his reply to this objection in so far as it is concerned with the humanity and divinity of Christ, we will consider how he treats the problem in relation to the theology of the Trinity. He is at pains to explain that the relations of origin which distinguish the three Persons do not mean that any of them has more power than either of the others. The reason is that the operations of the Trinity are common to all three Persons. The personal properties, which, as in the first book, he describes in concrete terminology, must not be called operations [52]. Where there is an operation, he argues, the cause precedes the effect; consequently, if the personal properties or relations were operations, generation and procession in God would not be eternal [53].

He then embarks on a discussion which is a veritable *tour de force,* such is the skill displayed in the management of words in spite of a complete avoidance of abstract terminology. His aim is, first to establish that the fatherhood of God is commensurate with the greatness of God Himself. He indicates that he could prove the same of the sonship and of the procession of the Holy Ghost, but for the sake of brevity restricts himself to one property, ' ut in uno trium naturam singulorum perpendamus '. The implication is that all three Persons are equal in power. The proof runs as follows: To be Father is nothing else than to be God having a Son. Now being Father, or God having a Son, cannot be an operation, since

51 ' Horum autem trium quisque sic illud potest quod ad se pertinet, ut non posset id quod ad alios pertinet: quomodo ergo una eademque est potestas omnium, quoniam id possunt singuli, quod non possunt ceteri? ' 807B.

52 ' quippe Filium gignere, seu gigni a Patre, demum ab utroque procedere, id operari non est '. 2807D.

53 *Ibid.* Cf. the Oxford MS. cited above, p. 49. Mathoud notes that on this question, which was much discussed at the time, Robert of Melun and Peter of Poitiers held the same views as Pullen. *P.L.* 1056B.

every operator is of greater worth and goodness than his operation; whereas no operator can be worthier or better than it is to be God having a Son [54].

He proceeds to state the principle, ' qualis est unaquaeque res, tale est esse rem ' — a kind of principle of identity, which we may translate, ' The nature of anything is the measure of the perfection involved in benig that thing. For example, says Pullen, the seriousness of the wickedness involved is the measure of the seriousness of being wicked [55]: ' Quam mala est iniquitas, tam malum est esse iniquum '; the goodness of the justice determines how good it is to be just: ' quam bona est justitia, tam bonum est justum ' [56]; the goodness of man determines how good it is to be a man: ' Prout bonus homo, bonum est esse hominem ' [57]. Hence, if we wish to measure the perfection involved in the divine Fatherhood, which is rendered in the phrase, ' esse Deum habentem Filium ', it is clear that it is the same as that described by the phrase, ' Deus habens Filium ' [58]. But the perfection involved in the latter phrase is infinite. It follows that the perfection implied by being God the Father, ' esse Deum habentem Filium ', is also infinite. Pullen does not here infer it, but leaves it to his readers to deduce, that the perfection implied by the divine sonship, ' Esse Deum habentem Patrem ', is also infinite. Similarly it could be established that the perfection involved in being the Holy Ghost is likewise infinite [59].

Having established the thesis, propounded at the beginning of the chapter, that the three Persons are equal in power, Pullen proceeds to affirm that, if we mean to distinguish the Persons, we must apparently distinguish in each His separate and eternal glory; for, unless we make a distinction between the glory of each of the Persons, we cannot speak of equality, but only of identity [60]. If, however, we do not mean to distinguish the Persons, but to consider their common substance, then the Persons are one in divinity, glory and majesty. Hence the author of the words in the Creed, ' sed Patris et Filii et Spiritus Sancti una est divinitas, aequalis gloria, coaeterna majestas ', was considering what is one in the divine Persons when he spoke of their one divinity, but when he

---

54 ' quis enim operator ille esse posset, qui melior jure esse deberet, quam sit esse Deum habentem Filium? ' 808A.

55 808A.

56 *Ibid.*

57 808A.

58 808B.

59 *Ibid.*

60 808C.

went on to confess their equality in glory and co-eternal majesty he was attending to their distinction as Persons [61]. When he commemorated their equality in glory it was equality between the Persons, not an equality between different glories that he had in mind, since these three equal Persons have but one glory and majesty, one immensity, one dominion, eternity and divinity. Just as there are not three glorious Gods, but one, so there are not three glories but one [62]. This is to be expected, he continues, since, seeing there is but one God, every divine perfection must be one [63], whereas the existence of three Persons demands the separate existence of the three properties which distinguish the individual Persons.

The next paragraph proposes a problem which, besides its intrinsic interest, is of importance because of the unmistakable way in which it sets Pullen in the ranks of the orthodox theologians and segregates him from the school of Gilbert Porreta. The problem is stated thus. Seeing that each of the divine Persons is God — all schools would have assented to this proposition — and conversely, that God is also each of the three Persons — against this Gilbert would have demurred — it follows that a property which belongs to God must also be a property of the Persons. Why, then, do we at one time speak of attributes of the divinity, at another of attributes of the Trinity of Persons? [64] Every property which is common to the three Persons may be predicated of God, he replies, seeing that the three Persons are God. Those, however, which are peculiar to each of the three Persons may with justice be spoken of as properties of the Persons. Two of these properties are that God should have a Father, 'habere Patrem Deum', and that God should have a Son, 'item habere Filium Deum' [65]. Each of these properties is a source of much glory. Although the properties are distinct from one another, the glory which they entail is not distinct, but one and the same. Similarly, both Father and Son are but one God, not different Gods. Moreover, just as the Son is equal to the Father, equal indeed as Son, for inasmuch as He is God, He is one and the same as the Father, so in the same way the glory of the three Persons is equal. It is said to be equal

61 808D.
62 809A.
63 'Omnis quoque, ut ita dicam, Dei forma aut proprietas una est'. *Ibid.*
64 809A.
65 809B.

because of their personal distinction, though in itself their glory is one and the same? [66]

So far Pullen has established that the three Persons are equal and have one and the same power by proving that the personal properties in virtue of which they are distinguished cannot be called operations. His argument assumed, as we have already noticed, that active generation is identical with Paternity: 'quod ipsum gignere, nihil aliud sit quam Patrem esse' [67]. Now he considers the hypothesis in which his assumption is not conceded. In this case active generation, 'Ipsum gignere', is regarded not as identical with the property of paternity, 'quod est Patrem esse', but as the cause of the existence in God of paternity [68].

This hypothesis, replies Pullen, is untenable; for no operation can be of such efficacy that in virtue of it the Father, who is God, should have being. Far more appropriate would it be for an operation to proceed from Him than He from an operation [69]. A person might admit, he continues, that the Son has a cause, seeing that He is 'Principium de Principio'; but it is impossible that the Father should have a cause, seeing that He is 'Principium sine Principio'. If it be replied that active generation ('ipsum gignere') is regarded as a cause, not of the existence of the Person of the Father, but only of His property of being Father, 'non quidem ut persona illa sit, verum ut Pater sit' [70], the answer is evident. Applied to men such a distinction would be valid, since there is a real distinction between personality and paternity, for personality exists before, or in the absence of, paternity. Applied, however, to God, the real distinction between personality and paternity is illegitimate, seeing that in God to be the person of the Father and to be Father is one and the same thing. The same holds good of the generation of the Son, and of the procession of the Holy Ghost. It is evident, therefore, that active generation, filiation, and procession may be appropriately called properties of the persons, but not operations [71].

---

[66] 'trium personarum aequalis est gloria, sed propter personas dicitur aequalitas, nam in gloria est identitas'. 809C.

[67] 809C. Cf. 809A.

[68] 809C.

[69] *Ibid.*

[70] 809D.

[71] 'respondeo apud nos quidem aliud et aliud est esse personam, et patrem, quia est persona, cum non est et quae non est pater: sed non ibi, id enim est esse illam personam, quod esse Patrem, et e converso. Gignere ergo ac gigni, atque demum ab utroque procedere, proprietates utique convenienter dicuntur personarum, non actiones earum'. 809D-810A.

Summing up the discussion, he remarks that only in consideration of the properties peculiar to the Persons, is it possible to say that One can do that which the others are unable to do, though, as is clear from what has preceded, he holds that these properties are not, strictly speaking, operations. This is emphasized when he adds that, although the power (' potestas ') of begetting God, which is proper to the Father is not the same as the power (' potestas ') of being begotten by God, which is proper to the Son, seeing that they are separate properties, nevertheless they are not two distinct powers, but one, just as God the Father and God the Son are not two distinct Gods, but one [72]. The implication of this statement is that the personal propterties which are identified with the Persons are really distinct from each other, but only virtually distinct from the divine essence. Pullen's position is substantially that of the later and more highly developed scholastic theology, although his terminology is defective. He concludes by observing that, if it be said that the various personal properties are derived from really distinct powers, we could no longer speak of one power or of one divine glory but of three, and it would follow that there are three who are powerful and glorious. As this formula is an innovation, he considers it safer to hold to his first statement that the three personal properties do not derive from three separate powers, but from one [73].

The words ' sed addit inde consequi ' are of interest. We have no clue which would tell ut to whom Pullen is referring. I am inclined to think that they refer to some *expositor* or commentator, and that this chapter developed out of a lecture by Pullen on the Athanasian Creed in which he used the work of the commentator as a gloss. It is known that in his day such lectures on the Athanasian Creed were given in the Schools, and much of the theology of the Trinity must have been based on the study of this creed with the aid of glosses. Apart from its intrinsic interest, this chapter, like that on the distinction of the Persons of the Trinity, is of value for the light it throws on the history of scholastic speculation on the divine relations at a time when only a fragmentary

---

72 810A.

73 ' Nisi quis dicat tres unam habere potentiam, majestatem, gloriam, et hoc ex unitate divinitatis quod indubitanter verum est: iterum quemque suam, et hoc ex distinctione suae proprietatis, quod forsan verum est. Sed addit inde consequi, ut trium tres sint potentiae, et totidem gloriae; indeque probari, ut ipsi sint tres et potentes et gloriosi; ... sed prior via minus scrupulosa, quia verba magis usitata '. 810B.

knowledge of Aristotelian philosophy was available in the theological schools. The development of the thought seems to be quite original.

THE DIVINE MISSIONS

Pullen's doctrine on the divine missions is contained partly in the first book of the *Sentences* [74], partly in the fifth book [75]. He distinguishes between the missions emanating from the Father and the Son by observing that the Father sends forth both the Son and the Holy Ghost, whereas the Son only sends the Holy Ghost. The Holy Ghost does not send forth any of the other divine Persons. The relation of the divine Persons in regard to a mission in the temporal order, he finds, is analogous to that of their eternal order of principality and procession [76].

Next he describes what he understands by a mission. Passively regarded, it is the manifestation of an invisible nature by some visible effect. Actively, it signifies the will of the Father and Son that the manifestation should be made [77]. Since the Son and the Holy Ghost were sent into the world by the will of the whole Trinity, certain authors, he adds, approve the expression that the whole Trinity sends the Son and the Holy Ghost. Nevertheless, he continues, we use another mode of expression, in order that we may distinguish what is proper to the several Persons [78]. We cannot say that the Son or the Holy Ghost is sent by Himself, but we can say that one of them is sent by the other, viz., He who proceeds by Him from whom He proceeds. He alone can be sent who is from another, and by whose will He is revealed to men through some manifestation of His presence. As for the difficulty from Isaias (xlviii. 16) *and now the Lord hath sent me, and his spirit,* Pullen interprets the text as follows: The Father decreed the Incarnation and the Son of Man was conceived by the power of the Holy Ghost. To the explanation he has given of the text he adds that the human nature assumed by the Word may be said to have been sent by the Holy Ghost, much in the same way as a good teacher is said to be sent by God [79].

---

[74] Cap. vii, 687B-C.

[75] Cap. iv, 831D-833A.

[76] 'Quemadmodum ergo se habent ii tres circa principium atque processum aeternaliter, ita quoque se habent in missione temporaliter'. 687B.

[77] 'Quod nutu Patris itemque Filii missio celebrata est,' *Ibid.*

[78] 'locutio variatur ut personae distinguantur,' 687B.

[79] 'humanitas suscepta merito dicetur a Spiritu quoque missa, sicut doctor bonus a Deo confirmatur missus'. 687C.

In the fifth book the mission of the Holy Ghost is treated in greater detail. The meaning of the expression 'mission of the Holy Ghost' as applied to the appearance of the Holy Ghost to the disciples at Pentecost, is that the invisible Spirit, who is omnipresent, was manifested in a visible manner. It was not the Spirit Himself that was perceived, but tongues of fire which symbolised his presence [80]. It was fitting that this manifestation symbolised the Spirit only, since it was He who came to give his sevenfold gifts.

The external mission is a symbol of the internal mission of the Holy Ghost. By his coming He brings his interior gifts of holiness; by his indwelling He conserves and increases these gifts [81].

Pullen's treatment of this question does not call for much comment. It is entirely orthodox as far as it goes, but incomplete, even as judged by the standards of his own day. Unlike Alcuin [82], Hugh of St. Victor [83], and Abelard [84], he does not attempt to examine explicitly why the Father is not sent. Presumably, he considered that the parallel he drew between the divine missions and the processions was sufficient answer to the question. We do not find any trace of an attempt to mingle Platonic with Christian elements in his discussion of the question, such as Abelard displays in his treatment of the same subject [85].

---

80 831D-832A.

81 'Nimirum ejus venire, id est, munera largiendo bonos efficere: ejus autem habitare, id est, munera data conservando augere: '832B. Pullen has already distinguished God's omnipresence in all things from his presence in the just by grace, 689 D., *supra* 70 f. He returns to the question in his treatment of justifiying faith, baptism, confirmation and penance, cf. 839, 841, *infra* 200, 232. For contemporary scholastic teaching see A. Landgraf, *Dogmengeschichte der Frühscholastik,* 1, ii, 41-56.

82 *De Fid. S. Trin., P. L.* 101, 41.

83 *De Sacr., P. L.* 176, 371.

84 *Theol. Chr. P. L.* 178, 1290.

85 *Theol. Chr., l. c.,* 1309.

CHAPTER IX

CREATION AND ORIGINAL SIN

The creation of the universe [1]

God created the universe, writes Pullen, in complete freedom. The moment of creation was freely chosen; the restriction of his creative work to one rather than to a number of worlds was self-imposed; the existence of the universe was not necessary for the well-being of an infinitely perfect Maker. God brought the universe into being out of nothing, in order that others might share in his goodness.

In Genesis, Moses said that the work of Creation took six days, but another text of Scripture (Ecclesiasticus, XVIII, 1) states that God created all things together. These statements are not irreconcilable. God first made the earth devoid of form, and waters and vapour enveloped it. When the earth became dry, God adorned it with many different living species. God may be said, therefore, to have created all things together, seeing that after the seventh day He added no new forms or matter to the universe [2]. The only exceptions to be noted are creatures, such as mules, which arise through the union of different species, or from the corruption of matter, for example, a certain kind of worm, or those monstrous births which are intended to remind men of the wondrous power of God [3]. In all these, however, it is but the form that is new. All normal creatures are manifestly akin to those first created from which they derive their substance and quality. All bodies are produced out of the original created matter; souls are created in the likeness of those made in the beginning. When, therefore, we read (Gen. ii. 2) that 'God rested on the seventh day' we are not to understand that God's activity came to an end, for this would be inconsistent with Our Lord's words (John, V. 17) '*My Father*

---

1 717C-719A.

2 See St. Augustine, *De Gen. ad Litt.* IV, 12.

3 See Abelard, *Expositio in Hexaemeron, P.L.*, 178, 769D.

worketh until now' but that all substances that later came into existence were either produced out of pre-existent matter, if they were corporeal, or in the likeness of those already created, if they were spiritual.

God made the earth to be man's dwelling-place; for the angels, and ultimately for man, God made heaven which is called the firmament. Philosophers teach that the firmament is a revolving sphere. How those that dwell thereon do not revolve along with it is difficult to understand, for the stars are certainly in motion. Bede's solution seems the best: beyond the heavens that are in motion there is a stable region to which Christ has ascended whither too the saints will be transported [4].

Heaven must be either a spiritual or a corporeal substance; only a madman would say that is an accidental form. For the angelic nature which is spiritual, a corporeal abode appears to be superflous; yet it seems requisite for the bodies of the saints in glory. To exclude the saints and the risen Humanity of Christ from the company of the angels in heaven would be to deprive them of their full glory. Heaven must be corporeal; to assert that it is a spiritual substance would be to run counter to scriptural authority and customary expression which recognise but three kinds of spirits: God Himself, good and evil angels and disembodied souls. The angels will be well-satisfied with this corporeal heaven which the Divine Artificer has made and adorned with wondrous and various beauty. It follows that, if heaven is corporeal, hell is likewise; were it not so, how could it contain those extremes of heat and cold which are the torments of the lost?

A comparison of Pullen's treatment of this subject with that of some of the better-known among his contemporaries shows that he is writing in the tradition of a school — that of Laon. The topics raised, the solutions suggested, are those to be found in the collections associated with, or derived from Anselm of Laon [5]. What Pullen contributes is a more advanced dialectical technique for the handling of the material, together with a more personal and elaborate literary presentation.

---

[4] i. e. The Empyrean. See Bede, *Hexaemeron*, I, *P. L.* 91, 18B-20A.

[5] See *Sententiae Divinae Paginae*, *Sententiae Anselmi* in 'Anselms von Laon systematische Sentenzen', ed. F. Bliemetzrieder, in *Beiträge*, XVIII 2-3 (1919) 12-14, 46-9. *Summa Sententiarum*, *P. L.* 176, 79C, 81A, 89-90. The material used in the school of Anselm was derived from patristic sources, especially from the commentaries of Ambrose, Augustine and Bede on the account of the Creation given in the book of Genesis.

Angels and Demons [6]

The angels are pure spirits. They are grouped in a hierarchy consisting of nine orders: angels, archangels, virtues, powers, principalities, dominations, thrones, cherubs and seraphs. Thus the term ' angel ' applies in general, in virtue of their function of divine messengers, to the members of all nine orders, and in particular to those belonging to the lowest order. To these and to the archangels is assigned more commonly the task of bearing messages, though beneficent operations affecting human life lie also within their charge. Three of the archangels are known by name: Michael, the protector of Christendom, who, along with each man's guardian angel offers the prayers of men to God; Raphael, the spirit of healing; and Gabriel, whose name shews that the superintendence of wars among men is part of his office. The seven superior orders are more concerned with action than with the communication of divine revelation. The virtues are entrusted with the operation of miracles; they also are called the angels of the Mass. The powers defend men from the assaults of evil spirits; principalities and dominations are names suggestive of authority within the angelic hierarchy rather than of specific functions. The thrones Pullen associates with the promulgation of God's judgments; and he conjectures that by their assistance human judges pronounce just sentence.

He cannot accept the opinion that the two highest orders, cherubs and seraphs are so rapt in contemplation of the Godhead that they are exempt from ministering to men, even though it is said that this was the teaching of the Areopagite. Scripture in several passages proves the contrary, notably in the text of Hebrews (i. 14), ' *Are they not all ministering spirits, sent to minister for them, who shall receive the inheritance of salvation*? ' Here it is of alla the angels that the Apostle is speaking, as is evident from the context of his argument. The name cherub, Pullen adds, means ' the fullness of knowledge '; it may, therefore, be by their aid that we advance in knowledge. Seraph signifies ' burning fire '. Material and and spiritual fire is the element in which they work. When God makes use of fire to destroy the wicked or purify the just, it would

[6] This paragraph contains the most important ideas of a series of disconnected chapters, cols. 881-7. The primary source of most of this doctrine, which was commonly taught, is St. Gregory the Great, *Hom xxxiv in Evang.* nn. 7-14, *P. L.* 76, 1249-55.

appear that His instruments are the seraphs. Spiritual fire is charity; hence it seems that seraphs are instrumental causes of God in the sanctification of men.

Evil spirits are fallen angels [7]. They too are grouped in a hierarchy of nine orders, as may be gathered from St. Paul's references to our spiritual enemies (Rom. viii. 38), even though, characteristically, the Apostle does not enumerate each single order. The gifts and functions belonging to the nine orders of angels are perverted towards man's destruction in their counterparts. From these proceed material and spiritual disasters of every kind, although for much of his misery man is himself wholly responsible. It may happen, where the evil is not the result of their suggestion, that the demons are ignorant of its existence, and can only become aware of it by outward manifestations.

The leader of the fallen angels was among the most glorious of those first created; most probably he belonged to the order of cherubs, as Ezechiel teaches (xxviii. 14). The same prophet also seems to confirm the opinion which maintains that after the fall the angelic nature was as much weakened in the evil spirits as it was strengthened in those who, remaining loyal, were admitted to the vision of God. (Ezech. xxviii 17).

The question, how was it possible for the angels to sin [8], can only be answered by considering the nature of their free-will and the extent of their knowledge of God [9]. Angels and men were both endowed by nature with free-will. In man this faculty was very powerful; in the angels, correspondingly more powerful. For freedom of action three elements must be present: discrimination, will-power, and unimpeded execution. The first (discretio) gives the power of moral judgments; will-power (voluntas) enables the soul to follow whichever course it pleases once the judgment is made; unimpeded execution (potestas), removes obstacles to the attainment of the end which has been chosen. For this reason free-will has been defined as a judgment concerning the will [10]. According as these three elements are present in greater or less force will be the power or weakness of free-will. Infants have not free-will, nor animals; men are deficient in one or other of the three elements

---

[7] 887-91.

[8] 720B-725A; 799A-800C; 743C-746A; 890D-891C.

[9] 720B-725A.

[10] By Boethius, *De Interpretatione*, ed. ii lib. P. L., 64, 492. On this question Pullen's thought is that of the School of Laon as represented by the *Sent. Div. Pag., ed. cit.* 27-8, *Sent. Anselmi, ibid.*, 49-50. See on this point O. Lottin, *Psychologie et Morale aux XIIe et XIIIe Siècles*, I, 22-24, 43.

that are requisite. The weakness of human wills is a consequence of the Fall, but even before the first sin, human freedom was weaker than that of the angels, since the nature of man is less spiritual than that of an angel. Human nature succumbed to a temptation from without; the more powerful will of the angels was its own tempter. So the different circumstances of the fall of man and of the angels made it equitable that the former should obtain forgiveness but not the latter. Free-will therefore, made possible the fall of the angels. This faculty was good in itself; its abuse evil [11]. It is also important, he continues, to consider what knowledge of God was possessed by the angels before their fall. If they enjoyed the vision of God it is hard to see how they could sin. If an angel saw God he must have understood partial truth in the vision of Truth Itself. Those doomed to fall must, therefore, have foreseen their own fall [12]. Unless this caused them pain they must have been insensible. Hence from the first moment when they saw God, the angels doomed to fall away were either unhappy or insensible. Pullen considers the suggestion that it is impossible to know truth as mirrored in the divine essence without being able to obtain a knowledge of all particular truths. Thus the angels now in Heaven do not know when the Day of Judgment will occur. So, theoretically speaking, the devil might once have had the vision of God without foreseeing his own fall [13]. That he actually did have this vision Pullen refuses to admit, since the beatitude of those who see God is incompatible with the state of sin [14]. At the moment therefore, of their creation the angels were given that knowledge of God which goes with faith. Those who persevered in faith were rewarded with the vision of God; the others never attained to that beatitude [15].

Although Pullen in the foregoing discussion maintains that those who see God will never sin, he does not venture to say that they cannot sin; it is a moral rather than a physical impossibility which he defends. Those who by the beatific vision are confirmed in grace retain the power of offending God; but, since they will never desire to use this power, sin is said to be impossible for them [16]:

---

[11] 721C. Cf. *Sent. Anselmi, ed. cit.* 78.

[12] The thought derives from Augustine, *De Gen. ad Litt.* XI, 17-19, ed. Zycha, *C. S. E. L,* 28, 319-352. It appears in a number of contemporary collections of *Sentences.*

[13] 722D.

[14] 723A.

[15] 723C-D. Cf. *Sent. Div. Pag., ed. cit.* 14; *Sent. Anselmi ibid.,* 53; Hugh of St. Victor, *De Sacr., P. L.,* 176, 252.

[16] 'Et quoniam longe longeque a peccandi distant voluntate, reputatur penes eos peccatum quasi impossibile'.

The reason why those who see God will never sin is that the vision of God once experienced precludes the will for ever from seeking evil [17]. Pullen's conception of the impeccability of the blessed resembles more closely the later Scotist view than that which St. Thomas Aquinas was to teach [18].

Pullen has little to say of the nature of the sin which caused the expulsion of the rebellious angels from Heaven. Lucifer in his pride, we are told, dared to compare himself with the Most High; he was, it is true, a mighty spirit, but his self-esteem went far beyond his real worth [19]. Those spirits which sided with the rebellious leader shared in his downfall [20].

The consequences of the fall of the angels were cosmic in their extent. They affected not only the fallen spirits themselves, but also the human race which came into existence after their fall [21].

The lost spirits from the moment of their fall have endured bitter punishment; when this world comes to an end their pains will be multiplied. In time they are a prey to torturing envy and anger and to certain noxious qualities experienced by them in this nether air which they now infest; after the Judgment they will be confined to Hell, and though their substance is incorporeal, they will be punished there with corporeal pains [22].

Once the rebellious angels fell from grace their wills were irrevocably averted from God and bent on evil; the good angels were rewarded with the vision of God and confirmed for ever in goodness. Until the number of the elect is complete, the demons are permitted to assault men for their spiritual profit; the angels, on the other hand, assist them in many different ways. The question

---

17 723-4.

18 Cf. Scotus, *Ordinatio,* I, D. 1, P. 3, Qq. 1-5; St Thomas, *Summa Theol.* I^a^, II^ae^, q. 4, a. 4; q. 5, a. 5. Pullen's teaching was common in the school of Anselm of Laon. See *Sent. Div. Pag.* 17f; *Sent. Anselmi* 54. It was, however, rejected by Robert of Melun. See O. Lottin, *op. cit.* 31 f.

19 890D.

20 891A.

21 745C.

22 723B-C; D. C. M. ed. cit. 203. The opinion that the fallen angels inhabit the air between heaven and earth, and only after the Last Judgment will be cast into hell was common in Pullen's day. See *Sententiae Divinae Paginae,* ed. cit. 16-17; *Sententiae Anselmi, ibid,* 53; *Summa Sententiarum, P. L.* 176, 84B. The foundation of this opinion was the interpretation given to II Pet. ii. 4 by certain of the Fathers. See Augustine, *De Natura Boni cap.* xxxiii, *P. L.* 42, 562; Gregory, *Moralia,* II, 47, *P. L.* 75, 590; Fulgentius, *De Trinitate,* viii, *P. L.* 66, 504. St. Thomas, *Summa Theol.* I, q. 65, a. 4 teaches that some of the demons are already in hell; those that are tempting human beings, though not actually in hell, nevertheless experience the torments that are their due.

arises, does this activity increase the demerits of the evil spirits and the merits of the good spirits? Pullen discusses the problem with his usual thoroughness [23]. He is aware of the difficulty of growth in merit or demerit, in goodness or wickedness, once the spirit is finally united to God or separated from Him for ever, but without condemning the opposite opinion considers it more probable that the angels and demons do not attain their final degree of goodness and malice respectively before the end of time [23a]. Pullen's solution of this problem was accepted by the Lombard, but rejected by St. Thomas [24].

A last question arising out of the fall of the angels is concerned with the relation of that event to the creation of the human race. It is credible, says Pullen, and commonly held, that the places of the fallen angels in heaven will be filled by the elect from among men. This suggests that, if all the angels had remained faithful, the human race would not have been created. In favour of this inference Pullen adduces a number of arguments, followed by others which tell against it. His conclusion is that, if the number of places in heaven available for the saints is exactly equal to the number of the fallen angels, the creation of man would not have been decreed by God unless He had foreseen the rebellion in heaven [25]. Pullen adds, however, that this numerical equality of fallen angels and saints is by no means certain [26].

Whatever be the numerical proportion of the elect to the fallen angels, this at least is certain: the merits of the saints in heaven far outweigh in worth what the heavenly court lost through the defection of the demons [27]. He proceeds to establish this assertion. The saints in heaven are to be made equal in dignity to the angels who remained faithful. The dignity of the spirits, which at the moment of their trial was equal to that of the fallen angels, is now far greater through the merit of their obedience [28].

That human beings should advance in dignity until they become equal to the angels is explained by the difficulty of the spiritual combat, in which, assisted by the grace of God men triumph over

---

23 799-800.

23a 800B.

24 See P. Lombard, *Sent.* II, D, xi, cap. 4, sqq; St. Thomas, *Summa Theol.* I, q. 62, a. 9.

25 745C.

26 742B-C. The *Sententie Divine Pagine,* is also uncertain on this question, *ed. cit.* 189.

27 743C.

28 743C-D.

their infernal enemies. The human race should, therefore, take heart for the struggle, looking forward to that future state of glory which so far surpasses what was lost by the sin of Adam. Now we have as the Head of the Body, that is the Church, Christ our Redeemer. With Him we have His Mother, Mary, Queen of Angels, Virgin Mother undefiled. These two shine like the sun and the moon in the heavenly Sion. If the merit and glory of the Virgin Mother has increased beyond any limit that is assignable, we, the brethren of Christ, may hope too to grow in merit and so become more worthy of God our Brother [29]. These considerations lead Pullen to extol the power and mercy of God, which are so evident in the restoration of the lost dignity of the human race. God's power, says Pullen, was exhibited very wonderfully in the work of Creation, but it shines forth with even greater splendour here, for to convert what is evil into what is good would seem to require greater power than the giving of existence where it was wanting before, since there is in creation no principle of resistance to the divine operation, as there is in an evil subject [30]. Just as in his dealings with men God's mercy is manifest, so in his treatment of the devil is his justice in evidence.

The creation of man

By fashioning the human body out of the slime of the earth, says Pullen, God desired to forestall human pride; by ennobling it with a soul as its formal principle He sealed it with His own likeness. The first body was made by the hands of God in order that from it all others might arise. Thus does man resemble his Creator who is the ultimate origin of all things. Seeing, therefore, that we all descend from one man who was made by God, we learn to revere one ultimate principle and lawgiver and to cherish one another because of the ties of natural kinship [31].

We read in the account of the formation of the first man that the soul was not infused by the Creator until the body was completely formed. By this we are to understand that in all human beings who descend from Adam the soul is not infused into the

---

29 'Namque semper virgo Maria, facta mater Salvatoris, ultra quam dici queat, crevit. Nonne ergo et sancti facti fratres Christi similiter crescunt? Utique crescunt ... facti igitur videntur et merito meliores, et fratre Deo digniores' 744C.

30 754A.

31 726A-B.

human embryo until it has attained its perfect shape. This conclusion is confirmed by the Mosaic legislation (Exod. xxi. 22) which decreed the death penalty against him who strikes a woman and makes her miscarry, provided that the perfect shape of the child is proof of the infusion of its soul. Where the embryo was undeveloped only a fine was imposed [32]. How explain, then, the shaping of the human body unless from the beginning it is informed by a soul? To say that the soul of the mother performs the office of informing principle would mean that one principle gives life to two beings, or more, if the conception is not single. It would follow, too, that the infant would be human before receiving its own soul. Yet in the absence of personal union between the embryo and the mother there appears to be no principle presiding over the shaping of the former [33].

What happens, apparently, surmises Pullen, is that from the beginning the embryo is dissociated from union with the souls and bodies of the parents from which its elements derive. Its shaping is to be ascribed to some natural energy analogous to that which enables a seed detached from the parent stock to develop into a complete plant or tree [34]. If the soul were infused before the

---

[32] Pullen's argument is not supported by the Vulgate text which reads as follows: 'Si rixati fuerint viri, et percusserit quis mulierem praegnantem, et abortivum quidem fecerit, sed ipsa vixerit: subjacebit damno quantum maritus mulieris expetierit, et arbitri judicaverint'. He is evidently relying on some version deriving from the Septuagint in which the legislation is set forth as he formulates it. Such a version was to be found in the Gloss, with which he was familiar. See *P. L.* 113, 257D-258A. The Gloss on this verse included a passage from St. Augustine's *Questiones in Heptateuchum, C. S. E. L.* Vol. XXVIII, sect. iii, p. 3, *P. L.* 34, 626, in which the text occurs in the following form which clearly derives from the Septuagint: 'Si autem litigabunt duo viri et percusserint mulierem in utero habentem, et exierit infans ejus non deformatus (*al.* nondum formatus: clearly the correct reading) detrimentum patietur; quantum indixerit vir mulieris, et dabit cum postulatione ... si autem formatus fuerit, dabit animam pro anima'. St. Augustine observes that the text gives rise to the question whether the soul is infused into the imperfectly formed body. The concluding words of his non-committal exposition as included in the Gloss apparently influenced certain theologians to accept the view that the rational soul does not inform an undeveloped embryo. See e. g. *Sententiae Anselmi, ed. cit.* 76. C. Vercellone, *Variae Lectiones Vulgatae Latinae Bibliorum*, I, (Rome, 1860) 25, observes that many writers from the ninth century onwards quote the legislation contained in Exodus xxi, 22, in the following conflate form derived from the Itala and Vulgate versions: 'Si quis percusserit mulierem praegnantem, et fecerit abortivum, si formatum non erat, mulctetur pecunia: quod si formatum, reddat anima pro anima'.

[33] 726C.

[34] 726D. For the embryo Pullen uses the word *seminarium*. His theory of generation is a curious one. Each parent, he held, contributed a liquid element,

embryo is fully formed it would either be linked in personal union with something which is not human; or, if not so linked, it would be unable to contribute to the growth of the embryo, and its presence would be superfluous [35]. Moreover, difficulties might arise for a soul in the general judgment if it had been united to an embryo which perished through miscarriage while as yet undeveloped. Another line of argument in support of his thesis which Pullen develops with much ingenuity depends for its validity on his theory of the mode of transmission of original sin [36].

Pullen defends the common Catholic teaching that the souls of all men are immediately created by God [37]. The opposite opinion, according to which the soul is transmitted by the parents along with the elements of the body, is known as the theory of traducianism. In rejecting this theory almost without exception the writers of the *Sentences* deriving from the School of Laon showed an unusual independence of their master, St. Augustine, who hesitated to pronounce definitely on this question. Pullen discusses the problem in his characteristic dialectical style. He excludes the possibility that the soul could proceed from one parent alone. His first argument is based on the simplicity of the substance of the soul which excludes division or composition on the part of the souls of the parents as a means of producing the souls of their offspring. Another means of refuting traducianism he finds in his favourite weapon of the *reductio ad absurdum*. If the soul is transmitted along with the elements of the body, it must remain extrinsic to them until they grow into the perfect embryo, as has already been proved. If the embryo perishes before birth, either the soul will remain without a body, with the anomalous consequence of souls greatly outnumbering bodies; or it will animate the bodily offspring of parents other than its own, in which case certain persons will have four parents, two of the body and two of the soul. Pullen finds theological support for his position in the text of the Epistle to the Hebrews; '*Moreover we have had fathers of our flesh for instructors, and we reverenced them*: *shall*

which was nothing else than blood which had changed colour under the excitement of coitus. From the union and coagulation of these elements the *seminarium* develops. The presence of male and female elements in the *seminarium* explains why physical characteristics of either parent are found in the offspring. See 729B, 726C-D. The theory is based on a passage of St. Augustine: 'ex sanguinibus enim homines nascuntur maris et feminae', In *Joann. Evangel. Tract. II, P. L.* 35, 1395A.

[35] 727B.

[36] 727D-728D.

[37] 728-731.

we not much more obey the Father of spirits, and live?' (xii. 9). This text appears to him decisive against the theory of traducianism [38].

A further question concerning the human soul discussed by Pullen, along with his contemporaries, was whether the soul is created in the body or outside it. He answers that the soul is created inside the body. This was the common opinion [39]. Pullen, as usual, discusses the question at greater length and with more subtlety than his contemporaries [40]. After disposing of the suggestion that the soul, if created outside the body, remains in proximity to it, in order to assist in its formation or to be conveniently placed for entering it at the appropriate moment, he rejects the opinion that souls descend from heaven as emanating from the 'philosophers' rather than from Scripture [41]. Moreover, a soul which had a pre-natal existence would possess wast stores of knowledge which presumably would be forgotten on its entry into a corruptible body. This, however, he comments, is nothing else than the heathen myth of the Cup of Bacchus [42]. The principal and most valuable knowledge which the soul would acquire would be that concerning the nature of God. With this knowledge it would grow in love and merit beyond what is possible for it when united with the body. Now it is unthinkable that God would allow such souls to be lost after incorporation, whether through their own guilt or through some mischance, since it is part of divine providence that when a soul grows, even in this life, unto perfect charity, God rarely permits it to be lost. Since, however, the loss of souls in this life is only too evident, it follows that they cannot have possessed this blissful pre-natal existence outside the body [43].

Granted, then, that souls are created within the body, and that as they proceed from the hand of God they are unstained by sin and unclouded by ignorance, how is it that they stand in need of a Redeemer? If, on the other hand, they are liable to these defects from the first moment of their union with the corruptible body, how can they be said to be good works of God? Pullen replies that the analogy of human creative work, in which the perfect form conceived by the artificer is but imperfectly realised be-

---

38 730D.

39 See *Summa Sententiarum, P. L.* 176, 92; *Sententiae Rolandi* ed. Gietl, 112; P. Lombard. *Sententiae* II, D. XVII, cap. 2.

40 731-3.

41 731B.

42 732A.

43 731-2.

cause of the imperfect material in which he works, enables us to understand how the soul, whose essence is good, is marred by the corruption it contracts from the body. Intelligence and rectitude belong to the soul in so far as it is the handiwork of God; obtuseness and depravity are the consequences of its association with the body which has been corrupted by original sin [44].

Human nature, criticism of Gilbert Porreta's doctrine

In the tenth chapter of the second book of the *Sentences* Pullen mentions and criticises a theory of the constitution of human nature which, he says, finds favour in certain circles [45]. According to this theory man is a composite entity made up of body and soul, a third nature different from each of its component parts [46]. Hugh of St. Victor describes the same opinion, though at greater length, and likewise takes sides against it [47]. Neither writer mentions by name those who hold the opinion in question. There can, however, be no doubt that they are attacking the teaching of Gilbert Porreta and his school. According to Gilbert and his followers, body and soul are united in such a way that a third nature (*subsistentia*) is formed, distinct from either taken separately. This nature or *subsistentia* was described as a substantial form [48]. It was known

---

[44] 733B-C.

[45] 733-4.

[46] 'Est igitur homo, ut quibusdam placet, quiddam ex anima et humano compositum corpore, ab utroque et natura diversum et numero tertium'. Ibid. 733C.

[47] Outlining Gilbert's theory Hugh writes: Hic autem solis verbis adhaerentes, ut non facile verborum involucra judicari potuissent, (Gilbert's terminology was notoriously involved and his meaning obscure), nisi in fine error se manifestus ostenderet. Dicunt hominem totum quoddam esse compositum ex anima et corpore, ita ut hoc totum nec anima sit, nec corpus sit, nec similiter anima et corpus; non enim totum ista esse, sed ex istis esse dicunt». *De Sacramen.* lib. II, p. l, cap. xi. *P. L.* 176, 406C.

[48] See Gilbert Porreta: *Commentaria in Librum de Duabus Naturis et Una Persona Christi, P. L.* 64, 1392D-1393C: 'Natura enim subsistentis est, qua ipsum subsistens aliquid est. Hae vero sunt substantiales formae, et quae illis in ipso subsistente adsunt qualitates et intervallares mensurae ... cum enim corpus animatur, vel anima incorporatur, fit hac corporis et animae conjunctione generatio animalis ... Unde animatio corporis et incorporatio animae subsistentiae videntur: et sunt utique, sed neque animae neque corporis, sed illius, quod ex his compositum est, animalis». Similarly the *Sententiae Divinitatis,* a work which follows Gilbert closely in the treatment of human personality: 'Quaedam vero junguntur per compositionem, ex quibus quiddam tertium redditur, ut anima et corpus in homine', ed. B. Geyer, *Beiträge* VIII, 2-3 (1909) 81.

as the *subsistentia* or *id quo*, that by which a person is a man, to distinguish it from the concrete person, the *subsistens* or *id quod,* who possesses manhood. Once the soul is separated from the body by death, says Gilbert, it is incorrect to speak either of the body or of the soul as a man; the man is merely a body and a disembodied spirit [49]. This refusal to recognise the disembodied soul as a man was sharply criticised by Hugh of St. Victor [50]. Along with the author of the *Summa Sententiarum,* Robert Pullen and Peter the Lombard, Hugh placed the essence of human personality in the soul. For these thinkers a man is nothing else than a soul which has a body [51]. The soul already constitutes a person before the body is brought into union with it. They admitted that the soul is wholly present, in every part of the body, but conceived this personal union as the apposition or association of two complete natures rather than as a union of two incomplete substances to form one complete human person or body-soul [52].

The thought of Gilbert Porreta was notoriously obscure to most of his contemporaries. His excessive realism brought him into conflict with ecclesiastical authority. Nevertheless his system contained much that was of value for future scholastic philosophy and theology. The Thomist theory of personality as developed in the thirteenth century under the influence of Aristotelian metaphysics

---

49 'Quicunque vero jam dissolutis anima et corpore non est homo, adhuc est et corpus et spiritus', *op. cit.* 1402D.

50 Outlining the theory under criticism Hugh writes: 'Quapropter quando homo moritur, et anima a carne separatur, divisis partibus totum ipsum quod ex eis compositum fuerat, jam nihil esse, ac per hoc ipsum hominem, qui hoc totum erat, similiter nihil esse, nec alicubi esse'. On this Hugh comments: 'Tales modos loquendi homines confingunt, et per falsas fictiones sermonum ad veras deceptiones errorum ducuntur. Quid enim stultius est quam dicere quod tunc homo esse desinat quando vere esse incipit, et tanto utique verius est, quanto est, verius in quo esse incipit?' *De Sacramentis,* Lib. II, p. I, cap. XI, *P.L.* 176, 407A-B.

51 'Quid enim magis est homo quam anima?' *De Sacramentis, l. c.* 407D; 'Quid est enim homo nisi anima habens corpus?' *Summa Sententiarum, P.L.* 176, 71A; 'Persona enim est substantia rationalis individuae naturae, hoc autem est anima', P. Lombard, *Sent.* III, D. cap. 5; 'Humana tamen caro dum animatur dici solet homo qui et de inanimato per animationem fit homo, et id permanet dum menti cohaeret' Pullen, *Sent.* 734C. Gilbert explicitly denies that the soul is a person, see *op. cit.* 1371D-1372A.

52 'Anima quippe in quantum est spiritus rationalis, ex se et per se habet esse personam, et quando corpus ei sociatur non tantum ad personam componitur, quantum in personam apponitur, *De Sacramentis,* 409B. 'Nugis igitur supersedentibus, naturas in homine duas personaliter cohaerere asseramus; duabus autem ex naturis hominem quasi tertium constare velut frivolum recusemus' Pullen, *Sent.* 734C.

is closer to the theory of Gilbert Porreta than to that of Pullen and Hugh of St Victor which was of Augustinian and Platonic ancestry.

According to the theory which he is criticising, says Pullen, the composite nature which is man is not affected by the quantitative changes of the body; rather is it on the same level as the soul, the other component element, as regards quantity[53]. This statement confirms the conviction that it is against Gilbert Porreta that Pullen is writing. In Gilbert's system personality-*id quo*-is a form or quality really distinct from the subsistent person-*id quod*[54]. Moreover, forms, whether accidental or substantial, are simple and invariable in essence. Though the elements which enter into composition do in a certain sense become greater by composition than they were beforehand, the form which is the result of composition is invariable and not subject to quantity[55]. Pullen seems to be thinking of this doctrine in his description of the theory which he is criticising.

Pullen's arguments against Gilbert's theory of a composite human nature are not very convincing. Firts he proposes philosophical reasons which he proceeds to support with a theological argument. If a man is something other than soul and body, he begins, we shall have to admit the existence of two entities in every person, entities which resemble each other so closely as to be in-

---

[53] 'Est igitur homo ... compositum, et natura diversum et numero tertium; quod nec unius partis additione augeatur, et alteri quantitati aequetur', 753C.

[54] See e. g. *Commentaria in Librum de Duabus Naturis et Una Persona in Christo, P.L.* 64, 1382B-C: '... si quis dicat, homo est risibilis; item, homo est individuorum forma: hominis nomen quidquid in una id in altera affirmatione significat: id est et id quod intelligitur homo, et id quo esse debet homo. Quorum significatorum illud, primum exposuimus, grammatici vocant substantiam. Illud vero quod secundo exposuimus, cujuscumque generis sit in omni facultate, qualitatem appellant. Sed in prima affirmatione non id quo est homo, id est nominis qualitas, sed is qui ea est homo, id est substantia nominis risibilis esse proponitur. In secunda vero affirmatione non is qui est homo, sed id quo est homo, id est nominis qualitas, individuorum forma dicitur'.

[55] In the *Liber Sex Principiorum* (a commentary on the last six of the ten categories of being) Gilbert writes; 'forma est compositioni contingens, simplici et invariabili essentia consistens. Compositio etenim non est, quoniam a natura compositionis sejungitur. Compositionum enim unaquaque alteri adveniens compositioni, majorem se conjunctam quodam modo efficit. In forma autem hoc minime est' *Cap.* I *De Forma,* ed. Albanus Heysse (Münster, 1929, recog. D. van den Eynde, 1953) 8.

St. Albert the Great who wrote a commentary on this work seems to be the first to assign its authorship to Gilbert Porreta. See S. Alberti Magni, *Liber de Sex Principiis,* Opera I (Paris, 1890) 305. The attribution is not incontestable.

distinguishable, since body and soul comprise each of them. It is useless to appeal to some difference between the two which is only perceptible to the eyes of the mind. There is no evidence for the existence of anything except a body which shows evident signs of animation by a soul. This, and this alone, is what we mean by a man. If any other entity exists every man is twofold, even as regards his body. Moreover, if what we see with our eyes is not a man, it follows that what we call a dead man never was a man[56].

This is ingenious enough as dialectic, but it fails to take account of Gilbert's distinction between *substantia* and *subsistentia,* between the person and the form by which he had personality. Pullen seems to imagine that the theory under review, in maintaining that the form or *subsistentia* of a man is different from that of a soul or body taken singly, makes some perceptible addition to the substance of the body. He is also misled by the fallacy that the human body has an independent and complete existence apart from its animation by the soul.

The theological argument is based on the words of the Athanasian Creed. « As the rational soul and the body are one man, so God and human nature are one Christ ». Pullen finds two arguments in this text in support of his position. The unity of God and human nature is not a unity of nature but of person; hence, infers Pullen, body and soul in man cannot be united in a single nature. Secondly, the text excludes all composition of the divine nature with human nature which would result in the production of a nature different from either; hence all composition of the human body and soul to form a distinct human nature is excluded. Body and soul are not parts of human nature but two natures united in one person[57].

The weakness of this argument from the Athanasian Creed lies in the supposition that the comparison between the hypostatic union and the union of body and soul in man holds good in every respect. This supposition is false. One point of difference which invalidates the argument of Pullen is that, whereas soul and body constitute one nature in man, the Word and human nature remain two distinct natures. Moreover, Pullen supposes that the union of body and soul to constitute one nature would mean confusion and alteration of the nature of each. This supposition is likewise

56 733D-734A.

57 ' Sicut ergo Deus et homo, homo totus, anima et corpus, unus est Christus, tribus substantiis non conficientibus quartam, sed convenientibus in unam personam; pari modo anima et caro unus est homo, conventu quidem naturarum, non partium ', 734C.

false, and was expressly excluded by Gilbert Porreta and his disciples who distinguished two different species of composition [58].

THE FACULTIES OF THE SOUL

Pullen's ideas about human psychology are a curious amalgam of Platonism, biblical exegesis and theological speculation. An attempt is made to conciliate the predominantly Platonic doctrine with some ideas derived from Aristotle's *Categories*. Running through the general theory there is a thread of polemic against the ideas of the School of Gilbert Porreta [59]. First, Pullen distinguishes three principal faculties of the soul: reason (*ratio*), the irascible passion (*ira*) and the appetitive passion (*concupiscentia*). Reason discriminates between good and evil; the two passions avoid or seek respectively those things which are harmful or beneficial to man's body or soul. In so far as the appetitive passion or concupiscence seeks the welfare of the body it is named sensuality. Sensuality is dependent for its activity on the operation of the five senses, but it is essentially a function of the soul. For this reason the soul is justly punished for the excesses of sensuality. For the same reason the soul is punished for the sins of the senses. Though these senses are powers of the soul, they are also to be considered instruments of the body. They serve the soul and body in different ways. Through them the body comes into contact with material objects, and, according to the quality of the contacts, the soul experiences pleasure or pain. Eating, for example, sets

---

58 'Duplex est modus unionis et diversi sunt modi sibi invicem conjungendi. Alia quidem per compositionem, ex quibus unum aliquid fit, alia per solam appositionem, ex quibus non fit unum; quae vero per compositionem, alia per commixtionem alterius vel utriusque, alia sine commixtione. Per commixtionem veluti cum mel et aqua commixtim funditur, neutram manet ... Quaedam vero junguntur per compositionem, ex quibus quiddam tertium redditur, ut anima et corpus in homine ... Haec enim manent nec aliquo modo vertuntur in alterutrum, sed nec unum in alterum nec in se invicem ... Quae vero sic junguntur per compositionem sine commixtione, quascunque rerum naturas retinent suisque imponuntur compositis, sicut corporis et spiritus natura non modo de corpore et spiritu verum etiam de homine vere dicitur. Omnis enim, ut dicit Boethius, natura partis natura totius'. *Sententiae Divinitatis, ed. cit.* 624. The parallel passages from Gilbert's commentary from which the passages in the *Sententiae Divinitatis* are taken are cited in the footnotes *ad loc.*

59 736-41. For a list of other theologians in whose works, all subsequent to Pullen's *Sentences*, may be found a classification of the powers of the soul see O. Lottin, *Psychologie et Morale aux XII*[e] *et XIII*[e] *Siècles*, I, 399 n. 1.

the body in movement, but gives pleasure to the soul; whereas, when the body is struck in battle the soul feels pain. So it is also with the operation of the other senses.

Plato, Pullen assures us, was aware that the soul contained within itself all the senses; for that philosopher, speaking in his usual enigmatic manner, said of the sensation of sight that the fire that is within us makes its way out through the eyes, becoming united to the fire that is without, and so united is borne to the material body that happens to be facing it. By repercussion from this body it re-enters the soul by the eyes, where it excites the sensation which we call vision. All that Plato intended by this description, explains Pullen, was that the centre of the sensation of vision is the soul, and that the function of vision is to illuminate visible objects. It does not pass out from the eye by local motion, but by the power of seeing (efficacia videndi). The exterior fire is light which co-operates with the faculty of vision. Plato also notes in the same treatise that the soul assists in sensation by certain movements. These movements are the senses which are located in the soul; they co-operate with the exterior instruments, such as the eyes, in the production of sensation [60].

Although the senses belong to the soul, Pullen continues, they are nevertheless corporeal, for, as Aristotle teaches, they are situated in and about the body [61]. They are corporeal, therefore, not because they inform the body, but because they cannot be present to the soul except through the medium of the body. A soul separated from the body has no senses. Hence a soul in hell will be tortured not by the anguish of the senses, but by realising the natures of its offences [62]. The senses are subject to sensuality or the appetitive faculty. In its turn this faculty is designed to be subject to reason, which is the instrument of moral judgements. Reason is a faculty of the soul. Is it conceivable that reason also belongs to man? This apparently odd question is intelligible if it is realised that Pullen has resumed his polemic against the theory which maintained that the nature of man is distinct from the nature of the soul or of the body considered singly. A glance at the description of that theory provided by Hugh of St. Victor makes it evident that Pullen has it in mind at this point. According to Hugh, the adherents of the theory against which he and Robert Pullen wrote, maintained that the properties of the com-

---

[60] 736A-B. Cf. Plato, *Timaeus* 45B-C.
[61] 736C.
[62] 736D.

posite nature which is man, were different from those of the parts considered singly. In particular the rationality that belongs to the complete nature of man is different from that which belongs to the soul, which is one of the component parts of that nature. So too with other qualities such as goodness[63]. In the present passage Pullen asserts that the only faculty of reason that we know is that which belongs to the soul, and that there is no distinct faculty of reason predicable of man, i. e. of a composite nature. He urges that it is difficult to see how one and the same faculty of reason can be both in the soul and the outward man, or how two separate faculties of reason could exist, one in the soul, the other in the outward man. If one and the same faculty is common to soul and body, how is it that it survives when this composite nature is dissolved by the death of the body? If the faculty of reasoning is similar, but distinct, in soul and body, then it is absurd to differentiate between the rationality of the soul and of the whole man[64]. Pullen pursues at some length this dialectical quibbling. Though ingenious it hardly touches the position of his opponents. It is vitiated by the supposition that the theory of Gilbert Porreta involves a duality of faculties and operations in man as a consequence of the union of soul and body in a third nature distinct from either soul or body considered separately[65].

Pullen attempts to secure the patronage of Aristotle for his essentially Platonic ideas. He refers to a passage in the *Categories*, in which the Philosopher taught that justice and injustice, irascibility and insanity, are qualities of the soul. When he went on to predicate them of the whole man, says Pullen, he was following the usage of popular speech, but, strictly speaking, these qualities, like those of skill in grammar or music or virtues like chastity, belong to the soul[66].

Not all the powers of the soul begin to operate at the same period. Concupiscence is active from the beginning, and is followed by irascibility. When the power of judgement is manifested then reason is present. Reason makes the soul like unto God;

---

63 'Postremo (dicunt) omnia quae in toto sunt diversa esse omnino ab his quae in partibus constant ... Itaque sicut rationalitas hominis alia est quam rationalitas animae; quia una totius est, et in toto est; altera partis est et in parte est; ita bonitatem totius quae in toto est, aliam esse dicunt, et bonitatem partis aliam, quia partis est et in parte tantum', *De Sacramentis*, Lib. II, p. 1. cap. II, *P. L.* 176, 406D.

64 737B-C.

65 738A.

66 738B. *Categoriae* 9b 34-10a 6. Pullen's citation of Aristotle derives

but if reason is not present in infancy, how can the soul be said to be made in the divine image? If it is present, why is the child unable to make use of it? A reason that is dormant can hardly be said to constitute anyone in the likeness of God. A soul in this state is hardly, it might appear, superior to the brute creation. Indeed in the activity and perfection of its senses the brute appears man's superior. Pullen answers that the superiority of the rational soul lies in its capacity for intelligence and virtue. This capacity will be fully perfected only in the next life when the creature that has merited heaven will behold the Creator face to face, and in Him all created reality[67]. Besides reason, the irascible and appetitive faculties, and the senses, Pullen numbers imagination among the powers of the soul. It is the power which enables the soul to represent absent objects. Along with all the other cognitive and appetitive faculties of man, with the exception of reason, imagination is common to man and the brute creation. This sharing in the faculties of cognition is proof that brutes have souls[68]. These souls are, however, irrational, and perish with the body they inform. Pullen proves in some detail that the survival of the brute soul would serve no useful purpose. He discusses its possible transformation into a rational soul and, as a pendant to this, the resurrection of its body, but dismisses both these fancies without hesitation[69].

Man in the state of original justice

Master Robert brings to the description of man's primal felicity in Paradise all the sources of his training in rhetoric. A rich vocabulary and sonorous and rhythmic sentences combine to build up a stately picture of the glory that passed from the human race with the sin of the first man and woman.

The earthly Paradise, so Pullen has read, lay towards the East. It was situated on a lofty plateau out of reach of the Deluge that came afterwards. It was protected from the extremes of heat and cold and from the pestilential variations to which our climate is subject[70]. Its soil brought forth fruits of every variety, and among

---

from the translation and commentary of Boethius. See *P. L.* 64, 248D.

67 739A-C.

68 740D.

69 740C.

70 Pestiferas nostri aeris vices omnes transcendit, 746B-C; cf. *D. C. M. ed. cit.* 209: 'pestiferas aeris immutationes'.

the trees that grew there was the Tree of Life, which by divine ordinance had the virtue of preserving from pain and death those who ate of its fruit [71]. Death is the penalty of sin. Had Adam not sinned, he and his posterity would have entered into eternal glory after their period of trial without the need of passing through the gate of death. His posterity would have included only those among men in the present order of Providence who are predestined to glory [72]. Now, however, besides the predestined there are among his descendants transgressors who will be lost. Their fate seems a necessary corollary of original sin; unless some men were lost, the elect would not sufficiently appreciate the mercy God has shewn them. If the number of the elect were less than those designed by God to be born in the event of a sinless human race, the ruin wrought by original sin would not have been fully repaired; if greater than that number, original sin might appear to have been positively advantageous [73].

Besides immunity from pain and death, man in the state of innocence enjoyed the privilege of integrity: evil desire and shame came after sin [74]. It is very probable too that the human body was much more beautiful than it is now; since we see that deformity and disease are sometimes punishments in those who have sinned personally after Adam [75].

To crown their happiness our first parents enjoyed the conversation of an angel, for that is what Scripture means when it says (Gen. iii. 8) that God walked and spoke in Paradise [76]. Therefore, as yet the man and the woman saw God only by faith, and not by vision.

THE FALL OF MAN AND ORIGINAL SIN

Although one positive precept only, that of refraining from the fruit of the tree which was in the midst of Paradise (Gen. iii. 3) was imposed on them, our first parents possessed freedom of will which they could abuse, and, indeed, did abuse in various ways. Both committed interior sins of pride before their outward act of disobedience. They had the assistance of divine grace, but this as-

---

[71] *Ibid.*
[72] 741B.
[73] 741B-C.
[74] 752B-753A.
[75] *Ibid.*
[76] 753C-D.

sistance did not compel their wills [77]. As a consequence of their interior sin the souls of Adam and Eve were corrupted. This corruption was communicated by the souls to their bodies, and these in their turn took their revenge by soliciting the souls with unlawful desires. In this way disharmony was set up in human nature, where before there had been peace; the soul lost its sovereignty over the body, and the body became subject to death. The discord then established between soul and body is the source of actual sins to which human nature is now so liable. Henceforth the mind of man is clouded by ignorance, his will enervated and shaken by passion, his senses enslaved by vanity. Concupiscence reigns in the soul, and it is only by the assistance of the healing grace of God that man can now rise superior to the wounds his nature has received from sin [78].

After describing the nature and consequences of original sin in the progenitors of the human race, Pullen proceeds to set forth his opinions on original sin as it exists in their posterity. The discussion is very involved and difficult to follow. On certain questions Pullen is somewhat hesitant. Here his conclusions will be put forward under three heads: the nature of original sin in the human race, the manner of its transmission, the reason why it is contracted.

Original sin is universal; for this reason it is called the sin of the world (John i. 29). In so far as it affects the soul of a newborn infant original sin, according to Pullen, consists chiefly, or even exclusively, in natural concupiscence. He makes this distinction because Scripture appears to say that all the descendants of Adam partook in some way in his original act of disobedience; whereas St. Augustine teaches that concupiscence is culpable until it has been condoned by the reception of baptism [79]. The only objection

---

[77] 750C-D.

[78] 754A-755C.

[79] 'Parvulis ergo originaliter reis concupiscentia aut maxime, aut sola originalis est macula'... 764B. 'Infans igitur duorum criminum reus, originali culpae implicatur et propriae, originali quia de Adam, inquit Apostolus: *in quo omnes peccaverunt*. Propriae, quia dicit Augustinus concupiscientiam cum parvulis nasci, baptismo a reatu solvi, ad agonem reliqui. Concupiscentiam ergo quoniam egeat venia liquet esse noxam: quoniam cum parvulis nata, et post baptisma remanet, liquet esse assiduam. Sed cum ratio non sinat citra discretionem, aliquid boni fieri vel mali, concupiscentiam necesse est accipi noxam, non utique actualem, verum quia cum parvulis nascitur, naturalem... merito igitur concupiscentia nuncupatur; quia concupiscendo est edita, et concupiscere movet illicita: quam si quis (quoniam in Adam praecessit, et ab ipso ad posteros defluxit) originale appellare malit, nec devius fortasse videatur nec absurdus'... 762D-763B.

to calling concupiscence original sin is that Scripture appears to speak of but one original sin, viz. Adam's act of disobedience. Pullen solves this difficulty by suggesting that Scripture equivalently and implicitly includes concupiscence under the term original sin [80]. Properly speaking the term original sin belongs to Adam's transgression, possibly because it gave rise to concupiscence and all evil [81]. On the other hand there is a difficulty in making Adam's descendants partakers in his act of disobedience, since they would then have a double guilt: in virtue of its generation from Adam an infant shares in the guilt of his sin of disobedience (but not in the other sins which he committed) [82]; it has in addition a personal guilt, since it is subject to concupiscence, which is culpable unless its guilt has been condoned by the sacrament of baptism [83]. In this double guilt that of concupiscence is graver than that which the soul incurs by participation in the disobedience of Adam. The participation was merely material; the soul itself could commit no actual sin before birth [84]. Nevertheless, there must have been some kind of participation for man to be made liable to the penalties of original sin [85]. There was a material participation in the sense that he who sinned was the ultimate source from which all the bodies

---

According to Pullen and his contemporaries original sin does not entirely destroy man's capacity for good: cf. 721A: 'In judicio praeceps, illicita affectans, piger et invalidus ad utilia, impetuosus ad inhonesta; liberum ergo arbitrium illiberabiliter est depressum, non tamen extinctum. Nam quemadmodum scintilla multo cinere pressa, quibusdam fomentis excitata, similis eluctanti, erumpit demum in flammam; ita mens nostra onere corruptae carnis gravatur quidem: attamen intenta sibi, nonnihil virium sibi restitisse residuum, in investigatione rerum demonstrat'. See A. Landgraf, *Dogmengeschichte der Frühscholastik,* 1, i, 100.

80 ... 'nisi forte quoniam dum et istud originale peccatum pronunciatur, bina originalia contra usum Scripturae inducuntur. Anne Scriptura dum alterum memorat, alterum subticendo negat? Est etenim illud originalis culpa, et dicitur; est fortasse et istud, sed non adeo dicitur: nonne tamen quoddamodo dicitur, dum cum parvulis nasci perhibetur; quippe cum parvulis non nasceretur, si parentes, et primi in nativa puritate perstitissent; non autem innasceretur omnibus nisi omnium esset. Nonne igitur originalis convincitur, eo quod omnes invadit ad quos a parentibus etiam primis profluit' ... 763B.

81 Alterum tamen sibi nomen hoc quasi proprium vindicavit. Sed quare? Ignoro; nisi forte quod et concupiscentiae et totius mali origo fuit: *ibid.*

82 'Igitur infans duorum criminum reus, originali culpae implicatur et propriae, originali quia de Adam, inquit Apostolus: 'In quo omnes peccaverunt' (Rom. v. 12). Propriae, quia dicit Augustinus concupiscentiam cum parvulis nasci in baptismo a reatu solvi, ad agonem relinqui. Concupiscentiam ergo, quoniam egeat venia, liquet esse noxam', 762D. See also 761A-C, 764D.

83 764C.

84 761-2.

85 761B-C.

of those who came after him were derived, and to that extent they were present when he sinned [86].

Original sin was transmitted to posterity by Adam and Eve through the act of generation. Their own bodies had been defiled by their sin; and the material elements derived from them, which went to form the bodies of their offspring, retained this corruption. On infusion, therefore, into bodies formed from these elements the souls of their offspring were at once infected with original sin [87]. In their turn the children of Adam transmitted a corrupt body to their descendants, and so the process has continued throughout human history. The corruption inhering in the material elements of man's corrupt bodily nature is increased by the concupiscence which accompanies the act of generation. But this increase of corruption is not transmitted; otherwise there would be a progressive growth in degree of original sin through successive generations of men [88]. Christ's body was immune from this corruption because of the miraculous manner of its conception [89]. Although human generation involves the transmission of a double corruption — of the soul and of the body — only that of the soul constitutes a state of sin [90]. Pullen considers his explanation of the manner in which the soul contracts original sin is sufficiently clear [91]. That bodies sprung from Adam should be subject to corruption he also thinks reasonable. What he finds impossible to explain is why souls immediately created by God and guiltless of personal sin should be defiled by contact with corrupt bodies. Here he acknowledges a mystery to which we cannot expect an answer in this life. In language which resembles that of William of Champeaux when faced with similar insoluble problems he bids us humbly confess our ignorance and await enlightenment in the life to come. Of only one thing can we be certain: God's ways are just [92].

---

86 '... quoniam ille solus in quo adhuc causaliter omnes seminaliterque coarctabantur, peccavit', 760C. 'Sic infans forsan peccator non ex eo quod adsit, sed quod in Adam praecessit, jam vocitatur. Ac per hoc, licet peccatum non habeat actu, habet reatu', 762B.

87 'Nam portiunculam corruptae massae detractam, ipsam quoque necesse est esse corruptam; ex qua, quasi vitiato ex semine vitiatus exsurgit fructus, homo, sed suis assimilatus parentibus', 755D-756A.

88 758D-759A.

89 756C-D.

90 759A.

91 759B.

92 'Quamobrem anima usque ad discretionem actualium exsors, solo participat originali, inde rea eaque juste quam occulte. Interim autem ignorantiam nostrae fragilitati debitam pie recognoscentes, nihil de occultis Filii

Pullen's theory of the nature and transmission of original sin shows the influence of the ideas of the School of Laon [93]. Among the ideas stressed by that School was the physical continuity of the human race with Adam, and the presence of concupiscence in the act of generation, as explanations of the transmission of original sin. Common to Pullen and the School of Laon is the affirmation that sins of Adam other than that of his disobedience do not affect his posterity, and the posing of the question regarding the justice of the act by which a soul is infected with original sin by the body.

The ultimate source of most of the speculations of this School is St. Augustine. In some respects Pullen was more faithful to the doctrine of St. Augustine than the compilers of the Laon *Sentences*. Unlike them, he did not make of concupiscence the sole formal element of original sin in mankind. He required with Augustine some participation in the guilt of Adam's sin. In including ignorance among the effects of original sin Pullen also manifests a closer dependence on the Augustinian system. The theories of the School of Laon came in for criticism at the hands of adherents of Abelard and Gilbert Porreta. Later theology was to revive the fruitful idea of St. Anselm of Canterbury that original sin as transmitted to the human race consists essentially in a privation of original justice. Although no great length of time separated the work of St. Anselm from that of the Laon School and of Robert Pullen, neither the anonymous collections of Laon, nor the *Sentences* of Pullen bear any trace of its influence.

---

contendamus, quoadusque manifestet occulta cordium et abscondita tenebrarum '.

93 On the theory of original sin current in the school of Laon see D. O. Lottin, 'Les théories du péché originel au XIIe siècle: 'L'école d'Anselme de Laon et de Guillaume de Champeaux', *R.T.A.M.* XI (1939) 17 ff.; and, on the influence of that school on Pullen, *ibid.* XII (1940) 240.

CHAPTER X

CHRISTOLOGY

THE INCARNATION

Pullen held that before the Redeemer came to save them, men had to learn by bitter experience their utter inability to know or do good without the assistance of divine grace. In the meantime God sent prophets to keep alive in their hearts the hope of a Saviour, and gave the Law to the Hebrews. From the infidelity of this people, which alone possessed the Law, all others could learn their own moral weakness [1]. Salvation was possible both within and without the Law; but the Law is rightly styled a law of death and servitude, since most of those who were subject to it were moved by servile fear and cupidity, so that ultimately they perished. Grace was offered under the Law, but sparingly in comparison with the New Testament dispensation, and temporal rewards were held out in order to secure a modicum of observance [2].

The purpose of Christ's incarnation was that He should offer his body as a new and sole sacrifice for sin, and inaugurate a priesthood worthy of so sublime a sacrifice, and a priestly law which would regulate its offering [3]. As his conception by a virgin was immune from concupiscence, Christ was untainted by original sin. The formation of his humanity was the work of the entire Trinity, although it is appropriated to the Holy Spirit as being a manifestation of divine love [4].

---

1 763-771.

2 'Lex ergo vetus servitutis est et mortis; nostra autem libertatis et gratiae; sub lege enim circumcisionis, tametsi gratia conferatur, longe tamen major baptizatis ... Tunc enim Spiritus timore turbavit, ut vel sic cogeret servituti. Nunc autem caritate donat, qua instructi tanquam filii obediant patri' 776D-777B.

Similarly Abelard in *Ep. ad Rom.;* but Richard of St. Victor reacted against the notion of the Old Law as a regime of fear. See A. Landgraf, Die Gnadenökonomie des Alten Bundes nach der Lehre der Frühscholastik, *Z. k. Th.* LVII (1933) 215-253.

3 778B.

4 781D.

To the question, at what precise moment was the hypostatic union effected, Pullen replies at the moment of the conception of Christ's body. Consequently, the union was effected before the infusion of Christ's soul [5]. In support of his opinion he appeals to the prayer, *Sancta Dei Genitrix, quae digne meruisti concipere quem totus orbis nequivit comprehendere,* and argues that, just as the conception of a man means the reception of the material elements of the human body, so the conception of God means the reception of God in personal union with the seminal elements of his human body. He alleges as a parallel the union between the divinity and the dead body of Christ in the sepulchre [6]. He deduces that this union of the divinity and the humanity is closer than that between soul and body, since it is prior to the union of soul and body, and is not dissolved by death. He insists on the reality of Christ's human soul, but firmly denies any confusion or composition of his human and divine natures, or of the three substances of Christ's body, soul and divinity [7].

So anxious is he to preserve orthodoxy of expression in his account of the hypostatic union, and to avoid any semblance of monophysitism, that at times he uses expressions which would almost lead one to think that he conceived the union to be an accidental one, after the manner of the third of the three explanations of the union mentioned by Peter Lombard [8]. This explanation is rightly attributed to Abelard [9], and logically leads to Nestorianism, as St. Thomas Aquinas demonstrated [10]. It cannot be

---

[5] Pullen held that the human soul was not infused into the body until the embryo had acquired a human shape. See ch. ix, *supra* pp. 168 ff. P. Lombard, *Sent.* III, d., and the author of the *Summa Sententiarum, P. L.* 176, 72, reject Pullen's view and maintain that the Word of God assumed a soul and body simultaneously, likewise later theologians with St. Thomas Aquinas, *Summa Theol.*, III, 33, 3. Pullen is prepared to admit that his reasoning is at fault on this point, and that the Word was simultaneously united to Christ's soul and body. See 791A, and cf. A. Landgraf, Das Axiom 'Verbum assumpsit carnem mediante anima' in der Frühscholastik, *Acta Pont. Academiae Romanae S. Thomae et Religionis Catholicae,* IX, Rome, 1944; id. *Dogmengeschichte der Frühscholastik,* II, i, 150-171.

[6] 782C-783B; 786C.

[7] 'Utraque enim natura id quod est, manet; nec unquam in alteram transit, sed alteri se conjungit, ut sit una persona substantiarum duarum, imo et trium, Dei animae et corporis. Nec enim verus homo esset absque anima, nec divinitatis officium est carnem vegetare' 784D.

[8] III *Sent.* d. VI. See A. Landgraf, *Dogmengeschichte der Frühscholastik,* II, i, 116-137.

[9] See *Theologia Schol. P. L.* 178, 1107-8; Joannes Cornubiensis, *Eulogium ad Alexandrum* III, *P. L.* 199, 1051-2.

[10] *In Sent.* III, d. VI, q. 3, a. 1; *Summ. Theol.*, III, q. 2, a. 6.

denied that there are some resemblances between Pullen and Abelard in their description of the question [11]. Yet Pullen, though making an essential distinction between the two natures, will not say with Abelard that the expressions God is ‘ flesh ’ or ‘ man ’ are not to be taken literally. He insists that Christ is not merely so called, but is essentially man and God, since He is but one person [12]. He is aware of the Abelardian distinction between proper and improper predication, but refuses to identify himself with it, insofar as it implies an irreverent criticism of the mode of expression used by the saints in treating of the union [13]. He holds that Christ is not merely the possessor of two natures, but is identified with them [14]. By this formula he would appear to exclude a merely accidental or dynamic union between the Godhead and the humanity. His considered conclusion is that one and the same person subsists in the hypostatic union in virtue of the union between Him who is one person in the Trinity and the entire humanity which has been assumed. Hence He subsists through a union of one person and two substances (the human soul and body). Further, as this person does not become incarnate without his (divine) substance, by which He is personally united to the other two, He is thus also a person of three substances [15].

In the union of the three substances Pullen sees the explanation of the unity of person in the hypostatic union. Just as in a man personal unity consists in the conjunction of his soul and body, so in Christ the unity of person consists in the much closer

---

11 Abelard writes: ‘Cum ergo ... spiritus sit Deus, nec unquam quod spiritus est corporeum fiat, ... quomodo proprie vel Verbum dicitur fieri caro, vel Deus homo? ’, *l. c.* 1107A-B. Pullen says: ‘Deus essentialiter homo non est, quia cum sit spiritus, non potest esse corpus; Deus homo personaliter est, quia, licet sit spiritus, nihilominus corpori hominis unitur. Unitur homini ut anima corpori ’, 786C.

12 ‘ Quoniam ergo non est nisi unus Christus, ipseque est non nuncupative, sed essentialiter homo et Deus, constat quod Christus, qui non est nisi unus, est tamen duarum substantiarum, imo et ambae substantiae; altera semper exstitit, altera esse coepit: qui erat infectus, is est factus: Creator factus est creatura 787A-B.

13 ‘ Auctorum tamen usum veneramur, sanamque sententiam, quoquo modo se habeant, verba, amplectimur, nec improprium dicimus quod sanctorum probat usus, magis tamen proprie aliud alio dici arbitramur ’. 788D.

14 *Supra* n. 12.

15 ‘ Mihi ita videtur proprie loquendum: persona una et eadem subsistit ex ea, quae est una in Trinitate persona et humanitate assumpta integre; ergo subsistit ex persona una et substantiis duabus: et quia ista persona non est incarnata, nisi cum sua substantia, qua reliquis duabus personaliter est unita, est quoque illa persona trium substantiarum ’. 792D-793A.

union of the divinity and the complete humanity[16]. This union is an effect of grace, so that although by nature God is not man, nor man God, they are so by grace[17]. Pullen affirms, therefore, that the union of the two natures (or three substances) constitutes personality in Christ[18]. By this statement he appears to mean that, though there are two natures (or three substances) in Christ, there is but one *suppositum naturae*; that Christ's body and soul are united to his divine nature in such a way that they belong to his personality. If this interpretation is correct, Pullen's view of the union is substantially the same as the second opinion mentioned by the Lombard, as expounded by St. Thomas[19].

Against this conclusion it might be objected that according to the second opinion, Christ is not only one person (*unus*), but also one subsistent reality (*unum*), since there is but one 'suppositum' of his two natures[20]; whereas Pullen appears to deny that Christ can be called *unum*. Examination, however, of Pullen's assertions make it evident that he is merely stressing the fact that there is no confusion or composition of the two *natures* of Christ[21]. He has no intention of asserting, as did the first view described by the Lombard, that Christ's human nature constitutes a reality which is additional to the reality conferred by its union with the person of the Word.

---

[16] 'Igitur personae unitatem, sicut in homine dicimus suam animae et carnis conjunctionem; ita et in Christo similem quidem, firmiorem tamen divinitatis, atque integrae humanitatis suam connexionem' 788B.

[17] 'Quare nec Deus homo, nec homo Deus per naturam est, attamen per gratiam est. Haec gratia Deum et hominem effecit unam personam, propter quam Deus et homo unus est Christus'.

[18] 'Hanc ergo connexionem arbitror proprie appellari personam'. 788B.

[19] 'Secunda opinio dicit, quod istae duae substantiae assumptae ita conjunguntur divinae personae quod pertinent ad personalitatem ipsius, adeo quod sicut persona verbi ante incarnationem subsistebat in natura divina; ita post incarnationem subsistit in humana et divina'. In III *Sent.* d. VI. Cf. *ibid.* Q. 1. a. 3. 'Secunda vero opinio dicit, quod constitutum ex duabus naturis tantum non est hypostasis subsistens, sed natura in qua subsistit verbum Dei unde non potest ponere, quod constitutum ex duabus substantiis tantum sit suppositum cui nomen imponitur, sed forma a qua imponitur, scilicet humanitas: illud vero cui nomen imponitur, quod est subsistens in humana natura, est persona verbi; et ideo nomen hoc *homo* comprehendit tres substantias; sed duas ex parte significati, tertiam ex parte suppositi'.

[20] Cf. St. Thomas, *ibid.* q. II a. 1.

[21] 'Quid est, homo est Deus, nisi unitus Deo? Quid autem est homo est unitus Deo, nisi homo et Deus est unus, imo anima, et caro et Deus sunt unus? Unus quidem, non unum; nam anima, et caro, et Deus, utique unus sunt, quia una persona sunt ... nulla ratione item unum sunt, quia una natura non sunt; procul dubio tria sunt, qui tres substantiae sunt'. 786C-D; cf. 734B.

Pullen further illustrates the unity of person in Christ by distinguishing different stages of the hypostatic union. These are, successively, the union of the divinity with the as yet inanimate body, with the animate body, with the dead body, and finally with the glorified body of Christ. These four conditions of the body do not, he says, involve the existence of four distinct persons. God was one person with the body and soul of Christ in their state of union, but not as a result of their union; otherwise He would be personally united with every man, since He is present in all men. Hence, as the union of Christ's body and soul was not the cause of his unity of person, so their separation could not be a cause of its multiplication [22].

Nor does the hypostatic union add a fourth divine person to the Trinity. The term ' person ' has different connotations when applied to the Trinity and the hypostatic union. In the Trinity there are in one nature (substantia) three eternal, co-equal persons. In the hypostatic union the term ' person ' connotes an operation of grace, by which three substances of God, a human body and a human soul are united in one person. One of these substances or natures is identical with one of the persons of the Trinity. Consequently the hypostatic union does not involve the existence of a fourth divine person [23].

One of the consequences of the hypostatic union is the communication of properties (*communicatio idiomatum*), in virtue of which the properties and operations of both the human and the

---

22 'Sed quoniam carni unitur Deus prius inanimatae, post animatae: item exanimatae, postremo ad immortalitatem ressuscitatae: num quatuor modis variata carne, quatuor quoque sunt personae? Absit! ... Verum quoniam tunc corporis divisio erat et animae, nonne divisae erant personae? Hoc quoque absit! Corpus namque et anima, una interim non erant persona. Sed Deus cum anima, licet non cum sola, una persona: Deus item cum corpore licet non cum solo, una persona; nec una et altera, sed una sola. Quippe carne et anima conjunctis, non pro tali conjunctione, Deus manens in illis, una est persona cum illis; alioquin una persona foret ex Deo et quovis homine: sed quoniam Deus naturae unitur utrique, est persona cum utraque '. 789D-790B.

23 ' Sed cum fide catholica Trinitatem docemur, quomodo quaternitas personarum inducitur? Tres personae sunt Pater, et Filius, et Spiritus sanctus; quomodo quarta est ex connexione Filii Dei, atque filii hominis et anima? Sed hanc cum illis numerandum non puto; quippe longe differenter hic atque ibi dicitur persona. Ibi namque tres personae sunt et una substantia, hic tres substantiae sunt et una persona; hic tres substantiae una persona sunt, ibi tres personae una substantia sunt ... Personam hanc conjunxit gratia, illae coaeternae sibi sunt ex natura; hanc ergo nec computes illis, nec reputes quasi unam ex illis; quippe una hujus personae natura una est in Trinitate persona '. 791C-D.

divine natures are attributed to the one *Person* of Christ. As Dr. A. Landgraf has remarked, the early scholastics were from the beginning familiar with this doctrine, and sought to explain and analyse it [23a]. Pullen expounds the doctrine with great precision, and justifies it by an appeal to the authority of Scripture and to daily usage [23b].

The endowments of Christ's human nature

Christ did not exclude from his human nature the limitations that belong to humanity. Sin, however, and ignorance, its consequence, He did exclude. Therefore, the text of Luke (ii, 52), which speaks of Christ as growing in wisdom and age and grace before God and man, must be read along with St. John's testimony (i, 14) that He was ' full of grace and truth ', and must be taken to mean that the plenitude of his gifts was daily more clearly manifested. Neither his office of Redeemer nor his human condition required Christ to progress from ignorance to knowledge. Had there been no original sin, it is probable that human beings would have had the use of reason from birth, although differences of intellectual capacity would still have existed as a consequence of differences of heredity. Certain results of the fall of man, such as liability to hunger and fatigue Christ accepted, and, had He not

---

[23a] *Dogmengeschichte der Frühscholastik* II, i, 138.

[23b] ' Non tamen fiebat caro, quomodo nec homo, versibilitate naturae, verum conjuntione. Non enim divinitas versa est in humanitatem, ne sit confusio substantiae; sed haec illi conjuncta est, ut sit unitas personae. Utraque auctoritas, altera per conceptum, altera per incarnatum, eumdem Dei Filium innotescit, mortuum atque sepultum: quod nunquam vere diceretur, nisi in unam convenirent personam Deus et mortuus sive sepultus. In hunc modum plerisque legendo locis invenies, matrem Dei Mariam concepisse Deum et peperisse, Deum passum, caeteraque magis congrua humanitati. Quoniam quoties diversae naturae personaliter uniuntur, consuevit et Scriptura et quotidianus usus, quod est alterius, alteri assignare. ... Deus ergo, nec sepultus nec mortuus, nec incarnatus, nec conceptus recte videretur, nisi conceptui atque carni, mortuo quoque ac sepulto, modo junctus personali intelligeretur. Sicut Filium Dei nunquam vocares filium hominis, nisi una persona Deum et hominem fuisset complexa. Deus factus est homo, et cum unum et alterum sunt, tamen unus; sic Filius Dei factus est filius hominis: et cum sint duae essentiae, et tamen unus, nonne etiam sunt unus Filius? Similiter sapiens Dei Filius, sapiens hominis filius, ita quoque Magister, Redemptor, Salvator, nonne ita duae sunt naturae, persona tamen una, ut sint Redemptor quoque unus et Salvator, Magister quoque et sapiens unus, juxta illud: Unus est enim Magister vester ':784A-C.

suffered a violent death He would have been liable to death through senescence [24].

Against pseudo-philosophers Pullen asserts, both in his *Sentences* and in his sermons, that Christ's birth left his mother's virginity intact. This was a prerogative which Christ shared with no other man, either before or after the fall. It was an effect proper to his state of glory, comparable to the beatific vision, which He possessed during his earthly life, and to his power of walking on the waters [25].

On the sanctity of Christ, Pullen remarks that, as He had from the beginning of his life the fulness of grace, his human nature did not advance in merit through the performance of successive acts of virtue. His virtues were continuously manifested, but they did not produce a corresponding increase of interior sanctity. In this He differs from the saints, who grow daily in holiness. As his charity was perfect from the beginning, so was his merit complete [26].

Christ's power was manifested by the miracles which He worked. These were worked by Christ in his human nature, just as in that nature He redeemed the world, and in that nature will judge it. Therefore, the human nature is also an object of our veneration [27]. Yet it is not the equal of the divine nature, either in power, wisdom or goodness. Texts of Scripture which suggest the contrary, such as, '*All power is given to me in heaven and in earth*' (Mt., xxviii, 18); are to be understood to mean that the human nature received these gifts from God to the limit of its capacity. Though it is immeasurably superior to any other created nature, it remains a creature infinitely inferior to the nature of God. This is indicated by such texts as, '*None is good but God alone*', (Mt. xviii, 19), and by the fact that God could have created other human natures in which the Father or Holy Spirit could have become incarnate, and which would have been equal

---

24 793A-795A. The question whether Christ's body was mortal by nature or by his free choice was much disputed in the twelfth century, and gave rise to many various solutions. It was due to Peter Lombard that the opposition between necessity and freedom was settled by his teaching that Christ freely assumed a body which was by nature mortal. See A. Landgraf, Die Sterblichkeit Christi nach der Lehre der Frühscholastik, *Z. k. Th.* LXXIII (1951) 257-312; *id. Dogmengeschichte der Frühscholastik*, II, i, 199-272.

25 793B-D; serm. 13: 'Philosophica namque ratio contraria est eternis bonis, et solum naturam sequitur, id est cursum nature, dum non patitur uirginem esse post partum, idem corpus in diuersis locis'.

26 798.

27 801-804.

in dignity to the human nature of Christ. It was not, however, fitting that a person of the Trinity should become incarnate as the Son of Man who was not already in the Trinity the Son of God [28].

Another question commonly raised in the schools was that of the impeccability of Christ. On this point Pullen observes that certain authors argue that, as Christ was made like to his brethren in all save sin, He possesed free will, and consequently had the power of sinning. That He remained sinless, though not impeccable, redounds all the more to his glory. However, most writers, adds Pullen, deny altogether that Christ could sin. He himself is content to say that such impeccability was the effect of divine grace; hence the goodness of the divine nature exceeds by far that of Christ's human nature [29].

The possibility of sinning, as of meriting, presupposes in Christ two wills, one human, the other divine. Pullen, along with all other theologians, sees the existence of these wills manifested in Christ's prayer in Gethsemane. Yet his prayer to be relieved of the chalice of his passion implied no derogation from the rectitude of his human will. His fear was deliberately permitted, in order to hearten the saints in their hours of unforeseen fears and repugnances [30]. On that occasion Christ's fear was not servile, since He was filled with the spirit of charity, but rather is to be attributed to the sentiment of reverence [31].

Among the theological virtues Pullen assigns to Christ in his human life charity, and, to some extent, hope. Christ's charity towards God was manifest, as also towards those who were to believe in Him. Yet Pullen finds it hard to explain in what sense Christ loved effectively those whom He knew would finally perish. He can do no better than suggest that Christ's outward expressions of love towards them were but the outward expression of a natural compassion for their ultimate fate, or were directed towards their ideal selves, to which they never attained [32].

---

[28] 801D-805C; 806B-807A; 810C-811A.

[29] 805C-806B. Pullen is not concerned here to decide between the opinion of the Abelardians, who maintained that Christ could sin, and their opponents, but to prove the superiority of his divine nature over his human nature. His own opinion that the sinlessness of Christ is due to the hypostatic union suggests that he sided with opponents of the Abelardians. See *supra* 102 f., and on the contemporary controversy A. Landgraf, Die Unsündbarkeit Christi in den frühesten Schulen der Scholastik, *Scholastik*, XIII (1938) 367-391; *Dogmengesch. der Frühscholastik* II, i, 320-370.

[30] 814B; 812C.

[31] 816C.

[32] 'Cum autem Judam Dominus noster amicum vocavit, non qualis esset, verum qualis esse deberet, expressit': 818B.

Instead of the theological virtue of faith, Christ, says Pullen, enjoyed the beatific vision of God throughout his life. He argues that if Christ had lived his human life by faith, his love of God would have been capable of increase when He attained to the vision of God, and in his earthly life He would have been surpassed in wisdom and charity by the least of the angels in heaven. Since both of these consequences are contrary to reason and authority, Pullen concludes that Christ's state on earth differed from that of the just, inasmuch as He already possessed God by vision instead of faith; his hope was restricted to his resurrection and ascension; and his charity, being aware of the ultimate fate of all men, embraced only those whom He foresaw were destined for salvation [33].

Along with contemporary and subsequent theologians Pullen was faced with reconciling his conclusion that Christ possessed the beatific vision with the sufferings incident to his earthly existence. He makes a distinction between the sufferings of the body and those of the soul; and asserts a corresponding twofold glorification. The glorification (stola) of the soul consists in the vision of God, which is granted to the just straightway after death; that of the body is the state of glory reserved for it until the end of time [34]. He solves his problem, however inadequately, by asserting that Christ possessed the former glorification in his lifetime, but imperfectly, since He could feel pain at the spectacle of human sin. The latter He did not possess until after his death [35].

The redemption

Pullen teaches clearly that Christ's death was a redemptive sacrifice [36]. He asserts that Christ could have redeemed mankind in some other way than by suffering a violent death; but sees in the price paid an index of his love [37]. Even if the Jews had not

---

33 818D-819C.

34 'Primam stolam, visionem scilicet Dei, animae sanctorum, exutis corporibus mox accipiunt' 819D. Pullen's thought and terminology anticipate the first definition on this subject to be made nearly two hundred years later by Benedict XII: 'animae sanctorum omnium ... mox post mortem suam ... vident divinam essentiam visione intuitiva'. Const. 'Benedictus Deus', 29 Jan. 1336, Denz. 530. Cf. *infra* 275 f.

35 820B-C.

36 '... sacrificium, scilicet, mei corporis inducens, dignumque tanto sacerdotium sacrificio': 778A. Cf. 821C.

37 820B-C; 712A-B, cf. *supra* 100-102. Pullen's insistence that the redemption could have been accomplished in some other way than by the crucifixion and death of Christ, distinguished his doctrine on this subject from that of

crucified the Saviour, the sufferings involved in his living a human life en earth would have been sufficient to reconcile mankind to God. Pullen emphatically denies that any ransom was due to the devil for man's redemption. To the argument that the price of the redemption had to be paid to him who held mankind captive, and that this was none other than the devil, he replies that the suggestion is impious; and in any case the devil would never have accepted a payment which was to deprive him of the power which he had been permitted to exercise over men for their chastisement. The devil would never have provoked the crucifixion if he had known who Christ was [38]. In fact, as soon as he became aware of this, he tried through the intervention of Pilate's wife to halt the process; but the passions he had aroused had become too strong for him to control. Christ, therefore, offered the sacrifice of his life to his Father, whose will He obeyed by the acceptance of suffering. God was pleased to accept this offering as a ransom for captive humanity, and thus humiliate the devil. By his endurance of suffering Christ also gave us an example that, as He suffered for the good of others, so we should not shrink from suffering on his behalf to our own spiritual profit [39].

In Pullen's denial that Christ offered a ransom to the devil there seems to be an allusion to a contemporary controversy — that between St. Bernard and Abelard — on the devil's power and rights over fallen man. Pullen, like Abelard, denied that the devil had any rights over mankind, but by his own denial that Christ offered a ransom to the devil showed that he was able to set its true value on the metaphorical language of such writers as Origen, who had spoken of the blood of Christ as a ransom paid to the devil [40].

Abelard. In certain other respects Abelard's views on the redemption seem to have influenced him, cf *infra* n. 38 and A. Landgraf: Literarhistorische Bemerkungen zu den Sentenzen des Robertus Pullus, *Traditio* 1 (1943) 216 f.

38 'Sed omnino absit nefarium illud nefas, quod salvator proditori, diabolo Deus se inclinans, pretiosam (quod utique idolatria foret), obtulerit mortem. Neque enim munus tale reciperet; unde se sciret potestate privandum; nimirum si cognovisset, nunquam dominum gloriae crucifixisset': 821B.

39 'Christus ergo, factus obediens Patri usque ad mortem, cui sacrificium passionis obtulit, nisi cui patiendo obedivit? Nimirum cui quis obedit, ei obedientiam ascribit. Hujus autem oblationis pro pretio placuit Deo captivos reducere, calumniatorem humiliare. Christus ergo ignominiosa tulit et aspera, ut neutrum expavescas pati pro Christo ad commodum proprium, quod ipse haud est pati dedignatus commodum propter alienum'. 821C.

40 Cf. Abelard, *In Rom. P.L.* 178, 833, 835; S. Bernard, *Ep. De Erroribus Abelardi, P.L.* 182, 1062-64; Origen., *In Rom.* 3, 7, *P.G.* 14, 945; *In Mt.* 16, 8, *ibid.* 1937.

The effect of Christ's passion and death was to obtain forgiveness of sins for all mankind. Whether they lived before or after Christ, men are justified only by faith in his passion. Many were thus justified before Christ's advent, says Pullen, but they did not receive recompense for their merits or forgiveness of their sins until Christ descended into hell after his death [41]. There they waited immune from suffering, except in the measure required for the expiation of their sins, until at the descent of Christ they were adorned with the perfection of justice which comes from the redemption. Only when their justice was completed by that of Christ was it a sufficient title to glory. Until his coming the just had been confined in the upper regions of hell. Thither Christ's soul descended, temporarily separated from his body, but ever united to his divinity [42]. Pullen sees in the descent of Christ into hell a further proof of his charity, as He could have liberated the just without descending into their infernal abode [43]. He thinks it probable that Christ freed all the just in hell, even those who had not as yet expiated all their sins. Some of those thus freed were permitted to resume their bodies for a time, in order to give testimony of Christ's resurrection. These, Pullen surmises, were probably the Hebrew patriarchs and prophets [44].

Christ's glorification

Accompanied by the souls of the just Christ's soul rose from hell, and rejoined his body, which now became glorified, immortal and impassible. During the forty days of his risen life on earth Christ tempered the glory of his body, in order that his disciples might be able to recognize Him and converse with Him [45]. During this period He taught his disciples, frequently appearing to them, and attended by the invisible band of the liberated spirits. At the Ascension He passed into heaven, and will not come again on earth until the day of judgement. Consequently all accounts of appar-

---

41 823A-B. 'Nostri, quoniam jam sunt redempti, jam sunt tales ut debeant in coelum ascendere. Nostri ergo plene fiunt justi, unde mox coelo honorantur. Antiqui autem nequaquam tempore suo plene justificabantur, unde vita aeterna differebatur ... Meritum antiquorum tunc est impletum quando merito Christi est adjutum, ut jam cum alio ad obtinendam gloriam sufficiat, ad quod ante (nimirum per se) non sufficiebat'. 823C-824A.

42 824C-D.

43 828A.

44 828D-830D.

45 829C.

itions of Christ to the saints must be understood either as visions of angels acting on Christ's behalf, or it must be supposed that the saints were granted a vision of Christ in heaven. In like manner it is not the saints themselves who have appeared to the living, but angels. Christ Himself is now seated at the right hand of God, which means, says Pullen, that He is reigning equal with the Father, or reposing after labour in the enjoyment of more excellent blessings, and from thence He sends forth his and his Father's Spirit for the perfecting of his disciples [46].

---

[46] 831D.

CHAPTER XI.

GRACE

THE NATURE OF JUSTIFICATION

Pullen does not use the term 'justification', but he does speak of 'justice' through which a man is worthy of eternal life [1]. The state of justice consists essentially in the possession of the virtue of charity [2]. Charity begets other virtues, and gives to all of them whatever worth they may have. The acquisition of other virtues, to which the way is indicated by the teaching of Scripture, increases the holiness which charity has inaugurated [3]. In particular faith and hope, if accompanied by charity, point the way to God [4]. Faith and hope are necessary in this life only: charity endures after death. Charity consists in the love of God above all things, and of one's neighbour above all else but God [5]. Under the term 'neighbour' Pullen expressly includes pagans and Jews, and all men of whose ultimate damnation we have no certain knowledge [6].

---

1 'Justus enim ex fide vivit, quod est, qui ex fide fit justus, ex justitia fit viva dignus:' 823D-824A.

2 'Sola caritas ea virtus est quae virum bonum creat: 854B.

'Species aromatum sunt diversa genera virtutum. Necessarium est, si volumus ut fumum compunctionis vel odorem bone opinionis he species de se generent, ut in igne caritatis, que mater et fundamentum est omnium virtutum ponantur:' Serm. 15: '... Nemo justus est nisi per caritatem: 860A.

3 'Caritatis pro initio, aliarum quoque virtutum accessio jam natam bonitatem accumulat, scientia scripturarum per omnia praestante ducatum: 854C.

4 'Excellentissimam nobis viam ad Deum Apostolus demonstrat esse tria haec: fidem, spem, caritatem. Cum quibus nemo est malus, sine quibus nemo est bonus: 816D.

Cf. Serm. 4: 'Si ergo volumus ut Deus sit in nobis, duo congregentur in nobis, id est, bona voluntas et operatio coniungantur, vel tres, id est, fides, spes, caritas simul habeantur, et tunc erit Christus in medio regens animam ut bene cogitet et bene velit, et corpus etiam, ut bene operetur'.

5 'Caritas quippe est amor Dei atque proximi, amplectens Deum super omnia, proximum autem super cetera: 816D.

6 'Proximus dicitur omnis homo vivens, quoniam omnes homines proximi nobis sumus, (sunt?) quia conditione naturae ad invicem cohaeremus'. 817A. Cf. Serm. 18: 'Hoc ideo commemoro quatenus caritate salutis optan-

Yet, following St. Augustine, he admits that it is not necessary to love all men with the same intensity and fervour. It is essential that we should desire the same spiritual blessings for all men, and assist all, as far as our resources permit, in their spiritual and temporal needs. There is evident in Pullen's spiritual works a genuine sympathy with the poor and the oppressed [7].

He defines faith with the author of the Epistle to the Hebrews (xi. 1) as *the 'substance of things to be hoped for, the evidence of things that appear not'*. Hence by faith doubt of the eternal blessings is excluded; by hope we trust we shall attain them through a holy life. Without faith there can be neither hope nor charity; and without charity faith and hope are vain [8].

The process of justification

Though justification consists essentially in the possession of charity, it is founded on faith, and has never been possible without faith, whether for Jews or Gentiles before the coming of Christ, or for those living under the New Law [9]. Those who lived before Christ were but imperfectly and incompletely justified. Their sins were not forgiven them; yet because of their faith in the Redeemer to come, they were not condemned to punishment. Only when Christ's atoning death had been offered for their sins did

---

de amicos et inimicos, paganos et iudeos non sicut ethnici, sed sicut Christiani discamus diligere. Cf. *Sent.* 818: 'Unde quos scimus reprobos, sive iam mortuos, ut Neronem, sive adhuc morituros, ut Antichristum, a nostro alienamus affectu'.

7 See especially *De Contemptu Mundi, ed. cit.* pp. 212-214.

8 'Fide nimirum quae nobis occulta est, condere arguimur, fide de aeternis quae sperantur bonis ambigere non sinimur, ac per hoc quodammodo certa in nobis firmaque subsistunt; bona autem quae credendo futura exspectamus, bene vivendo adipisci speramus. Fidem imprimis habere necesse est, sine qua nec quid speres, nec quid ames intelligis. Sed quid prodest more impiorum bona malave credere futura, absque spe adipiscendi bona, effugiendi mala? Spes autem semper vana est, nisi merito caritatis digna est obtinere quod optat. Quare quoniam per fidem nondum cognita, quasi per speculum in aenigmate videmus; per spem autem nondum comprehensa expectamus:' 817A-B.

On the development of the scholastic doctrine of sanctifying grace from the commentaries of the early scholastics on the Pauline teaching on justification by faith see A. Landgraf, *Dogmengeschichte der Frühscholastik,* 1, i, 203-219; id. Die Erkenntnis der heiligmachenden Gnade in der Frühscolastik. *Scholastik,* III (1928) 28-64.

9 'Et ante et mosaicae legis tempore, salus est ex gentibus. Unde?... utriusque ex fide:' 771B.

they achieve forgiveness and the perfection of justice which belongs to the New Law [10]. It is evident from the contrast which Pullen draws between the justice of the Old and the New Covenants that he considers the latter to be an imparted, intrinsic justice, and not merely an imputed extrinsic justice. The latter appears to be his notion of the justice attributed to the just of the old Law up to the time of the Redemption.

Faith in one God and in a Redeemer to come was sufficient to save those who lived before Christ. For Christians, however, the articles of saving faith are wider. They include the virginal birth of Christ, his passion, resurrection and ascension, and explicit faith in the Trinity [11]. Yet neither Christians nor others can attain salvation by faith alone. Charity and good works are

---

[10] 'Neque enim id virtutis eorum merita habebant, ut quod mala ad inferna traxerunt, eos bona ad coelos sublevarent, donec veniret Christus, cujus merita praecedentium patrum insufficientiam supplerent; ut merita antiquorum per Christum accepta Deo, digna tandem fierent munerari coelo. Interim autem neque bona retribuebat, quippe tanto praemio non satis digna; neque mala condonabat, quoniam nondum pretium erat datum; sed neque puniebat quos fides venturi excusabat. Itaque quasi induciis positis, praecedentium delicta sustentabat, ut in morte Christi remitterentur, atque in hoc tempore justitia plena antiqui illustrarentur. ...Antiqui itaque sancti quod prius non habent, tempore gratiae consequuntur; eam videlicet perfectionem, quam nostri sancti nostro tempore adipiscuntur: 823B-D. Cf. 822A: 'Justus ex fide fit, in fidei justitiaeque signum, conservationem atque incrementum suscipiens baptismum atque opus bonum; jam perfecte sanctus, tanquam passione redemptus.

[11] Cf. Serm. 5: 'Ratio igitur, cum tandem convalescit, fidem excitat et de morte resuscitat. Quod innuit ubi ait: Numeravit ccc & xciii vernaculos. Tau autem apud Hebreos, que figuram habet crucis Christi, trecentos significat. Per trecentos igitur passionem Christi intelligimus, per quam nos liberari et salvari confidimus. Sed attendendum est quod tres dicendo insinuet nobis quedam ita de Christo esse credenda, videlicet natum, passum resurrexisse. Per centum autem qui sequuntur ascensionem dedit intelligendam, et congrue. Centenarius enim numerus apud compotistas ex leva transit in dexteram. Et Christus in ascensione a leva ad dexteram, ab hoc mundo transivit ad patrem. Unde in Canticis: Leua eius sub capite meo, et dextera illius amplexabitur me. Qui igitur credit Christum natum de uirgine, passum resurrexisse, addat et ut credat eum ad celos ascendisse, et sic numerauit trecentos. Non solum autem trecentos, sed et xviii Abraham numerauit, per quod fidem Trinitatis cum bonis operibus habendam designauit. Constat enim xviii ex senario multiplicato per ternarium. Per ternarium igitur fidem Trinitatis, per senarium bona opera intelligere debemus. Dominus enim sex diebus operatus est, et septimo requieuit. Et notandum quod ternarius precedit, et senarius sequitur. Nichil enim prosunt opera que sine fide fiunt... Per hoc quod dixit, numerauit, partes fidei nostre distinguendas et memoriter retinendas insinuauit. Uerbi gratia, si credimus unum deum, tamen

also necessary. Otherwise faith is dead and profitless. Speaking of those justified before the coming of Christ he observes that they were justified by no other faith than ours, for faith is one, as baptism is one. As justifying faith for Christians includes charity, so it did for all others. Those thus justified receive the Holy Spirit [12].

For the justification of adults actual faith and charity are required; infants are saved by the sacrament of baptism which, with Augustine, he calls the sacrament or symbol of faith [13].

Given this actual faith and charity, justification is received even before the reception of baptism by adults, or, in the case of the recovery of justice, before the reception of the sacrament of penance. The implications of this doctrine for Pullen's sacramental theology will be considered later. Numerous texts in the *Sentences* attest Pullen's view that adult catechumens are justified before baptism by faith informed by charity. Baptism symbolises justification already received [14]. Yet a person justified

---

non sufficit nisi tres personas esse credamus, et eas unum esse deum ... Hac ratione Iudeis ut rudibus, unitas praedicatur in ueteri lege, ut ibi: Audi, Israel, deus tuus, deus unus est; Christianis, uero, ut adultis, trinitas in euangelio ac si diceretur: Audi Christianae, deus tuus, deus unus et trinus est. Si ergo uolumus ut noster Abraham nostrum Loth reducat, non solum partes fidei nostre que incarnationi pertinent distinctas firmiter teneamus, uerum etiam Trinitatem in unitate et unitatem in Trinitate ueneremur'. In this allegorical exposition Abraham symbolises faith, and Lot the soul.

12 'Sed una est fides, sicut et baptisma procul dubio nostra quae per dilectionem operatur. Haec est lex nova:' 771B, cf. 839-A-D: 'Fides ergo quae per dilectionem operatur, sola virum bonum parit ... Non id meretur fides otiosa, quae est daemonum, sed diligens, quae est sanctorum ... Ergo ante baptismum Spiritum Sanctum acceperunt, ut magnificarent Deum, ac per hoc jam credentes justi erant'. Cf. *De Contemptu Mundi* ed. cit. 222.

For Pullen's doctrine of the divine indwelling cf. *supra* 159, n. 81. On the biblical sources of the early scholastic doctrine of justification by faith and charity see A. Landgraf, Glaube und Werk in der Frühscholastik, *Greg.* XVII (1936) 515-561; id. *Dogmengeschichte der Frühscholastik*, i, ii, 14-24.

13 'Quippe ut salvetur quis, aut necessaria fides est adultis, aut sacramentum fidei, qui est baptismus, parvulis. Nam absque utroque nemo salvari potest. Puer ergo, quoniam credere nescit, sacramentum credendi requirit': 844D. Cf. Aug. Ep. 98, C. S. E. L. 33. Elsewhere (703B-C) Pullen suggests that even baptised infants who die before attaining the use of reason must make an act of charity when the soul is separated from the body, if they are to be saved. This theory is of Abelardian origin. Cf. Abelard, *In Ep. ad Rom.* P. L. 178, 838; A. Landgraf, Literarhistorische Bemerkungen zu den Sentenzen des Robertus Pullus, *Traditio*, 1, (1943) 217; *Dogmengeschichte der Frühscholastik*, 1. i, 44 f.

14 'Quod fides facit, baptismus ostendit; fides peccata delet, baptismus deleta docet, unde sacramentum dicitur: 840D.

by faith, who through disobedience neglected to receive the sacrament afterwards would lose the grace of justification. Pullen argues that the case of such a catechumen is parallel with that of a sinner who has received forgiveness by his humble contrition of post-baptismal sins. Unless the latter subsequently submits his sins in confession to the power of the keys he will lose the forgiveness already obtained through his contrition [15]. First justification in adults is, therefore, secured by faith informed by charity; second justification (or the recovery of justification) is obtained by contrition which is based on faith and likewise informed by charity [16]. The sacraments of baptism and penance respectively, in addition to other effects, manifest what has already

---

Liquido constat ante lavacrum hominem fuisse justum, nec enim poterat fidem quae per dilectionem operatur obtinere et injustus esse: » 838B.

'Sicut ergo sanctorum patrum Abraham prius ex fide justificatus post sacramentum circumcisionis in signum interioris jam perceptae accepit, ita filii ejus per fidem, ex fide prius justificantur, post sacramentum ablutionis in signum interioris jam perceptae assumunt: » 838C.

'Non ergo baptismum, sed Spiritum per fidem comitatur justitia atque salus; ex martyrio quoque est salus, ubi non antecessit baptismus: ' 839D.

'Illud ergo decretum (nisi quis renatus fuerit ex aqua et Spiritu Sancto, non intrabit in regnum coelorum) ... neque de illis agit quos fide praeclaros necessitas a sacramento disjungit: ' 840B.

'Nam sicut adulti, si morte praepropera excludatur baptisma, sola ex catechizatione credentes salvantur, ita parvuli, licet catechumeni absque baptismo certa ratione damnantur: ' 844C.

Hence in the case of infants if there is a doubt about a previous baptism the ceremony must be repeated; but this is not so essential in the case of adults, who possess faith: 'Nam quoties baptisma ambigitur, si puer est, quoniam absque lavacro perderetur, omnimodis baptizetur. Sancti enim haud judicant iteratum, quod ignoratur patratum. Si adultus est, fidemque habet, nihil periculi est, si non est baptizatus, dum aut domestici mentiuntur renatum, aut tacent, verum; nam more omnium se in pueritia baptizatum credit; 844D-845A. 'Itaque res (i. e. justification) sacramentum suum comitatur in pueris, antecedit in adultis': 845D.

The same ideas regarding the justification of an adult catechumen by baptism are found in the *Epitome Theologiae* of Master Herman, ed. Cousin, p. 580, and in Hugh of St. Victor, *De Sacramentis Fidei, P. L.* 176, 448.

15 'Et sicut ille in percepta jam justitia non permaneret, si mandatum Dei negligens circumcidi respueret, ita isti prius justi, si contra oboedientiam baptizari recusarent. Sic cordi contrito et humiliato mox venia conceditur peccati necesse tamen est postea confiteri. Si quis tamen corde contrito ante confessionem morte fuerit preoccupatus, ne pereat compunctio intercedit. Quare, qui jam justus est ex fide, ne pereat de via justa, baptizetur in fide; si enim lavacrum spernit, jam ab ea fide excidit que per dilectionem operatur. Quod si morte praeventus a lavacro regenerationis praepeditur, quia extra fundamentum non est, perire non potest': 838D.

16 *Infra* 205 f.

been obtained by faith and charity [17]; and only physical impossibility excuses a person from the necessity of receiving these sacraments subsequently [18].

Pullen's account of the preparation required for justification, though unsystematic, is, nevertheless, very orthodox, and quite devoid of any suggestion of semi-pelagianism. He notes that normally the occasion of the origin of faith in adults is the hearing of the preaching of the gospel; but the assent of faith is produced by the grace of God [19]. Faith is therefore a gratuitous gift of God; it is due neither to a believer's own previous merits, nor to the merits of parents in respect of their offspring [20]. Before the advent of faith personal merit is impossible, since no man can do good until he is united with Christ [21]. Supplication on the part of the Church and the just may obtain faith and conversion for infidels and sinners, as appears from the allegorical interpretation of the miracles worked by Christ at the instance of Jairus (Mk. v. 22), the centurion (Mt. vii, 5) and Martha and Mary (Jo. xi, 5), as well as from the conversion of St. Augustine, and the saving of Peter from drowning (Mt. xiv, 30). Nevertheless, the efficacy of such supplications is not to be attributed to merit in such a way that grace is excluded. In the first place it is grace

---

17 'Ex quo quis paenitet, Deus remittit; peccata postmodum confitenti minister Dei absolvendo remittit. Et quid est absolvendo remittit; nisi quod sacramentum remissionis et absolutionis facit? Absolutio quae, peracta confessione super paenitentem a sacerdote fit, sacramentum est, quoniam sacrae rei signum est. Et cujus sacrae rei est signum, nisi remissionis et absolutionis? Nimirum confitentibus a sacerdote facta peccatis absolutio remissionem peccatorum, quam antea peperit cordis contritio, designat'. 910B-C.

18 Cf. *supra* n. 15.

19 'Intentio praedicationis religio est Christianae conversationis. Origo religionis fides est, quippe juxta Apostolorum ipsa spiritualis aedificiis fundamentum est ... Fides autem ex auditu nasci in Apostolo docetur. Sed quomodo ex auditu, si testimonio ejusdem ipsa non est ex nobis, Dei autem donum est, non ex operibus? ... Nimirum praedicator verba fundit, verborum autem sensum, immo fidem menti Deus infundit; nam sensus exercitio Scripturarum perspicax sententiam plerumque ex verbis perpendat, sententiae autem fidem nonnisi per gratiam adhibeat: ' 834B-D.

20 'Auditores ergo praedicatores suos diligant, quorum per officium, Deo intrinsecus operante, irradiantur fide non pro meritis parentum. Dei enim donum est, non ex operibus, ut ne quis glorietur. Non hoc Apostolus diceret, si quodlibet cujuslibetve opus Deus consideraret, quare cuipiam quasi ex merito fidem recompensaret: ' 835A.

21 ' Opera nimirum, quamvis magnifica, nihil sunt ante fidem: Nam non est qui faciat bonum, non est usque ad unum, id est nemo facit bonum usquequo veniat ad Christum: ipse enim est unus, id est solus, in quo bene faciat'. *ibid.* B.

which inspires these supplications; in the second, their efficacy is not such as to extort from God the grace of faith or conversion for others, as from one who owes that grace in justice. Such supplications are to be regarded as appeals to the divine mercy, by which God is moved freely to grant graces of faith, conversion and perseverance[22]. His accuracy of expression on the relation of grace to the beginning of faith and to merit argues a close acquaintance with the works of St. Augustine[23].

The influence of the African doctor is again apparent in Pullen's description of the justification of an adult who is justified by penance after post-baptismal sins. In eloquent language he describes a sinner who, though desirous to shake off the burden of his sins, finds himself powerless to put his desires into effect. Such a man experiences in himself the conflict of two wills, one good, the other evil; and the evil will prevails. He must call on God for assistance, and his prayer will be heard; he must devote himself to works of mercy and penitence. The very desire he has of conversion is a grace of God. If he is instant in prayer the grace of conversion will follow. As yet the sinner is not justified, but by the grace of God he is filled with the fear of hell, and from this fear he can rise to charity by which he will be justified. Pullen explains how this is accomplished. In this life

---

22 'Quid est ergo quod parentes pro filiis, imo tota Eclesia pro convertendis orat, orantem pro credituris imitata Dominum Jesum? Quid, inquam, pro nondum credentibus aut facinorosis orat, si nec illis fidem nec istis justitiam impetrat? Sed sanctorum supplicatio filiis, imo et aliis et infidelibus fidem et pravis aequitatem promeretur': 835C-D. 'Ipsa namque (gratia) trahit ad fidem, et pravitati implicitum ducit ad emendationem. Et utrumque agens modo in id, per se nativa dulcedine incitatur, modo supplicationibus (quas etiam gratia parit) provocatur: neque enim supplicationes cujusquam id promereri queunt apud Deum, ut ex debito necesse sit aut credituris, aut vitio purgandis gratiam suam conferre, quod utique non jam esset gratiam dare, sed debitum reddere. Nimirum supplicationes haud quidpiam quasi sibi debitum postulant. Verum quibusdam incitamentis misericordiam implorant unde universum Christianae religionis studium supplicatio potius quam meritum nuncupari debet, quoniam *non sunt condignae passiones huius temporis ad futuram gloriam* (Rom. viii, 18). Merita ergo hominum haudquamquam sibi Deum districtione judicii obligant, verum devota supplicatio pium judicem movet, ut gratuito beneficio suo, idolatrae fidem, distorto aequitatem, bono in proposito perseveranti, largiatur salutem:' 836D-837A. Cf. 838A. See A.Landgraf, *Dogmengeschichte der Frühsch.* I, i, 281.

23 'Nisi verius est, quod sicut ex gratia initium est fidei, ex fide autem justitiae initium, ex justitia, vero et initium bonorum et prosecutio; ita ex bono opere merito obedientiae et fides incrementum sumat, et justitia; Deo juxta augmenta mensurae munera distribuente, nec fiet quis justus nisi ex fide, fiet autem justior ex opere: 822C. Cf. *supra* 48, n. 64.

God is wont to bestow gifts of three kinds. The first kind comprises purely temporal gifts, which are often lavished on the wicked; the second, among which is the fear of hell, is intended to promote the conversion of sinners; the third consists of meritorious works which follow justification. The second class of gift is an appeal and a preparation for the third [24]. A sinner who under the impulse of this fear detests his sin and desires to be rid of it, is no longer wholly evil, nor is he as yet good, since he is still burdened with his sin. His state is an intermediate one; until he is free of his sins his works merit neither reward nor punishment [25]. A sinner in this state, though still without justifying charity, has within him the first sparks of that virtue. This initial charity will gradually inspire him to perform works of greater worth, which are the genuine offspring of charity [26]. Hence his condition is quite different from that of one who is quite devoid of charity; for there can be no charity where there is an attachment to even one sin [27]. Even if he is unable through

---

[24] 'Anxiatur ex sorde, desiderat benefacere, consueti tamen dulcedine mali revocatus, quod bene cupit implere nequit': 892A.

'Petat ergo assidue, petat devote, ad opera misericordiae refugiat, disciplinam apprehendat, et qui dedit ut exire ardeat, dabit tandem ut exeat:' *ibid.* B...

'Homo ergo malus, sed volens fieri bonus, propter quaedam sua, imo Dei bona, respicitur a Deo et liberatur a malo. Deus enim bona hoc in saeculo largitur aut terrena, quae abundantius contingunt perditis; aut altera, inter quae est timor gehennae, quibus peccator commutatur a via sua prava; aut tertia, quibus vir jam justus dignus fit corona. Prima dantur ut inde in terra vivatur, secunda supplicationes et quaedam via sunt, ut ad illa quae remunerabilia sunt pertingatur. Hujusmodi ergo bona quodammodo vigent vivuntque: quamvis enim nondum bonus fit is a quo fiunt, tamen ideo fecit ut per minora bonis majoribus atque retribuendis locus praeparatur; et sic bonus fiat:' *ibid.* B-C.

[25] 'Illa autem quae suo anxia de germine noxio tristatur, atque de extirpando meditatur, jam mala arbor non est, quoniam malum germen suum detestatur; bona nondum est quoniam, licet invita, malo germine oneratur. Medium ergo tenens statum, quod est exsecrabile putat; quod non est ardenter exoptat; sed valetudine morbi tardatur. Quae ergo interim recte quodammodo agantur, ea agenti nec poenam nec praemium ingerunt, id tamen merito suae dignitatis, nisi a proposito defecerint, certa ratione acquirunt ut, vitiis devictis, ea tandem obtineas unde mercedem speres:' 892C-D.

[26] 'Sed non omnino alienatur a caritate qui sibi displicet bonusque fieri satagit. Unde quoniam quibusdam caritatis praeventus est primitiis, primitiva quoque quaedam operatur bona, quo caritate ipsa tandem inflammatus, condigna caritate meliora atque veriora superaddat bona: 893A.

Similar ideas are found in a 'sentence' of the Laon School, in Walter of Mortagne, and especially in Robert of Melun. See A. Landgraf, *Dogmengeschichte der Frühscholastik,* 1, ii, 152-156.

[27] Nam ubi nihil caritatis adest, quod contingit quoties scienter una macula amatur, ibi nihil boni viventis atque valentis esse potest': *ibid.* On the sig-

ingrained habit to throw off all his sins at once, he should try to overcome them one by one. Provided he is desirous of abandoning all of them, and regrets all of them, he is worthy of pardon, even if he cannot achieve what he desires. In contrast, a person who hates and abandons only some of his offences is not yet sufficiently disposed to receive forgiveness [28]. There is, indeed, no hope for those who are so attached to one or more sins that they do not desire amendment, unless by the grace of God their wills are so changed that they conceive a desire of conversion or at least a longing for such a desire [29].

A clear distinction is drawn by Pullen between a natural and a supernatural love of good and hatred of evil. The former is completely inefficacious, and serves only to convict a man of sin; the latter is an effect of grace, and is never without effect, provided that the human will co-operates with the divine initiative [30]. It is due to this grace that the human will is led to will good, and to cease from sinning, to ask and receive forgiveness of sins, and to embark on meritorious good works [31]. The salutary fear inspired by grace is fear of God, and not of men. Moved by this fear a sinner will renounce all sins. If to this fear be added right notions of belief and conduct, hope of pardon, prayer and charity, he has arrived at the moment of justification. Even if he were to die before making confession, such a sinner would be saved, provided he did not disdain the obligation of confession [32].

---

nificance of Pullen's teaching for the interpretation of the scholastic axiom '*Facienti quod in se est* ... see A. Landgraf, *l. c.* 253.

28 893A-B.

29 *Ibid.* D.

30 'Inest unicuique naturae beneficio hujuscemodi voluntas, qua quodammodo quod iniquum est abominatur; quod justum, amplexetur; adeo infirma, ut per eam nemo promoveatur, quisque accusetur ... Sed voluntas quae ex gratia Dei inspiratur, tantae virtutis est, ut nunquam absque effectu sit, nisi cum ipse homo gratiae defuerit:' 894A.

For similar early scholastic teaching see A. Landgraf, *Dogmengeschichte der Frühscholastik,* I, i, 107, 114-128.

31 'Quisquis autem hujusmodi voluntate praeditum se sentit, dono Dei aggratuletur, obnixe gratias agens, promoveri petens. Quare si in malitia degens adhuc, bene velle saltem desiderat, bene velle petat. Si autem jam bene vult, ad effectum properans de malitia exire contendat; ex quo peccata dimiserit mox veniam postulaturus; qua a judice pio absque difficultate accepta, jam tempus est sanctam vitam sanctitatisque praemium exposcere:' *ibid.*

32 'Per quam (gratiam) si quis vitam corrigere satagit, ante omnia inspicere debet, utrum de patratione vitiorum, non quorumdam, sed omnium, timore Dei, non mundi, ingemiscat; adeo ut nulla ratione velit fecisse aut facturus esse, illa aut alia. Quisquis autem se hujusmodi perspexerit, fidei mo-

It is the movement of love of God as a father, and the desire of heaven that characterises justifying charity. Fear is a usual pre-disposition, but so long as it is the sole motive for conversion it is insufficient. Yet it is a gift of God, and provided a sinner renounces all his evil ways, and strives to fulfil his duties to God, he will infallibly receive the gift of justifying charity. Fear of God by itself is an insufficient disposition for justification because without charity it only avails to prevent the act of sinning; it does not expel from the heart all attachment to sin. A man moved by fear alone would sin if he could do so without punishment; he does good under compulsion, acting as a slave, rather than as a son[33]. The effect of charity is to induce a man to renounce evil, even if he could sin with impunity[34]. The fear, therefore, which Pullen is considering is, apparently, what later theologians call *timor serviliter servilis.*

---

rumque normam sincera rerum notitia comprehendens, quia in his *ignorans ignoratur* (quippe cum in fide erroneam, aut in moribus foedam sententiam quemadmodum et vitam tenens jure damnetur) is si veniam sperat, et orat, caritateque polleat, poenitentia contritus, cognitione salubrium perspicuus; is inquam, et non alius, jam et non prius, gaudeat concivis regni coelestis ascriptus sanctis: ' 896A-B.

[33] ' Sed paenitentiam plerumque parit timor, in illo qui timet ardere, non peccare. Vir certe malus, quoniam vir bonus plus horret culpam quam gehennam. Ille praevidens poenam reprimit culpam; si impune liceret, repressam exerceret. Nec potest bonus esse quisquis illicita vellet si auderet. Quodam enim modo cujusque voluntas affectat, quidquid solum ex necessitate recusat. Nam quod coactus facis, id te facere verum est, id te velle falsum est... Qui ergo ex timore poenitet, adhuc est servus, quoniam flagra formidat; nondum filius qui, patrem amans, sperat haereditatem. Servus autem de habitaculo Sarae ejicitur, quippe haeres non futurus. Quamobrem quisquis dum paenitet, solum timore angitur, nondum per paenitentiam veniam meretur. Verum qui largitur timorem ut ex timore necessitatem incutiat, is cum paenitentia largietur amorem, ut sit paenitens venia dignus, tanto initio sapientiae praeventus largitori suo prout decet gratus existat: ' 852D-853B. Cf. 776C, 892B, 815C.

' Timor a Deo infunditur ut prava deserantur. Caritas superaddita ornat bonam vitam. Timor a manu non corde agit iniquitatem. Iniquitas sedit cordi, et si impune liceret faceret. Timor deserit mala quae diligit, sicut facit (bona) quae odit, malletque non esse vindictam quae frenat voluptatem. Qui ergo timet poenam odit justitiam. Servus tamen ejiciendus; nec enim haereditatem quaerit; solum poenam fugit. ' *De Contemp. Mundi, ed. cit.* 219.

[34] ' Et quoniam mala actu, mente amamus, initium sapientiae jam adest sapientia ipsa adhuc abest; adveniet autem cum male agere nolueris, quamvis impune liceret. Sed voluntas haec coelica caritate famulatur: ' 815C.

On the early scholastic doctrine of servile fear see A. Landgraf, Die Lehre der Frühscholastik von der knechtischen Furcht, *Div. Th. Fr.* XV (1937) 160ff; id., Familienbildung bei Paulinenkommentaren des 12. Jahrhunderts, Biblica xiii (1932) 1917.

A difficulty arises here. If the fear which leads to the abandonment of the outward sinful deed is consistent with an inward attachment to it, it is hard to see how it can be a disposition towards justification. It would appear to constitute yet another sin, and indeed is now so regarded according to the common teaching of theologians. Moreover Pullen himself, as we have already seen, clearly teaches that those who cherish an attachment even to a single sin cannot hope for pardon [35]. It seems, therefore, that Pullen in his discursive unsystematic manner has two grades of the fear of God in mind when he is considering a sinner's progress towards justification. In certain contexts he is treating of merely servile fear. In common with Peter Lombard he regards this as useful and salutary [36]. Elsewhere he is describing what Peter Lombard calls ' initial fear '. This fear, as we have seen already, includes the first sparks of charity, and excludes deliberate complacency in sin [37]. It corresponds to what later theologians were to call *timor simpliciter servilis.* But the distinction between the two types of fear is less marked in Pullen than in the Lombard, in the author of the *Summa Sententiarum*, and in certain collections of *Sentences* of the Laon School [38].

The question of the motive of sincere and efficacious repentance was much studied by theologians contemporary with Robert Pullen. Most influential among them was Peter Abelard. Admitting, along with the Laon school the place of fear as a first step towards justification, Abelard developed in a number of works the theme of the necessity of charity for the acquisition of actual justification [39]. Many contemporary writings bear the influence of Abelard's thought on this question. In particular it was due to him that theologians began to distinguish clearly two principal questions, that of the origin of repentance, and that of the psychological motive of efficacious contrition. The citations given in this

---

[35] 893D.

[36] Cf. P. Lombard. *Sent.* III cap. iv; ' Timor autem servilis est, ut ait Augustinus, cum per timorem gehennae continet se homo a peccato, quo praesentiam judicis et poenas metuit, et timore facit, quidquid boni facit, non timore amittendi aeternum bonum, quod non amat, sed timore patiendi malum, quod formidat. Et succedit initialis timor, quando incipit quod durum erat amari; et sic incipit excludi servilis timor a caritate '.

[37] Cf. *supra* 204.

[38] Cf. *Summa Sententiarum, P. L.* 175, 115A; *Sententie Anselmi,* ed. Bliemetzrieder, 105-106.

[39] See P. Anciaux, *La théologie du sacrement de pénitence au XIIIe siècle,* 154-159; A. Landgraf, *Dogmengeschichte der Frühscholastik,* I, i, 131, 164; I, ii, 57, 137 f.

chapter appear to show that Robert Pullen was not immune from the influence of Abelard on these points.

We may conclude this account of Pullen's ideas on the process of justification by noting with what care he distinguishes the respective roles of grace and of the human will. The offering of grace is due to a wholly gratuitous divine liberality. If the grace fails of its effect, this is due to fault of the creature. If it is accepted the human will is again at work, but the primary factor in the acceptance is the grace of God [40].

Thus Pullen clearly distinguishes prevenient grace which stimulates the will to desire and do good, and subsequent grace, which enables men to persevere therein [41]. Grace does not destroy human freedom [42]. Yet so great is the power of grace that without doing violence to the will it can completely alter and transform the perverse will of a sinner [43]. From all this it is clear that Pullen was familiar with the notion of what was later to be called efficacious grace ' in actu primo ', if not with its technical name. Man's merit and responsibility lie in the free submission of his will to the freely offered grace of God. With his master, St. Augustine, Pullen held firmly that man's merits are in the first place God's gifts [44].

---

[40] 'Non enim ipse (Apostolus) solus, sed gratia Dei adjutus laboravit: quae angelis omnibus, primis quoque hominibus pariter bene creatis proposita, ab alio repulsa, ab alio libertate arbitrii suscepta est; sed vitii proprii erat, quod paratum sibi auctoris adjutorium, ille refutavit: quod autem is cohaesit, et ex propria prodiit voluntate, et primo ex datoris largitate', 894C. 'Unde non solum gratia quae a Deo missa nostram pungit pigritiam, verum quoque ipsum assentire co-operarique gratiae, quod utique ex nobis est, verum eo modo quod nonnisi gratiae praevenientis auxilio fieret, nec factum, nisi gratiae subsequentis subsidio maneret opus quodammodo Dei est. Opus ergo bonum omne quod agimus, non soli nos, imo cum Deo facimus'. 895C.

Of twelfth-century speculation on the relation of grace to free-will see A. Landgraf, *Dogmengeschichte der Frühscholastik*, 1, i, 65-82; id. Die Erkenntnis der helfenden Gnade in der Frühscholastik, *Z. K. T.* LV (1931) 208-238.

[41] 'Unde patet quod omnium bene gestorum prima praecipuaque causa gratia est; quippe quae bona coepta praevenit ut subsistant, subsequitur ut maneant': 895A.

[42] 'Nostrum autem apud arbitrium, nonnulla, verum secundaria, recte agendorum auctoritas conversatur... Nam quamvis gratia revocat errantem, perducat obedientem; trahit tamen voluntarium, nec cogit invitum': 895A.

[43] 'adeo valens, adeoque vigens, ut quamlibet perversi voluntatem, vitamque in quantumlibet emendationis gradum absque omni difficultate et coactione, quoties libuerit immutet': *ibid.*

[44] 'Unde nostrarum elegantia actionum, et gratia est et meritum; gratia tamen tanquam duce per omnia sibi vindicante primatum. Unde quidquid meriti est, rite gratiae accomodatur, quae illud et ut sit promovet, et ut maneat comitatur': *ibid.* C.

GROWTH IN CHARITY.

Charity has various degrees. In beginners it is weak; strong enough to guarantee admission to heaven, but not necessarily adequate to secure victory over all temptations [45]. It can, however, develop to so high a degree that its possessor will not be lost or even sin gravely [46]. This perfect charity which 'never falleth away' (1 Cor. xii, 8), is extremely rare. Pullen speculates that certain persons such as David, Solomon, and St. Peter who had possessed it, did indeed fall, but only temporarily. Their ultimate conversion was always assured. The explanation of their return lies in the fact that, even when it has been lost through sin, this mature charity leaves behind it a root, through which it is revived by the continual prompting of divine grace[47]. If after a temporary grave lapse the possessor of such charity were to die, Pullen admits that he would be lost; but he maintains that whoever has attained to so high a degree of charity has thereby merited not to be allowed to die in his sin [48].

The doctrine that for adults eternal life is at once a gift of God and the reward of merit is frequently stressed by Pullen both in the sermons and in the *Sentences* [49]. He insists that only

---

45 'licet tamen non absurde intelligi, quod caritas circa bene vivendi primordia quamdam soleat obtinere teneritatem, jam quidem digna coelo, gravi tamen nondum idonea bello, aut tentationis aut persecutionis': 860C.

46 'Unde caritas hoc etiam in saeculo illum videtur emereri gradum, quem quisquis vel semel attigerit, nunquam postea criminaliter delinquit, neque perit': *ibid.* D.

47 'Unde David, atque Salomonem, Petrum quoque, quos jam illum caritatis gradum apprehendisse nefas credere non est, sed nec fas indubitanter affirmare, constat viros optimos pessime deliquisse.

Sed caritatem quae vitio pulsata fugit, quoniam ea erat quae vel semel habita, postea hominem perire non sinit, quamdam post se sui credibile, est dereliquisse radicem, unde reorum conscientia puncta atque repuncta, quietem haud unquam permittat, donec sua de radice caritas per gratiam pullulans inquietum refoverit': 861B.

This suggestion is an original contribution of Pullen to a question which was much debated in his day. See A. Landgraf, *Dogmengeschichte der Frühscholastik,* 1, ii, 157.

48 'Usque eo tamen nonnunquam debilitari videtur, ut si interim contigerit quempiam mori, contingat quoque damnari. Verum caritatis illud aiunt esse meritum ex maturitate, ut suos mori non sinat in crimine': *ibid.* D.

49 'Inter haec duo gratiarum genera medium tenent merita locum. Atque haec quidem ea bona sunt, unde dicitur *Nullum bonum irremuneratum*... Merita ergo recte inter utraque collocantur, quoniam muneribus ad meritum, merito venitur ad praemium; meritum quoque Dei semper est donum, nonnunquam autem et praemium': 859D.

those good works are meritorious, which are done in union with Christ by those who have charity. Moreover, the meritorious value of the works is in proportion to the charity which informs them, and is not merely measured by the excellence or difficulty of the work done [50]. Attachment to a single grave sin is sufficient to extinguish charity and the power of meriting and to deprive a person of all the merits previously acquired by him [51]. A right intention of pleasing God is also necessary if a good work is to be reckoned meritorious. Sinful motives completely corrupt men's good deeds. Mixed motives render them profitless, but after repentance the merit inherent in them can revive [52]. If the reprobate perform any good works they receive their reward in this life. After death whatever good deeds they may have done will not avail even to secure for them a mitigation of their punishment [53].

---

[50] 'Nam ubi nihil caritatis adest, quod contingit quoties scienter una macula amatur, ibi nihil boni viventis atque valentis esse potest, sed juxta caritatis augmenta augentur et operum merita': 893A.

Cf. *De Contemp. Mundi.* ed. cit. 214: 'Quia discretor mentium affectum ponderat, non censum'; and on the same topic *Sent.* 871B: 'Unde paupercula mulier plus divitibus misit, quia quod minus erat in re pensabatur ex voluntate'. Similer teaching is found in Abelard and Hugh of St. Victor. See A. Landgraf, Die Bestimmung des Verdienstgrades in der Frühscholastik, *Scholastik* VIII (1933), 1-40.

[51] 'Nimia ergo vis mali, quoniam tanquam pessimum fermentum non solum quae fiunt, sed et quae antea praecedunt bona corrumpit, ac mortua reddit, nec reviviscunt, nisi per paenitentiam fermentum ipsum, unde origo mali est, diluatur': 859A.

[52] Cf. *De Contemp. Mundi*: *ed. cit.* 217: 'Cavendum nobis magnopere est ne dum quid bonum agimus mala intentione corrumpamus ... Quidam enim dum bene agunt partim Deo, partim intendunt mundo, querentes per idem sibi in celo Deum placare in mundo lucrum et famam comparare, et quia eundem cultum deo exibent et lucro, indignatus parem recusat seruitutem ... Sed quia Deus in parte extitit causa, si alteram partem penitentia liberauerit, quod prius mortuum fuerit iam uiuit.

[53] 'Qui autem ad tempus bene agit, ad tempus et donatur. Is nihil speret in futuro, nam infernus quo properat nulli pensat praemium ... Nimirum dives flamma cruciatus, stilla saltem exoptans refrigerari, audit apud inferos non solum munera negari, verum nec poenas per merita mitigari': 858B.

CHAPTER XII.

THE SACRAMENTS.

THE SACRAMENTS IN GENERAL.

There is no systematic treatment of the sacraments in general in Pullen's *Sentences,* but by gathering together certain of his opinions, expressed in his treatment of different sacraments, we can form an idea, however incomplete, of his general sacramental doctrine.

He does not state the number of the sacraments of the New Law. Some years were to pass after the composition of Pullen's *Sentences* before the sevenfold number gained general acceptance. Pullen treats of six sacraments. Neither in his Sentences nor in his sermons does he mention Extreme Unction. Nor does he provide a definition of a sacrament of the New Law. Yet he distinguishes clearly enough rites to which the term *sacramentum* applies strictly. A sacrament is an efficacious sign of grace. With St. Augustine he speaks of the outward sign as the *sacramentum,* and of the inward effect as the *virtus* or *res sacramenti* [1].

The Eucharist is the principal sacrament of the Church because of the excellence of the gifts which it signifies and confers on those who receive it piously [2]. He admits the existence of sacraments under the Old Law. Here he uses the term sacrament in a wide sense to signify a sacred sign. In this sense even the strugg-

---

[1] 'Aliud nimirum est sacramentum ipsum videre; aliud quid sacramento agatur inspicere. Sacramentum oculis se offert; res ipsa mente vestigatur. Sacramentum fit in corpore, virtus autem sacramenti in mente': 842B.

Speaking of baptism he notes that the inward effect is withheld in unworthy recipients until they repent: 'Ergo percipiunt sacramentum nec percipiunt sacramenti fructum: percipiunt autem cum mollita mente abscedet impoenitentia, nunquam tamen iterato sacramento': 846B.

[2] 'Mensa ergo Domini non solum ipsius passionem, imo et conformitatem, et ut dictum est, Ecclesiae designat unitatem. Habe caritatem et eris hoc vinculo tam capiti constrictus quam membris, jure ergo praecipuum Ecclesiae judicatur sacramentum, quod tam sacra, habet insinuare, imo et rite participantibus conferre': 965B-C.

les and wars of the Jews against their enemies were sacraments, as they foreshadowed the spiritual struggles of Christians [3]. Certain of these signs prefigured Christian sacraments to come. Thus Baptism was foreshadowed by the cloud of the Exodus and by the Red Sea, and the Eucharist by the manna, and by the water which gushed from the rock struck by Moses [4]. Pullen asserts that the Old Testament sacraments, which included the rite of circumcision, produced the same effects of grace, while the old dispensation lasted, as the sacraments of the New Law, but in a different manner. He admits that there was no intrinsic reality of grace in the sacraments of the Old Law, but argues that the blessings which they were unable to confer of themselves were granted to men through their instrumentality, provided they had faith in and hope of the reality which was prefigured by these older sacraments. Under the New Law the faithful receive the same effects directly from the sacraments which were symbolised by the Old Testament signs [5]. Notable among the sacraments of the Old Law was the rite of circumcision, for Jewish male children, by which they were freed from original sin. For Jewish female children, as well as for the children of Gentiles, Pullen holds that salvation was assured through the faith of their parents. In similar fashion were saved Jewish males who died before the eighth day after birth, and all those who died in the womb, whether Jews or Gentiles [6].

Under the New Law the minister of the sacraments acts as the vicar of Christ, who may be truly said to baptize, or to consecrate the Holy Eucharist [7]. Hence even if a pagan were to baptize

---

[3] 779A.

[4] 959C-960C.

[5] 'Sacramenta igitur corporis et sanguinis Domini veteri in populo praecesserunt, et idem credentibus, ut auctores fatentur, valuerunt; non quod figura rei vires habere possit, sed quoniam Deus qui nihil non potest, quod modo conferre placet per veritatem, tunc dare volebat per umbram': 960C.

'Sed verius arbitror id officii figuras habere, ut res suas insinuent, fidem autem in figuris latentem figuras suscipientibus, revelante Deo, detectam id contulisse per spem, quod modo fidelibus ex significatis confertur per rem': 961B.

[6] 766-769B. Cf. Gregory the Great, *Moralia,* IV, 3, *P. L.* 75, 635.

[7] 'Sed temetsi nullus adesset patrinus, imo nullus omnino foret in mundo, tantum vel paganissimus morem Ecclesiae tenens baptizaret, nihilominus virtute sacramenti servatus, apud Christum, qui solus baptizat, misericordiam inveniret': 845C.

'Dominus virtute benedictionis suae, et per se et per ministros panem in corpus suum, vinumque in sanguinem suum convertit': 965C.

in case of necessity the sacrament would be valid, provided he observed the customary rites of the Church [8]. Pullen does not require an internal intention in the minister of conforming his action to the mind of the Church in the sacramental action. All he demands for the validity of the sacrament is that the outward rite be correctly applied. He concludes, therefore, that, even if the minister of Baptism act in jest, the sacrament is valid. He applies the same principle to the person receiving this sacrament. If he were to approach the sacrament in a spirit of mockery the sacrament would be valid, although fruitless. In the same context Pullen maintains similar views regarding the administration of penance and the contract of matrimony. A penitent who confesses his sins sincerely and makes due satisfaction receives forgiveness, even if the confessor acts mockingly towards him. In marriage a plea that the contract was entered on in jest does not avail to secure separation [9].

---

[8] *Ibid.* This conclusion is in harmony with the general doctrine of the early scholastic theologians who held that the power granted to priests over the sacraments was a ministerial one only. This power did not directly affect the guilt of sin, whether in the sacrament of baptism or of penance, but only indirectly through the ministration of the sacramental signs. Cf. *infra* 216 f., 229-232, 237-240; and see A. Landgraf, Der frühscholastische Streit um die potestas quam Christus potuit dare servis et non dedit, *Greg.* XV (1934) 524-572.
quidem ut non baptizetur, verum ut baptizando non emundetur ».

[9] ' Nec obest quidquam quominus baptisma dicatur aut lavantis perversitas aut loti. Lotus nullomodo nocetur aliena, aliquo modo propria; non quidem ut non baptizetur, verum ut baptizando non emundetur ».

' Quid ergo? Joco atque risorie unus baptizat, alter baptizatur, numquid hujusmodi dicemus baptizatum? Sed dum ille joco baptizat, iste serio baptizatur. Quid inde perdit? Nonne quod ad se pertinet facit, dum more ecclesiastico lavacrum suscipit, licet ille in hoc offendat quod irrisorie lavat, cum tamen regulam baptizandi non excedat. Sic si quis peccata confitentem sacerdos irrideat, nihilominus tamen irriso recte consulat, reus discrete confitens diligenterque satisfaciens a reatu nihilominus absolvitur. Contra si quis catholice per omnia baptizat, baptizandus autem irrisorio animo accedat, nonne irrisio sicut fictio rem sacramenti tollit; ipsum tamen sacramentum tollere nequit. Baptizatus ergo non mundatus videtur. Sic licet quis conjugium quasi ludo contraxerit, nihilo magis tamen ludi objectio conjugium initum separabit. Sic ergo hinc inde tota baptismi actio irrisorie agitur, tantum ordo sacramenti teneatur, cur ea quae per se sacramento nihil officiunt, conjuncta extinguunt? '. 841D-842B.

Pullen even admits that those who baptise each other in jest while bathing receive the sacrament validly, but, owing to their irreverence, without fruit: an infant baptised in the same circumstances would be validly and fruitfully baptised: 842C-D. The question was current in the schools in Pullen's day. See P. Lombard, IV *Sent* D. vi, c. 5. The Lombard rightly rejects Pullen's solution of the question on the ground of lack of a requisite intention. On

It is clear that Pullen does not sufficiently distinguish between the moral qualities required in the minister of a sacrament and the intention required of him. By his time it had been established that neither faith nor moral excellence were necessary for the *validity* of a sacrament, but the necessity of an internal intention on the part of the minister, as distinguished from an external intention of merely celebrating the outward rite, had not yet been authoritatively established. Pullen, therefore, considers the problem of a fictitious internal intention under the general category of the moral character of the minister. Not only when treating of Baptism and Penance, but also in discussing the Eucharist Pullen is insistent that unworthy ministers can administer valid sacraments [10]. This doctrine makes it clear that he places sacraments in a different category from other priestly activities. The sacraments have an intrinsic efficacy independent of the worth of the human minister, and depending on Christ their author. In contrast private prayers of unworthy ministers are profitless for those on behalf of whom they are said [11]. It is clear that Pullen in this context, as in his discussion of the respective efficacy of the sacraments of the Old and the New Law, is almost in possession of the doctrine of the efficacy of the sacraments *ex opere operato*.

He notes that three sacraments — Baptism, Confirmation and Holy Order — may not be repeated, owing to the permanency of their effect. As Christ's saving death was but one, so too is baptism, which is its efficacious sign. The doctrine of the sacramental

---

the history of this question among the early scholastics see A. Landgraf, Beiträge der Frühscholastik zur Terminologie der allgemein Sakramentenlehre, *Div. Th. Fr.* XXIX (1951) 3-34.

10 'Possunt quidem indigni vita conficere; sed necesse est ritum ecclesiasticum servare. Indigni namque, licet damno suo, attamen conficiunt; sed nunquam aliter nisi conficiendi disciplinam aemulentur': 968A.

In his treatise, *De Contemptu Mundi* he says of a confessor: 'Sacerdos cui assistis ne tibi vileat: qualisqualis est, summi pontificis uicarius est. Sacramento suo rex ipse non deerit, si regio caractere indutus miles humilis adveneris': *ed. cit.* p. 205.

11 'Quid susceptum officium orandi primum pro se, deinde pro populo relinguere nequeunt, et si faciunt indigni tanto officio malo sui faciunt. Affirmare non audeo malum esse quod huiusmodi homines pro peccatis aliorum orationes faciunt. Illud autem dico: pro uero estimo quod orationes bone sunt, nec utiles. Quis enim est ille seruus, qui suo dominum pro conseruo suo intercedere presumat, cum ipsum dominum contra semetipsum iratum sentiat? Re uera, si facere presumeret, non solum conseruum domino irato non reconciliaret, sed etiam contra illum ad maiorem iram dominum prouocaret': Serm. 15.

character is here implicit, but did not become explicit until sometime later [12].

Baptism.

According to Pullen this sacrament was not only instituted by Christ, but was administered during his public ministry, although up to the time of the passion the rite of circumcision was still permitted [13]. The baptism of John was a distinct rite; it marked a break with the old Law, and, on the occasion of its reception by Our Lord, foreshadowed the effects of Christian baptism [14].

The essentials of the rite of baptism are a triple immersion in water, and the invocation of the Trinity. The invocation of the Trinity and the use of water are required for validity; the triple immersion is prescribed but is not necessary for validity [15]. The external rite symbolises the interior regenerating activity of the Trinity, an activity which is attributed by appropriation to the Holy Spirit. In water there is a natural aptitude for the symbolism [16]. A triple immersion is enjoined out of reverence for the

---

12 'Sed licet non liceat sacramenta quaedam iterari, quoniam semel sumpta ad omne sufficiunt tempus, sunt tamen alia quae nisi saepius percepta non sufficiunt illi qui supervivit': 847C.

'Baptisma nunquam repetitur, nec confirmatio': 846D. On Holy Order: 'Notandum autem quod sacramentum semel impositum cum vita permaneat, bono utique bonum, malo autem ad malum': 927C.

'Cum ergo una sola morte Christi uniusque solius efficacia baptismatis, venia tibi praesto est, quotiescunque poenitentia haud abest; sicut mors Christi nunquam repetitur, nec mortis similitudo baptisma, unquam repetatur': 846C. See A. Landgraf, Zur Frage von der Wiederholbarkeit der Sakramente, *Div. Th. Fr.* XXIX (1951) 257-283.

13 'Sed ut auctoritas baptismi post resurrectionem privatim injuncta claresceret, ante resurrectionem sacramentum lavacri coram Domino publice celebratur': 849B.

'Sed tempora divisa sunt circumcisionis atque baptismi. Tempus namque circumcisionis, sicut et legis, usque ad passionem Domini': 847C.

14 780B.

15 840A: 841C.

16 'Aqua dum lavat, Spiritum Sanctum mundantem designat; corpus dum lavatur, mundatio animae designatur': 843A.

The passage is of interest as illustrating Pullen's contribution to contemporary attempts at a definition of baptism. Some, with Hugh of St Victor, said that baptism consisted in water sanctified by the invocation of the Holy Spirit. Others, with Abelard and the Porretanists, decided that it was an ablution under a prescribed form of words. Pullen took the ablution to be understood passively, and his solution appears to have been adopted by the

Blessed Trinity, and to symbolise the three days during which Christ lay in the sepulchre [17]. The purpose of the immersion is to signify our death to sin, not merely by the remission of guilt, but also by the assuaging of the troublesome effects of sinful habits [18]. Further, as Christ rose from the grave, so the newly baptised arise to a new life [19].

Treating of the effect of baptism, Pullen observes that by it all infants are liberated from the guilt of original sin, even though God foresees that some will afterwards lose their souls for subsequent sins [20]. As we have seen, in treating of his teaching on grace, he held that adults are justified by faith informed by charity, even before the actual reception of baptism. Nevertheless, he considers that baptism is not merely a symbol. It adds something to what faith and charity have already secured. Faith, he says, averts (spiritual) death; baptism sows the seed of life; faith frees the soul from eternal punishment; baptism removes the debt of temporal punishment which remains after the guilt has been forgiven [21], and consequently works of satisfaction are not demanded of one who receives this sacrament [22]. Further, baptism manifests what faith has obtained [23]. He concludes, therefore, that baptism is rightly said to forgive sins, since it frees a man from the punishment due to sin, signifies that he is free of the guilt

---

Lombard. See A. Landgraf, Die frühscholastische Definition der Taufe, *Greg.* XXVII (1946) 200-219.

'Virtus enim Trinitatis adest sacramento baptismatis, quod dum Christus baptizaretur nobis est insinuatum': 848A.

17 843C.

18 'Jure immersio insinuat remissionem peccatorum, quoniam id est immergi, quod peccato mori atque sepeliri. Et quid est peccato mori aut sepeliri, nisi non solum culpa expiari, verum etiam molestias pravae consuetudinis sedari?': 844A.

19 844B.

20 700B.

21 'Post fidem, qua mors propellitur, succedit baptisma, ut vita vegetetur': 840D.

'Homini peccata remittit fides ne damnetur; baptismus, ne puniatur': *ibid.*

22 'Quod expositor ita explanat: Gratia Dei in Baptismate non requirit gemitum vel planctum, vel opus aliquod, nisi solum fidem, et omnia gratis condonat. Dona ergo Dei, id est remissio peccatorum in baptismo facta, non requirit paenitentiam, id est purgatoriam poenam post remissionem. Nimirum cor contritum quod baptisma praevenit, et humiliatum quod sacramento obedientem submittit, ita reum purgat, ut pro poena sufficiat': 849D.

23 'Quod fides facit, baptismus ostendit; fides peccata delet, baptismus deleta docet, unde sacramentum dicitur': 840D.

of sin, and strengthens the life which has its origin in faith. The vivifying Spirit is given when a person is justified by faith informed by charity; at baptism He is given more fully, to be a shield against sin; in confirmation He is conferred with even greater fulness, to promote holiness of life [24]. By baptism the antecedent actual sins of adult recipients are forgiven in addition to original sin, and in this effect Pullen sees another proof of its superiority to the rite of circumcision [25]. Therefore, to the newly baptised heaven is open, a truth which was symbolised by the opening of heaven at the baptism of Christ [26]. The same effects are assigned to martyrdom [27].

After baptism concupiscence remains, but is no longer imputed as a sin, unless it be consented to [28]. As we have seen, Pullen placed the principal element of original sin in concupiscence [29]. In the baptised it provides the material for moral effort [30]. Darkness of mind, or ignorance, also remains after baptism. Pullen

---

24 'Recte ergo in remissionem peccatorum baptisma sumitur, quod a poena peccati solvit, et absolutum insinuat, et vitam ex fide natam confortat. Quid ergo Spiritum sanctum recipit per fidem, eum magis obtinet in regeneratione, praecipue habiturus eundem in confirmatione, hoc namque est Spiritum quasi quibusdam gradibus suscipere, per augmenta promoveri bonae vitae': 841A.

25 'Item baptisma tanquam propositum adultis actualia etiam contra peccata (praeterita tantum) sumitur remedio in tantum fortasse, ut nullam expiationis gratia requirant poenam post lavacrum': 849B. Pullen, therefore, explicitly rejects the opinion of certain of his contemporaries of the Porretanist school that the efficacy of baptism extends even to the post-baptismal sins of the elect. See A. Landgraf, Zwei Probleme der frühscholastischen Sakramentenlehre, *Z. k. Th.* LXVI (1942) 132-140.

26 848A, 850B.

27 850A.

28 'Notandum autem considerationem alteram et alteram esse ante baptismum et post. Nam ante, delictum damnabile judicatur fomes ipse peccati cum suis sordidis foetibus; damnatur enim parvulus, quoniam naturalem habet concupiscentiam, quanto magis adultus, quoniam et concupiscentiam habet et concupiscit. Quare ante lavacrum fomes ipse peccati imputatur;; imputantur quoque motus mali ex fomite noti, qui cum sint valde valdeque multi, multum multumque damnandis coacervant cruciatum. Sed post baptismum; *Beatus vir cui non imputavit Dominus peccatum* (Ps. xxxi, 2): habet utique peccatum concupiscentiae et motuum, sed non imputatur, nisi ad consensum usque deviatur; virtus enim baptismi id efficit, ut hujusmodi solum jam sint ad infirmitatem, quoniam prius erant et ad mortem': 863D-864D.

29 *Supra* ch. viii.

30 'Haec omnia cum fomite, unde quasi ex mala radice pullulant, ante lavacrum, sicut de concupiscentia perhibet Augustinus, ad damnationem trahunt, in baptismo a reatu solvuntur, post baptismum ad agonem relinquuntur': 854C-D.

distinguishes three kinds of culpable ignorance. The first is an effect of original sin, the second is due to the corruption of the body and to concupiscence, the third is a consequence of deliberate personal sin. Before baptism all three are culpable; after baptism only the third kind [31].

Numerous practical instructions are given for the administration of the sacrament. Adult baptism is held on the occasion of solemn festivals. Any delay that this may involve is not dangerous, since it is presumed that the catechumens are already justified by faith [32]. Infants should be baptised as soon as possible, especially if they are in danger of death [33]. In this case a layman may officiate, if no cleric is at hand. The father of the child may baptise in such extreme necessity; and he need have no fear of incurring an impediment of spiritual relationship which would preclude marital relations with his wife [34]. Sponsors are required at infant baptism to vouch for its accomplishment, to answer the catechesis on behalf of the child, and to ensure the fulfilment of the pact made between God and man. He notes that parents are usually excluded from the Church at the baptism of their offspring. He conjectures that this custom is a relic of the days when numerous infants were baptised simultaneously. It was possible then for a parent to receive from the font his own child, instead of that of another at whose baptism he was assisting, and as a consequence incur the impediment of spiritual relationship in reference to his wife. To avoid this contingency, it was enacted that parents should not be present at the baptism of their children [35].

---

[31] 'Jure haereditaria ignoramus, ignorantiam terrena inhabitatione aggravamus, aggravatam interminatis excessibus cumulamus ... Est combinatio originalis maculae sua cum ignorantia. Est altera motuum carnis, item fortasse cum sua, Est tandem, absque forsan tertia, qua malefacimus, et male faciendo prave intelligimus. Omnes tres imputat Deus ante conversionem, duas quidem occulto judicio, tertiam vero manifesto; ultimo autem, soli, regeneratione suscepta, intendere videtur, nisi per apostasiam praevaricato foedere foederis gratia subtrahatur': 869B-C; cf. 875, 876C-877B, 962B.

[32] 844C, 846A.

[33] 846A.

[34] 929A-C. By the canon law of the time this impediment arose between the officiant and the parents of the child, as well as between him and the child.

[35] 844D-845A, 929C-D. Basing their conclusion on the authority of St Augustine, many early scholastics resolved the problem of reconciling the doctrine of justification by faith with its impossibility in infants by appealing to the faith of the sponsors at baptism. See Aug. *De Libero Arbitrio*, 23, *P. L.* 32, 1304; A. Landgraf, Kindertaufe und Glaube in der Frühscholastik, *Greg.* IX (1928) 337-372.

The catechetical interrogations that precede the actual baptism are essential at the baptism of adults, in order to ensure the presence of actual faith. If faith is wanting the baptism is without fruit; so too if they have an attachment to sin. Once, however, they repent of these impediments to grace the sacrament will produce its effect without it being necessary or lawful to repeat it [36]. Finally, he notes that after the ceremony it is customary to make an offering to God. It is fitting that the faithful make these offerings, but priests are not to demand them [37].

Confirmation.

Pullen notes that, like baptism, this sacrament is never repeated. It is called confirmation because it strengthens the good effect of baptism, and arms the recipient in advance to contend against the powers of evil. It also forgives sins [38]. Unlike baptism, it is not absolutely necessary for salvation. Consequently it is not so essential for infants, but it should be conferred on them as a preparation for the future. For this reason Christ laid his hands on the children when they were brought to Him (Mk. x, 13), and the words which he spoke on that occasion: *Suffer the little children to come unto me,* were a decree enjoining the confirmation of infants. Any negligence in providing this sacrament for children is, therefore, sinful. Even before they arrive at the age of reason children will be benefited by this sacrament, since by it the glory of eternal life, of which they have a pledge through baptism, is increased by the rite of confirmation. This sacrament is superior to baptism, inasmuch as it is a more excellent thing to be an athlete than merely to be healed of disease. Baptism is a sacrament of healing; confirmation invigorates the soul, once it has been healed. Because it is a more excellent sacrament than baptism its administration has been reserved to bishops from apostolic times.

The holy Eucharist.

The chief heads of Catholic doctrine concerning this sacrament are clearly expounded by Pullen. He frequently refers to the real

---

36 846B.

37 929D-930C.

38 'Quae recte confirmatio dicitur, quoniam super hoc quod peccata ipsa quoque dimittit, in bono etiam confirmat, et quasi athletam contra spiritualia nequitiae praearmat': 846D.

presence of Christ in the sacrament, and contrasts the spiritual communion with Christ's divinity which the angels enjoy in heaven with the physical reception of his body by the faithful in Holy Communion [39].

He does not use the term transsubstantiation, but clearly holds the doctrine. He teaches that the presence of Christ in the Eucharist is effected by a conversion of the substance of the bread and of the wine into the body and blood of Christ. Though the substance of the bread and of the wine cease to be present, their outward appearances and qualities remain [40]. The conversion is an effect of divine omnipotence, and is effected by Christ through the sole ministry of priests [41].

The doctrine of concomitance is well stated. In virtue of the words of consecration the bread is not converted into Christ's blood, nor the wine into his body, nor either of these into his soul or divinity. Yet body, blood, soul and divinity are received in communion even under one species. The reason is that Christ has no other body or blood except those in union with each other and with the divinity [42].

Treating of the institution of the Holy Eucharist, Pullen notes

---

[39] 'Hic panis de caelo, hic panis angelorum merito dicatur; quoniam illum designat qui cum sit refectio et gaudium angelorum, de caelo descendit ut carne assumpta fieret et hominum panis. Quem ergo angeli, utpote fortiores, manducant in divinitate, homo infirmus eundem manducat in carne': 959C-D.

[40] 'Cum autem panis in carnem, vinum quoque virtute Christi vertatur in sanguinem, substantia utique vini et panis desinit esse quod fuerat, idque fit quod prius non erat; proprietates tamen amborum transeuntium manent, unde fit ut id quinque sensus nostri post consecrationem inveniant, quod ante consecrationem inveniebant': 966D.

[41] 'Dominus virtute benedictionis suae, et per se et per ministros, ita ut neque panis neque vinum id quod ante erat remaneat, verum in alteram transeat naturam; panis in carnem, vini in sanguinem': 965C.

'Transit itaque substantia, sed remanet forma; neutrum miraris, sed omnipotentem contemplaris': 697A.

'Non ab aliis quam sacerdotibus, neque ab ipsis contra statutum Ecclesiae accedentibus, altaris sacramenta conficiuntur. Possunt equidem indigni vita conficere; sed necesse est ritum ecclesiasticum servare': 965A.

[42] 'Itaque neque panem in sanguinem, neque vinum in carnem, imo neutrum in animam aut in divinam naturam arbitraris benedicendo vertendum ... Vinum tamen efficitur sanguis, is quidem qui per carnem est diffusus, quia alium non habet Christus': 964A-B.

'Panis transit in corpus verum; non exsangue, sed plenum sanguine; non mortuum, sed anima vivificatum Deoque unitum': 967C.

'Utique sub utraque specie totus Christus suscipitur, si speciem, speciei amica verba prosequuntur': 968A.

that Christ first partook of the Jewish Pasch before instituting the sacrament of which the Pasch was a type. In giving the sacrament of his body and blood as a memorial of the redemption, he terminated forever the old dispensation [43]. So anxious is Pullen to prevent any reintroduction of Old Testament rites, that he inveighs at length against a custom of partaking on the evening of Maundy Thursday of a meal additional to the one sanctioned by ecclesiastical law during Lent [44].

The effects of the reception of this sacrament by the faithful are a quickening of spiritual life and mutual union. These graces are symbolised and effected by each of the sacramental species. The only difference between them is that the perfection of the soul is more particularly signified by the partaking of Christ's blood, and that of the body by the reception of his body [45].

The Eucharist produces these effects only in worthy recipients. Others, whether infidels or sinners, partake of this sacrament to their destruction [46]. Sacrilegious recipients are reckoned guilty of deicide, and their punishment in hell will be that meted out to those who crucified Christ [47]. Those who are in good dispositions should partake of the sacrament without anxiety, becoming by

---

[43] 'Antiqui ergo paschae, tam sibo meta ponitur quam potui, in coena Domini. Coenam ergo Domini, neque in vino neque in azymis, sicut neque in esu agni, quoniam haec Dominus terminavit, nemo reducat; alioquin judaizat. Extrema pars coenae, quae ita novo debetur homini quemadmodum prima veteri, qua Dominus suis sacramenta corporis et sanguinis distribuit, ipsa saepius est repetenda, auctore Domino, qui post novae coenae, novique paschae distributionem ait apostolis, et per eos aliis: *Hoc facite in meam commemorationem*': 971A.

[44] 973C-974B.

[45] 'Eadem significatio in calice est, nisi quod sanguis quo anima nonnunquam declaratur, ea refectione animam indicat recreandam; corpus vero carne, ut quoniam corpore et anima constamus, in utroque virtute coelestis cibi perficiamur; et sicut corporali cibo corporaliter, ita spirituali spiritualiter confortemur': 961D-962A.

[46]. 'Alii namque mors est, nisi qui verum Ecclesiae est membrum': 961D.

'Qui ergo non manducat, vitam non habet; qui autem indigne manducat, mortem habet. Malum est ut vita careas, pessimum autem ut mortem incurras. Quid est ergo consulendum? Ut vitam corrigas, et communices. Sin autem nondum vis bonus esse, minus mali est non communicare. Bonus autem es mala si non habes mortifera, tametsi habes quotidiana, id est si mens in affectu peccandi non sit': 962D.

[47] 962B. Cf. *De Contemp. Mundi et cit.* 221: 'Quid ergo, sacrilege quid insultas homicidis? Alii, hominis; tu, dei homicida es; alii, hostem; tu interemisti patrem, et quotiens ad mensam domini inconsulte accessisti tot parricidiorum reatus contraxisti ».

it stronger to do good and resist evil, and better able to discern between the one and the other [48]. The Eucharist is, therefore, the food of the strong; by receiving it the good become better, and the wicked worse [49]. For reasons of reverence towards the sacrament Pullen held that it should not be administered to criminals condemned to death. By its reception a criminal will become the temple of God; yet he will not on that account be spared by his judges. Better, then, argues Pullen, that the criminal should forego the consolation of Holy Communion than that men should lay violent and sacrilegious hands on the temple of God, and bury him in unconsecrated ground. When the criminal has repented of his sins his salvation is not endangered. A further justification for this apparently rigorist practice, urged by Pullen, is that men are likely to be deterred from committing capital crimes, if they know that they will not be allowed to receive the sacraments of penance or the Eucharist before their execution [50].

The frequency of communion, says Pullen, is a matter of custom, and varies with different persons. The Fathers enjoined the reception of the sacrament three times a year, at Christmas, Easter and Pentecost. This is to be regarded as a minimum for laymen; but priests should communicate more often. Local usage can be a guide, but the important thing is to approach worthily [51]. Pullen is insistent that the sacrament under the form of viaticum for the dying is so necessary, that a person who fails to receive it through his own negligence departs this life badly [52].

Treating of the administration of the sacrament Pullen states that priests have the duty of deciding who are to be permitted to receive, and who are to be prohibited. Notorious public sinners must be excluded, if this can be done without provoking dissensions; for if they are suffered to communicate those who are weak in faith will be scandalized, the unworthy recipients will be lulled into a false sense of security, and the priest will be guilty of exposing the sacrament to irreverence. Other sinners

---

48 963A.

49 963A.

50 904B-C.

51 966D.

52 'Nam qui cibum hunc habere potuit et neglexit, male de hac vita abit': 962D. Pullen, therefore, teaches equivalently that the reception of the Eucharist is necessary *necessitate praecepti*. Certain of his contemporaries, chiefly from the Porretanist school, taught what amounted to a *necessitas medii*. See A. Landgraf, Zwei Probleme der frühscholastischen Sakramentenlehre. *Z. k. Th.* LXVI (1942) 119-121.

should be admonished privately to refrain from sacrilegious reception. If they reject this counsel they may be suffered to approach the altar, lest the priest, in denying the sacrament, be thought to be acting out of personal animosity. A priest compelled to administer the sacrament under these circumstances commits no sin; he may take comfort from the thought that Christ did not cast out Judas from the supper [53].

Regarding the question of reception under one or two species, Pullen prudently remarks that the decision has been left by Christ to the judgement of the Church. Custom and convenience have combined to decide that the laity should receive under one kind only. There would be danger of irreverence if they were to partake of the chalice of Christ's blood in crowded churches, and the danger would be accentuated if the chalice had to be carried about the parish for distribution to the sick. Yet he who receives under one kind receives as much as one who receives under both, since Christ's body and blood are not separated. To dip the host in the chalice before distribution argues a want of faith in this truth. Moreover, such a practice is contrary to Christ's ordinance, seeing that He administered the host and the chalice separately. It is no defence to reply that the practice of communicating the laity under one kind only is also contrary to Christ's example. The custom has in its justification a valid reason, already stated, which is equally cogent against the practice of intinction. It is significant, remarks Pullen, that at the Last Supper the only person to receive bread by intinction was Judas. Pullen admits that the practice is customary in numerous places for reasons of alleged convenience, but concludes that it is different from Christ's practice, and that innovation on the present discipline is strictly forbidden by the authority of Rome.

Pullen makes a brief reference to the practice of spiritual or symbolic communion. He enquires whether the popular opinion is well founded that those who partake of bread blessed, but not consecrated, at Sunday Mass in lieu of the Eucharist, or, if they are unable to receive the bread, at least partake of grass, receive the same spiritual blessings as are conferred by the actual reception of the sacrament. He replies that there is no authority for such a persuasion, and that it would be temerarious to encourage it. No argument in its support can be adduced from the efficacy of the Old Testament types of the Eucharist, since these have now

---

53 968B-D.

54 964A-B.

been abrogated[55]. The custom of distributing blessed bread to those unable to communicate was common in the Middle Ages, and in some regions has lasted until modern times. The reference to making a spiritual communion at the hour of death by partaking of three blades of grass is confirmed both by numerous *chansons de geste* from the twelfth century onwards and by some historical documents[56].

Pullen's treatment of the Eucharist as a sacrifice is brief, and not clearly distinguished from his discussion of it as a sacrament. In several places he expressly calls it a sacrifice[57]. Commenting on the text, *Sacrifice and oblation thou didst not desire ... then said I, Behold I come* (Ps. xxxix, 7-8), he remarks that, in the person of the prophet, Christ is declaring his will to institute a new sacrifice in place of those of old, one in place of many, the reality in place of the types. This is to be a sacrifice of his body, and it was to have a priesthood worthy of it, and a priestly code to regulate its offering[58]. By its means the world is to be reconciled to the Father[59]. It is the sacrifice and salvation of the Church[60]. This new sacrifice was inaugurated by Christ at the Last Supper, when He gave his body and blood to his disciples for them to partake of. The body which He gave them was mortal, and doomed to die, as the future forms of the words which Christ

---

55 'Ergone vulgi decretum hujus rei consideratione confirmatur, scilicet panem benedictum die Dominica libantibus; vel praeoccupatis herbam saltem quasi Eucharistiam sumentibus, idem valere et pro eucharistia esse? Quis hoc absque auctoritate inducere audeat. Praesertim cum postquam res est, ipsam ratio sit esse per se; ante autem quam sit, figuram valere': 960D-961A.

56 See W. Sylvester, The Communions with Three Blades of Grass of the Knights-Errant, *Dublin Review*, CXXI (1897) 80; A. Landgraf, Literarhistorische Bemerkungen zu den Sentenzen des Robertus Pullus, *Traditio* 1 (1943) 221f.

57 'Sacrificium autem hoc corpore et sanguine celebratur, ut eo participans totus vegetatur. Ad hoc sacrificium diversa grana conveniunt, quoniam diversis Ecclesiae personis praeparatur': 961D.

58 'Venit autem ut legem finiret; sicut ipse in propheta ad Patrem loquens testatur: *Holocaustum et pro peccato non postulasti; tunc dixi: Ecce venio;* quasi diceret: Cum tibi placuit ut legis sacrificia cessarent... tunc veni in mundum, ut facerem voluntatem tuam, unum pro multis, novum pro veteribus, rem pro figuris, sacrificium scilicet mei corporis inducens, dignumque tanto sacerdotium, sacrificio, legemque sacerdotum, jura sacrificii perdocentem': 778A-B.

59 'Domino, ut per stultitiam fidei salvos faceret credentes superbosque confutaret, placuit, sicut per lavacri regenerationem, ita quoque per corporis et sanguinis sui refectionem mundum Patri suo reconciliare': 959C.

60 961D; 963A.

used make clear [61]. The reception of Christ's body and blood under separate species at the supper signified their physical separation to come by his passion and death. Hence the Last Supper was not by itself a complete sacrifice; but needed to be completed by the passion. Like the Supper the Eucharist is a representation of the passion but in retrospect. In the Supper the passion was represented in Christ's mortal body; in the Eucharist in his immortal body [62]. In this understanding of the Eucharistic sacrifice the Communion is of supreme importance. It is by the communion of Christ's body and blood, in which there is a separate reception of the sacred elements by the priest, that the passion is signified. This separate reception was enjoined by Christ on the disciples present at the Last Supper, and on other priests [63]. In Pullen's explanation, therefore, of the Mass, there is a sacramental or mystical immolation of Christ in the communion of the priest who consecrated the sacred species by the power of Christ. The Mass (like the Last Supper) symbolises Calvary and for this reason those who communicate should always recall to mind the significance of their action, endeavouring to make some recompense to Christ [64]. In addition, union with Christ's body in Communion signifies union with Him in mind and will, and, consequently, the union of the members of the Church. Further, this symbolism

[61] 'Dominus discipulis suis mortale corpus, et quod plus est moriturum (unde ait: *Quod pro vobis tradetur*: sicut et de sanguine, *qui pro multis effundetur*), manducandum exhibuit': 964C. Many theologians of Pullen's time held that Christ gave his immortal body in Communion at the Last Supper. See A. Landgraf, *Dogmengeschichte der Frühscholastik*, II, i, 199ff; id. Die Sterblichkeit Christi nach der Lehre der Frühscholastik, *Z. k. Th.* LXXIII (1951) 257-312.

[62] 'Quod in Christi mortali corpore gerebatur sacramenti perceptione, id in ipsius consequenter passione completum est; quod autem modo in mensa Christi representatur, in praeterita ejus passione agebatur. Illa ergo quod adhuc erat futurum, ista autem refectio quod jam est praeteritum designat. Ibi in mortali carne passio futura, hic in immortali praeterita insinuatur': 963A.

[63] 'Dum caro manducatur, et ori sanguis infunditur, passio Domini et corpore afflicti et sanguine perfusi insinuatur ... Et quidem Christus discipulis, et per discipulos sacerdotibus reliquis qualiter ab ipsis mensa Domini sit participanda declaravit, dicens: *Accipite et comedite*: *Hoc est corpus meum*: et post: *Bibite ex hoc omnes; hic est sanguis meus.* Itaque primo corpus, post sanguis a presbyteris est sumendus. Institutio Christi mutanda non est quippe decreti sanctione hoc modo firmata: *Hoc facietis in meam commemorationem.* Itaque non aliud, sed hoc fiat': 963C-D.

[64] 'Quamobrem quoties sacramento participamus, significatae rei memores esse debemus; quare enim memores nisi ut quid pro nobis tulerit attendamus, quidve rependi oporteat, minime praetermittamus?': 963C.

is efficacious. The reception of the Body and blood of Christ confers the graces of union which it signifies. For this reason the Eucharist is accounted the principal sacrament of the Church [65].

Pullen's explanation has the merit of indicating the organic relation of Communion to the Eucharistic sacrifice, and of the Eucharist to the sacrifice of Calvary. The Eucharist and Calvary are not two distinct sacrifices, each with its own real immolation. The Eucharist is essentially a sacramental sacrifice. It needs Calvary for its completion as a sacrificial rite; only in the passion is the immolation real and physical. Calvary requires the Eucharist as a perpetual and efficacious sign, and as a mystical renewal of Christ's saving love [66].

Penance.

During the course of the twelfth century the theology of the sacraments was developed and systematised to a remarkable extent. This is especially true of the sacrament of penance, to which the masters in the schools paid particular attention. At the opening of the century apart from Lanfranc's *Libellus de Celanda Confessione* [67] and the anonymous *De Vera et Falsa Paenitentia* [68] there were no systematic theological treatises on the sacrament of penance. In the construction of their syntheses the masters in theology had at their disposal a number of canonical collections dealing with the practical administration of the sacrament, which embodied many patristic texts and material from the earlier penitential books, as well as papal and conciliar decisions. Faced with this unsystematic mass of material, and with the problem

---

[65] 'Unio perceptionis unionem significat mentis; quippe dum carnem Christi in nobis suscipimus, quid aliud quam templum Christi nos insinuamus? Tunc autem Christi templum sumus, cum tanto inhabitatore moribus atque fide pollemus. ... Mensa ergo Domini non solum ipsius passionem, imo et conformitatem, et, ut dictum est, Ecclesiae designat unitatem; habe caritatem et eris hoc vinculo tam capiti constrictus quam membris. Jure ergo praecipuum Ecclesiae judicatur sacramentum, quod tam sacra habet insinuare, imo et rite participantibus conferre': 963B-C.

[66] Those familair with the explanation of the sacrifice in the *Mysterium Fidei* of Père M. de la Taille, will find not a little confirmation in Pullen of the author's claim that his theory is well grounded in the teaching of antiquity, in spite of certain differences of treatment.

[67] *P. L.* 150, 625-632.

[68] *P. L.* 40, 1113-1130. This work was composed probably about the middle of the eleventh century. It was thought to be the work of St. Augustine up to the fifteenth century.

of reconciling many apparently contradictory texts, it is not surprising that the early twelfth-century theologians propounded imperfect, obscure and not infrequently mutually contradictory solutions of the problems which they undertook to solve. Yet their work was to lay the foundations of the scholastic theology of the sacraments. Among the most influential of the masters who dealt with the theology of penance in the first half of the century were Peter Abelard, Hugh of St. Victor and the masters of the school of Laon. The solutions of Abelard were often explicitly contradicted by Hugh, but after they had been pruned of their excesses they were destined to have a wider influence, largely through their adoption by Peter the Lombard. Robert Pullen's work on penance is of considerable importance. He inclined more to the opinions of Abelard than to those of the school of St. Victor, but developed them in an original and fruitful manner which was not without influence on later theologians.

Pullen's treatment of the sacrament of penance is more detailed than of the other sacraments. It is developed in his sermons, as well as in his *Sentences*. In the *Sentences* the theological problems are studied in a series of loosely connected chapters in books V to VII. As with other topics there is a somewhat haphazard arrangement of material, and a certain amount of repetition and overlapping. Like Hugh of St. Victor, Pullen begins his treatment of penance by dealing with confession. This he defines as a second refuge for those who have sinned after baptism [69]. He insists that sincere contrition for all sins and a firm purpose of amendment must precede confession if it is to be profitable [70]. We have already examined this preliminary contrition in connection with Pullen's account of the preparation required for justification [71]. He explicitly includes confession among the sacraments [72]. This is contrary to the opinion of Abelard and others that penance was not a sacrament, and against those contemporary

[69] 'Quoniam pactum baptismi subditi adhuc vanitati non servamus, secundum post naufragium nobis refugium constituitur confessio': 851D. Tertullian speaks of penance as « naufrago tabulam », *De Paenitentia.* IV, 3, *P.L.* I. 1233.

[70] 'Nihil ergo valet confessio oris, nisi pretium sumat ex affectione mentis': 852A. Cf. *De Contemptu Mundi,* ed. cit. 204: 'Nam ante omnia opus est compunctione, ut in quocumque deum offendisti toto corde displiceas, ita ut preterita omnio defleas, et deflenda cavere ulterius proponas'.

[17] *supra* 204 ff.

[72] 'Sed licet non liceat sacramenta quaedam iterari, quoniam semel sumpta ad omne sufficiunt tempus, sunt tamen alia quae nisi saepius percepta, non sufficiunt illi qui supervivit. Unde confessionem et eucharistiam crebro repetimus': 847C.

authors who held that only public penance was sacramental. In accordance with his general sacramental theory Pullen reckons confession a sacrament because it signifies a sacred gift. The effect or gift here is the forgiveness of sins already granted to the penitent by God because of his contrition. Pullen also uses the expressions, 'the sacrament of binding and loosing', and 'the sacrament of absolution and remission', as equivalent to the term 'the sacrament of confession' [73]. This notion of priestly absolution as the outward sacramental sign of the divine remission already granted to the contrite penitent had already been adumbrated by earlier writers, but it was first formulated explicitly by Pullen, and in the form in which he elucidated it was echoed by later writers [74].

If therefore, as Pullen and many other writers admitted, the guilt of sin is remitted by contrition the question arises as to the necessity of confession. Pullen is emphatic in a number of passages both in the Sermons and the *Sentences* that confession is absolutely necessary if it can possibly be made [75]. Just as an adult catechumen who has already been justified by saving faith is bound under pain of grave sin to receive the sacrament of baptism, so a penitent justified by contrition must afterwards confess his sins to a priest [76]. Unwillingness to accept this obligation makes forgive-

---

[73] 'Is nimirum peccata dimittit, qui virtutes dimissioni superponit; qui utrisque vitam aeternam retribuit, quid ergo apud homines est peccata remittere, aut peccato absolvere, nisi sacramentum remissionis et absolutionis celebrare? Ex quo quis paenitet, Deus remittit, peccata postmodum confitenti minister Dei absolvendo remittit. Et quid est absolvendo remittit: nisi quod sacramentum remissionis et absolutionis facit? Absolutio quae peracta confessione super paenitentem a sacerdote fit, sacramentum est quoniam sacrae rei signum est. Et cujus sacrae rei est signum, nisi remissionis et absolutionis? Nimirum confitentibus a sacerdote facta a peccatis absolutio remissionem peccatorum, quam antea peperit cordis contritio designat': 910B-C.

[74] e. g. by Simon of Tournei, Odo of Ourscamp, Stephen Langton, See P. Anciaux, *La théologie du sacrement de pénitence au XIIe siècle,* pp. 375, 494, 518, 606, 609.

[75] *Serm.* 2: 'Qui autem preuenti fuerint morte antequam soluantur, procul dubio dampnabuntur. Sed qui statim post confessionem, siue in parte peracta satisfactione, obierit, antequam conplere eam possit saluabitur iste, *sic tamen quasi per ignem*'.

De Contemp. Mundi, ed. cit. 205: 'Et quidem penitentiam talem esse decet que sola sufficit, siquidem confessionem, satisfactionemque extrema necessitas, non uoluntas, excludit: quod sensit qui dicit: *dixi confitebor aduersum me iniusticiam meam domino, et tu remisisti impietatem peccati mei.* Id est proposui uicario dei iniusticiam que est ex me confiteri, nil michi parcens, et tu, merito huius propositi statim impietatem remisisti'.

[76] 'Quemadmodum autem post compunctionem, ubi ab ipso Domino susci-

ness impossible; neglect to fulfil it nullifies the remission received [77]. Pullen notes that the necessity of confession is inculcated by Scripture, and urged by the Church [78]. To the objection that St. Peter and St. Mary Magdalene received forgiveness without confession, he replies that the privileges of individuals do not constitute a general law [79]. Confession must therefore be as complete as possible, and free both from exaggerations and excuses. Essential circumstances of the sin must be mentioned. Along with contrition and confession there must be hope of pardon and amendment of life [80].

Pullen suggests three reasons for the necessity of making confession of sins to a priest. The first is the duty of obedience to ecclesiastical law; this reason was unanimously admitted by theologians, but some allowed Abelard's opinion that if confession were to result in a grave scandal for the Church it could be omitted. Unlike Pullen they found justification for this opinion in the supposition that St. Peter found forgiveness without making oral confession [81]. The second reason advanced by Pullen is that the priest, after hearing the confession, might impose a suitable penance, by the performance of which the penitent would be saved from enduring the far more severe pains of purgatory [82].

---

tatur Lazarus, necessaria est confessio, ubi officiis ministrorum ligamentis mortis, id est corpore peccati absolvitur; ita post fidem qua mors propellitur, succedit baptisma, ut vita vegetetur': 840C-D.

77 'Quisquis enim facinora sua sacerdoti pandere noluerit, aut timore mundi perterritus, aut inhonestate rei verecundatus, is nulla ratione veniam impetrat; aut si prius confiteri optabat, jam id agit ut impetratam perdat': 896C.

78 'Confessionem autem obnixe et Scriptura mandat, et Ecclesia statuit': 897D. This definite assertion is remarkable in view of the uncertainty of a number of the early theologians as to whether confession is of divine or ecclesiastical institution. See the text cited from the Gloss on the *Digestum Vetus* by A. Landgraf, Grundlagen für ein Verständnis der Buszlehre der Scholastik, *Z. k. Th.* LI (1927) 167.

79 'Nam privilegium paucorum non facit legem': 898A.

80 'Qui vere utiliterque confitetur, is prout res gesta est persequatur, nec ultra quam res se habet turpitudinem suam exaggeret, nec ipsam abhorrens verborum appositione excuset': 900D. Cf. *De Contemp. Mundi, ed. cit.* 205.

'Plerumque enim quid in gestione negotii contingit gesto negotio aut prevalet, aut reatum adjungit. Ratione ergo tali: *Revela Domino viam tuam, et spera in eo et ipse faciet ...* Opus est sperare, quia sine spe non est impetrare. Verumtamen si quis vitam non corrigit, et veniam sperat, is frustra sperat': 900D-901A. Cf. *De Contemp. Mundi. ed. cit.* 208.

81 Abelard, *Ethica*, c. 24. See Anciaux, *op. cit.* 179.

82 'Est quoque opus illis quoniam praesens poena diligenter suscepta, a futura longe graviore defendit purgatoria': 908C.

This reason was also commonly admitted, especially by Abelard and his followers, who admitted no intrinsic connection between the sacerdotal absolution and the remission of the guilt of sin. Their opinion was controverted by the Victorines, who contended that by the absolution there was not just a declaration that the guilt was forgiven by God, but an efficacious absolution from the eternal punishment due to sin. Pullen's third reason for making confession indicates that he held a position intermediate between that of Abelard and Hugh of St. Victor. This reason is said to consist in the fact that in the rite of confession worthily celebrated there is an absolution from sins [83].

To understand the nature of this absolution, says Pullen, it is first necessary to understand how men are so bound that they require loosing. Their bonds are spiritual, either of sin, or of the punishment due to sin. The latter consists either in penitential exercises, or in the punishment of excommunication. A person separated from the Church and its benefits by excommunication is absolved from this bond by the rite of reconciliation. The former bond, that of sin, binds a man as long as he has his heart set on it, and even after he has forsaken it, inasmuch as through a habit of sin his will has become enfeebled and sluggish in doing good [84]. To illustrate the nature of the sacerdotal absolution Pullen adapts to his purpose a much used allegorical interpretation of the scriptural account of the raising of Lazarus from the dead. As he lies motionless in the tomb Lazarus is a type of a sinner who of himself is powerless to regain the life of grace which he has lost. Summoned to arise and come forth from the tomb, he represents the sinner who by the grace of contrition has been restored to spiritual life. As he emerges with his face covered by a veil, and his limbs constricted by the winding sheet, he symbolises the sinner, who, in spite of his restoration to spiritual life, is still a prey to mental blindness and weakness of will, which are the wounds left by his sins. Finally, when he is freed from his bands by the disciples and

---

83 'Opus quoque est confessione, quoniam in ipsa digne celebrata peccatorum est absolutio': 908C.

84 'Sed ut absolutionis ratio manifestius declaretur, prius quid sit ligari, ut solvi necesse sit, praevideatur. Ligantur homines vinculis spiritualibus aut peccati aut poenae peccati Poena autem peccati, sicut modo accepimus, aut lamenta sunt paenitentium, aut sequestratio excommunicatorum: sed qui extra Ecclesiam, imo et Ecclesiae beneficia, ligamine anathematis detinetur, is reconciliatione foederata absolvitur. Vinculo peccati constringitur quisquis aut dum amat culpam a recto itinere praepeditus, aut si vitium jam deposuit, quasi a languore qui recenter convaluerit, ita a vitio noviter curatur, consuetudine mala libere quid agat retardatur': 908D-909A.

suffered to depart, Lazarus represents a penitent who has been absolved by a priest. The effect of the absolution is that the penitent receives strength gradually to overcome the crippling effects of his sins, and is thus prepared to walk in the way of truth [85].

Confession, therefore, should be made without delay, even by him who is justified by contrition. Only thus will light and strength be granted him that he might emerge from the darkness and stupor which are the result of his sins. Absolution, therefore, does not merely manifest the forgiveness of sin; it contributes to it, in the sense that it provides grace to heal the wounds of sin [86]. There is thus a parallel between confession and adult baptism. The latter does not only manifest the reception of justification by faith; it strengthens it. Moreover, just as confirmation by its invigorating grace is the complement of the healing grace of baptism, so satis-

---

[85] 'Qui vero fructibus paenitentiae nondum expletis poenae obnoxius tenetur, is, ea peracta, ut jam dignus sit requie, absolvitur. Ex proprio contrahit homo ut morte praevaricationis gravatus, e loco ad vitam per se moveri non possit. Hic est Lazarus immobilis in tumulo. Virtute autem divina fit ut flagitiis pressus, onere mortifero se subtrahat. Hic est Lazarus a tumulo clamore Domini evocatus, qui Deo suffragante a morte ad vitam redit. Is, vita reddita, quam quasi ex antea habita morte vestigia aliquandiu reservans, quodammodo torpet et hebet, dum humanae fragilitatis inopia, quae agenda sunt discutiens, minus videt, et utcunque discussa et cognita ut oporteret minime exsequi valet. Hic est Lazarus resuscitatus, facie velatus, institisque circumligatus. Quisque vero justitiae restitutus, praeteritae ignominiae molestia, quasi quibusdam institis a recto gressu retardatur, is sacerdotali confessione, ad viam veritatis tenendam praeparatur; sicque difficultas bene agendi, quae prius inerat, paulatim consuetudine boni alleviatur. Hic est Lazarus discipulorum officio solutus et abire permissus': 909A-B.

[86] 'Valde ergo opus est ut nemo ad confessionem sit piger; quoniam licet quisque corde contrito et humilato a morte animae reviviscat, attamen torpore quodam post recessum mortis residuo et ad ea quae mortis sunt tametsi invitus incessanter retorquetur, et ab officiis vitae cum moestitia detinetur; donec per confessionem absolutio id efficiat, et ut facies mentis sudario peccati, non jam ut prius quasi per sudarium, sed aptius magis ac modo magisque verum cernat, et ut cetera membra constricta prius quibusdam languorum quasi ligamentis, et per hoc quamvis rediviva, vix tamen ad vitam palpitantia, jam gradu libero, liberiore in progressu futuro, acie rationis per omnia ducatum praebente, inoffensum vitae callem suo quaeque modo incedant. Impedimenta hujusmodi infert interitus, quisque suo in genere praecipuus; vita rediens dum illa luctatur evincere, proficit quidem, sed parum donec adjuta confessione confessionisque opere, vires, recipiat et augeat, quibus se expediat et crescat. *Sit ergo omnis homo velox ad confitendum,* quoniam sic promptus fiet ad bene agendum': 909C-D.

'Nam sedulitas confessionis, maxime sacerdoti facta, nominatimque expressa, id virium obtinet, non solum ut reus expietur, verum quoque ut vitiorum crebra impugnatio retundatur, protervitas inquietationis hebetur': 897B.

faction by penitential exercises completes the effect of confession [87].

Pullen's teaching that confession loosed the bonds of sin by healing its wounds, was taken up by other theologians, including Odo of Ourscamp and Stephen Langton [88].

According to Pullen the contrite penitent who has received absolution in the manner and with the results already described, remains bound by the temporal punishment due to sin until he has performed condign satisfaction. When the priest imposes a penance for sin he exercises his power of binding. Absolution from this bond does not belong to the priest but to God, since the human agent, whether priest or penitent, cannot know for certain when condign satisfaction has been made. If the satisfaction enjoined by the priest, and performed by the penitent, is insufficient, further satisfaction will be required by God, either in the form of sufferings endured by the penitent in this life, or hereafter in purgatory. When God is content with the satisfaction that has been performed the sinner is fit to enter heaven. For this reason the Church has not enjoined any special form of absolution from the bond of tem-

---

[87] 'Quemadmodum autem post compunctionem, ubi ab ipso Domino suscitatur Lazarus, necessaria est confessio, ubi officio ministrorum ligamentis mortis, id est torpore (corpore) peccati absolvitur; ita post fidem, qua mors propellitur, succedit baptisma, ut vita vegetatur. Et quomodo quolibet tempore *charitas operit multitudinem peccatorum*, ne sint ultra ad damnationem, compunctio vero, quam charitas parit, atque satisfactio, quam importat compunctio, eadem operit, ne exigantur ultra ad poenam; ita homini peccata remittit fides, ne damnetur; baptismus, ne puniatur. Quod fides facit baptismus ostendit; fides peccata delet, baptismus deleta docet, unde sacramentum dicitur': 840D.

'Recte ergo in remissionem peccatorum baptisma sumitur, quod a poena peccati solvi, et absolutum insinuat, et vitam ex fide natam confortat. Qui ergo Spiritum Sanctum recipit per fidem, eum magis obtinet in regeneratione, praecipue habiturus eundem in confirmatione, hoc namque est Spiritum quibusdam gradibus suscipere, per augmenta promoveri bonae vitae ... Fides more paenitentiae suscitat, baptismus more confessionis sanat, confirmatio more satisfactionis vegetat': 841A.

[88] See Anciaux, *op. cit.* 423, 494. Langton says that the wounds of sin are loosed. 'per exhortationem sacerdotis'. Odo of Ourscamp attributes this effect to the words of absolution, and says that it is intermediate between absolution from guilt and absolution from punishment. Pullen seems to have regarded it as appertaining to absolution from punishment, in so far as the weakness consequent on sin is a punishment for the sin. Cf. 913C-D: 'Trifaria namque participatione quilibet a peccatis absolvitur: aut dum ipsa corde contrito indulgentur; aut dum moles ex peccatis nata, et post peccati abscessum vinctis in mendicitate et ferro molesta, succurrente Domino, sedatur; aut tertio dum quam meruit culpa, cessat disciplina. Sed prima dimissio id efficit, ut non sit ad damnationem culpa, secunda vero cum tertia ut a peccati discedat poena'.

poral punishment. No certainty can be had of full satisfaction except in the case of a purely ecclesiastical penalty [89]. Pullen considered that works of satisfaction spontaneously undertaken were more praiseworthy and meritorious than those enjoined by a confessor, since they were more likely to be motivated by love and not by fear [90].

In imposing a penance the confessor is to review carefully the circumstances of the case [91]. He can err either by laxity or excessive severity [92]. Account must also be taken of the strength of the penitent in determining the type of austerity to be imposed. Alms-

---

89 'Quisquis vero per confessionem poenitentiae fructibus intendit (quod jam potest ea quae in confessione fit absolutione roboratus) is usque ad peractos, obligatur poenae. Poenam autem peccati quoad protelari oportet, quandove terminari, ille novit cui satisfit per poenam': 909D-910A.

'Peracta autem paenitentia, (non semper quam homo imponit sed quam Deus pronovit; quippe si homo minus quam docet facit, Deus purgatoriis id supplet poenis, aut in hoc saeculo; nec nostra superfluit satisfactio, quoniam si plena est, omnino tollit: sin vero diminuta, partim imminuit flagellum Dei nostrae praevaricationi debitum), peracta, inquam paenitentia, reus per Deum absolvitur; non solum ut non amplius pro peccato puniri oporteat, verum etiam ut purgatione facta coelo fiat idoneus. Hujusmodi absolutionem homo non facit, quia quando eam fieri conveniat, nemo novit. Unde statuta Ecclesiae id minime decreverunt, quod sicut completam confessionem, ita quoque peractam satisfactionem consequatur. Novit enim ex ore confitentis et ex modo se habendi utrum a culpa absolvat. Sed nulla experimenti ratio comperta est, unde certum sit quando a poena culpae solvi oporteat, nisi forte ab illa quam imposuit ipse'.

Sicut autem sacerdos solvit, ita et ligat, dum utriusque sacramentum celebrat. Sacerdos ergo ligat poenae. ... dum illum pro delictis usque ad tempus post confessionem onerat': 910D-911B.

90 Cf. *De Contemp. Mundi, ed. cit.* 216: 'Nemo tunc tantum disciplinam noxarum speret purgatoriam cum quod a sacerdote injungitur ipse inplere conatur: immo quod per se addiderit preclarius puto. Nam quod ibi necessitas cogit, hic accumulat uoluntas. Illud timori, istud sepius deputandum amori. Illud post mortem a pena liberat: istud coronam procurat, et, si quid minus a sacerdote inponitur, consummat'. The principle that works of supererogation are more meritorious than those of obligation appears in a number of early scholastic texts; see A. Landgraf, *Dogmengeschichte der Frühscholastik,* 1, ii, 104-110.

91 'Qui autem consulere debet praepedito, is aggressurus opus, quod vix a quoquam satis diligenter beneque peragitur, invocata divina opitulatione se praemuniat; deinde attendens: *Quis, quid, ubi, quibus auxiliis, cur quomodo, quando* fecerit. Nam juxta harum qualitatem circumstantiarum, qualitas ipsa negotii perpenditur, et vel levior, vel gravior culpa aestimatur. Cognita autem causa ... sacerdos poenam condignam reo impositurus excogitet': 901D.

92 'In moralitate peccat qui quod ligandum est soluit, uel quod soluendum est ligat, et plus uel minus quam modum quantitas rei exigit indiscrete peccatorem liberat uel onerat': Serm. 19.

giving of one's own abundance is good, but painful enough to satisfy the obligation of penance. As a priest will have to render an account of his flock he should take care to impose such satisfactions as will preserve his penitents from further punishment in the life to come [93].

By the absolution from sin which he has received a penitent will receive strength to perform his penance [94].

He must not try to obtain a milder penance by deliberately seeking a simple rather than a prudent confessor [95]. If he fails to perform his penance through negligence, he will forfeit the remission he has obtained [96]. Prudence however, must be his guide in doing penance, and he should not undertake more than he can bear [97]. There are three principal ways of making satisfaction: discipline, prayer and almsgiving. Besides expiating sins, these are acts of religion, and merit the vision of God [98]. Discipline is equivalent to what later writers call mortification. It may be either interior or exterior, either self-inflicted or imposed from without. Pullen describes interior discipline as the endurance of solicitude and anxiety involved in the performance of works of zeal

---

[93] 'Considerans quid cujusque vires valeant, quid ferre recusent, quod culpae jure debeatur, ut ita reus humilietur, ostendat; quod tamen tolerari possit, imponat. Alius jejunium, alius virgam, alius frigora, alius labores, tandem alius hoc, alius illud perferre potest ... Unde praeter opera misericordiae, quae nostra de sufficientia nostro sine labore ministramus egenis, opus est ardore fornacis, unde rubigo consumatur pravitatis. Hic autem ardor aut in praesenti suscipitur, aut in futuro non effugietur'.

'Sacerdos ergo de his quibus rationem est redditurus, praesentem provideat poenam, ut evitent futuram': 902A-B.

[94] 'Quisquis vero per confessionem paenitentiae fructibus intendit (quod jam potest ea quae in confessione fit absolutione roboratus)': 909D.

[95] 'Peccator quoque si scienter ad simplicem et non prudentem confessorem eat, ut pro multis et magnis peccatis leuem et insufficientem satisfactionem faciat, procul dubio procul a raphidim habitat. Nullum quippe peccatum remanet impunitum': Serm. 19.

[96] 'Sicut enim compunctio nihil est sine spe, nec utrumque sine confessione; ita tria simul inefficacia sunt, si cum tempus suppetit et possis, aut a presbytero poenitentiae lamenta non recipis, aut recepta peragere parvipendis. Licet enim confessionis puritate acceperis veniam, si postmodum negligis satisfacere perdis acceptam': 901A-B.

[97] 'Quisquis tamen caveat onus importabile sibi assumere, ne necessitas cogat sub fasce a presbytero non recte imposita succumbere ... quod enim importabile est usquequaque recusari debet: *ibid.*

[96] 'Post confessionem et absolutionem, opus est (causa satisfactionis, imo et religionis) disciplina, oratione, eleemosyna. His tribus impetratur visio Dei, et prius venia peccati': 911C-D.

and charity [99]. Exterior discipline consists in the endurance of all kinds of suffering which spring from external causes [100]. His principal rule for the practice of self-discipline is the elimination of vices by their contrary virtues [101]. Humility can compensate for inability to endure condign external chastisement [102]. Among all forms of external austerity he ranks fasting highest, because it is sanctioned both by the practice of the Old and the New Testament [103].

The second form of making satisfaction consists in the practice of prayer, which, says Pullen, cannot fail to be of profit to a contrite and humble heart. Deliberate distractions rob one of the benefits of prayer, unlike those arising from human frailty. The mere effort to pray well is meritorious [104]. Prayer should be made for worthy intentions [105]. Temporal blessings may be requested, such as health, but spiritual blessings are more fitting objects of petition [106]. Sometimes the reason why our prayers are not heard

---

99 'Disciplina interior est multiformis animi anxietas, et curarum exercitatio, varia atque frequens utraque, cum ratione suscepta. Curarum edacitatem, sollicitudo omnium ecclesiarum, in Apostolo pariebat': 914B.

100 'Disciplinam exterius habemus cum molestiam aut extraneis de rebus, aut de charis nostris, aut postremo nostro de corpore, natam patienter toleramus': *ibid.*

101 'Necesse est enim ut quod voluptate deliquimus, castigationis amaritudine detergamus ,nihilque convenientius videtur, quam ut contrariis contraria opponamus remedia': *ibid.* C.

102 'Si tamen tanta est fragilitas praevaricatoris, ut nec qualitatem nec quantitatem ferre queat satisfactionis, aliquid tale inquirendum est, quod nec vires recusent, et reum excruciet. Est ergo satisfactio quaedam quam cujuslibet natura tolerare fere valeat, aspera tamen et tanto Deo gratior, quanto humilior, cum quilibet sacerdotis prostratus ad pedes, se caedendum virgis exhibet nudum': 914D.

103 914D-915C.

104 'Quod si dedita vanis mens vagatur, quid prodest labia concutere? Utique parum, aut potius nihil. Cum enim cuipiam loqueris et alio mentem vertis, nonne si distractio tui animadversa fuerit, locutio tua contemptibilis erit? Verum si conatu cum toto constringis animum cum verbis, unde tamen invincibili infirmitate distraharis, nonne id non tibi, sed tuae imputabitur fragilitati, ut jam tu non opereris illud, sed peccatum quod in te est? Quod si assiduitatem precum devotionis attentio prosecuta sese illi aequaret, felix utique esset. Nunc vero dum attentus aeque devotus fieri labores, contraque tuum luctaris morbum, ipso certamine beatus es, laurea tandem dimicationis triumphante donandus': 915C-D.

105 'Is quoque qui petit talis esse debet, taleque quod petitur esse oportet, ut hujusmodi non conveniat negari': 916A.

106 'Si autem oro, si opera misericordie inpendo, ut nec ego nec cari necessariis uite destituamur, quemadmodum ecclesiam pro temporalibus etiam commodis, et ne infirmi deficiant nouimus interpellare, non malum, puto, est. Quod

is our sinfulness [107]. Words are not essential in praying, since God reads our hearts; but we make use of them for the edification of our neighbour, for the overcoming of our natural slothfulness, and for the consecration of all our faculties to God [108].

The third means of satisfying for sins is by the practice of almsgiving. There are spiritual and corporal alms. The latter should be given generously, but not extravagantly [109]. Goodwill is of more account with God than pecuniary expenditure [110]. Spiritual alms include prayers for the living and the dead [111]. Corporal works of mercy which are specially commended are visiting the imprisoned, succouring those in need of sustenance and clothing, and assisting travellers [112]. In all these works of charity due order is to be maintained, in such a way that those more immediately dependent on us are first to be provided for, in accordance with the text, *He set in order charity in me* (Cant. ii, 4) [113].

The foregoing account of Pullen's teaching on the necessity of confession and satisfaction is evidence enough of the contemporary conviction of the important part played by the priest as the minister of the sacrament of penance. During the first half of the twelfth century, largely owing to the influence of Abelard, the precise nature and efficacy of the power of the priest came in for closer examination at the hands of theologians. Among other questions theologians enquired whether the plenary power of forgiving sins, which Christ granted to the Apostles, has descended to all bishops, including those of indifferent lives? [114] It was Abelard's opinion that only those notable for sanctity and prudence could lay claim to this power. After he had been condemned at the Council of Sens in 1140 he retracted his opinion, admitting that even the unworthy retained their power as long as the Church tolerated them [115]. It may be in allusion to the opinion of

si nobis uel proximis benefacientes salutem corporis exposcimus aut mentis, in illo bene in isto optime fieri non ambigimus': *De Contemp. Mundi, ed.* cit. 217.

107 916A.

108 *ibid.*

109 'Ut tanquam dispensator prudens sic in presens sis largus, ne in futurum habearis inprouidus': *De Contemp. Mundi, ed. cit.* 214.

110 'Quid ergo de paupertate querimus, quasi unde deo seruiamus non habentes? Non pecunia, set uoluntas pia apud deum perornat'. *ibid.*

111 916A-917B.

112 917B-C.

113 ibid. *De Contemp. Mundi,* 212-214.

114 See Abelard, *Ethica,* c. 25.

115 *Apologia,* ed. Cousin, t. II. 722.

Abelard that Pullen explicitly affirms that the power of binding and loosing, and of forgiving sins was given to all the successors of St. Peter and the Apostles, and to priests, as well as to bishops [116]. Abelard did not allow that priests possessed the power of binding.

Another question which was raised concerned the number and the nature of the powers signified by the metaphor of the keys. Abelard maintained that, though used in the plural, the term 'keys' signified but a single power, that of binding and loosing. Others such as the author of the *Summa Sententiarum,* saw in the plural form a proof that one of the keys consisted in the knowledge and prudence required for judging sinners, while the other was the power of binding and loosing. Yet others maintained that there were three keys, as binding and loosing were distinct operations. Pullen does not treat of this controversy in any of his surviving works, but his opinion was sufficiently well known to be mentioned by several later writers. We gather from these writers that, according to Master Robert Pullen the keys signify the judicial power of the priest. The plural form is used to signify the twofold effect of this power, binding and loosing. The requisite prudence or knowledge is not a key, but a necessary condition for the right use of the power of the keys. It may be compared to the handle of a knife, of which the blade signifies the power of binding and loosing. To make proper use of the power a priest must possess the necessary knowledge. On the penitent's side acceptance and performance of works of satisfaction are necessary. These are symbolised by the two thongs which bind the blade to the handle. On this explanation all priests receive the power of the keys. It is, therefore, different from the theory of Master Peter Abelard who asserted that few possess the keys, in so far as they include necessary knowledge as well as the power of binding and loosing, since there are few who can rightly discern between those who should be bound, and those who should be loosed [117]. Those who

---

[116] 'Sacramentum tamen ligandi atque solvendi penes ipsos Dei vicarios, id est, sacerdotes Ecclesiae est. Unde Dominus: *Quorum remiseritis peccata, remissa erunt; et quorum retinueritis retenta sunt.* Et item: *Quodcumque ligaveris super terram, erit ligatum et in coelis,* etc. Illud communiter omnibus, istud Petro, et per Petrum proponitur omnibus. Quamobrem auctoritate Domini, apostoli eorumque successores, peccata hominum retinent, ac per hoc ipsos solvunt': 910A-B.

[117] Ms. Bamberg Cod. Patr. 128, f. 15, cited by A. Landgraf, Some Unknown Writings of the Early Scholastic Period, *The New Scholasticism,* IV, (1930) 12: 'Ex predictis constat claves dici scientiam discernendi et potentiam iudi-

make use of the power of the keys without the necessary knowledge, says Pullen, do harm. They are like a man who holds a knife by the blade when cutting bread [118].

Pullen, therefore, is in accord with Abelard in maintaining that the keys signify a single power, that of binding and loosing. He differs from him in separating the possession of this power from the possession of the knowledge requisite for its use.

On the question of the nature of the power of binding and loosing Pullen's teaching also shows some important modifications of Abelard's opinions. With Abelard, as we have already seen, he teaches that sins are forgiven by God before confession as soon as the sinner is moved by contrition. Unlike Abelard, who did not hold that penance was a sacrament, and who made the efficacy of the power of binding and loosing dependent n the moral character of the minister [119], Pullen, saw in the priestly absolution a sacramental

---

candi, M(agister) R(obertus) Pollett aliter dicebat, Asserebat enim claves tantummodo dici potentiam iudicandi, que potentia dicebatur claves in plurali numero, non clavis propter duos effectus, scilicet propter potentiam ligandi et potentiam solvendi. Ille autem claves iuxta illum alligate sunt manubrio, ut usus clavium firmius habeatur. Est autem illud manubrium scientia discernendi. Alliguntur claves manubrio duabus corrigiis, que sunt voluntas satisfaciendi et executio operis. Et quod sic fit (?) verisimile. Nam secundum hoc omnes sacerdotes has habebunt claves, id est potentiam ligandi et solvendi. Secundum Magistrum Petrum pauci habent claves, scilicet scientiam discernendi et potentiam ligandi et solvendi. Pauci enim sciunt discernere, qui sint ligandi et solvendi ... F. 16: *Claudere et aperire,* id est solvere vel ligare augetur propter gratiam collatam in dignitate sacerdotii. Si premissam sententiam M(agistri) R(oberti) Poldi vel(is) tenere, omnes sacerdotes has claves recipiunt, scilicet potentiam ligandi et solvendi, sed quidam carent manubrio id est scientia discretionis'.

118 Peter the Chanter, *Summa,* Ms. London, B. M. Harley 3253, f. 121v., cited by A. Landgraf, l. c. p. 13: 'Magister Robertus, ut dicitur, dicebat quod scientia est quasi manubrium, potestas vero ligandi et solvendi sicut lamina cultelli. Et sicut lamina manum incidit, cum tenetur sine manubrio ad scindendum panem, ita potentia ledit sine scientia, que est quasi temperamentum lamine'.

Odo of Ourscamp closely follows the teaching of Pullen on the keys: Quaestiones, II, 34 (p. 34). See P. Anciaux, *op. cit.* 541. Pullen's doctrine is explicitly referred to by Robert Courçon: Bruges cod. 247, f. 19vb-20va, cited by P. Anciaux, l. c. 569: 'Tertii, ut magister Polanus et eius sequaces, dicebant quod clauis duo habet, scilicet scientiam precedentem et potestatem ligandi et solvendi subsequentem. Sicut in cultello duo sunt, scilicet manubrium et ferrum. Per manubrium tenetur ferrum. Sicut ergo ferrum secat manus tractantis, ita potentia ligandi uel soluendi que est quasi ferrum, ledit prelatum nisi in eo precedat scientia discernendi inter lepram et lepram, qua teneri habet potentia talis'.

119 See P. Anciaux, *op. cit.* 293.

sign of the divine forgiveness [120], and maintained that its efficacy was independent of the moral character of the officiant [121].

The priest exercises his power of binding by imposing a penance on the penitent or by refusing absolution to an obdurate sinner. Just as absolution manifests the remission of sin by God, so its denial signifies that it is retained by Him. God will only ratify just sentences. A priest who makes arbitrary or unjust use of his power thereby deprives himself of it. Great care should, therefore, be taken by the priest before absolving a sinner to verify that he has already been raised to life by God like Lazarus. As the priests of the Old Testament merely certified that men were infected by leprosy or free from it, and accordingly either excluded them from the people or admitted them to their company; so priests of the New Testament have the office of judging, but not of determining, the condition of penitents, and of admitting them into the Church or excluding them therefrom. Nevertheless, the exercise of this declarative power does affect the penitents for better or worse [122]. We have already seen how the absolution of the

---

120 ' Sed, *Quis potest dimittere peccata nisi solus Deus*? Is nimirum peccata dimittit qui virtutes dimissioni superponit; qui utriusque vitam aeternam retribuit. Quid ergo apud homines est peccatum remittere, aut a peccato absolvere, nisi sacramentum remissionis et absolutionis celebrare? Ex quo quis poenitet, Deus absolvendo remittit. Et quid est absolvendo remittit; nisi quod sacramentum remissionis et absolutionis facit? Absolutio quae peracta confessione super poenitentem a sacerdote fit, sacramentum est, quoniam sacrae rei signum est. Et cujus sacrae rei est signum, nisi remissionis et absolutionis? Nimirum confitentibus a sacerdote facta a peccatis absolutio remissionem peccatorum, quam antea peperit cordis contritio designat': 910B-C.

12 *Supra*, 214.

122 ' Sicut autem sacerdos solvit, ita et ligat, dum utriusque rei sacramentum celebrat. Sacerdos ergo ligat poenae, ligat culpae, dum illum pro delictis usque ad tempus post confessionem onerat. Istum autem a malo cessare nolentem, non posse veniam consequi denuntiat, et sic retinet peccata, retenta quoque apud Deum. Sicut e contra cessanti et confitenti absolvendo remittit peccata, remissa quoque apud Deum. Ait enim vicario suo Petrus: *Quod expedit ligabis, quod expedit solves;* exponens, videlicet Dominici sententiam decreti, eo usque scilicet apostolicam pertingere potestatem, ut liget vinculis constringendum, absolvat absolvi dignum. Nam qui indebite solvit aut ligat, propria potestate se privat. Non enim quod ipse agit ita fieri Deus consentit. Ligat anathemate super terram immeritum, et non ligatur apud Deum; anathemate super terram indignum absolvit, et non erit solutus in coelis ... Nemo ergo institis constringat vivum, nec absolvat mortuum; ne aut inferat constringendo necem, aut eliciat absolvendo fetorem ... Sacerdos tempore legis si quem intra castra leprosum comperisset, proditum ejiciebat; ejectum, si quando sanum vidisset, in castra revocabat; nec leprosum nec mundum efficiens, tantum utrumque discernens. Pari ratione putant Ecclesiae prelatos id ex potestate habere, ut Ecclesiae membra integra a pu-

priest contributes in Pullen's view to the remission of sin by its healing effect on the wounds left by evil habits.

Certain restrictions of the jurisdiction of the ordinary priest in the use of the power of the keys are noted by Pullen [123]. He should not administer the sacrament of penance to any but his own parishioners, except in cases of necessity. Public sins which have given scandal are to be expiated by public penance, and absolution is reserved to the bishop [124]. In assigning to ordinary priests absolution from secret sins Pullen dissociates himself from certain other unnamed writers who, he says, maintain that all sins must be submitted to the bishop. In favour of his opinion he argues that, if the sin were secret, the penitent would shrink from avowing it in public; that bishops would not have time to deal with the great numbers involved; and that penitents would be unwill-

---

tridis dijudicent, dijudicatione facta ab aliis alia disparare satagant. Sed quamvis nec mundos nec immundos sui sit efficere ministerii, quoniam alterum virtus Dei, alterum facit deformitas rei, attamen dum solvunt aut ligant, id inde contigit, aut ut melior, aut deterior reus fiat; dum aut si quasi leprosus extra dejicitur, aut ille, quoniam sanus inventus est, intra castra excipitur': 911B-912C.

Like so many others among his contemporaries who saw in the absolution of the priest a declaration of a divine remission already granted in view of a sinner's contrition, Pullen was influenced by certain patristic texts which had been incorporated in collections of canons and *florilegia,* and which served as « authorities » in the elucidation of theological problems. Among the most influential of such texts were, St. Jerome, *In Matt. lib. III, c. 16, P. L.* 26, 118, and St. Gregory the Great, *In Evang.* lib. II, hom. 26, 5-6, *P. L.* 76, 1200-1201. Both writers were concerned to exclude arbitrary and unjust use of the power of the keys. In adapting the biblical prescriptions for the treatment of lepers, and the account of the raising of Lazarus from the dead, they appeared to many early scholastics to restrict the powers of priests in the sacrament of penance to a simple declaration that sinners had been already forgiven, or were still bound by their sins. In consequence twelfth-century theologians were much exercised to find reasons for the necessity of confession in addition to that of obedience to the Church. In the passage under consideration Pullen's indebtedness to Gregory is evident.

The passage also illustrates the distinction made in Pullen's day between a juridical or corporeal separation from the Church through excommunication, and a moral or spiritual separation which might or might not be accompanied by the former one. See A. Landgraf, Sünde und Trennung von der Kirche in der Frühscholastik, *Scholastik* V (1930) 210-247.

[123] 902B. Pullen praises penitents who seek a confessor other than their local priest in order to obtain better counsel, provided they have received permission to do this, or have first accepted the penance enjoined by their own parish priest: Gratian, *Decretum,* dictum post c. ii D. VI De Paenitentia, Friedberg, I, 1244, makes the same concession.

[124] 907C-D.

ing to open their conscience to bishops who at the present time are devoted to worldly preoccupations [125]. Among sins which require public penitence is perjury committed by a plaintiff in a capital charge, in which the defendant's innocence is established through trial by ordeal [126].

If such a sinner refuses to submit to penance he is visited with ecclesiastical penalties. Several allusions are made in the *Sentences* and the Sermons of Pullen to the power of the Church to impose censures and penalties in virtue of the power of the keys. Excommunication is a punishment to be used in the last resort, when a sinner is deaf to admonitions. It is a power belonging to prelates, whom Pullen in one of his sermons likens to the watchdogs of Christ. He observes that not all these watchdogs are moved by worthy motives when they attack men [127]. He distinguishes two kinds of excommunication, one in which certain persons are specified by name, the other in which anathema is pronounced against any who perpetrate certain crimes, and against their accomplices. In the latter type no particular persons are named, either because the offenders are unknown, or known only under the seal of confession. Excommunication of particular persons is warranted by Our Lord's precept (Matt. xviii, 18) and St. Paul's practice (1 Cor. v, 5). An excommunicated person is handed over to Satan, to be vexed by him with bodily afflictions or spiritual defilement. He is to be avoided by the faithful, except by those who in virtue of social or family ties cannot be separated from him. Such a sentence must be founded on certain knowledge, and only

---

[125] 907C-D. Cf. Ivo Carnotensis, *Decretum* Pars XV, cap. 4, *P. L.* 161, 857: 'Ne presbyter clam episcopo reconciliet paenitentem'. This regulation, cited from the third council of Carthage, is also referred to by P. Lombard, *Sent.* IV D. xx cap. 6.

[126] 'Qui autem ut accusatio verisimilis habeatur super reum jurat, si divino examine is postea absolvitur, ille plane perjurat. Et quoniam capitis arcessit, dolensque non perficit; praeter perjurium quod patrat ipsa re, homicida est conatu et voluntate. Is autem quoniam publice peccavit, publice poeniteat; aut, si id neglexerit, ut dignum est, ecclesiasticae disciplinae succumbat': 905B.

[127] 'Solent esse canes socii pastorum, qui simul cum pastoribus, in die oves a raptoribus, nocte a furibus custodiunt. Pastor noster Iesus Christus, qui de se ait, *Ego sum pastor bonus.* Huius pastoris ouile est ecclesia, ubi non hedi, sed oues sunt, id est simplices in malicia. Habet iste pastor canes adiutores, prelatos ecclesiae ... Sed hoc debent agere canes, id est, mordere, peccatores increpatione et lacerare iusticia, ut eas comedant. In comestione saturitas et delectatio designatur, que in peccatoris conuercione habentur ... Non autem omnes canes hac intentione mordent peccatorem et lacerant ut eum, sed ut sua comedant, uel ut ire sue satisfaciant': Serm. 4.

put into effect where the offender is contumacious. Its purpose is to secure a sinner's conversion and amendment. If it were exercised out of malevolence it would do more harm to the Church than to the excommunicated person. The indeterminate kind of excommunication is founded not so much on scriptural precept as on ecclesiastical usage, to which obedience is due [128]. These two types correspond to what was later called *poenae ferendae sententiae* and *poenae latae sententiae.*

Pullen provides some pastoral advice for priests charged with the administration of the sacrament of penance [129]. They should realise that the sick and dying require different treatment from those who are in good health. Among the latter a priest will find men accused of crimes who are afraid of death or mutilation. These should be instructed not to allow their fear of the world to affect them to such an extent that they are prepared to offend God. If an accused is to undergo trial by ordeal he should be warned not to perjure himself. Better to suffer patiently God's punishments in this life, and thus escape eternal punishment, than to escape now by perjury and suffer eternally hereafter [130]. If the accused rejects this counsel the confessor must let matters take their course, as he is bound to preserve the secret of confession. Pullen suggests that such trials by ordeal should be abolished, but notes that, if they result in the accused being convicted of perjury, a confessor should stay away from him [131]. From the

---

128 898D.-900A. Pullen held that grave sin alone did not deprive anyone of membership of the Church. For this a sentence of excommunication was necessary. Until this was pronounced a sinner retained some spiritual life, and was protected from the assaults of Satan by the efficacy of the good works of the Church. See 899A. For contemporary teaching see J. Beumer, Ekklesiologische Probleme der Frühscholastik, *Scholastik,* XXVII (1952) 183-209.

129 903-905.

130 'Quippe qui inspiciens anteactam vitam suam corde conteritur et humiliatur, is si poenam qualibet pro culpa sibi oblatam patienter suscipit, futuram eadem de culpa effugit. Sic Sodomitas, sic mari rubro submersos; sic denique in deserto prostratos punivit in praesenti ne puniret in aeternum': 903C-D. Cf. P. Lomb. *Sent.* IV, D. xv; Gratian, *Decretum* C. XXXIII, De Paen. dist. iii, Friedberg, 1225-1226.

131 'Si autem reus convenienter a presbytero instructus, carni consentiens, id potius eligat ut perjurio patrato in ambiguum periculi, atque salutis praeceps ruat; sacerdoti, qui hujusmodi judicia ab Ecclesia Christi putent (putet?) exterminanda, nihil aliud restat, nisi ut omnibus more ecclesiastico celebratis, id permittat fieri, quod per confessionem culpa cognita minime potuit castigari.

Quod si eum qui ex confessione est reus, reum quoque divina pandant judicia (judicia enim Dei abyssus multa) non videtur ad sacerdotem pertinere ad hujusmodi accedere debere': 905D-906A.

moment when he is convicted he is handed over to a secular judge, and should confess to him, for confession is to be made to him from whom punishment is received. If a priest were to visit such malefactors they would be encouraged in their evildoing by the hope of obtaining from him confession and communion [132]. Pullen urges lofty motives of religion for this harsh counsel. If a criminal is permitted to receive the Eucharist he becomes the temple of God. Yet he will not on that account be spared by his judges. Better then that the criminal should forego the consolation of Holy Communion than that men should lay violent and sacrilegious hands on one who is the tabernacle of Christ. Provided the criminal duly repents of his sins his soul is in no danger. Further, would-be offenders are likely to be deterred if they know that a priest will not be allowed to visit them in the event of their capture [133]. A further reason for denying the Eucharist even to repentant criminals is the shameful character of their death and their burial in unconsecrated ground. A person who ventures to admit a repentant criminal to confession and communion, and then denied him Christian burial would be guilty of grave sin [134].

Pullen's counsels are evidence of a rigoristic practice in the administration of penance. Refusal of the sacrament of penance to condemned criminals was authoritatively condemned by the Council of Vienne (1311-1312) [135]. Yet the practice lingered on in France until the early sixteenth century [136]. In England explicit provision had been made in the ecclesiastical legislation of English and Danish kings from the ninth to the eleventh century for the hearing of confessions of criminals condemned to death [137]. In 1261 the Archbishop of Canterbury, Boniface of Savoy, held a Council at Lambeth in which the right of prisoners to the sacrament of penance was again affirmed. The practice of denying it was denounced as inhuman and unchristian [138]. On the question of denying the Eucharist to condemned criminals medieval opinion was divided. The rigoristic practice was common in France, largely owing to the influence of judicial authorities, who saw in

---

132 904A.
133 904C.
134 905A.
135 C. J. C. Clem. V. 9, 1: Friedberg, II, 1190.
136 H. Mathoud, Observationes, *P. L.* 186, 1091 A.
137 Wilkins, *Concilia Magnae Brittaniae*, I, 203 (Alfred, Edward the Elder, Guthrum), 307 (Canute).
138 Wilkins, *op. cit.* 754.

the denial of the sacrament a deterrent to wrongdoers [139]. It is interesting to note that Gilbert Porreta, Bishop of Poitiers and Pullen's predecessor in the chair of theology at the Cathedral School at Paris, also alleged the reason of reverence to the sacred species in counselling the denial of Communion to a criminal condemned to death [140]. However, Gilbert allowed that he should make his confession before execution. Pullen's theory that forgiveness of the guilt of sin was normally due to contrition, and prior to confession, allowed him to dispense with confession to a priest, in the case of a criminal, yet, as we have seen, he suggests that there will be a confession to a secular judge. This practice of confession to a layman in cases where a priest could not be had was commonly advocated and practised in the Middle Ages. Authority for the practice was found in a work, composed probably about the middle of the eleventh century, which was known as the *Liber de Vera et Falsa Poenitentia,* and which until the fifteenth century passed as a genuine work of St. Augustine. In this treatise confession was extolled especially for the element of shame involved in making avowal of sins. It was considered that the difficulty of the avowal constituted a considerable amount of the satisfaction required of a sinner. The author of this work, and those who afterwards advocated the practice, admitted that laymen had not the power of the keys, but maintained that where recourse to a priest was impossible the effort of making confession to a layman would be accepted by God as a sign of repentance and humility [141]. Outside such a case of necessity confession to laymen was permitted by Pullen, and theologians in general, only where the sins were venial. These confessions could either be specific or general [142].

---

[139] J. Corblet, *Histoire du sacrement de l'eucharistie* I 335, Paris, 1885.

[140] Martène-Durand, *Thesaurus Novus Anecdotorum,* I, 429, Paris, 1717.

[141] 'Tanta itaque vis confessionis est, ut si deest sacerdos, confiteatur proximo. Saepe enim contingit, quod poenitens non potest verecundari coram sacerdote, quem desideranti nec locus nec tempus offert. Et si ille cui confitebitur potestatem solvendi non habet, fit tamen dignus venia ex desiderio sacerdotis, qui socio confitetur turpitudinem criminis. Mundati enim sunt leprosi, dum ibant ostendere ora sacerdotibus, antequam ad eos pervenirent. (Lc. xviii, 14). Unde patet Deum ad cor respicere, dum ex necessitate prohibentur ad sacerdotes pervenire': *Liber de Vera et Falsa Poenitentia, P. L.* 40, 1122.

[142] 'Sed confessionem unam licet fieri co-aequalibus; altera, nisi extreme urget necessitas, debetur sacerdotibus. Si quotidianis, et his sine quibus non vivitur urgeris, sufficit hujusmodi confiteri comparibus, imo nonnunquam et minoribus; quo more presbyteri et quotidie indifferenter circumstantibus confitentur. Sed confessionem si non singulatim, quoniam prae multitudine raro

A priest is strictly bound by the seal of confession. So strict is the obligation that he may not exclude from Holy Communion those whom he knows from confession to be unworthy [143]. He may, however, pronounce an indeterminate excommunication, in which there is no mention of particular persons, against the perpetrators of crimes and those who have cognisance of them even if he has confessional knowledge of their guilt, if two conditions are verified. These are that the guilty parties have refused to answer an ecclesiastical summons, and that the priest has been directed to pronounce such a censure [144].

Another question on which Pullen adopted a rigorist position was that of the return of sins. The problem discussed by many twelfth-century theologians was whether the guilt and punishment due to sins which had been forgiven through penance would be again imputed by God against a sinner who after forgiveness again fell into sins. It was not just a question of the greater gravity of the subsequent sins, owing to the ingratitude apparent in them, but of the withdrawal of forgiveness already granted by God. Certain texts of the Fathers appeared to suggest that forgiveness was thus withdrawn, at least in the event of subsequent sins against fraternal charity. These were commentaries of St. John Chrysostom and St. Augustine on the parable of the wicked servant in Matthew xvii, 23-35 [145]. Further, a much used text of Gregory the

---

fieri potest ... *Confitemini alterutrum peccata vestra et orate pro invicem ut salvemini.* De illis, juxta hujus expositionem, peccatis mandatum tradens, sine quibus non vivitur': 897A-B. Pullen here refers to the gloss on Jac. V. 16 which cites Bede: 'coaequalibus quotidiana et levia, graviora vero sacerdoti pandamus ». (*P. L.* 93, 40).

143 'Non enim quos per confessionem novit indignos, detegere publica accusatione licet, nec a communione communiter cunctis scandalo indicto illos quos aestimat sontes repellere decet. Unde Dominus Judae, dignus inter dignos, indigno sacramenta corporis sui distribuit, subdolum parricidamque sciens, sed detegere cavens, exemplum ministris suis proposuit': 898C. Cf. St. Augustine, *Serm.* 351, 10. *P. L.* 39, 15: 'Nemo arbitretur, fratres, propterea se consilium salutiferae huius paenitentiae debere contemnere, quia multos forte advertit et novit ad sacramenta altaris accedere, quorum talia crimina non ignorat. Multi enim corriguntur ut Petrus, multi tolerantur ut Judas, multi nesciuntur, donec veniat Dominus, qui illuminet abscondita tenebrarum et manifestet cogitationes cordis'.

144 898C.

145 St. John Chrysostom, *In Mt.* xviii, 23, n. 7: 'Non erraverit quis si hoc peccatum (i. e. injuriae memoriam) omni peccato gravius pronuntiet. Alia enim omnia veniam impetrare poterunt, istud solum adeo non potuit veniam adipisci (a patre familias), ut jam deleta et jam extincta (debita) iterum renovarit'. *P. G.* 51, 29.

Great seemed to imply that the efficacy of penance depended on perseverance in good dispositions [146]. The problem was not merely a speculative one. Those who maintained that sins could return in the event of a relapse tended to urge that they should once again be confessed, since all held that confession was a necessary condition of forgiveness. The result was a multiplication of general confessions, and the growth of extensive formulas of self-accusation. Twelfth-century theologians were divided on the speculative question. Peter Lombard leaves the question open [147]. Abelard denies that sins return [148], and among others who assented to his opinion were Gandulphus of Bologna [149] and Roland Bandinelli [150]. Those who held that sins return included Hugh of St Victor [151], Robert Pullen [152] and, it would appear, the canonist Gratian [153]. They were followed towards the end of the century by Alan of Lille [154].

In favour of his opinion, Pullen refers to the parable of the wicked servant, and, apparently, to the text of Gregory the Great, when he remarks that forgiveness is not valid when its necessary condition is violated [155].

St. Augustine, *De Baptismo cont. Donatistas,* I, 12, 20: 'Redire dimissa peccata, ubi fraterna charitas non est apertissime Dominus docet de illo servo' (*Mat.* xviii, 27-35).

146 St. Gregory the Great: *Hom. in Evang.* XXXIV, 15: 'Paenitentia est praeterita mala flere et flenda non committere', *P.L.* 76, 1256B. Cf. St. Isidore of Seville: *Synon.* 1, 77: 'Inanis est paenitentia, quam sequens culpa commaculat', *P.L.* 83, 845.

147 *Sent.* IV, D. XXII, cap. i.

148 *Expos. in Ep. ad Rom., P.L.* 178, 864, 872.

149 *Sent.* IV, n. 196, ed. J. de Walter, 498.

150 *Sent.* ed. A. Gietl, 249 ff.

151 *De Sacr.* II, XIV, 9, *P.L.* 176, 570-578.

152 'Quisquis cordis compunctione fit contritus, seu confessionis patefactione purgatus, si reversus ad vomitum pactum refutat, is dimissis jam flagitiis denuo se obligat': 896C.

153 *Decretum* II, C. XXXIII, Q. 3, Dist. 4, Friedberg, 1229-1238.

On this question see A. Landgraf, Die Frühscholastische Streitfrage vom Wiederaufleben der Sünden, *Z. k. Th.* LXI (1937) 534.

154 *Liber Paenitentialis, P.L.* 210, 303.

155 'Ita enim facta pacti dissipatione pacto dimissa repetuntur, sicut plura servo nequam, quoniam veniam rogarat, debita prius dimissa postmodum exiguntur; quoniam quod oportuit conservo pauciora debenti commisereri respuit. Utique vera ratione interim dimittebantur, quod patet quoniam ab interim defunctis minime requirerentur. Sed dimissio vires non habet, nisi dum contra ejus legem non agitur. Unde patet quod confessione peccatorum valde est opus': 896C-D.

Pullen was acquainted with the text of St. Gregory in which a definition of penance is given, as appears from his own definition in the *De Contemptu*

In spite of this severe teaching he does hold that in this life all sins can obtain forgiveness, provided there is true repentance. The sin against the Holy Ghost (Mt. xii, 32) is only irremissible in so far as it signifies final impenitence [156]. After death there is no forgiveness for mortal sins, but venial sins may be expiated in purgatory [157].

HOLY ORDER.

Pullen speaks of the permanency of this sacrament, which like baptism may not be repeated [158]. Therefore, a suspended cleric is not re-ordained when after doing penance, he is re-admitted to the ministry. If a suspended priest, or one who for a graver offence has been permanently degraded, should presume to exercise his office, his actions are valid, although unlawful [159].

Admission to the clerical state depends on a man's free choice, but the candidate must be a freeman, literate and not committed to military or judicial duties. The social character of the clerical office requires as a further condition that no one should be ordained whose appearance is unbearably repulsive [160]. Admission to the

---

Mundi: 'ut preterita omnino defleas, et deflenda cauere ulterius proponas', ed. cit. 204.

156 '... qui peccaverit in Spiritum Sanctum ... neque in hoc seculo neque remittetur ei in futuro ... Quare? Quoniam impoenitens in vita permansit': 913A.

157 'Nimirum offensae quaedam veniam merentur in praesenti, quod de omnibus in quibus graviter erratur, si ad veniam veniunt, intelligendum puto. Nam quae venialiter admittuntur, ea fortasse, non etiam alia, post mortem veniam consequuntur ... Unde nostrorum traditio est doctorum, quod praeter illam quae in praesenti fit peccatorum remissionem, altera detur in altero saeculo, sed nonnisi de levibus. Nam quae gravia sunt nisi in hoc saeculo condonantur, frustra in postmodum veniam expectatur': 913A-C.

158 'Notandum autem quod sacramentum semel impositum cum vita permaneat, bono utique bonum, malo autem, ad malum: unde rebaptizari aut re-ordinari non licet': 927C, cf. Ivo, *Decretum,* VI, 82. *P. L.* 161, 453.

159 'Dum autem sententia suspensionis aut degradationis manet, quid si interim officium interdictum agatur? Utique propter potestatem quae non aufertur, sicut boni, ita quoque et prohibiti videntur sua uti posse, verum malo suo, omniumque qui intus ita sunt ut prohibitionem contemnant': *ibid.* D; cf. Ivo, *Ibid.* 224, P. L. 161, 493.

Pullen does not explicitly consider the question of the validity of the ministrations of an heretical priest. His general principles, however, suggest that he held them to be valid but unlawful. On the contemporary controversy see A. Landgraf, Zur Lehre der Konsekrationsgewalt des von der Kirche getrennten Priesters im 12. Jahrhundert, *Scholastik,* XV (1940) 204-227.

160 'Non statim admovendus est choro (clero?), si forte visu intolerabili sit; non quod tali de causa a Deo fiat remotior, propter, quam in societatis communicatione solum exstet deformior': 922B-C.

various orders, as distinguished from the reception of the tonsure, does not depend on a man's own choice but on the bishop and the archdeacon, who have the duty of deciding which clerics are to proceed to orders [161].

It is unlawful to ordain those who have no title to a definite church in which they are to serve. If after ordination a cleric repudiates the obligation of service in a church to which he has pledged himself he is guilty of sacrilege and apostasy [162].

Marriage is unlawful for those who have been promoted to any of the major orders of the sub-diaconate, diaconate or priesthood. Marriage of priests was abrogated with the abrogation of the Old Law and its rites. Priests who claim the right to marry are clearly at variance with the existing law of the Church, which freely admits the sons of laymen to orders, but only after a period of probation those of priests [163]. Under the Old Law priests refrained from marital relations during their periods of service in the Temple; under the New Law when priests are continually occupied marriage is altogether forbidden. The ancient priesthood separated themselves from their wives when they were engaged in offering the body and blood of animals, yet there are among us, says Pullen, priests whose daily duty it is to offer the body and blood of Christ, and who still think it lawful to keep company with harlots. This is Pullen's blunt description of those irregular unions to which he refuses the name of marriage, as they are dissolved at will, and are prohibited by law. In spite of the canonical laws against them they would appear, both from Pullen's invective and from other sources, to have been fairly prevalent in the England of his day [164].

The abode and dress of a priest are rich in promise of good,

---

[161] *Ibid* D.

[162] 923B.

[163] 'Qua ratione sacerdotes sibi jura connubii intorqueant, cum lex nostra laicorum libere, sacerdotum nonnisi cum mora filios ad ordines promoveat': *ibid.* D. Cf. Ivo, *Decretum*, VI, 410, *P. L.* 161, 533. 'Presbyterorum filios a sacri altaris ministratione removendos decernimus, nisi aut in coenobiis, aut in canonicis regularibus religiose probati fuerint conversari'.

[164] 'Antiqui quando a ministerio templi cessabant, ad uxores accedebant; nostros, quoniam saepe praesto esse oportet, nunquam amplexibus vacare licet. Illi, dum animalium carnem et sanguinem bajulant, tactum abhorrent conjugum; nostri vel ad suum vel ad opus aliorum ex officio habent carnem Domini et sanguinem quotidie tractare, licitosque putent amplexus etiam meretricum. Apud nos enim sacerdoti nulla copulatur conjugio, quoniam quandolibet eam dimittere licet. Praeterea copula hujusmodi praevaricatrix est; quoniam generali sanctione interdicta': 923D-924A.

adds Pullen. Let each one beware lest this promise be falsified in himself [165].

A priest should be exemplary in life and doctrine [166], but this is impossible unless he studies the Catholic faith, listens to teachers, and is diligent in searching the Scriptures, from which truth is extracted after much studious effort, in much the same way as a fish is taken by an angler from the water [167]. Neglect of these counsels leads to ignorance, injustice and impurity [168]. Examples of evil are to be seen in those disedifying priests who, though continuing to perform their duties of chanting, celebrating masses and saying office, then set off on horseback to take part in hunting and hawking. There are others who spend the day playing chess or pass the time in dalliance with women [169].

Parish priests must insist on faith in the Trinity and the Incarnation, and instruct the faithful on the necessity of baptism, and its lawful administration by a layman in cases of necessity [170]. They must also teach the faithful the doctrine of morals, explaining the nature of virtues and vices, and showing their growth and goal. Along with this theoretical teaching the priest must use his authority to secure good conduct. However, owing to the number and power of offenders he will often find it inexpedient to have recourse to sanctions, the only effect of which would be to provoke schism in the Church [171].

Matrimony.

Pullen treats at some length of this sacrament, but remarks that he cannot deal fully with it, as the solution of one question at

---

165 924A.

166 928B.

167 'Sed quomodo sciunt illi dominum, qui nec Catholicae fidei veritatem, nec doctores audiunt, nec scripturas scrutantur, de quibus fidei veritas, ut piscis de aqua multo labore et studio eruitur': Serm. 6.

168 'Ignorata veritate, ingerit se falsitas, quam comitatur iniusticia et uite inmundicia': *ibid.*

169 'Hi erigunt archam domini iuxta Dagon, quanquam perseuerantes in prauitate uite aliqua faciunt que docet sacra scriptura; ut clerici qui cantant, missas celebrant, horas dicunt, sed postea equos ascendunt, uenantur, et in auibus celi ludunt, in scacis diem expendunt. Que non in laicis sed in clericis uitia sunt, et omnio prohibita. Alii mulierculas amplexantur, collocuntur, libidinis ardores accedunt': *ibid.* See also *supra* 47 f.

170 928D-929A.

171 930C.

once gives rise to others without number [172]. Like all his contemporaries he is dependent on St. Augustine for the main lines of his teaching, but in two important points he excels them by the manner in which he develops St. Augustine's doctrine. St. Augustine nowhere explicitly states that there is a special grace attached to the sacrament of matrimony, and the mid-twelfth century scholastics such as Hugh of St. Victor, Walter of Mortagne (to whom is attributed the treatise on matrimony in the *Summa Sententiarum*) and Peter Lombard, made no advance on this point. Writing before the Lombard Pullen says that marriage entered on for a right motive is legitimate, but that human infirmity is such that venial sin may occur unless God grant his succour [173]. The implication is that such succour is given to those who enter on marriage with a right intention. This conclusion is confirmed by his assertion that those who go through the ceremony of marriage with an interior intention contrary to any of the three blessings of Christian matrimony — offspring, conjugal fidelity, and the sacrament (i. e. indissolubility) — receive the sacrament indeed, but without profit. They are married in the eyes of the Church, and as their evil intention has not been manifested outwardly, their union will be regarded as valid. Inwardly they are living in concubinage, and this will continue as long as they reject any of the three blessings [174]. The « profit » (utilitas) or effect (res) of mar-

[172] 'Nam plene de conjugio agere, sicut nec fere de ulla re, minime nos sufficere arbitramur, ubi una quaestione absoluta, innumerae usu ipso novae suboriuntur': 956C.

[173] 'Qua enim ratione illum damnabo, qui quantum potest Deum quaerit, tametsi fragilitas trahit, non ut aliquatenus fornicari, sed ut conjugio delectari desideret; quod etiam abhorreret, nisi Deus infirmis permisisset; trahit non ut mundi rem aut honorem, contempto Deo; sed sicut concessum est infirmis exoptet. Verum bonis mala vicina sunt, *ut opitulante Deo solum* in inquisitione rerum falli nequeas': 960A-B.

[174] 'Conjux vero, si id vere vult esse quod dicitur, quamvis filios suscipere non aestimet, minime tamen id agat quare non suscipiat; alioquin quemadmodum qui fictus baptizatur, habet utique baptismum perceptione, sed non utilitate; ita haec sacramento conjux non re ... Est fides conjugii sine sacramento; sacramentum item nonnunquam est absque fide; quod accidit quoties conjugandi, aut torum inter se immaculatum servare disponunt, sese tamen relinquere meditantur; aut conversari simul more conjugii volunt, nisi quod undique fornicari desiderant. Qui animo tali conveniunt quoniam a se bonum conjugii repellunt, si ambo sunt tales, ambo sunt inter se scortatores. Si unus solus est talis, alter solus est conjux. Hujusmodi conjuges nunquam erunt donec vitiis quae conjugium fieri non sinunt eliminatis, bona conjugii amplectantur ... Quidquid enim in animo lateat, dummodo coram Ecclesia quoad dignum est conjugio fiat, utique conjugium reputatur. Licet enim conjugium nondum sit utilitate, est tamen sacramentum veritate. Quod contra conjugium

riage which such spouses fail to receive can hardly be anything else than sanctifying grace. It can scarcely be merely the bond, since Pullen compares the status of such married persons with those who receive the sacrament of baptism without the requisite dispositions. (ficti). As the latter received the sacramental character, so the former were linked by the bond of marriage, though in neither case was the sacrament profitable. The doctrine is in keeping with Pullen's general sacramental theory that corrupt intentions do not invalidate a sacrament, provided the outward forms have been correctly observed. As the Church requires such baptised persons to fulfil the obligations they have taken upon themselves, so with such married persons, although their marriage would not have been permitted if their corrupt intentions had been manifested at the time of the ceremony [175].

Another point of Pullen's teaching in which he differs explicitly from Peter Lombard and Walter of Mortagne, (on whom the Lombard drew for his doctrine), is his clear assertion that matrimony, if entered on with an intention of pleasing God, is not merely free from sin, but also merits a reward [176]. This is a notable advance on the doctrine of Walter of Mortagne [177] and of Peter Lombard [178] who, misunderstanding St. Augustine [179], held that marriage

---

est, cubat in corde; quod cum conjugio est sonat in ore. Coram Ecclesia, quia more Ecclesiae uxorem ducit, quidquid ineptiarum corde premat, nihil inde conjugio derogabit. Potest utique esse ut nihil aut parum prosit, non tamen potest esse ut conjugium non sit'. 957D-958B.

[175] 'In conjugio tamen praedicta mala sunt maxime vitanda quorum contraria summopere tanquam bona conjugii sunt appetenda. Si enim sermo conjungendorum haec bona abdicaverit, dispensatio Ecclesiae conjunctioni fornicariae contradicit. Sicut baptizandum vetustati nolentem renuntiare non recipit, sacramenta tamen quoque modo hinc inde dato debita requirit': 958B-C.

[176] 'Sed qui ita conveniunt, num bono conjugii a voluptate tori excusantur? Utique qui statutum Christi sequens uxorem ducit, ne contra Dei prohibitum fornicetur; aut (si ita acciderit) ut soboles propter Deum educetur tali mente ut nullam propter molestiam, quod Deus conjuxit homo ipse separet, is per bonum conjugii a malo tori liberatur: imo quoniam ne offendat Deum, et uxorem ducit, et dimittere non quaerit, non consulens carnem sed Dei voluntatem, *procul dubio praemium adipiscitur*. Is, si cum uxore dormit ut filios procreet, ut fornicationem evitet, aut ut sociae debitum reddat; vere Domini pro nutu se habet, malum ardoris qui bonum propositi prosequitur omnino condonatur': 958C-D.

[177] *Summa Sententiarum*, *P. L.* 176, 155C-D.

[178] *Sententia*, Lib IV, D. xxvi, c. 2: 'Si non peccassent primi homines, sine carnis incentivo ac fervore libidinis ipsi ac successores eorum convenirent; et sicut remunerabile est aliquod bonum opus, sic coitus eorum bonus esset et remunerabilis. Quia vero propter peccatum talis concupiscentiae lex mem-

was a meritorious state of life only in man's primitive state of innocence. After the fall the presence of concupiscence makes the marriage act sinful, but those are excused from sin who seek in marriage the three blessings of offspring, conjugal fidelity and indissolubility.

Pullen's fidelity to the Augustinian doctrine is also evident in his assertion that those who, without excluding the essential blessings of matrimony, are led by an immoderate desire of pleasure do not sin mortally but only venially[180]. Mortal sin is committed by those who seek to prevent offspring from their union, or who meditate divorce or infidelity. With Augustine Pullen asserts that those who thus exclude the blessings of matrimony are not spouses but fornicators. If only one of them is thus ill-intentioned, the other is truly married[181]. The sin of those who ex-

---

bris nostris inhaesit, sine qua carnalis non fit commistio, reprehensibilis est et malus coitus, nisi excusetur per bona conjugii'.

ibid c. iii: 'Indulgentia vero, quia meliora non eligit, remedium habet, non praemium'.

ibid. c. iv: 'De minoribus bonis est conjugium, quod non meretur palmam, sed est in remedium'.

179 St. Augustine, while asserting that virginity was a more meritorious state than matrimony, did not say that in the present state of human nature matrimony was without merit. Cf. *De Bono Conjugali* XI, 13, ed. J. Zycha, *C.S.E.L.* 204-5; *P.L.* 40, 382: 'Quod ergo ait: *quae innupta est, cogitat ea quae sunt Domini, ut sit sancta et corpore et spiritu,* non sic accipiendum est, ut putemus non esse sanctam corpore christianam conjugem castam ... proinde illud dictum est secundum ampliorem sanctitatem innuptarum quam nuptarum, cui merces etiam debetur amplior secundum quod isto bono illud est melius, quia et hoc solum cogitat, quomodo placeat domino'.

180 'Sin vero talis (ut nostra est fragilitas) ad amplexus nonnunquam voluntate devius fertur hic utique *salvus erit, sic tamen quasi per ignem.* Neque enim qui secundum Deum uxorem tenet et suscipit, propter voluptatem tori perit. ... Nam vir etiam bonus fragilitate praeventus, voluptate nonnunquam trahitur, sicut ad cibum, ita quoque ad coitum; sed nolit Deus ut propter invincibilia damnetur peccata vir toto proposito bonus': 958D-959A. Cf. Aug. *De Nuptiis et Concupiscentia* I, XV, 17, ed. C. F. Urba & J. Zycha, *C.S.E.L.* 229: 'Sed tamen aliud est non concumbere nisi sola voluntate generandi, quod non habet culpam, aliud carnis concumbendo adpetere voluptatem, sed non praeter conjugem, quod venialem habet culpam, quia, etsi non causa propagandae prolis concumbitur, non tamen huius libidinis causa propagationi prolis obsistitur siue uoto malo siue opere malo'.

181 'Conjux vero, si id vere vult esse quod dicitur, quamvis filios suscipere non aestimet, minime tamen id agat quare non suscipiat; alioquin quemadmodum qui fictus baptizatur, habet utique sacramentum perceptione, sed non utilitate; ita haec sacramento conjux non etiam re': 957D.

'Est fides conjugii sine sacramento; sacramentum item nonnunquam est absque fide; quod accidit quoties conjugandi, aut torum inter se immaculatum servare disponunt, sese tamen relinquere meditantur; aut conversari simul more

clude the blessings of matrimony from their union is only less than that of those who do the same outside of marriage, since the latter incur the additional guilt of an external scandal in the Church [182].

As marriage was instituted by God, God's purposes should be sought by those who enter on this state of life. With St. Augustine Pullen teaches that marriage was instituted by God in order that children might be born, and educated to worship God, and as a remedy for concupiscence [183]. Provided God's purposes are their first consideration, other motives such as personal attraction, or family alliances are legitimate [184]. If, however, such secondary motives are alone intended, the parties should be corrected by the Church if they manifest their intentions, but they are not necessarily to be prevented from marrying, as such alliances are to be preferred to scandalous concubinage [185]. He presumes that such persons will not positively exclude the three blessings of marriage. He defines these as fidelity, the safeguard of marital chastity; offspring, for the increase of the Christian religion; the sacrament which excludes the rupture of the marriage bond by divorce [186].

---

conjugii volunt, nisi quod undique fornicari desiderant. Qui animo tali conveniunt, quoniam a se bonum conjugii repellunt, si ambo sunt tales, ambo sunt inter se scortatores. Si unus solus est talis, alter solus est conjux': 958A. Cf. Aug. *De Nuptiis et Concupiscentia,* I, XV, 17, *ed. cit.* 229-230: 'Nam qui hoc faciunt quamuis uocentur coniuges, non sunt nec ullam nuptiarum retinent ueritatem, sed honestum nomen uelandae turpitudini obtendunt ... prorsus si ambo tales sunt, coniuges non sunt; et si ab initio tales fuerunt, non sibi per connubium, sed per stuprum potius conuenerunt. Si autem non ambo sunt tales, audeo dicere; aut illa est quodam modo mariti meretrix aut ille adulter uxoris'.

182 'Quoties ergo bona conjugii evanescunt, voluptas tori nullatenus excusatur, nisi quod levior damnatio subsequitur; quoniam ita peccatur, ut Ecclesia non scandalizetur': 960A.

183 'Te ergo conjugem fieri oportet aut ut filiorum generatione cultum Dei multiplices; aut ut carnis tuae incontinentiam modifices': 956D.

184 'Neque nocet; imo fieri oportet, ut post primam considerationem minime praetermittas sequentem; quatenus tibi sponsam hujusmodi provideas cujus formae intento minime sit opus aliis provocari. Ratio quoque est talem tibi procurare affinitatem unde in saeculo habeas defensionem': 957B.

185 'Si vero in conjugio nihil nisi divitias aut voluptatem aut hujusmodi aliquid quaeras, idque etiam loquendo prodas, error tuus erit ab Ecclesia arguendus, sed non ideo videris mihi a nuptiis arcendus; melius namque est vel sic convenire, quam scandalo Ecclesiae passim stupro inservire': 958C.

186 'Convenientes autem, simul cum connubio bona connubii suscipiunt tria haec, fidem, prolem, sacramentum. Fidem ut adulterino amplexu nuptiarum puritas non foedetur; prolem ut religio Christiana augeatur; sacramentum ne quo divortio copula disrumpatur': 957C. Cf. Aug. *De Gen. ad Litt.* IX, 7, ed. J. Zycha, *C. S.E. L.* 275 f. *P. L.*, 34, 397; *De Nuptiis et Concupiscentia,* I, XI,

Treating of marriage in Old Testament times he maintains that as originally instituted by God it was a union of two only, and that if man had not sinned this would have been its perpetual form, to the exclusion of polygamy, whether simultaneous or successive [187]. Polygamy was permitted to the Israelites to ensure the propagation of the worshippers of the true God, whose numbers were often reduced by constant wars with idolaters [188]. Divorce was also allowed for a multiplicity of reasons [189]. Concubinage was practised lawfully by the patriarchs, but was abrogated by the Law, although plurality of wives continued to be lawful [190].

In treating of the Pauline privilege Pullen holds the same doctrine as Hugh of St. Victor. Both writers maintained that the convert Christian is free to dismiss the pagan partner of a marriage previously contracted in infidelity, not only in the case when the latter refuses to co-habit peaceably, but even when he is willing to remain. The reason alleged by Pullen is that the idolatry of the pagan partner is equivalent to spiritual adultery. In either case the Christian may contract a fresh marriage. He justifies this unusual doctrine on the ground that only Christian marriage is indissoluble; the marriages of Jews and of pagans are liable to dissolution. However he advises the retention of the pagan party where this is possible, in order that he or she may be converted and the marriage thus become a Christian union [191]. Gratian and Peter Lombard differ from Pullen and Hugh of St. Victor in allowing the right of re-marriage only in the case where the unbeliever refuses peaceable cohabitation. Apart from this case the Christian can claim no more than separation [192].

Divorce was abolished by Christ, who allowed permanent separation in the case of adultery [193]. For this step, which is option-

---

13, ed. C. F. Urba & J. Zycha, *C.S.E.L.* 225, 231; *P.L.* 44, 421, 424; *De Bono Conjugali* 32, ed. J. Zycha, *C.S.E.L.* 226-228; *P.L.* 40, 394.

187 945C. Cf. P. Lomb. *Sent.* IV D. xxxiii, cap. 1-2; *Summa Sententiarum, P.L.* 176, 157.

188 946A-C; Cf. Aug. *De Bono Conjugali* XXV, 33, ed. J. Zycha, *C.S.E.L.* 288, *P.L.* 40, 395; *Contra Faustum* XXII, 48, ed. J. Zycha, *C.S.E.L.* 640f; *P.L.* 42, 429f; Gratian, *Decretum* C. XXXII, Q. IV, c. 6, Friedberg, 1129; P. Lomb. *Sent.* IV D. xxxiii, cap. 1-2.

189 946C. Cf. P. Lomb. *Sent.* IV D. xxxiii, cap. iii.

190 947A. Cf. P. Lomb. *ibid.* cap. 4.

191 947A-D. Cf. Hugh of St. Victor, *De Sacramentis,* Lib. II cap. xiii, *P.L.* 176, 508.

192 Cf. Gratian, *Decretum* II, Dictum ad c. 2, C. XXXVIII, 2, Friedberg, I, 1090; P. Lomb. *Sent.* IV, D. XXXIX, cap. v.

193 950B.

al, not compulsory, legal proof is required, and it is pen only to an innocent party, whether husband or wife. Both parties are bound to continence after separation. Where this is impossible the innocent party should recall the offender [194]. Separation is also allowed for what Pullen calls spiritual fornication. By this he means the crime of idolatry or solicitation to evil in such a way as to endanger the salvation of the other party. Here separation is essential, but in the event of repentance the guilty party should be recalled. Although separation for spiritual fornication was not mentioned by Christ, Pullen asserts that in the Gospel Christ was only dealing with grounds for separation which were based on acts of injustice towards man. Elsewhere in Scripture, he says, there is a precept enjoining withdrawal from all company which endangers salvation [195].

Besides separation for matrimonial infidelity there is a voluntary separation which married persons may by mutual consent freely undertake with the intention of living in continence. Such a resolve may be the object of a vow, either private or public. These vows must be observed. God will judge their violation if they are but private vows, but if they are public the Church will also intervene. The husband must make proper provision for his wife, but he should not so separate without the most careful previous consideration [196].

On the question of impediments to marriage he observes that consent, which normally seals marriage, fails of this effect where there is an impediment which is known to both parties. If it is known to one party only the marriage is valid only for the other. If each party is invincibly ignorant of the impediment, the marriage is valid as long as their ignorance persists. On the impediment becoming known the parties are to be separated, and may normally contract other unions [197]. Hugh of St. Victor also speaks of these putative marriages as true marriages, as long as the impediment remains secret, and defends at some length their right to be called marriages, even though at some later date they will be dissolved [198]. Pullen notes that some persons call them quasi-marriages, since true marriages are indissoluble [199]. He further states that Christ left to be determined by the Church which are the im-

---

194 950C-D.

195 951B-952A.

196 949C-950B.

197 952B-C.

198 *De Sacramentis* Lib. II, p. xi, c. 11, *P. L.* 176, 497 ff.

199 956C.

pediments to Christian marriage. Among those in force in his day he mentions disparity of worship, a public vow of chastity, religious profession, major orders, consanguinity, affinity and spiritual relationship. He adds that, if any of these impediments supervene after marriage, they will normally not provide a ground for its dissolution [200].

A question of considerable practical importance in Pullen's day was, whether a person who had promised marriage under oath to one person, but who before the ceremony could take place had contracted marriage with another, was to be regarded as the legal spouse of the first or the second of these two. Behind this question lay a long history with roots both in the Roman and the Germanic legal systems [201]. In the Western Church betrothal was regarded as strictly binding, and its fulfilment was required under ecclesiastical penalties. Among the Germanic peoples it was regarded rather as the initial stage of the matrimonial contract than as an agreement which, though preparatory, is nevertheless distinct from it, and different in character [202]. The question was complicated up to the middle of the twelfth century by division of opinion among canonists on the question of the determining factor in the completion of the contract of marriage. Under the influence of Lombardic marriage law, and misled by a corrupt text of St. Leo [203], Gratian and the Bologna canonists saw in consent only a *matrimonium initiatum*. For a *Matrimonium ratum* consummation was required. They also held that consent *de futuro* as given at betrothal, was equally efficacious as consent *de praesenti* to effect a *matrimonium initiatum*. Against this opinion the theologians of the twelfth-century Paris School taught that, whereas consent *de praesenti* sufficed for the full formation of marriage, even apart from consummation, consent *de futuro* in no way constituted marriage, but only betrothal. This difference of theory led to diversity of practice in the settlement of matrimonial disputes. In Italy, even in Rome, the opinion of the Bologna canonists prevailed up to the second half of the century. A woman who, after pledging herself to one man, but without consummating the union, subsequently contracted and consummated a marriage with another, was adjudged to be the wife of the second. In France, if the consent was *de praesenti*, she was held to be the wife of the first [204]. Unanimity of prac-

---

[200] 952D-954C.

[201] See G. H. Joyce, *Christian Marriage*, ed. 2, London, 1948, 84ff.

[202] Joyce, *l. c.* 86.

[203] *Ep.* 167 ad Rusticum, *P. L.* 54, 1204. See Joyce *l. c.* 57.

[204] Joyce, l. c. 63.

tice was finally established by the legislation of Alexander III (1159-1181), who issued decretals in which the doctrine of the Paris theologians was upheld. In his *Summa Rolandi* he had previously maintained the doctrine of the Bologna School, but already before his election to the papacy he had adopted the teaching of the Paris School in his *Sententiae.*

It is in the light of these controversies that the 39th chapter of the seventh book of Pullen's *Sentences* is to be read. He notes that, according to some, if it could be established that a man had promised marriage under oath to one woman, and afterwards in violation of the oath contracted marriage with another, the man must be compelled to return to the first woman. According to others, as consent is the effective formative factor of marriage, the latter union must prevail over the betrothal, even though this had been made under oath [205]. The two opinions represent the teaching of the Bologna and Paris Schools respectively. Pullen comments that such a betrothal should have been given effect, provided there were no legal impediments. He then proceeds with much dialectical subtlety to discuss the moral issues involved in the taking and observance of oaths [206]. On the question at issue he is very cautious in proposing a solution. In favour of the betrothal is the wrong done by its non-observance, and its aggravation by marriage with another person. Against the betrothal is the fact that many wrongs are done which cannot be altered, and the fact that marriages are not dissolved [207]. Pullen prefers to leave the theoretical question open. In practice one must be guided by ecclesiastical legislation. If the decrees of the Catholic Church state that those who have been betrothed under oath are not to be separated, then they must be adhered to. If not, then the subsequent marriage must stand, seeing that it was not unlawful [208].

---

205 'Asserunt etiam nonnulli quod si quis media fide alicui conjugium promiserit, idque probari possit, matrimonium cum alia post fidem datam contractum minime servari debere, sed ad priorem redeundum esse. Alii autem autumant consensum utriusque, quoniam is est conjugii effector, praevalere sponsioni, quamvis juramento confirmatae': 954C.

206 954C-955C.

207 'Si tamen interim aliunde matrimonium contrahatur, injuriam sponsioni faciendam arbitrantur; lex conjugii injuste est suscepta, et tamen non destruenda. Nimirum multa utique (inique?) fiunt, et tamen facta immutari nequeunt. Et, ne de eadem re exeamus, si coram Ecclesia, quae ante conjugium fieri debent, transigantur omnia, conjugio autem assensus non praebeatur, nonne injuria est quod pactio nuptiarum contemnitur, major autem si aliunde nuptiae contrahantur? Et tamen copulam matrimonii nemo dissolvit': 955C-D.

208 'Inter has partium contentiones, id mihi tenendum videtur quod eccle-

Pullen's caution is intelligible. In his day there was no authoritative solution of the problem. In the eleventh century promise under oath was generally held by theologians in the Western Church to constitute a marriage, and decisions based on this view were made by Pope Alexander II in 1066-67, and by Pope Gregory VII in 1074 [209]. When Pullen wrote, about 1140, this opinion was still defended by the Bologna School, but rejected by the School of Paris. Walter of Mortagne [210], Hugh of St. Victor [211], and Peter Lombard [212], in treating of the question here discussed by Pullen, have no hesitation in deciding that a promise of marriage *de futuro*, though made under oath, does not constitute a marriage.

Two causes for which a marriage may be either dissolved or allowed to stand are mentioned by Pullen. The first is that of a man who has been deceived into taking a woman of servile condition as his wife, while under the impression that she was a freewoman. In this case the man can either ratify the marriage by accepting the obligation which he has undertaken, or seek a solution from the ecclesiastical court. If his plea is upheld both parties are free to re-marry [213].

The second cause permitting a dissolution at the discretion of the partners is impotence, whether natural or produced by the spells of sorcerers. If it is established that this defect is perpetual, the parties may either live together in continence or seek a dissolution, and the unaffected partner may contract a fresh marriage [214].

---

siasticis non obviat decretis. Catholicae ergo consulenda puto Ecclesiae decreta, quae si responderint nec cognatos debere sociari, nec fide media obligatos posse disjungi, mos Ecclesiae non praetereatur. Sin autem res aliter se habeat, quis audeat quod factum est immutare conjugium, quando quidem id fieri nunquam fuit prohibitum?': 955D-956A.

[209] Joyce, *op. cit.* 87f.

[210] *Summa Sententiarum, P. L.* 176, 160.

[211] *De Sacramentis*, Lib. II, p. xi, cap. 5, *P. L.* 176, 485-488.

[212] *Sent.* IV. D. xxviii, cap. 1-2.

[213] 956A.

[214] *Ibid.*

CHAPTER XIII

CHURCH AND SOCIETY

THE TWO SWORDS.

The Church is the body of which Christ is the head [1]. Allegorically, Christ is typified both by the peaceful Solomon and by the warlike David [2]. Scripture (Cant. iii, 7) alludes to the Church as the bed of Solomon, since in the Church sinners are justified and begotten in Christ [3]. In the Psalms the Church is spoken of as a city. This city is encompassed by enemies, human and infernal. Its defenders are the prelates of the Church, and their chief weapon is the sword of the Spirit, the word of God which they should not merely know, but be able to use [4].

Besides the word of God, there are in the Church two swords symbolising respectively spiritual and temporal power. The hilt of a sword is in the form of a cross; and this signifies that spiritual or temporal power must be invoked when causes worthy of the

---

1 'Nimirum sancta Ecclesia quae illius capitis corpus est, quae etiam contra mundum certamen suscepit': 905D.

2 '*En lectulum Salamonis ambiunt sexaginta ex fortissimis Israel* Salamon, qui pacificus interpretatur, Christus est qui terrena pacificauit atque celestia, reconcilians deo et angelis suis. Quid, licet sit Salamon, alibi tamen Dauit, id est manu fortis dicitur. Nouit enim Christus parcere subiectis et debellare superbis': Serm. 14.

3 'In hoc lecto Salamon noster generat filios et requiescit. Filios gignit cum pios de impiis, iustos efficit de iniquis. In eo requiescit quando perseuerant et proficiunt in bonis': *ibid.*

4 'Unde in psalmo: *nisi dominus custodierit ciuitatem, frustra uigilat qui custodit illam.* Quod prius lectus ecce modo ciuitas nominatur. Lectus quantum ad pacem habentes; ciuitas quantum ad eos qui muris iusticie repellunt inimicos. Habet ergo custodes qui eam ambiunt, id est circumquaque custodiunt, ne in parte aliqua hosti aditus pateat. Custodes isti prelati sunt ecclesie... Sequitur: *singuli tenentes gladios in manibus et docti ad bella.* (Cant. iii, 8). Per gladium euangelium accipimus. Ait enim apostolus: *et gladio* (sic) *spiritus est uerbum* dei. (cf. Eph. vi, 17). ... oportet autem scientiam scripturarum habere in cordis memoria. Item, quia possent scientiam habere et nescire uti ea, additur *et docti ad bella,* ut sciant quid, quibus, et quantum et quomodo dicere debent': *ibid.*

cross of Christ are at stake. One of these swords belongs to the clergy, the other to the laity. If both swords were entrusted to either one or the other of the two powers neither would be fittingly used [5]. The temporal power rules the body; the spiritual power, the soul. The former will use bodily penalties to coerce recalcitrant subjects to maintain peace, the latter spiritual ones [6].

If spiritual weapons were sufficient to ensure peace and the correction of evildoers in the Church, and if she were not assailed by enemies from without, there would be no need for the intervention of the temporal sword of kings in the Church [7]. As matters are at present a king may, and should, protect the Church from its enemies. A king who acts thus in equity and justice is worthy of his title; otherwise he is a mere tyrant [8]. Though a prelate is concerned with healing the wounds of the soul, and a king with redressing external wrongs, yet each should, where necessary, help the other in the exercise of his office. Further, spiritual power is as much to be preferred to temporal power as the soul is to the body. Moreover, just as the body cannot dispense with the guidance of the soul, so kingdoms are heading for disaster, unless they are supported by the counsels of the priesthood. A king should obey a priest where the commandments of God are concerned; a prelate should be subject to the king in worldly matters, according to the text: *Render,* therefore, *to Caesar the things that are Caesar's; and to God, the things that are God's.* (Mt. xxii, 21) [9]. All power is from God, Pullen admits, but not always in the same way. Sometimes God allows a tyrant to rule over a people in punishment for its sins. Even in this case obedience is due, but no internal assent is to be given to the evildoing of the ruler. A distinction must be made between his power and his error. As his power is from God it is good, and those who obey

---

5 'Nimirum sancta Ecclesia, quae illius capitis corpus est, quae etiam contra mundum certamen suscepit, gladiis eget duobus in congressu, utroque signum crucis exprimente. Quippe nihil aliud aut defendere, aut oppugnare licet, nisi illud quo salva crucis reverentia fieri conveniat. Gladiorum alter deputatur clericis, alter laicis. Si enim uterque uni committitur, neuter ut oportet exercetur': 965D.

6 'Sacerdotalis ergo dignitas, saecularisque potestas, hos inter se duos dividant gladios. Haec sibi corpus, illa spiritum proprie ditioni subjugari arbitretur. Reum ergo feriat altera corporali caesione, altera corrigi nolentem spirituali': 966A.

7 920B.

8 *ibid.* C.

9 920D-921A.

out of reverence for God preserve themselves from implication in his wickedness [10].

Pullen's doctrine of the relation of the two authorities spiritual and temporal is very moderate. He is far from suggesting that both swords belong to the Church, even though with Hugh of St. Victor [11], he maintains that spiritual power is as superior to temporal power as the soul is to the body. We are as yet far from the exaggerated interpretations of the passage in Luke xx, 38), *here are two swords,* which polemical writers on one side or the other were later to make in the interest of Church or State respectively [12]. Pullen's doctrine is traditional, and adds nothing essential to the ideas of St. Peter Damian [13] or Hildebert, Bishop of Mans [14].

Corrupt acquisition and exercise of power, whether spiritual or temporal, are strongly condemned [15]. In particular, simoniacal transactions are denounced; and the distinction made between the ecclesiastical office, for which alone payment is made, and the spiritual power attached to it, is rejected [16]. Undue influence in the conferring of ecclesiastical preferment is likewise condemned [17]. In the case of those who have obtained Holy Orders by simony the only course allowable is for the cleric concerned to resign his office; less grave offenders may retain their positions after doing penance, provided no scandal is thereby given [18]. The clergy are warned to avoid committing simony in the exercise of their ministry. Offerings from the faithful after baptism or confession may be accepted, but they may not be demanded either for these sacraments or for others [19]. If a cleric refuses his spiritual ministrations without payment the laity, except when in grave spiritual need, should refuse to pay, under penalty of sharing in the guilt of simony [20]. Similar warnings are addressed to the civil authority [21]. Corruption is avoided by the payment of legitimate dues

10 919C-920A.

11 *De Sacramentis, P. L.* 176, 418C.

12 See J. Lecler, L'argument des deux glaives (Lc. xxii, 38), *R.S.R.*, XXI (1931) 299-339.

13 *Sermon* 69, *P. L.* 144, 900.

14 *Ep.* 18, *P. L.* 171, 227.

15 904C-D; 921C.

16 926C-927C.

17 924C-D.

18 927A-C.

19 929D-930A.

20 930B.

21 921B.

and taxes. Tithes are paid to the clergy to enable them to devote themselves to their spiritual activities [22]. Tribute must be paid to the king of soldiers required for the maintenance of peace. In return the king has a duty of protecting his loyal subjects [23].

The members of the Church.

The Church, says Pullen, is divided into three classes of persons: prelates, celibates and the married, typified respectively by Noe, Daniel and Job [24]. Of bishops, or prelates, as he usually styles them, Pullen has much to say both in the *Sentences* and the Sermons. They are to be severe in repressing abuses, not hesitating to punish their erring subjects [25]. They should choose suitable archdeacons as their coadjutors, and appoint parish priests of learning and good character [26]. To them belongs the guidance of the other two classes in Church both by doctrine and example [27]. They should not be ambitious of the office of a bishop, nor seek in it dignity and emoluments, but the honour of God and the good of souls. Martha should be their model, not those who covet advancement, and, when they achieve it, despoil and fleece their flocks [28]. They should be well versed in Scripture and skilful in

---

22 918B.

23 In his *Medieval Humanism in the Life and Writings of John of Salisbury,* London, 1950, pp. 23f, H. Liebeschütz notes that in the *Policraticus,* Books V and VI, John, in dealing with the relations of kings and priests, and the duties of judges, knights, peasants and merchants follows the same order of treatment as does Pullen, his former teacher, in his *Sentences.* Another noteworthy resemblance is to be seen in the strictures of both writers against venality and corruption in the exercise of ecclesiastical and civil power.

24 931A. Cf. St. Augustine, *De Peccatorum Meritis et Remissione,* lib. II, cap. x, *P. L.* 44, 158.

25 *Serm.* 3, 4, 6: 'Ad litteram: fuit iste Heli, qui etsi filios suos castigat, tamen in castigatione eorum est usus paterna magis pietate quam uindicaria potestate. Iste gerit personam episcoporum, qui presides sunt et prelati aliorum sacerdotum. Episcopi igitur, audientes casum Heli, timeant et ipsi suam ruinam nisi castigauerint eos quibus sunt prelati. Sicut enim de manibus sacerdotis requiritur sanguis populi, ita de manu episcopi non solum sanguis populi sed et mors sacerdotum et captio arche Domini'.

Serm. 19: 'Pastor qui legam honorat, nec in uirga ferrea quos regit castigat, Moysen sine uirga in colle collocat ».

26 *Serm.* 8, 9.

27 933A.

28 '*Qui episcopatum desiderat bonum opus desiderat.* Opus dicit non dignitatem, ut insinuet non gloriam quaerendam in prelatione sed laborem. Rogandus dominus ut mittat operarios in messem suam. Et hoc idem est quod Martha ait: *Dic ergo illi ut me adiuuet.* Et respondit, *Martha, Martha,*

its use [29]. Whatever their personal shortcomings, they are still channels of spiritual profit to their subjects, and are entitled to their obedience [30]. If they are faithful to their charge they will merit a double reward for their personal holiness and pastoral zeal. Though there are examples of private persons who excel prelates in holiness, it remains true that as a rule a good superior is more holy than a good subject. In like manner a man of good intelligence is likely to excel in charity, although it often happens that by the assistance of grace the simple surpass their superiors in this virtue [31].

By the term celibates Pullen refers to those who have embraced the religious state. Like those in the world they can only be saved by the virtue of charity, but in their state of life charity expresses itself in contemplation rather than in action [32]. Pullen warns the wearers of the religious habit against hypocrisy [33]. Some leave the world, not out of hatred of its moral corruption, but in order to seek fleshly comfort in religion. There is also to be found the man who, seeing he has no hope of advancement in the world, dons the religious habit with the intention of attaining eminence by a superstitious show of religion. There is the lukewarm, brutish character who performs all his duties out of mere routine. There are the proud and the envious, despisers of others, who put an evil interpretation even on good deeds [34]. Some,

---

solicita es et turbaris erga plurima. Solicita Martha non ut illi qui uruntur solicitudine ut preficiantur; prefecti laborant, et totam curam suam impendunt lac emulgere et uellera omnibus diripere': Serm. 9.

29 Serm. 14.

30 'Qualiscunque agricola sit, quid ad te, cum ab ejus manu, nisi accipere neglexeris, vita tibi sit proventura? Si pravus fuerit, sibi utique erit. Quid autem inde tibi nocumenti surgit, cum a deo, si bonus fueris, etiam per ministrum malum tibi, quod opus animae tuae est procuretur? *Tu quis es alienum servum,* imo praelatum tuum, ut iudices? *Domino stat aut cadit*': 933B.

31 'Facilius tamen est, et saepe fit, ut qui bene regit, bene recto melior sit, sicut qui bene intelligit, si caritatem habet, plus diligere solet; quamvis minus sciens, opitulante gratia, plerumque superiores amando excedat': 934A.

32 940C.

33 'Hujusmodi autem magnopere caveant ne in vestimentis ovium apparentes, intrinsecus sint lupi rapaces; opus extra obtendentes bonum, cor intra celantes pravum': 940D.

'Uerbi gratia, si quis in conuentu monachorum ieiuniis, uigiliis, orationibus, et laboribus corpus suum affligat, et in peccatis criminalibus uiuens uoluntatem dimittendi non habeat pro labore suo regnum celorum sibi dari rogat procul dubio incassum laborat': Serm. 15.

34 'Quidam enim quaerentes quae sua sunt, non quae Jesu Christi; usurpative aut solitariam vitam ingrediuntur, aut ingressum servant; fessi plerumque saeculo, carni satisfacere quaerunt in claustro. Qui in conversatione

out of a mistaken sense of charity, are afraid to admonish their brethren of their faults, or even encourage them, and thus partake of their guilt. Others are disobedient to their superiors. It is no excuse to say that the superiors are not good men. Once the superiors have been legitimately appointed they have received authority from God, and must be obeyed. The most that can be done is to ensure that evil men are not appointed to office [35].

The third group in the Church, that of the married, includes farmers, merchants, soldiers and all others who follow a lawful calling. These will be saved if they labour, not for love of this world, but in order to please God in the sphere of activity which He has pre-ordained for them. On the foundation of faith, which God has laid for them by the ministry of their teachers, they have to build a spiritual house [36]. If they are detached in spirit from their possessions they may be said to *build upon this foundation gold and silver* [37]. In these precious metals, good works, the connatural fruit of charity, are to be set. Those who build thus have little or nothing to fear in purgatory. If, however, they are attached to the world they are said to build wood, hay or stubble on the foundation of faith, and they will be punished either in this world or in purgatory [38].

The three orders in the Church are hierarchically arranged. There can be ascent from the married state to that of celibacy, or from either of these to prelacy, but no descent [39]. If married persons by mutual agreement are desirous of practising continence, they may do so either in their own homes or in religion. In neither case is the marriage bond dissolved. If one partner enters religion, and is afterwards reclaimed by the other, he must return to her, unless mutual consent for a separation was made publicly. In the event of his outliving his partner after quitting religion for this reason, he should fulfil his vow by returning to the cloister [40]. If a slave has been ordained or received in a monastery without the necessary consent of his master, he must either be returned

---

saeculi diffidit exaltari, religionis habitum nonnumquam invadit, superstitiose agens ut possit sublimari. Alius, neque frigidus neque calidus, pecudum more consuetudinem sequens, omnia negligenter facit. Alii superbia laborantes, aut invidia aestuantes, omnes praeter se pariter contemnunt; bene enim gesta sinistre accipiunt': 941A.

[35] 941B-D.

[36] 942B-D.

[37] Cf. 1 Cor. iii, 12.

[38] 943D.

[39] 934A.

[40] *Ibid.* B.

to him or bought from him [41]. Transition from the married state to religion may be made on one's own initiative or on the advice of others, but prelacy should only be accepted under compulsion from the Church, and not even then by a man who knows that he is unworthy [42]. Everyone must be subject to his own prelate. Those whose lives are spent in transit from one locality to another, such as pilgrims, merchants and students are subject to the prelate of their temporary residences [43].

To the three orders in the Church there correspond two kinds of life, the active, of which Lia and Martha are types, and the contemplative, symbolised by Rachel and by Mary, the sister of Martha. The active life merits heaven by the service of God and one's neighbour; the contemplative life is already a foretaste of heavenly joys [44]. The two, however, cannot be completely separated here below; contemplation must be joined to action [45]. In neither is a person immune from the attacks of the devil [46]. The contemplative life is more suited to those who have abandoned the world for the religious state; the active life is more appropriate for the rest of mankind. Prelates, however, should give themselves both to action and contemplation. In contemplation they will find inspiration for their activity, and renewal of spirit after their labours [47].

---

[41] 934C-935A.

[42] 935A. Cf. Serm. 9: 'Non ergo nisi inuitus et uocatus tanquam Aaron preficitur. Quod fit quando certo ordine obseruato, aliquis in prelationem eligitur, in quo illi qui eligunt maxime notandi sunt, et qui eligitur; ut sint qui eligunt uiri religiosi, querentes Dei honorem et salutem populi non suam utilitatem, ille qui eligitur sit talis qui habeat uires et scientiam, et inuitus tandem accedat. Quod si eum abeuntes post carnis desideria eligunt, nec tractus ueniat, sciemus quia non est a Deo uocatus'.

[43] 935D-936A.

[44] 936B. Cf. Serm. 9.

[45] 937B-C.

[46] 'Qui prius Jacob propter actiuam postea Isrel per contemplatiuam uitam uocatus est, quoniam ut uir simplex in tabernaculis habitat a predicto hoste, cui tale displicet studium, grauiter infestatur': Serm. 19.

[47] 938B. Cf. Serm. 9. 'Optimum est deo uacare, uoluntatem eius attendere, proprie saluti consulere. Quod si intermittatur a prelato, non tamen auferatur ab eo. Debet enim prelatus in idipsum redire aliquando ab exterioribus curis, ut receptus in ocium et in secretum de deo cogitet, uias eius et iusticias consideret, et sic a fonte uite hauriat quod aliis propinare ualeat'.

Cf. 939D-940A: 'Exutis saeculo commoda est contemplatio; involutis, concordat actio; praelato autem utraque incumbit, quatenus contemplando addiscat quid in subditos agat, agendo fatigatus atque ideo recreandus, ad fomenta confugiat contemplationis'.

On the controverted question which of the two states is superior, Pullen remarks that, if they are evaluated by their scriptural types, contemplation is more excellent, as Rachel and Mary are clearly preferable to Lia and Martha. Yet the excellence of the active life appears in this that it was the life of Christ and his Apostles. Though the Apostles practised contemplation and Christ was the greatest of contemplatives, yet it was their activity that commended them to God and made them profitable to the world, and Christ's activity that constituted Him Saviour of the world and won for Him exaltation in heaven [48]. Likewise the martyrs were united with God and exalted in glory above the contemplatives by their active imitation of their Master. Pullen concludes that contemplation is more agreeable than activity, and is superior to it in that it is the life of the world to come. In this world it is also more excellent where the lives of private persons are in comparison. Where, however, the activity is that which belongs to the life of a prelate it is superior to the contemplative life, since the heavenly reward of this activity is the highest of all [49].

---

[48] 938D-939B.

[49] 'Actio igitur privata merito et dignitate subest contemplationi; contemplatio autem nostrae mortalitatis meritis est inferior fructibus actuosae praelationis, quae summum a Deo speret gradum in coelo. Nam *super omnia bona sua constituet eos,* ut auctoritas tradit non quod soli, sed quod prae ceteris habituri': 939C.

CHAPTER XIV

ESCHATOLOGY

THE END OF THE WORLD AND THE RESURRECTION OF THE BODY.

Pullen brings his *Sentences* to a conclusion with an elaborate treatment in twenty-two chapters of the end of the world and the second coming of Christ. He begins by asserting that before the end of the world Elias and Enoch will return to the earth, and will convert the Jews [1]. By that time most of the gentiles will have grown corrupt in faith and morals, and will have adhered to Antichrist. With the conversion of the Jews there will be no further vocation of the gentiles, and those of their number who have been wholly deceived by Antichrist will be definitively excluded from salvation [2].

The mission of Elias and Enoch will be twofold. They will prepare men for the conflict with Antichrist, and announce the coming of Christ as Judge of the world. Like that of Christ their ministry will last for a little over three years. Besides converting the Jews, they will fortify the Church to face the imminent transformation of the world. Tradition teaches, says Pullen, that in those days the Jews will return from all parts to their own land, to hear and accept the word of God, and to suffer persecution for Christ's sake at the hands of Antichrist [3]. After fulfilling their mission Elias and Enoch will be among the first to be slain by Antichrist [4]. He will then reign undisturbed for about three and a half years after having subdued the world [5]. Only the most saintly will survive the persecutions of that time, but in the end Christ will slay him, either personally or through the agency of

---

1 977C. Cf. St. Augustine *De Civitate Dei* Lib. XX, cap. 29, *Adsonis* Monachi, *Liber de Antichristo, P.L.* 40, 1131-1134, *P.L.* 101, 1290-1298.

2 978B.

3 978C-979A.

4 979B; Adso, *op. cit., P.L.* 40, 1134.

5 *Ibid.*

Michael the archangel [6]. Before this time there will be a great falling away of the nations. First they will lapse from their obedience to the Roman emperors. Afterwards there will be a great apostasy from the spiritual empire of the Roman Church. This apostasy will immediately precede the manifestation of Antichrist. He will set himself up as God, placing his throne in the temple, by which is to be understood either the Church or the Jewish Temple, which will have been rebuilt [7]. Alluding to St. Paul's treatment of the topic in Thessalonians, ii, 7, Pullen follows the Gloss in suggesting alternative factors which delay the manifestation of Antichrist, among them the power of Rome, which he describes in terms reminiscent of a famous passage in Irenaeus [8]. With the Gloss too and St. Augustine he maintains that the signs and wonders to be worked by Antichrist will either be magical delusions, or, if real, permitted by God [9].

From the book of Daniel, another source of much speculation on Antichrist, he gathers that forty-five days' space for repentance will be granted after his death to those who had wavered during the persecution. For those who yielded there will be no pardon [10]. They will be destroyed in the great conflagration which will follow the days of repentance. In this fire will also perish all other living creatures, and fire and water, as they are now known will be no more. The whole substance of the universe will be transformed and adapted to the condition of mankind after the resurrection from the dead [11].

The fire will endure as long as is necessary for the purification of the faithful. In it they will die, and then arise to glory along with all the just. The reprobate will also rise with incorrupt-

---

6 'Cito enim post regnum illum Dominus Jesus *interficiet spiritu oris sui*, id est, potentia jussionis suae sive per se, sive per Michaelem. Occidetur enim, ut doctores tradunt, in monte Oliveti in papilione et solio suo, illo in loco contra quem Dominus ascendit in coelum': 979C-D. Cf. Adso, l. c. and the note of the editors: 'Adsonis Ms., *occidetur in papilione et in solio suo, in illo loco contra quem ascendit Dominus ad coelum*'. Pullen's use of Adso's work is manifest. The *De Antichristo* of Adso dates from the tenth century.

7 980B. Cf. Augustine, *De Civ. Dei*, lib. XX, cap. 19.

8 'Vel, *qui detinet illum*, id est, *potestas Romae ad quam adhuc omnes undique quasi ad caput confluunt*': 980C; cf. Irenaeus, *Haer.* III, 3, 2: 'Ad hanc enim Ecclesiam, propter potentiorem principalitatem, necesse est omnem convenire ecclesiam, hoc est, eos qui sunt undique fideles'.

9 980D. Cf. Aug. *l. c.*

10 980B-C.

11 981B-982C. Cf. Aug. *In Ps.* CI, *P.L.* 37, 1313f.

ible, but not glorified bodies [12]. The glorified bodies of the just will be wanting in no natural perfection. Grace will supply whatever deficiencies existed in their earthly condition, and the power and wisdom of God will ensure that everyone will receive back his own members, each in its own place, and with the same name as before [13]. Christ's resurrection is, therefore, not only the pledge, but also the pattern of ours [14].

The statement that in the resurrection all will receive back their own bodies is not without its difficulties. There are, says Pullen, two theories put forward about the constitution of the human body. The first of these maintains that the parental seed does not develop from within; the human frame is built up by the reception of food which is joined extrinsically to the minute seed, until adult stature is attained. On this view very little in the human body derives from the parents, and nothing at all from man's original ancestors [15]. The second theory maintains that the total quantity of an adult is due to the intrinsic development of the semen. Food assists development, but is not converted into human nature. The seminal elements received from the parents grow into the full stature of a human body without incorporating any extrinsic matter. A parallel is to be found in the production of Eve's body from the rib of Adam [16]. Both of these theories are open to objection. On the first view non-human substance will by incorporation into human nature partake of the resurrec-

---

12 985A. 'Resurgent autem incorrupti tam boni quam mali, unde sequitur: *Et nos immutabimur,* quasi diceret: *Incorruptio communis est; immutatio* autem nostra, *id est sanctorum est'.* Cf. Aug. *De Civ. Dei,* lib. XX, cap 20.

13 983D-984A: 'Singula igitur membra, aut ad sua redibunt nomina, aut alienis in praemium, persolventur nominibus. Sed membra sua minime amittent nomina; Job namque de Deo dicit: *Quem visurus sum ego ipse, et non alius, et oculi mei conspecturi sunt.* ... Unde similitudinis argumento consequitur quod reliqua quoque membra propria resument nomina'. Cf. Aug. *De Civ. Dei,* lib. XXII, cap. 19-20.

14 984B: 'Christi resurrectio nostrae sit non causa solum verum quoque et exemplum'.

15 985A: 'Juxta hanc sententiam semen humanum in sua parvitate permaneat, tantum autem sibi aliena quaedam assumens, ex assumptis quantitatem compleat hominibus debitam. Homines ergo primi de humo facti sunt, posteri autem, sed remotiores, neque ex humo, neque ex primis, sed tantum ex cibis facti sunt'.

16 'Haec sententia fomenta pueritiae dicit, ignem, balnea, vestes, cibum quoque atque potum; haec interius, illa fovent exterius. Verumtamen, sicut nec illa in humanam vertuntur naturam, ita neque ista; imo juxta dominicam sententiam *omne quod intrat in os, in ventrem vadit, et per secessum emittitur.* Itaque sicut tota Eva, prius in costa coarctabatur, ita universa posteritatis copia in lumbis Adae continebatur': 985B.

tion; on the second it would appear that as all humanity is materially descended from Adam alone, his will be the only body to qualify for the resurrection [17]. The second of the two theories was developed through a misunderstanding of a passage in the *De Civitate Dei* of St. Augustine [18]. It was held by the author of the *Summa Sententiarum* [19], Hugh of St. Victor [20], and Peter Lombard [21].

It found favour with these authors because it appeared to offer an intelligible explanation of the unity of humanity, and particularly of the solidarity of the race in original sin with Adam. It also emphasised the unity of the primary creative principle, and the correlative obligations of obedience to God and mutual love on the part of men. The first of the two opinions is attributed by Peter Lombard to certain sophists — *verborum sectatores* [22]. Pullen adopts the second theory, but admits that the seminal elements contributed by parents, and the rib of Adam, do not return to their original sources at the resurrection. Only what is necessary to the full perfection of the human body will be restored [23]. Here Pullen reproduces the substance of Augustine's doctrine [24], as also his opinion that men will rise with bodies endowed with the perfection found at the age of thirty years, *the measure of the age of the fulness of Christ* (Eph. iv, 13) [25].

The bodies of the just will differ from those of the reprobate not in quantity but in quality. They will be glorified bodies, after the pattern of Christ's body, but of varying degrees of splendour [26]. They are called spiritual because they will be entirely subject to the spirit, and because they will enjoy prerogatives proper to a

---

17 'Haec sententia gaudet dicere, nihil nisi humanam substantiam resurgere; altera minime abhorret porcinam carnem aut ejusmodi alimonia, in humanam tamen substantiam conversam, aut solam resurgere aut ex maxima parte.

Sed si resurrectio unicuique sua restituet membra, num usque adeo, ut Adam redeat costa? Sed jam non est Eva; ut ad parentes redeat effusio seminum, sed jam nulli existent filii; et erit Adam in resurrectione solus; quod absit': 985C-D.

18 Lib. XXII, cap. 14.

19 Tr. III, cap. 10. *P.L.* 176, 105f.

20 *De Sacr.* I, vi, 37, *P.L.* 176, 285ff.

21 *II Sent.* D. xxx, cap. 15.

22 *II Sent.* D. XXX, cap. 14.

23 986B-C. For others on this topic see A. Landgraf, *Dogmengesch.* II, i, 146ff.

24 *Enchiridion*, cap. 89; *De Civ. Dei*, lib. XXII, cap. 19.

25 988A-B. Cf. Aug. *De Civ. Dei*, lib. XXII, cap. 15.

26 989A.

spirit, such as agility, lightness and immunity from the use of food and vesture [27].

The different degrees of bodily glory will correspond to different degrees of perfection in the vision which the just will have of God. The more perfect vision of God will also carry with it a deeper knowledge of created truth, such as the nature of the soul and of heavenly spirits. In the vision of God the mystery of the Blessed Trinity will be understood. If in this life growth in faith in Christ brings a more profound understanding of divine truth, it is easy to see how much more sublime will be the knowledge to be attained in the vision of God [28].

The general judgement.

After the universal conflagration Christ will appear as Judge. He will be heralded by the sound of the trumpet, by which the voice of the archangel Michael is to be understood. This is the signal for the resurrection of the dead. Pullen here indulges in a very involved dialectical discussion of 1 Thessalonians iv, 14-16, 1 Cor. xv, 51-52 and a number of other texts with a view to determining the exact order of events immediately prior to the judgement [29]. The same literal interpretation of the scriptural texts provides him with further scope for his dialectical discussion of the eschatological texts in the synoptic gospels [30]. He concludes that the signs and portents there described will find a literal fulfilment shortly before the universal conflagration. To those in the fire, both just and reprobate, Christ will appear on high, but He will be beyond the reach of the flames, which will rise no higher

---

27 989A-B.

28 989B-D: 'Juxta exterioris gloriam hominis, gloria quoque dabitur interiori, ut qui plus habet in corporis decore, plus quoque habeat in Dei visione; et qui plus de Deo sentit, plus quoque in notitia rerum capiat ... Nimirum instructi in agnitione Dei, per hoc veniunt in omnes divitias, id est copiam; intellectus pleni, ut perfecte de humanis et divinis habeant intellectum, ut de anima et de supernis spiritibus. *In agnitione Dei,* non dico quantum ad opera, sed mysterii Dei, ut scietur quod est secretum et a paucis cognitum de essentia Dei Patris Christi, ut sciatur quod alia persona sit a Filio, quamvis idem in substantia cum eo. Ad quam agnitionem quisquis tendit, ad Christum tantum recurrat. Quanto enim quisque in fide appropriat Christo, tanto magis ex Christi ditatur thesauro. Quod si juxta augmenta fidei notitia augetur, quanto magis celsiores specie, celsiores fient rerum omnium cognitione'.

29 990-995.

30 997-998.

than did the waters of the flood[31]. Christ's coming will be in majesty. The sign of the cross will appear in the heavens as an emblem of his victory. His angels will gather the just and the unjust from the four quarters of the world, and after the judgement will convey the latter to hell[32].

At the judgement all mankind will gaze on Christ with their bodily eyes. The just will be on high with Christ the unjust assembled beneath them. Pullen confesses that there can be no certainty about the time or place of judgement, but considers it probable that it will take place in the air above the spot whence Christ ascended into heaven. The matter of judgement will be largely the practice of fraternal charity. This is exercised by the performance of the corporal works of mercy, but much more perfectly by spiritual works such as the instruction of the ignorant, the conversion of sinners and the consolation of the afflicted[33]. At the judgement the sins and virtues of all will be made manifest. Nor is there anything repugnant in the notion of the just being thus given a knowledge of all historic events and the natures of all things, seeing that they will be admitted to the more sublime knowledge of the Trinity[34]. The simultaneous knowledge of all events will be made possible by a marvellous transformation of the human mind in virtue of which it will grasp the divine immensity in one continuous intuition[35]. Even the hearts of the wicked will be enlarged sufficiently for them to take in all good and evil events at the day of judgement[36].

At the day of judgement both the just and the wicked will behold Christ in his human nature, but only the former will be able to contemplate Christ in his divinity. Pullen argues strongly against certain unnamed commentators that not merely those just

---

[31] 997-998.

[32] 998C-999B.

[33] 1001: 'Magnum est corporaliter oppresso quolibet modo subvenire, longe majus est spiritualibus liberalem esse necessitatibus. Ibi charitatis est inchoatio, hic autem consummatio'.

[34] 1002A-B: 'Num id usque adeo universaliter intelligendum est, ut sanctis quibus dabitur notitia Trinitatis nihil prorsus negetur noscendum in creaturis; quatenus comprehendant rerum omnium tam naturas quam eventus? Utique facillimum puto post notitiam Dei posse notitiam habere, si ita opus est, cujusque rei'.

[35] 1003B: 'Mens enim nostra nobiscum mirum in modum mutanda tantae capacitatis efficienda, ut immensitatem uno et perpetuo contempletur intuitu divinam, nihil mirabitur omnia, ita quod, integra singula simul et interminate complecti possit'.

[36] 1003B.

whose souls have already gazed on the divinity in heaven will on the resumption of their bodies continue to contemplate it at the judgement, but also that the remainder of the elect will enjoy the same vision as soon as they have received their glorified bodies [37].

Both from this passage and others it is evident that Pullen held that even before the day of judgement the just are in heaven, where they enjoy beatitude in the vision of God. However, he adds that this beatitude is to be perfected only after the resurrection [38]. On this question of the abode of the just between the time of their death and the final resurrection there had been some hesitancy in patristic literature. Pullen is faithful to the tradition of the majority of writers in assigning heaven as the resting place of the saints even before the last judgement. He is more definite than a number of patristic writers, and certain theologians of his own day, such as St. Bernard and the Lombard, by explicitly asserting that the just in heaven will enjoy the vision of God straightway after death [39]. His assertion that the beatitude of the just in heaven will be increased after the resurrection is common doctrine in patristic literature.

Although there can be no certain knowledge of the number and identity of the elect and the reprobate before the day of judgement, Pullen remarks that in this life we are not left entirely in ignorance on this question. Those who refuse to believe are destined for perdition. Of the remainder those who have left all things for Christ are destined for heaven; those who retain their goods, and use them to good purpose will also be saved. Of the former it may be said that their salvation is already known; of the latter that it is as yet uncertain. Even here, however, reservations must be made. Of those who have left all for Christ some will fail to persevere, as will many of those who do not rid themselves of their possessions. Though the proportion of the elect is greater among those who observe the evangelical counsels than among the remainder, their actual number is likely to be less. It is to the just who have practised the evangelical counsels that the text of scripture seems more properly to apply which promises

---

37 1004D. 'Ergo commune aliquid dicendum videtur. Et quid potius quam ut iis qui obviam Christo in aera rapiendi sunt, ex quo ad ipsum ventum erit, cum ipso pariter clarescant corpore, splendeant mente, habentes carnem decore sibi debito conspicuam, spiritum visione Dei illustrem'.

38 1028A-B: 'Quamquam enim interim etiam in coelo dum minus habent, minusque sciunt, tandem tamen plene beandi, plene quoque sperant doceri'.

39 819D; 1004A-D; 827A-B.

that they shall sit in judgement with Christ at the Day of Judgement. (Mt. xix, 28) [40].

This judgement will only be exercised by the saints over the wicked, and will consist in their participation in the sentence of condemnation to be pronounced by Christ against the wicked, which will be carried into execution by the angels [41].

Heaven, hell, purgatory.

After judgement the saints will enjoy eternal bliss, but the lost will suffer eternal punishment. The saved will be aware of the fate of the lost, and thus will realise their own good fortune. Likewise the lost will be painfully aware of the glory of the saints, but will not behold it. To give an adequate description of the bliss of the saved or the misery of the lost is beyond the power of the human mind. It is known, however, that infinite extremes of heat and cold will afflict those in hell. Evil passions and desires which defiled them on earth will remain to make them worse in hell. In contrast, the habits of virtue of the just will be perfected in heaven. But in neither the wicked nor the just will these interior dispositions issue into outward works. The reason is that good works imply laborious effort, which is out of keeping with the state of heavenly bliss of the just who have no further need of merit. Evil deeds, on the other hand, would be a source of satisfaction to the lost, and must be denied them, lest there be thereby any mitigation of their sufferings [42]. As the punishment of the lost is eternal, Origen erred in imagining that men and even demons would be freed from hell after a certain length of time [43]. In like manner the just will always abide in bliss without danger of defection. But between the endless misery of the lost and the endless joy of the blessed there will be this difference, that the former will admit of temporal alternations of various sufferings, whereas the latter will consist in one unchanging moment of happiness, in which past and future will have no place, but only one perpetual present [44].

---

[40] 1005C-1007B.

[41] 1007B-1008B.

[42] 1008B-1010A.

[43] 1010A; 999C; cf. Aug. *De Civ. Dei,* lib. XXI, cap. 17.

[44] 1010A-B: 'Boni quorum incessanter *adesse festinant tempora* (Deut. xxxii, 35), sicut eorum quorum erit *participatio in idipsum* (Ps. cxxi, 3), nullum timebunt casum, apud quos *aliud et aliud* non inveniet locum, quoniam perseverabit in idipsum: *fuisse et futurum esse* nemo dubie inter eos

Pullen's ideas on purgatory deserve mention. Under the Old Law, before the descent of Christ into Hell, souls in need of purgation occupied a position intermediate between the souls of the lost, and the saints who awaited the coming of Christ in the state of peace designated by the expression ' Abraham's bosom ' [45]. Once they had made sufficient satisfaction for their sins, they ascended to the company of the spirits in Abraham's bosom. After the descent of Christ the purgatorial state continues to exist, but Pullen confesses he is ignorant of its precise location. Heaven is a definite corporeal place above the earth [46]. Likewise hell is a real place situated beneath the earth [47]. Neither hell nor heaven appear to be suitable locations for purgatory. But it is certain that there is a place of purgation, and that souls will be detained there until they have made adequate satisfaction for their sins [48]. The pains of purgatory will be proportionate to the sins to be expiated, but the expiation demanded will be more severe than that which would have sufficed on earth, which is the proper place for doing penance [49]. Indeed the pains of purgatory are more severe than any earthly sufferings, and are only surpassed by those of hell [50].

A question of interest raised by Pullen concerns those souls who have made adequate satisfaction for their sins in purgatory. Are they then admitted to the vision of God? There was no authoritative solution in Pullen's day of this problem. Not until the Constitution of Pope Benedict XII, ' Benedictus Deus ', was it defined

---

cogitet, sed *esse* tantum admiretur; quoniam ibi nihil praeteribit, nihil venturum erit. Quod enim ibi est, semper ita esse necesse est. Apud inferos temporum varietas intelligatur ubi tormentorum mutabilis miseria perseverabit '.

45 824D-826C.

46 *Supra* ch. VIII, 249f.

47 823B: ' Infernus equidem locus est tam deterior terra quam inferior '; cf. 825A: ' Infernus autem subter est, juxta Isaiam, quippe in inferioribus terrae collocatum '.

48 ' Sed disciplina haec ubi fit? Num in coelo? Num in inferno? Sed nec coelum tribulationi, nec tartarus correctioni, praecipue nostro tempore competere videtur. Nam si solum boni debentur coelo, nonne solum mali debentur inferno? Et si coelum omne excludit malum, quomodo infernus ullum recipit bonum? ... Ergo ubi sunt poenitentes post mortem? In purgatoriis. Ubi sunt ea? Nondum scio. Quamdiu ibi sunt? Usque ad satisfactionem '.

49 827B: ' Quare pro modo culpae expiatio intelligitur major, minorve, longa sive brevis. Semper autem acrior succedit, quoniam tempore suo satisfactio in vita non praecessit '.

50 826B; cf. De Contemptu Mundi *ed. cit.* 199.

that such souls were at once admitted to the vision of God. Pullen's friend and contemporary, St. Bernard, believed that the vision of the Godhead was reserved until the resurrection of the body [51]. Pullen, following the tradition of St. Gregory the Great, argues strongly in favour of the opinion that as soon as their state of purgation is ended they enjoy the vision of God. He is at pains to refute the objection that, whereas those who have made sufficient satisfaction for their sins before death are worthy of immediate admission to the vision of God, the remainder, who have made their expiation in purgatory are detained in some place of rest outside heaven until the resurrection from the dead [52]. He replies that these souls would not be fully reconciled to God, seeing that something was lacking in their satisfaction. Further, it would appear unjust that souls who died as long ago as the time of the Apostles with a small debt to be paid in purgatory should be deprived of heaven until the resurrection. It would also be anomalous if one person should be excluded from heaven for so long after a lifetime of meritorious religious observance, merely because he had to pass a period in purgatory, while another could gain immediate admission, if he had no debt to expiate, even though his merit was much less [53].

He concludes that the souls which have made sufficient satisfaction in purgatory, which is no longer located in hell, ascend at once to heaven, just as those who made satisfaction in hell before the descent of Christ were received into the region known as Abraham's bosom [54].

---

51 See B. de Vregille: L'Attente des saints d'après Saint Bernard, *N. R. T.*, LXX (1948) 225ff.

52 827A.

53 *Ibid.* B.

54 *Ibid.*: 'Unde peracta purgatione poenitentes, tam nostri, ex purgatoriis (quae extra infernum) ad coelos, quam veteres ex purgatoriis (quae in inferno) ad sinum Abrahae refrigerandi, jugiter conscendere videntur'.

CHAPTER XV

CONCLUSION

Pullen's theological achievement.

The preceding account of Pullen's theological ideas may be concluded by a brief appraisal of his work as a whole. It is evident that he had a gift for abstract speculation. This is seen especially in his treatment of questions concerning the nature of God. Along with this went great fertility of mind, which enabled him to examine every aspect of a problem. Underlying this superstructure of speculation and dialectical ingenuity there is a solid knowledge of Scripture and traditional theological teaching. He was a master of the theological culture of his day, well-informed on the questions debated in the schools. Inevitably many of the topics he raises and the solutions which he advances are common property. It could hardly be otherwise in the work of an orthodox teacher of theology. Yet even in treating of such questions his highly personal style makes his work always readable.

On debated points of doctrine he did not hesitate to propose his own solutions. Some of these were taken up with profit by later theologians. He appears to have had some influence on the work of Peter Lombard, though not to the extent claimed by his seventeenth-century editor H. Mathoud[1]. Among the questions where his influence is discernible in the Lombard's *Sentences* are the discussions of the conciliation of God's mercy and justice and of the existence of moral evil and divine omnipotence. It was, however, his doctrine on the sacrament of penance which seems to have had most effect on his successors. This is not surprising considering the amount of consideration which he gave to this topic both in his ascetical works and in his *Sentences*. Later writers echoed, as we have observed, the doctrine which he first explicitly formulated of priestly absolution as the outward sing of this sac-

---

1 See A. Landgraf, Literarhistorische Bemerkungen zu den Sentenzen des Robertus Pullus, *Traditio*, 1 (1943) 213-215.

rament. Also of importance for later theology was his teaching that this absolution, besides manifesting the remission of sins by God, contributes to it by obtaining grace for the healing of the wounds in the soul left by sin. His theories on the number and nature of the power of the keys were also remembered by later writers.

On other points it is harder to determine his influence. Some of his ideas were to gain acceptance though in his day they had weighty names against them. Among these was his opinion that matrimony was a meritorious state of life, if entered on with a right intention. This opinion was to prevail over the contrary opinion defended by Peter Lombard. Another instance of the soundness of his teaching appears in his insistence that the beatific vision is granted before the resurrection of the body, as soon as souls are sufficiently purified after death. On this point Pullen's view was later defined as of faith, and the contrary opinion held by St. Bernard became no longer tenable.

Worthy of attention too is his teaching on grace. His knowledge of the writings of St. Augustine preserved him from all trace of semi-pelagianism. Among other of his interesting speculations mention may be made of his discussion of the unity, simplicity and omnipresence of God, the problem of evil, the equality of the divine persons, the creation of man and original sin, the hypostatic union, the sacrament of the Eucharist, the relations of the temporal and spiritual power, and his elaborate eschatological theology.

St. Bernard's description of his theology as 'sane' was well-merited. Inevitably some of his opinions are obsolete, for example that concerning the return of sins once forgiven, and his doctrine of the intention requisite for valid administration of a sacrament. In his day these were still open questions. His unusual and subtly argued opinion that the Father and Son are two principles of the Holy Ghost is explicable on the ground that he wrote more than a century before the Council of Lyons defined that they are one principle.

Pullen's theology was orthodox in intention, though he felt free to speculate where questions had received no authoritative solution. Along with his great contemporary Hugh of St. Victor he derives from the school of Laon. There is, however, no evidence of a verbal dependence on any of the extant fragments of the Laon school. His method was to take ideas current in that school, and develop them by the aid of his subtle dialectical technique. In this respect he may certainly be reckoned among those who contributed to the development of the scholastic method in theology.

Among his contemporaries the three most influential were undoubtedly Hugh of St. Victor, Peter Abelard and Gilbert Porreta. Each of these may be regarded as the head of a school of theological thought which had considerable influence on later development. Pullen belonged to none of these schools, although he shared much in common with each of them. Nor did he found any school of his own. He stood, it would apear, somewhat apart from all of them, although on the whole closer to Hugh of St. Victor than to either of the others. He differs, however, from the Victorine school by his denial that an intuitive knowledge of God is possible in this life, and unlike its adherents does not attribute any probative value to the usual analogical arguments for the existence of the Blessed Trinity.

There is little reason for attaching Pullen to the school of Abelard. The nineteenth-century French savant, B. Hauréau, erred seriously in asserting that Pullen closely followed Abelard and borrowed from him to the extent of plagiarism [2]. His only justification for this accusation is a reference to Pullen's *Sentences,* Book I, chapter 15, and to Mathoud's notes on the discussion. If he had taken the trouble to read with attention either Pullen's text or Mathoud's notes he would have perceived that Pullen was citing Abelard only in order to refute his opinions on the divine omnipotence. On other questions also Pullen was at variance with Abelard, He defends against Abelard the doctrine of the substantial omnipresence of God as opposed to a mere potential presence. He differs from Abelard in his explanation of the nature of moral evil, and, unlike him attaches no importance to analogical or any other natural arguments as a proof of the existence of the Blessed Trinity. He separates himself from Abelard's doctrine on the hypostatic union, in spite of certain superficial similarities of expression. On the theology of the sacrament of penance Pullen is closer to Abelard than to Hugh of St. Victor, but he differs from him on some important points and develops certain ideas of Abelard in an original and fruitful manner. Against Abelard's opinion, retracted after the Council of Sens in 1140, that unworthy bishops had not the power of forgiving sins, and against his denial that ordinary priests possess the power of binding, he taught explicitly that the powers of binding and loosing were given to all the successors of St. Peter and the Apostles, to simple priests as well as to bishops.

[2] 'Il le suit de très près, et lui fait quelquefois des emprunts qui pourraient passer pour des plagiats'. *De la philosophie scolastique,* 329 (Paris, 1850).

He also differed from Abelard in his explanation of the meaning of the power of the keys, and modifies considerably Abelard's opinion on the nature of binding and loosing. The two authors also differ on the question of the return of sins once forgiven.

In theological method Pullen is closer to Abelard than to Hugh of St. Victor. The resemblance to Abelard is seen in the copious and skilful use of dialectic for the marshalling of arguments to establish a position, refute an opponent or harmonize apparently conflicting texts. There can however, be no certainty of any dependence on Abelard, who was by no means the only able dialectician of his day. A noteworthy difference between the style of these two is the greater brevity and conciseness with which Pullen treats his questions.

Gilbert Porreta was Pullen's predecessor in the chair of theology at the Cathedral school of Paris. It has been argued in this study that Pullen seems to have aligned himself with the opposition to Gilbert's trinitarian theology which came to a head at the Council of Rheims in 1148, two years after Pullen's death. It has also been contended that another less well-known theory of Gilbert, that concerning the constitution of human nature, was also controverted by Pullen, and by Hugh of St. Victor.

The survival of forty-five of his sermons is an argument that Pullen enjoyed a contemporary reputation as a preacher. It may well be that it was this reputation and the existence of these sermons that were responsible for the statement in the *Continuatio Bedae*[3] that he preached the word of God with great fruit to the people of Oxford during his five years sojourn in the city. However, the surviving sermons appear to have been delivered to clerics and religious rather than to townspeople. In quality they compare favourably with similar contemporary academic sermons.

If sermons and theological writings are an index to the character of their author, Pullen emerges as a man of serious, even stern, temperament, outspoken, ascetical, conservative in outlook, a scholar who valued learning only as an instrument for the penetration and dissemination of the word of God. He was primarily a teacher and known and valued as such.

---

[3] *Supra*, 6.

INDEX OF PERSONS

INDEX OF SUBJECTS

" ANALECTA GREGORIANA „

cura Pontificiae Universitatis Gregorianae edita

I. - **Schwamm, H.: Magistri Ioannis de Ripa doctrina de praescientia divina.** — 1930, in-8°, p. XII-228.

II. - **Adamczyk,** Stanislaus: **De obiecto formali intellectus nostri secundum doctrinam S. Thomae Aquinatis.** — editio altera correcta, 1952, in-8°, p. XVI-152.

III. - **Druwé, Eugenius S. J.: Prima forma inedita operis S. Anselmi « Cur Deus homo ».** — Textus, cum Introductione et notis criticis — 1933, in-8°, p. XII-150.

IV. - **Bidagor** Ramon, S. I.: **La « Iglesia Propria » en España.** Estudio historico-canonico. — 1933, in-8°, p. XXII-176.

V. - **Madoz,** José S. I.: **El concepto de la Tradición en S. Vincente de Lerins.** — 1933, in-8°, p. 214.

VI. - **Keeler** Leo W. S. I., **The Problem of Error from Plato to Kant.** — 1934, in-8°, p. 284.

VII. - **De Aldama** J. A., S. J.: **El Simbolo Toledano.** — 1934, in-8°, pag. 167.

VIII. - **Miscellanea iuridica** Iustiniani et Gregorii IX legibus commemorandis, cura Pont. Univ. Gregorianae edita. — 1935, in-8°, p. 185.

IX et X. - **Miscellanea Vermeersch** — Scritti pubblicati in onore del R. P. Arturo Vermeersch, S. I. — 2 vol., 1935, in-8° — I vol. p. XXIX-454; II vol. p. 406.

XI. - **Bévenot** M., S. J.: **St. Cyprian's de Unitate. Chap. IV.** — 1938, in-8°, p. LXXXV-79 et 6 tab.

XII. - **Gómez Helin, L.: Praedestinatio apud Ioannem Cardinalem de Lugo.** — 1938, in-8°, p. XII-191.

XIII. - **Daniele,** Ireneo: **I documenti Costantiniani della « Vita Constantini » di Eusebio di Cesarea.** — 1938, in-8°, p. 219.

XIV. - **Villoslada,** Riccardo G., S. I., Dr. Hist. Eccl.: **La Universidad de París durante los estudios de Francisco de Vitoria** O. P. (1507-1522). — 1938, in-8°, p. XXVIII-468.

XV. - **Villiger,** Iohann, Dr. Hist. Eccl., Prof. in Fac. Theol. ad Lucernam: **Das Bistum Basel zur Zeit Iohanns XXII.,** Benedikts XII, und Klemens VI. (1316-1352). — 1939, in-8°, pag. XXVIII-370.

XVI. - **Schnitzler** Th.: **Im Kampfe um Chalcedon.** Geschichte und Inhalt des Codex Encyclius von 458. — 1938, p. IX-132, in 8°.

XVII. - **Sheridan** Ioannes Antonius.: **Expositio plenior hylemorphismi Fr. Rogeri Baconis, O. F. M.** — 1938, in-8°, pag. XVIII-176.

XVIII. - **Boularand** Ephrem S. I.: **La venue de l'Homme à la foi d'après Saint Jean Chrysostome.** — 1939, in-8°, p. 192.

XIX. - **De Letter** Prudentius S. I.: **De ratione meriti secundum Sanctum Thomam.** — 1939, in-8°, p. XVIII-152.

XX. - **Haacke** Gualterus: **Die Glaubensformel des Papstes Hormisdas im Acacianischen Schisma.** — 1939, in-8°, p. 150.

XXI. - **González** Severino, S. I., Prof. de Dogma en la Fac. Teol. de Comillas: **La fórmula** Μία οὐσία τρεῖς ὑποστάσεις en **San Gregorio de Nisa.** — 1939, p. XX-146, in 8°

XXII. - **Gosso** Francesco, Dr. Hist. Eccl.: **Vita economica delle Abbazie Piemontesi.** (Sec. X-XIV). — 1940, in-8°, p. 216.

XXIII. - **De Mañaricua** Andrés E.: **El matrimonio de los esclavos.** — 1940, in-8°, p. 286.

XXIV. - **Mazon** Cándido S. I., Prof. de Derecho en la Pont. Universidad Gregoriana y en el Pont. Inst. Oriental: **Las reglas de los religiosos,** su obligacion y naturaleza juridica. — 1940, in-8°, p. XVI-360.

XXV. - **Aguirre Elorriaga** Manuel S. I.: **El Abate de Pradt en la emancipación hispanoamericana** (1800-1830). — 1941, in-8°, p. VII-377.

XXVI. - **Ghiron** M.: **Il matrimonio canonico degli italiani all'estero.** 1941, in-8°, p. 164.

XXVII. - **Reuter** A., O. M. I.: **Sancti Aurelii Augustini doctrina de Bonis Matrimonii.** — 1942, in-8°, p. XII-276.

XXVIII. - **Orbàn** L.: **Theologica Güntheriana et Concilium Vaticanum.** — Vol. I, 1942, in-8°, p. 208 (Hoc volumen non venit separatim sed cum tota collectione).

XXIX. - **La Compagnia di Gesù e le Scienze Sacre.** — Conferenze commemorative del IV Centenario della fondazione della Compagnia di Gesù, tenute all'Università Gregoriana: 5-11 novembre 1941. — 1942, in-8°, p. 270.

XXX. - **Bertrams** W. S. I.: **Der neuzeitliche Staatsgedanke und die Konkordate des ausgehenden Mittelalters.** — Zweite verbesserte Auflage, 1950, in-8°, p. XVII-192.

XXXI. - **D'Izzalini** Luigi, O. F. M.: **Il principio intellettivo della ragione umana nelle opere di S. Tommaso d'Aquino.** pag. XVI-184, 1943, in-8°.

XXXII. - **Smulders** Pierre. S. I.: **La doctrine trinitaire de S. Hilaire de Poitiers.** — 1944, in-8° p. 300.

XXXIII. - **Rambaldi** Giuseppe, S. I.: **L'oggetto dell'intenzione sacramentale, nei Teologi dei secoli XVI e XVII.** — 1944, in-8°, p. 192.

XXXIV. - **Muñoz P., S. I.: Introducción a la síntesis de San Augustín.** 1945, in-8°, p. 351.

XXXV. - **Galtier P., S. I.: Le Saint Esprit en nous d'après les Pères Grecs.** 1945, p. 290, in-8°.

XXXVI. - **Faller O., S. I.: De Priorum saeculorum silentio circa Assumptionem B. Mariae Virginis.** p. XII-135, 1946, in-8°.

XXXVII. - **D'Elia P. M., S. I.: Galileo in Cina.** Relazioni attraverso il Collegio Romano tra Galileo e i gesuiti scienziati missionari in Cina (1612-1640) — p. XII-127; 1947, in-8°.

XXXVIII. - **Alszeghy Z., S. I.: Grundformen der Liebe. Die Theorie der Gottesliebe bei dem hl. Bonaventura.** — 1946, p. 300. in-8°.

XXXIX. - **Hoenen P., S. I.: La théorie du jugement d'après St. Thomas d'Aquin.** — Editio altera, recognita et aucta, 1953, p. XII-384, in-8°

XL. - **Flick M., S. I.: L'attimo della giustificazione secondo San Tommaso.** — 1947, p. 206, in-8°.

XLI. - **Monachino V., S. I.: La cura pastorale a Milano, Cartagine e Roma nel sec. IV.** — 1947, in-8°, p. XX-442.

XLII. - **Vollert C., S. I.: The Doctrine of Hervaeus Natalis on Primitive Justice and Original Sin.** — 1947, p. 335, in-8°.

XLIII. - **Hoenen P., S. I.: Recherches de logique formelle. La structure du systeme des syllogismes et de celui des sorites. La logique des notions « au moins » et « tout au plus ».** — p. 384, 1947, in-8°.

XLIV. - **Selvaggi Fil., S. I.: Dalla filosofia alla Tecnica. — La logica del potenziamento.** — 1947, p. XII-278, in-8°.

XLV. - **Klotzner Iosef., Dr. Hist. Eccl.: Kardinal Dominikus Jacobazzi und sein Konzilswerk.** — 1948, p. 300, in-8°.

XLVI. - **Federici Giul. Ces., S. I.: Il principio animatore della Filosofia Vichiana.** — 1948, in-8°, pag. 220.

XLVII. - **Nanni Luigi: La Parrocchia studiata nei documenti lucchesi dei secoli VIII-XIII** — 1948, pp. XVI-234, in-8°.

XLVIII. - **Asensio Felix, S. I.: « Misericordia et Veritas »** — El hesed y'émet divinos: su influjo religioso-social en la historia de Israel. — 1948, pp. 344.

XLIX. - **Ogiermann** Helm. Aloysius, S. I.: **Hegels Gottesbeweise.** — 1948, pp. 230.

L. - **Orban** Ladislas: **Theologia Güntheriana et Concilium Vaticanum.** — Vol. II, 1949, in-8°, pag. 218.

LI. - **Beck,** G. J. Henry: **The Pastoral Care of Souls in South-East France, during the Sixth Century.** - 1950, in-8°, pag. LXXII-415.

LII. - **Quadrio**, Giuseppe, S. D. B.: **Il Trattato « De Assumptione B. Mariae Virginis » dello pseudo Agostino, e il suo influsso nella teologia Assunzionistica latina.** - 1951, in-8°, p. XVI-432.

LIII. - **Schmidt**, Herman A. P., S. I.: **Liturgie et Langue vulgaire. Le problème de la langue liturgique chez les premiers Réformateurs et au Concile de Trente.** - 1950, p. 212, in-8°.

LIV. - **Galtier**, Paul, S. I.: **Aux origines du Sacrement de Pénitence.** - 1951, p. XII-228, in-8°.

LV. - **Broderick**, John F., S. I.: **The Holy See and the Irish Movement for the Repeal of the Union with England** (1829-1847). - 1951, p. XXVIII-240, in-8°.

LVI. - **Williams**, Michael E.: **The Teaching of Gilbert Porreta on the Trinity, as found in his Commentaries on Boethius.** - 1951, p. XVI-134.

LVII. - **Hanssens** Ioannes M., S. I.: **Aux origines de la Prière Liturgique - Nature et Genèse de l'office des Matines** - 1952, p. VIII-180, in-8°.

LVIII. - **Asensio**, Felix, S. I.: **Yahveh y su Pueblo** - Contenido teológico en la historia bíblica de la elección. - 1953, p. 260 in-8°.

LIX. - **De Haes**, Paul: **I a Résurrection de Jésus, dans l'Apologétique des cinquante dernières années.** - 1953, in-8°, p. XVI-320.

LX. - **Mori**, Elios Giuseppe (R. D.): **Il motivo della Fede, da Gaetano a Suarez,** con Appendice di Fonti Manoscritte. - 1953, in-8°, p. XVI-280.

LXI. - **Laurin** Joseph-Rhéal, O.M.I.: **Orientations Maîtresses des** Apologistes Chrétiens de 270 à 361. - 1954, in-8°, pp. VIII-500.

LXII. - **Bernini** Giuseppe, S. I.: **Le Preghiere Penitenziali del Salterio.** - 1953, in-8°, p. XXIV-324.

LXIII - **Hoenen** Petrus, S. I.: **De Noetica geometriae origine theoriae cognitionis** - 1954; in-8°, pp. 300.

LXIV. - **Courtney** Francis, S. I.: **Cardinal Robert Pullen** († 1146) - **An English Theologian of the twelfth Century** - 1954, in-8°, p. XXIV-296.

LXV. - **Orbe** Antonio, S. I.: **En aurora de la exegesis del IV Evangelio** (Ioh. I, 3) (Estudios Valentinianos vol. II). - 1954, in-8°.

LXVI. - **Villoslada** Riccardo Garcia, S. I.: **Storia del Collegio Romano dal suo inizio** (1551), **alla soppressione della Compagnia di Gesù** (1773) - 1954, in-8°, p. 360.